Sacred Sites in North Star Country
Places in Greater New York State
(PA,OH,NJ,CT,MA,VT,ONT)
That Changed the World

By Madis Senner

Mother Earth Press
Syracuse, New York
www.motherearthpress.net
motherearthprayers@gmail.com

Cover Design by Linda Donaldson of Imagine Design.
Cover Pictures. Front cover clockwise from upper left; Scotts
Bluff, Stone Arabia Church, South Hill, Foundation of Light.
Back cover clockwise from upper left; Grafton Peace Pagoda,
Wisdom's Golden Rod, Swami Vivekananda's Cottage Thousand
Islands, Wisdom's Golden Rod.

Illustrations are by Linda Donaldson of Imagine Design.
Photographs by author; except for Schoharie Presbyterian by
Loraine Mavins.
Maps courtesy of Maps-© OpenStreetMap contributors, www.
openstreetmap. org.
Icons by the Noun Project.
ISBN 978-0-9908744-1-6

To the Spirit Keepers
To you oh great ones,
That kept the beacons burning
bright.

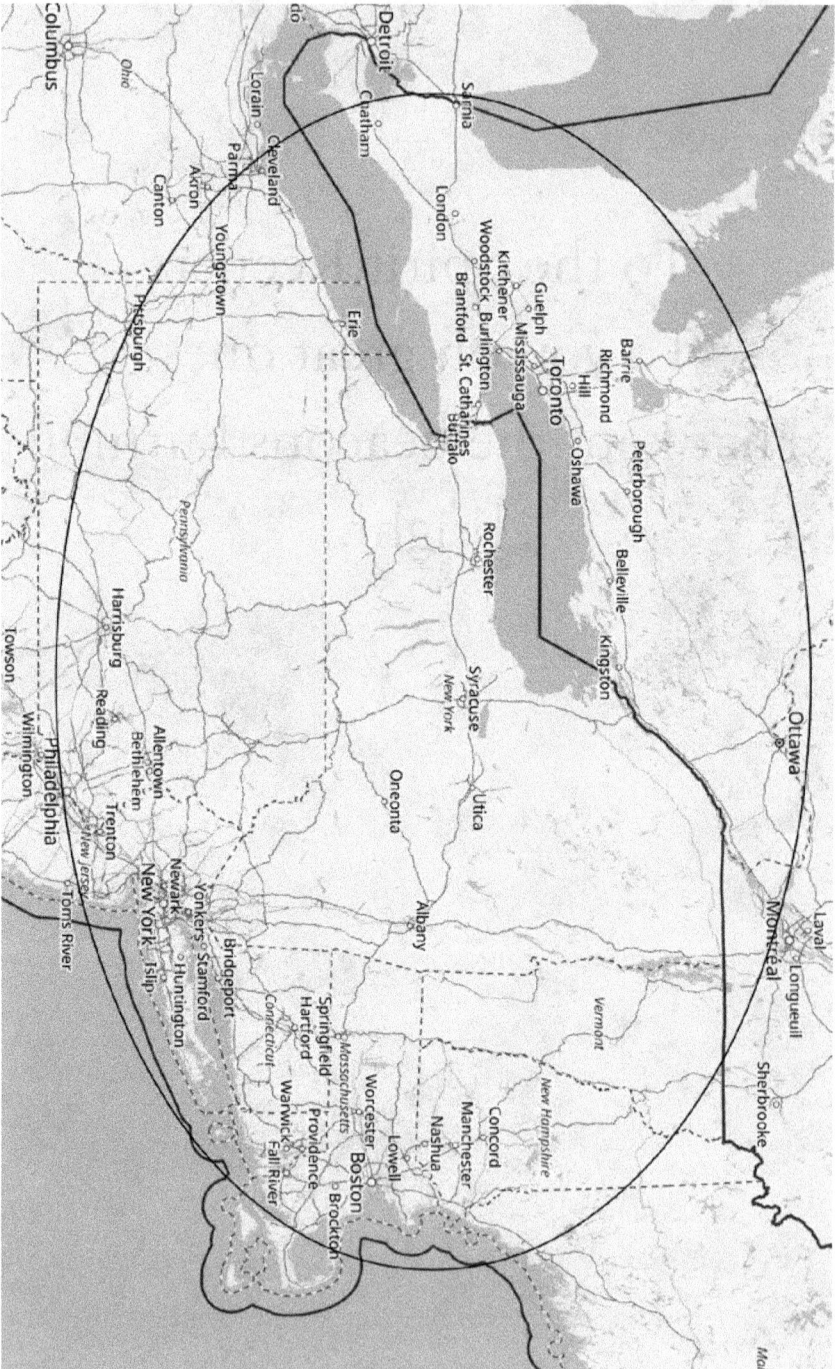

There was a time when our hearts and minds were focused not on profit or plunder, but upon making a better world, of achieving freedom and equality for all, of exploring new ways of spirituality, of making Heaven on Earth. Well, that time may be gone, but that place where all this happened still exists. Because you see my friend, place can be just as important as time in determining history. Come explore.

Table of Contents

XI

Part III Conclusion and Appendix

Preface

In 2002 I felt called to get people to pray around Onondaga Lake in Syracuse, NY. A sacred lake to the Haudenosaunee (Iroquois) where the great prophet the Peacemaker planted the Tree of Peace and gave them the Great Law of Peace, which helped shape the USA constitution.

On that quest I came to learn about the many movements and causes born in upstate NY, and others that found their most strident voices there, particularly during the Antebellum period; the Women's Movement, abolitionism, America's Second Great Awakening, food reform.... I learned the area was called the Burned-over District, America's Psychic Highway, North Star Country and more.

I found out that many great souls were either born in upstate NY, or drawn there. People like Harriet Tubman, Susan B. Anthony, Fredrick Douglass, Elizabeth Cady Stanton, Gerrit Smith, Matilda Joslyn Gage...

I learned of great souls that had epiphanies in upstate NY; Charles Grandison Finney (Revivalist, America's Second Great Awakening), Clara Barton (American Red Cross),...

I came to see that the Dalai Lama's Tibetan Buddhists had their headquarters in Upstate NY, as did others.

I created a website (www.motherearthprayers.org) and began cataloguing sacred sites on it.

As I progressed on my quest, my focus and connection to Mother Earth got increasingly stronger. Then one day, I had an insight, arguably an epiphany about Mother Earth. A formation, or aspect, of Mother Earth's unseen body (subtle body) what I call 'Fields of Consciousness' was revealed to me.

I found Fields of Consciousness at the homes of great leaders and places where social justice took place. I was not sure whether these people were drawn to the Fields, or were influenced by them; probably a little of both. I came to realize Fields of Consciousness had an affect upon humankind's consciousness. I have since concluded that they play a critical role in shaping our individual and collective souls. I wrote *Sacred Sites in North Star Country* to educate about places where Fields are found and to encourage people to visit and pray, or meditate in them; because this empowers them and makes them stronger.

To better explain myself it was necessary to introduce several new concepts regarding Mother Earth as I did in *Vortices and Spirals*. Because this is not a book about Mother Earth's cosmology I have kept new concepts to a minimum.

In many ways I am breaking new ground by arguing that place shapes history. I relied on the work of Carl Jung, the New Unconscious and the work of Dr. Michael Persinger and Todd Murphy to make my point.

In order to tell my story I have included Haudenosaunee (Iroquois) history. The challenge was that at times there are many variations of Haudenosaunee history and legends; from Peacemaker's narrative to things such as where the Seneca people were born—Bare Hill, or South Hill. I apologize if the narrative selected offends anyone. Out of respect to the Haudenosaunee I refer to the Peacemaker, as the Peacemaker, and not his Native American name.

All of the sacred sites listed have Fields of Consciousness.

Several of the sacred sites listed are historical homes, or places that are not conducive to spiritual practices such as prayer, or meditation. I have also included places of worship whose accessibility may be limited to worship services once a week. I did this because I want to provide pilgrims with as many options as possible, to show the link between Fields and the influence upon people and to offer a broad array of choices. I also hope that communities that have Fields of Consciousness will take it upon themselves to make them more accessible, and work to enhance them.

Many of the sacred sites listed lack a palpable sense of presence. In other words, they seem indistinguishable from the place across the street; in that there is nothing special about them. But all the places listed have Fields of Consciousness, and while some of the Fields may be muted, they can be significantly improved through prayer, meditation and ceremony. It is incumbent that people work to improve and enhance space; this is critical if we are going to make a better world, as I explain in the Conclusion.

Given that so many reform and religious movements were born here, as were many great souls, the question was what to call my book. I settled on North Star Country, after the North Star that so many Freedom Seekers followed to freedom, because it was the most encompassing. North Star is also what Fredrick Douglass called his abolitionist newspaper.

Because this is a labor of love, there may be too many reviews and some may be too long, or wordy. I apologize; I was only following my heart.

Since I have been surveying North Star Country for over a decade many people have helped me on my quest; local historians, government employees, clergy and more. The bibliography for individual sites mentions some of those people.

My thanks to Lorraine Mavins, who was a fellow student, explorer and traveler through much of my sojourn. Thanks to Judy Wellman for historical help and with providing contacts. Over the years the staff of Paine Branch Library have been a big help with research and inter-library loan; a special thanks to Renate Dunsmore, Karen DiNatale, Rose Zeppetello, Galina Levina and Lorraine Mavins.

Several people provided me with helpful suggestions for potential places to survey. Thanks to author, storyteller and puppeteer Melanie Zimmer for her detailed emails of listings and numerous suggestions. Thanks to Marilyn Gang of Toronto Dowsers for providing me with suggestions to consider in southern Ontario. Thanks for fellow lover of Mother Earth Reverend Timothy Lake for taking the time to send me recommendations of sacred sites.

Thanks to Dr. Steve Wechsler for his many suggestions, most notably the Himalayan Institute.

I owe a debt of gratitude to Gina Barkovitch and Lorraine Mavins for reading my Western NY draft and providing input regarding the format of this book. Thanks.

I would like to thank Leola Sutton for input on editing. Thanks to my student Janice Carr for editorial help and for accompanying me on long excursions from Massachusetts to Ohio, and Pennsylvania and New Jersey. I don't know how I would have been able to do it without your help.

Introduction-How To Use this Book

This is a book about sacred sites in greater New York State that changed our collective soul. The premise is that place matters and can affect our individual, as well as our collective being and consciousness; and that certain places of Mother Earth in particular have a profound affect upon us. All of the places listed contain an aspect of Mother Earth called Fields of Consciousness; which I refer to in an abbreviated form as FOC. I will also call them Fields. They emanate Mother Earth's highest aspirations for humankind—love, compassion, selflessness, and forgiveness—and make up Mother Earth's Soul.

It is hoped that you will come visit and pray/meditate/do ceremony at the various sacred sites listed. In doing so Mother Earth will nourish your soul and raise your consciousness, in the process you will also strengthen Her.

It is important to realize that we need Mother Earth to achieve our fullest potential and She needs us to achieve Hers. We have a symbiotic relationship. Through good acts and positive intentions we make Her shine and in the process improve what she nourishes us with, through negativity we sully and damage Her.

Unfortunately many of the Fields of Consciousness have lost their vitality and are sullied. Praying/meditating/doing ceremony on Fields will help cleanse and reinvigorate them at a particular location. It is a critical task, because the consciousness emanating from Fields of Consciousness is carried to the farthest corners of the world to nourish humanity's soul.

Praying and meditating in FOC have helped raise my consciousness and enhanced my spiritual growth. They have also had a dramatic influence upon my community.

When I returned to Syracuse in 2000, after living 21 years in New York City, I was amazed at the level of violence in the city, particularly the number of murders. I prayed and prayed to God to please direct me what to do to help. In the fall of 2002 God answered my prayers and encouraged me to organize a prayer vigil on Onondaga Lake (Syracuse, NY), a sacred lake to the Haudenosaunee (Iroquois), in a place that is now called the 'Peacemaker's Sanctuary.' At the time I had limited knowledge of sacred space and was questioning why this place?

On November 29, 2002, the Friday after Thanksgiving, twenty-five of us gathered for a prayer vigil and ceremony at the Peacemakers Sanctuary. I would continue to go there and pray everyday until the first murder in the city of Syracuse on January 19, 2003. That was one of the longest, if not longest, periods without a murder in Syracuse (the last murder was November 14th) in quite some time. The year 2002 would mark the peak in the number of murders in Syracuse until 2016.

I cannot say with certainty that it was our efforts that brought an end to violence; but I believe it helped a lot.

I mention this because I believe it shows the potential power of reinvigorated FOC to bring peace and healing to locations throughout the world.

This book is made up of three parts.

Part I Before You Visit. Contains information explaining FOC and North Star Country, as well as advice on using this book and on visiting the sacred sites listed. In Chapter 1 you will learn about the significant influence that North Star Country has had upon the world. Chapter 2 will explain why and how place matters. In Chapter 3 you will learn about Fields of Consciousness and the Spirit Lines (Ley Lines) that originate from them and the role they play in shaping human consciousness.

I strongly suggest you prepare before visiting sites, especially if you are coming some distance. Chapter 4 gives some advice on preparing for your visit. This will help you build momentum and excitement over your upcoming visit; which will help instill reverence within you for your visit. Reverence and respect are critical to visiting a site, because it is the intention you bring to a place that will help set the tone, or vibe that remains there after you leave. Preparation is also about practicing spiritual exercises before you come. Just as you would physically exercise and train before a big sporting event such as a long distance run, you need to similarly get your spiritual self in shape; particularly if you are going to be spending hours meditating. It is also about your gear; knowing what you are going to bring you if you plan on going in the woods. Things like having hiking boots, a meditative cushion and how to dress.

In Chapter 5 I talk about Experiencing Sites. Not only will I provide some suggestions on how to visit a place, but also teach you about the impact that your visit will have upon place. And why it is so critical to nourish a place with love and compassion. This section provides advice on how to use the surveys and what places to visit if you are attempting to sense consciousness, or have interest in a particular issue such as Women's Rights, abolitionism, peace....

Part II Listing of Sacred Sites The reviews of sacred sites begins in Part II and is listed by geographical location. They indicate where the FOC are located. In other words, where you should meditate, pray or do ceremony. Many of the reviews contain historical and biographical information and a bibliography for further reading. Basic information about visiting a place from directions, hours of operation, admission charges, etc. are included. Please be aware hours change and places close.

Part III Conclusion and Appendix Part III Contains the Conclusion as well as helpful information such as suggested tours and contact information for local tourist bureaus. There are also some prayers, meditations and mantras that you may wish to use. It also contains a glossary for quick reference.

Part I
Before You Visit

Chapter 1

North Star Country—You Shall Know Them By Their Fruits

North Star Country, the area of greater New York State (Pennsylvania, much of Massachusetts, and parts of Vermont, New Jersey, Connecticut, Ohio and southern Ontario, Canada; and maybe even parts of New Hampshire, Maine, Delaware and Maryland) has played a critical role in shaping America and the world; spiritually, democratically and in social justice/rights. I call it North Star Country because that is what the many Freedom Seekers escaping slavery called it.

We are not used to thinking that a place, even a sacred place, can elevate our consciousness, let alone transform our collective soul. Consider the words of Jesus who taught that you shall know a false prophet by the fruit that they bear (Mt 7.16), meaning that we are judged not by our words or appearance, but by our deeds.

North Star Country has borne a bounty of fruit by transforming individual souls and making a better world. It is the birthplace of the Women's Movement, birthplace of American democracy, a place where prophets walked and religions were born, a bedrock of abolitionism and home to numerous Utopian communities. It has been called the Burned-over-District because the spiritual wildfires and revivalism were once so strong here that the area had been scorched so badly that there was nothing, or no one left to convert. Arguably it is the home to America's Second Great Awakening and even the First Great Awakening that took place at its periphery.

Clearly North Star Country has been an area of great social change and spiritual growth.

Historians will tell you that these social changes took place during the tumultuous Antebellum period preceding the Civil War and were a function of the time and transformation the United States was undergoing then. Clearly time matters—but so does place, as I will explain in the next chapter.

Many have recognized that there is something special to North Star Country, particularly its heart center, upstate New York as folklorist Carl Carmer noted:

"It is a broad psychic highway, a thoroughfare of the occult.. east of Albany to west of Buffalo... In no other area in the western Hemisphere have so many evidences of transcending mortal living been manifest...

Until its evidences of enchantment have been academically explained away I shall prefer to believe that special quality of this strip of land has made it the track that leads to things seldom in men's knowing." [1]

Historian Whitney Cross in his classic *Burned-over District, The Social and Intellectual History of Enthusiastic Religion in Western New York, 1800-1850*, detailed the enthusiasm of people for spiritual experimentation and social reform saying, "upon this broad belt of land congregated a people extraordinarily given to unusual religious beliefs, peculiarly devoted to crusades aimed at the perfection of mankind and the attainment of millennial happiness."[2] A passion and fervor which was like no other in America that drew people to a variety of ism's[3]; Revivalism, Spiritualism, abolitionism, Swedenborgianism, Mesmerism, Fourierism....

My purpose in writing this book is to encourage you to visit and to pray, meditate, or do ceremony at the sacred sites listed, because it will raise your consciousness. In doing so you will also strengthen the FOC located there, and in the process help raise humankind's collective consciousness and transform our collective soul.

Fields of Consciousness are unique to North Star Country and are found at the homes of great leaders such as Fredrick Douglass, Susan B. Anthony, Harriet Tubman and others. These FOC played a role, most likely a dominant role in the social changes that took place in North Star Country.

Another factor in Mother Earth also contributed in fostering dramatic changes in North Star Country; the imprints, impressions, or memories of those that had previously lived there. People leave imprints, or memories of their thoughts and actions wherever they go—sometimes these can have a powerful influence upon us. Because many are unfamiliar, or skeptical that imprints can influence human behavior, in the next chapter I will go into greater depth in explaining why this is so.

North Star Country

In the last few decades the area considered to be the Burned-over District, synonymous with the social changes in upstate New York, has expanded from the central western New York corridor (Utica to Buffalo) to stretch from western New England to the Ohio reserve. North Star Country stretches farther north to Canada and farther to the east and to the south.

For our purpose North Star Country is where FOC are located. This is because FOC greatly contributed to the dramatic social transformations in North Star Country by influencing the participants through their emanations. The consciousness emanating from Fields are a transformative force that nourishes our soul with altruism, love, compassion, selflessness and forgiveness.

While FOC are found throughout North Star Country their potency varies as you shall learn in Chapter 3. The most potent area is located between Utica and Rochester, next the rest of New York State, as you fan out their potency begins to diminish.

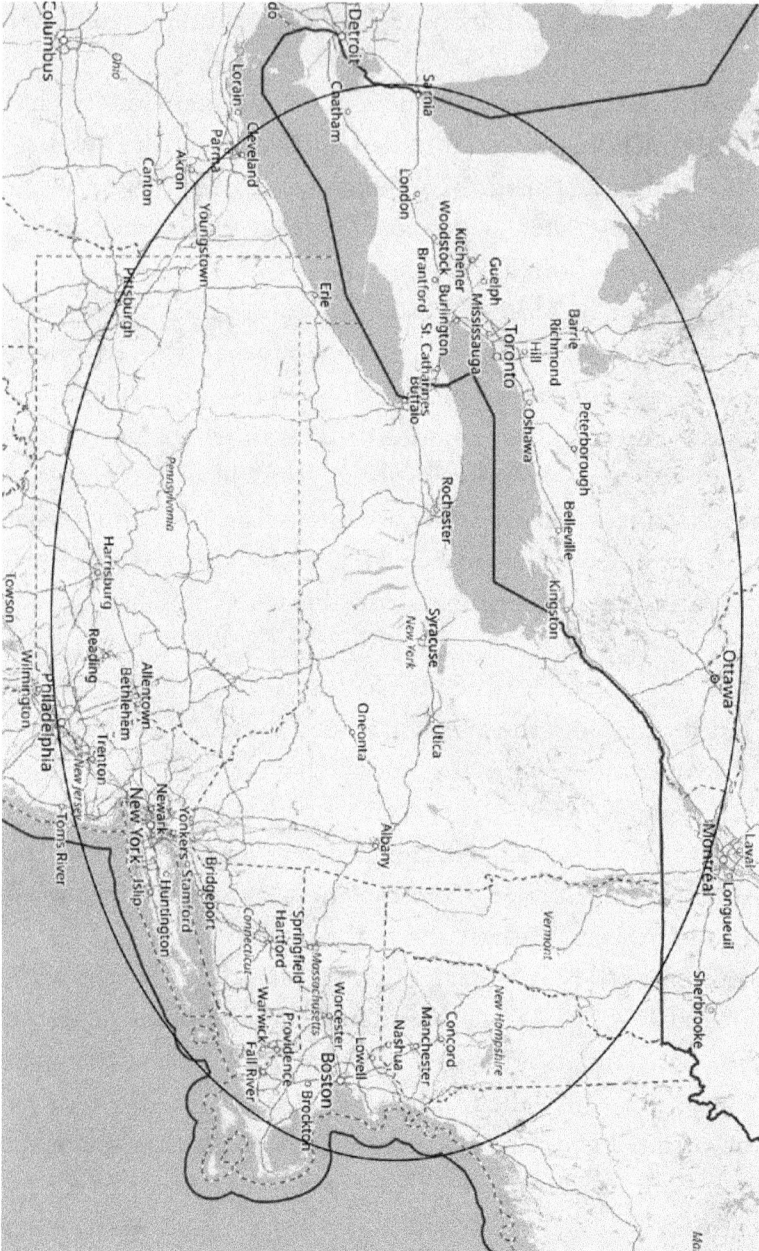

Exhibit 1.1, Map of North Star Country. The circle is the approximate geographic area that North Star Country covers. Maps-© OpenStreetMap contributors, www. openstreetmap. org.

Exhibit 1.1 shows the geographical scope of North Star Country. It is an approximation, but I have found FOC from Boston to Cleveland, southern Ontario, Canada to southern Pennsylvania.

FOC have been a powerful force in transforming humankind.

The Birthplace of Democracy

Before Europeans came to America there was a great prophet in North Star Country, the Peacemaker; a messenger of God who united the five warring tribes (Cayuga, Mohawk, Oneida, Onondaga and Seneca) forming the Haudenosaunee, or Iroquois Nation. He planted the Tree of Peace (white pine) on the shores of Onondaga Lake (Syracuse, NY) and gave the people The Great Law of Peace. The Great Law of Peace greatly influenced the Founders, and arguably the US Constitution is based upon it.

If we honestly and openly examine The Great Law of Peace and compare it to American democracy and our founding texts the similarities become apparent. When the Tree of Peace was planted an eagle soared high in the sky and landed on the white pine tree clutching five arrows representing the five nations. Similarly the US National Seal behind the one dollar bill shows an eagle clutching thirteen arrows representing each of the colonies.

Both allowed for freedom of religion; interesting since the Great Law of Peace is a spiritual document, yet it allowed people to believe anything they wanted to, as long as they obeyed it. Both allowed freedom of speech and provided a route to naturalization. Chiefs were to be servants of the people and have thick skins.

The Haudenosaunee confederacy was an inspiration to several of the Founders. As Benjamin Franklin wrote to James Parker:

"It would be a very strange thing if Six Nations of Ignorant Savages should be capable of forming a Scheme for such an Union and be able to execute it in such a manner, as that it has subsisted Ages, and appears indissoluble, and yet a like Union should be impracticable for ten or a dozen English colonies."[4]

11

As Gregory Schaaf writes

"Benjamin Franklin, Thomas Jefferson and the other Founding Fathers were impressed by the Iroquoian political structure, which featured three branches of government and a system of checks and balances, as well as many freedoms now protected by the Bill of Rights."[5]

The importance of the Haudenosaunee and the Great Law of Peace upon the Founders and American Democracy was not recognized for over 200 years. Finally on October 21, 1988 the Senate passed Hr. Cons. Res. 331,

"to acknowledge the contribution of the Iroquois Confederacy of Nations to the development of the United States Constitution...the original framers of the constitution, including, most notably, George Washington and Benjamin Franklin, are known to have greatly admired the concepts of the Six Nations of the Iroquois Confederacy....the confederation of the original Thirteen Colonies into one republic was influenced by the political system developed by the Iroquois Confederacy as were many of the democratic principles which were incorporated into the constitution itself."[6]

Birthplace of the Women's Movement

Yet there are differences between the Great Law of Peace and American Democracy. For one, the Haudenosaunee are a matrilineal society where clan mothers watch out for their clans and hold enormous power. Women elect leaders and can impeach them. They also have the power to decide whether to go to war because, as the Peacemaker noted, women are more hesitant to send their sons off to war.

The status women held in Iroquois society was a big influence to the leaders of the Women's Movement that was born in North Star Country with the first Women's Rights Convention in Seneca Falls in 1848. Author, feminist and scholar Sally Roesch Wagner was so impressed by this influence that she wrote a book about it, *Sisters in Spirit, Haudenosaunee (Iroquois) Influences on Early American Feminists*. She notes how Lucretia Mott's "feminist vision was inspired by her first hand experience of women's political, spiritual, social and economic authority in the Seneca community."[7]

In particular, Wagner details how the Haudenosaunee women shaped the thinking of the more radical early feminists such as Elizabeth Cady Stanton and especially Matilda Joslyn Gage. Interestingly within a few years of learning about the Matilda Joslyn Gage home in the outskirts of Syracuse (Fayetteville) Wagner started a nonprofit, raised money and purchased the home. The Gage home and that of other prominent leaders of the Women's Movement, Elizabeth Cady Stanton and Susan B. Anthony are listed as sacred sites in Part II.

When I think of the relationship of men and women in the Haudenosaunee culture I am reminded of the Mohawk men and their famous haircut—The Mohawk. It is probably one of the most, if not the most virile symbol of a warrior, of toughness, fearlessness and the like donned by sports figures, soldiers and warriors of various ilk before battle. Yet as much as Mohawk men exuded ferociousness they would get guidance from women and needed their approval to go to war—the exact opposite to cultures around the world today.

What welled up in North Star Country regarding female emancipation was broad and pervasive; particularly in religion and spirituality. When I say broad and pervasive I mean it was not just a few activists or subtle changes made, it was if a fever for social reform and spiritual exploration burned in North Star Country. In other words, it was if everyone caught the fever and the collective psyche of the people was being transformed.

For example, early on in the revival movement men and women were not segregated, but sat together.[8] New religions such as Spiritualism empowered women and gave them leadership roles, unheard of at the time. Women started religions and led religious movements in North Star Country.

There were numerous reforms and religions born in North Star Country as seen in Exhibit 1.2, as well as a place where many great souls and prophets lived.

Exhibit 1.2 The Fruits Born From North Star Country	
Movements	Women's Movement, Second Great Awakening, New Age Movement, Perfectionism, Social Gospel, Niagara Movement (predecessor to the NAACP), First Great Awakening*, Conservation* (Environmentalism with Transcendentalism's focus on Nature.)
Religions	Spiritualism, Mormonism, Millerism/Seven Day Adventists, Transcendentalism*, Theosophy*, Universalism*.
Prophets	The Peacemaker, Handsome Lake (18th century Seneca prophet.)
Abolitionists, Women's Rights	Fredrick Douglass, Harriet Tubman, Susan B. Anthony, Gerrit Smith, William Seward, Jermain Loguen. Elizabeth Cady Stanton, Matilda Joslyn Gage, Sojourner Truth*, William Lloyd Garrison*+,...
Utopian Communities	Oneida Community, Skaneateles Community, Sodus Bay Phalanx, Inspirationalists of Buffalo Creek, Kiantone Domain,...
Other	Birthplace of (American) Democracy, food reform, clothing reform, Anti-masonry, Peace Society,...
*Outside of the core of North Star Country, but still within it. + Garrison's home in the Roxbury section of Boston, now in private hands, sits on a FOC.	

Not only was North Star County a passionate birthplace but also a cauldron for reforms from other places. Benevolent Societies, as Whitney Cross notes, were not unique to the Burned-over District having long roots in the past and were national in scope. But the campaigns to circulate bibles, to found Sunday Schools, to encourage temperance and to enforce Sabbath "all spurted so suddenly here and so intensified and broadened their appeals in this region that they became in their proportions veritable peculiarities of this time and place in American history."[9]

The Marriage of Spirituality with Reform

One of the features of social reform in North Star Country was that it was inseparable from spirituality/religion, a sharp contrast to our modern society. Syracuse University professor Michael Barkun in *Crucible of the Millennium, The Burned Over District of New York in the 1840's* noted the strong linkages between social reformers, community builders and revivalists, often in the same individual, and how difficult and misleading it is to categorize ventures as either religious, or secular.[10] In many ways spirituality/religion drove social reform.

The most vocal voices for social reform within Christianity were Ecclesiastical Abolitionists, who were committed to sanctifying the religious and political processes of Antebellum America by creating purified organizations.[11] They broke free from traditional denominations that were connected to southern churches that advocated slavery and created anti-slavery, or abolition churches.[12] They also helped create the Liberty Party, the first reform minded party in America. Ecclesiastical Abolitionism adhered to the doctrine of Perfectionism, to become better and more moral; not necessarily to become perfect, but being closer to God in thought and deed.

Many Spiritualists were reform minded. Spiritualism, the belief that the deceased can and wish to communicate with the living, was born in Hydesville, NY in 1848. It began when the Fox sisters heard mysterious rapping noises supposedly from a deceased peddler. Soon the peddler was answering questions by the number of his rappings, one was no, two was yes. Eventually it was

15

realized that the Fox sisters could call up other spirits. They became mediums and took their abilities on the road.

Spiritualism saw converts into the millions. Many social reformers joined its ranks. Noted abolitionists and Women's Rights advocates Amy and Isaac Post, Hicksite Quakers and neighbors of the Fox Sisters embraced Spiritualism and introduced it to many other Quakers.

Spiritualism stirred many other reforms, empowered people and liberated them from the control of the church that saw itself as the sole medium to the divine. It offered hope and intimacy with the divine and salvation compared to the Calvinist doctrine of predestination. Spiritualism said that we are all evolving and could determine our own destiny. It also offered the hope to communicate with deceased relatives at a time of high mortality, particularly after the Civil War.

Most importantly, Spiritualism empowered women. Mediums were primarily women and were given prominence and spoke publicly which was unheard of at the time. As Director of Women's Studies in Religion at Harvard Divinity School Anne Braude has written and lectured on the role women have played in religion. In her book *Radical Spirits, Spiritualism and Women's Rights in Nineteenth Century America*, when published in 1989 brought to light how intertwined Spiritualism was with the Women's Movement. Braude said that Spiritualism was a "central agent of feminism."[13] She notes how the "American Women's Rights Movement drew its first breath in an atmosphere alive with rumors of angels." She goes on to say; "While not all feminists were Spiritualists, all Spiritualists were women's advocates."[14] In the introduction to her second edition, Braude notes that what distinguished advocates that were Spiritualists was their radicalism; the more radical members of the Women's Movement were Spiritualists.

When we think of Spiritualism we envision mediums, psychics and channellers looking to profit. However, that was not the case for much of Spiritualism during its early days. While Spiritualism drew many fraudsters and profiteers, others saw it as means to bring about reform.

Theologian John Buescher notes how many reformers saw Spiritualism as a vehicle for social reform. They felt that contact with the divine, or with beings in other realms could help bring about a better world:

> "Many...who turned to Spiritualism sensed a biblical millennium, which manifested itself in plans for egalitarian Utopias where humans mingle with angels or become angels themselves. Thus, Spiritualism was not just a means of contacting the spirits of the deceased or of exploring the afterlife. Rather, it meant the opening wide of a gate between a perfect Heaven and an imperfect Earth. This idea provided a link between spiritualism and social reform. "[15]

Spiritualism drew large audiences for other radical causes besides feminism as Braude[16] notes: Abolitionism, Free Speech, Abolition of capital punishment, land monopoly......

The religious fervor of reform that brewed in North Star Country not only gave us new religions and sects, they were religions led by women; Mother Annie Lee, Shakerism; Jemima Wilkinson, Society of Universal Friends; Madame Blavatsky, co-founder of Theosophy. Theosophy itself was a rebellion against traditional religion and was based upon the belief in the equality of sexes and races.

Religiously minded social reform would transform into the Social Gospel of the latter half of the nineteenth and early twentieth century. The Social Gospel believed Jesus teachings to help the poor, the sick, the old, and the widower and to visit the prisoner should be applied to social issues. Today we would call it social justice. Many of its dominant leaders were from North Star Country; Walter Rauschenbusch, Washington Gladden, Charles Monroe Sheldon ("What would Jesus Do?) and Richard T. Ely.

The Social Gospel would go on to inspire leaders such as Martin Luther King Jr.

Abolitionism, Underground Railroad

Abolitionism was a powerful force in North Star Country. Several of the routes, or tracks, of Underground Railroad passed through it. Many of its leaders lived here: Fredrick Douglass, Harriet Tubman, Gerrit Smith, William Seward and leaders of the Women's Movement.

In the center of North Star Country (Syracuse) lived Jermain Loguen an escaped slave, minister and conductor on the Underground Railroad. It is estimated that he and his wife Caroline assisted 1,500 passengers (probably more than anyone else) on the Underground Railroad, helping Syracuse earn the nickname, 'Canada of the North.'[17]

The core of North Star Country (aka the Burned-over District) seized leadership of the abolition crusade; and had a powerful influence upon the enlarged antislavery agitation of the forties and fifties and ultimately the Civil War.[18] An expanded view of North Star Country includes much of the North.

Utopian Communities

Steeped in North Star Country was the belief that a better world was possible. Many looked to achieve this by forming Utopian communities. The Shakers and the Oneida Community (both listed as sacred sites in Part II) believed that communal living improved human behavior. There was also Thomas Lake Harris and the Brotherhood of New Life, John Murray Spear and Kiantone.

Many embraced millennialism—the second coming of Christ and a 1,000 year reign of peace, or Heaven on Earth. The most infamous was William Miller and the Millerites. Miller predicted the end of the world would come between the spring equinox of 1843 and 1844. When Christ failed to appear, it was called 'The

Great Disappointment' and did little to deter believers. Detecting an error in calculations a new date was determined, October 22, 1844. When Christ failed to return it led to the 'Second Disappointment' and the dissolution of believers; still the Millerite movement would give birth to Seven Day Adventists. Miller's home and ascension rock in Whitehall, NY still stands.

As Barkun notes of Utopian communities, "they derived their value, as far as many Utopians were concerned, from the fact that they were instruments bringing the millennium nearer. It could be achieved here and now, if only in miniature." [19]

New Age Movement

While the New Age Movement was not recognized, or categorized until the 1960's or 1970's, its nascent formation took place in North Star Country in the nineteenth century. It is so North Star: spiritual exploration and new forms of its expression, self seeking/help, esoteric, occult, the influence of Eastern traditions, alternative beliefs, emphasis on the mystical, the belief in other, or alternative realities and inhabitants thereof.

Spiritualism, as previously noted, empowered people to seek their own spirituality through communication with other realms of reality; in doing so it not only broke from the traditional church (the middle man), but it recognized that there was another, or alternative reality to our existence. Spiritualism played a key role in shaping the New Age Movement.

Theosophy born at the edge of North Star Country in New York City, is probably the dominant stock in the soup called the New Age Movement. Theosophy placed emphasis on occult and esoteric knowledge. It taught about alternative realities and its inhabitants. It has no firm beliefs, only that all of life is indivisible, and required no firm membership, or doctrine; instead it advocated a new spiritual freedom of self-exploration. Theosophy has a strong emphasis on the mystical.

Transcendentalism (eastern edge of North Star Country) and Theosophy added Eastern influences to the soup that would become the New Age Movement. Introducing beliefs such as all of creation is connected and we are one, and spiritual practices such as Yoga and meditation. The coming to America by mystics such as Swami Vivekananda added doctrine and spiritual practices such as meditation to the New Age soup. Two of his main teaching grounds are listed as sacred sites in Part II.

Transcendentalism added the love of Nature.

Professor Joscelyn Godwin of Colgate University, who many call the grandfather, or dean of occult and esoteric knowledge, mentions several other esoteric and spiritual explorers in North Star Country in his *Upstate Cauldron*. Truly the New Age was born in North Star Country in the nineteenth century.

Heaven on Earth, The Fire Still Smolders

North Star Country has played a powerful role in shaping our collective being. The fires of spiritual exploration and social reform that burned brightly in the nineteenth century still smolder. The famous social activists of the 1960's and 1970's, the Berrigan brothers and Chris Hedges (his childhood church in Schoharie, NY is listed) currently one of the most strident progressive voice as well as others hail from North Star Country. As does the Fellowship of Reconciliation an ecumenical peace and justice group that has played a pivotal role in peace and justice for over a hundred years. Therapeutic Touch an alternative healing modality (energy healing) was born in North Star Country; its base in Pumpkin Hollow in Craryville, NY is listed as a sacred site.

While much of what was born in North Star Country adhered to the prophetic spirit, there were exceptions, most notably Mormonism. It failed to embrace social reform; polygamy was an early church practice and to this day it still does not ordain women. Mormonism did not admit blacks until 1978.

Heaven on Earth, or Perfectionism, would be the omnibus classification to encompass all that was born in North Star Country. The belief that a better world is possible and that there is a greater reality beyond the material world, helping us to achieve such, is at the core of North Star Country.

References and Recommended Reading

1. Carmer, Carl, *Listen for the Lonesome Drum, A York State Chronicle*, David McKay, NY 1950. pages145-146

2. Cross, Whitney, *Burned-over District, The Social and Intellectual History of Enthusiastic Religion in Western New York, 1800-1850*, Cornell University Press (1950) reprinted by Harper Torchbooks, New York, NY, 1965. Page 3.

3. Ibid, Page 202.

4. Johansen, Bruce; Letter from Benjamin Franklin to James Parker, 1751, in Chapter 4, *Forgotten Founders*, Harvard Common Press, Boston, Ma.,1982.

5. Schaaf, Gregory, "From the Great Law of Peace to the Constitutions of the United States: A Revision of America's Democratic Roots", American Indian Law Review, Vol. 14 No.2 (1988/1989)

6.http://www.senate.gov/reference/resources/pdf/hconres331.pdf.

7. Wagner, Sally Roesch, *Sisters in Spirit, Haudenosaunee (Iroquois) Influences on Early American Feminists*. Page 44
Women's Rights National Historic Park http://www.nps.gov/wori/learn/historyculture/frederick-douglass.htm

8. Whitney Cross talks about this in the *Burned-over District*, page 178.

9. Ibid. Page 126.

10. Barkun, Michael; *Crucible of the Millennium. The Burned Over District of New York in the 1840's*, Syracuse University Press, 1986; Page 2.

11. Strong, Douglas M.; *Perfectionist Politics, Abolitionism and the Religious Tensions of American Democracy*, Syracuse University Press, Syracuse NY 1999 Page 4.

12. Slavery was a contentious issue that divided denominations by regions, the North and South. Timothy L. Smith in *Revivalism and Social Reform, in Mid-Nineteenth Century America*, Abingdon Press, Nashville, Tennessee, 1957; Page 216. notes "But no avenue of propaganda could have been devised more effectively to harden Northern antipathy toward slavery than the pulpits and the pens of such men. Nor could any have so deeply enflamed Southern pride." To many northerners the bible was an anti-slavery document, while to many southerners it was a pro-slavery document.

13. Braude, Anne; *Radical Spirits, Spiritualism and Women's Rights in Nineteenth Century America*, Indiana university Press, Bloomington, 1989, 2001; Page 192

14. Ibid. Page 58

15. Buescher, John B., *The Other Side of Salvation: Spiritualism and the Nineteenth Century Religious Experience*, Skinner House Books, Boston, Ma. 2004, Page 123.

16. Braude, Page 69.

17. Sernett, Milton C., *North Star Country, Upstate New York and The Crusade for African American Freedom*, Page 179.

18. Cross, Page 217.

19. Page 68 Barkun

Chapter 2

Place Matters—The Influence of North Star Country On Our Collective Consciousness

Place matters, our physical location can have a profound influence upon us. The dramatic social changes that took place in North Star Country during the Antebellum period—Women's Rights, abolitionism, Utopian communities, and religions borne—were greatly shaped by Mother Earth.

The reason this sounds outrageous to many is because we have lost our connection to the land.

We are intimately connected to Mother Earth, She shapes us and nourishes us, physically and spiritually. We also affect Her. Our progress and the transformation of our souls, is contingent upon Her transformation. We are bound to Her in all that we do.

One of Her special parts is the greater Upstate New York region, what I call North Star Country. It is here where Her soul resides, I say this because so much good and so much that has advanced our collective being came from this area. She has touched and nourished the souls of so many great people here.

Each of us has a special place that evokes strong emotions; a childhood home, a park or woods, where we went to college, our grandparent's home. While many of the world's religions do not recognize the influence that Mother Earth has upon us, they all have sacred places. Islam has Mecca, Judaism the Temple Mount, Christianity Bethlehem, Hinduism Varanasi, Buddhism the Bodhi Tree where Buddha achieved enlightenment. There are also pilgrimage places such as Lourdes where people flock to each year for miraculous healings. Place Matters.

Regionalism

In 1968 Kevin Phillips was a strategist for the Nixon Presidential Campaign. Ever since the New Deal in 1930's Republican conservatism had suffered at the hands of Democratic liberalism. Yet in 1969 he published a book, *The Emerging Republican Majority*, which predicted the rise and dominance of Republican conservatism for decades to come.

Phillip's book would help shape what became the Republican's Southern Strategy; play to Southern white Democrats dissatisfied with the Civil Rights Act of 1964 and benefit from the migration west and to the south. At the time it was considered ground breaking and today it is thought to be one of the great books of American politics, mostly because he was so prescient and correct in his prediction.

In his book Phillips gave a variety of reasons why Republicanism would surge. He felt that American politics had played in clear cycles of ideology, population movement and regionalism; with the 1968 Republican Victory a turning point that would last 30 to 40 years as other cycles had. He also felt that white Democratic voters dissatisfied with Johnson's Great Society and the Civil Rights Act of 1964 would switch in droves to the Republican party.

While immigrant fluxes and religious affiliations influence voting choices, Phillips felt "the basic roots of American voting patterns have long rested in the regionalism of Civil War loyalties."[1]

Phillips saw the liberal northeast and its big cities political influence was waning because of population shifts from cities to suburbia, both local and distant.[2] He felt the population booms in Texas and Florida would continue, and combined with the migration flow to the new urbanized cities of the South would increase the South's share of the national population.

Phillips was right, the population of the South has surged and conservatism has steadily grown with it. The region's electoral votes has gone from 120 (1970) to 190 (2010.) Yet Republican voting has consistently held steady. Why?

For example, Georgia saw its population double from 4.6 mil (1970) to 9.7 mil (2010), its electoral votes rise from 12 to 16 in that same period. Yet its voting record remained consistently conservative Republican with the exception of when southern native sons Carter and Clinton ran for president. Not everyone moving to Georgia was a conservative Democrat that switched party allegiance to conservative Republicanism. There were liberals, independents, middle of the road people and immigrants.

No doubt other factors such as the rise in conservatism nationally and the advent of a free market economy played a role. But something more had to account for why such a surge in population would embrace the regions traditional Civil War allegiances. Was it the land?

The Collective Unconscious

To understand how the land can influence us we turn to Swiss born psychiatrist Carl Jung who gave us concepts such as archetypes and the collective unconscious. Jung was a nature lover who felt the earth was a living organism that had a spirit and a mind; similar to the beliefs of indigenous people. He said it could be a healing force saying that when people get dirty from too much civilization all they need to do is take a walk in the woods; because, "whenever we touch nature we get clean."[3] Similarly when we touch nature , we touch our unconscious .

Jung saw the land influencing who we are, saying the mind was "a system of adaptation determined by the conditions of an earthly environment."[4] In other words, we are at the mercy of the earth and its laws.

On a trip to America's Middle West[5], while watching workers leaving a factory, Jung commented to a friend on how he would have never imagined that there was such a high percentage of Native American blood in the workers. His companion laughed and said that they had no Native American blood. Years later Jung called this the "Indianization" of the American people; in other words the American people behaved like Native American, not from their frequent contact with them, but because the had absorbed their characteristics (archetypes, behaviors) from the land.[6] Similarly, the South retained its conservative roots and voted conservative Republican in the face of massive migration into it because the land consumed the immigrants.

In Jung's view, nature was identical to the collective unconscious and contained our archetypes[7];

"For it is the body, the feeling, the instincts which connect us with the soil. If you give up your past you naturally detach from the past; you loose your roots in the soil, your connection with the totem ancestors that dwell in the soil."[8]

Clearly Jung felt that the earth had a strong grip upon us. We see this in his writings about America and how he felt the land had conquered the European conquerors, in other words it took over control and changed them. He said "the foreign land assimilates its conqueror ….Our contact with the unconscious chains us to the earth and makes it hard for us to move."[9] In the telling Jung points out how Australian Aborigines believe one cannot conquer a foreign soil, because the ancestor-spirits that dwell in the soil will reincarnate in the invader.

Jung believed that the collective unconscious shaped humankind. It contained the psychic life of our earliest ancestors and the successive generations that followed. He described the evolution of our psyche by comparing it to a multistory building. Its upper story was constructed in the nineteenth century, its ground floor in the sixteenth century and its masonry reveals that it was reconstructed in the eleventh century. In the cellar we find

Roman foundations and under the cellar is a cave with Neolithic tools in the upper layer and remnants of fauna from the same period in the lower level. Jung felt we live in the upper story and are only aware of the lower story. We remain totally unaware of what lies below the earth's surface.[10]

The same multistory building that Jung uses to describe the evolution of our psyche is contained in the earth. It is a reservoir of the memories and actions of those that have walked its soil. It is a repository that exerts tremendous influence upon us individually and collectively. We keep adding more floors over time.

Jung's view on the unconscious has received a rebirth, in what many call the 'new unconscious.' While most adherents believe that the unconscious lies in the human brain and is not linked to the earth, they do agree with Jung that it has a tremendous influence upon us.

American physicist Leonard Mlodinow has authored five NY Times bestsellers, including one with Stephen Hawking (*Grand Design.*) In his book *Subliminal, How your Unconscious Mind Rules your Behavior* he talks about the power of the unconscious. He notes that that we do not operate like straightforward number crunching computers and calculate results. Instead our brains are made up of many modules, most of which lie below our consciousness and greatly influence our judgment, feelings and behavior.

Imprints, Land Memories and Impressions

National Public Radio did a segment on how a change in the environment was responsible for the remarkable success of Vietnam veterans to remain drug free after kicking their heroin addiction. Reporter Alex Spiegel interviewed and relied on the research of Lee Robins. Robins noted that 20% US Vietnam veterans were addicted to heroin. Instead of returning home and seeking treatment, they remained in Vietnam and were not allowed to return home until they had kicked their habit. What she found was startling; recidivism rates were about 6% compared to about 90% for the public at large.[11] These results were so remarkable that many people doubted Robins and she had to spend years defending her work.

It was the change of environment that helped the Vietnam Vets stay off of heroin. David T. Neal, PhD who along with USC professor Wendy Wood, PhD write a blog for Psychology Today says, "[P]eople, when they perform a behavior a lot — especially in the same environment, same sort of physical setting — outsource the control of the behavior to the environment." His fellow blogger Wendy Wood agreed and noted how we are oblivious to the environments saying, "We don't feel sort of pushed by the environment." Noting at the same time "But, in fact, we're very integrated with it."[12]

When Jung talks about our 'ancestral totems' are in the land, or when researchers say we 'outsource' our behavior to the environment, the implication is that the land retains our thoughts and deeds—both our collective and individual thoughts and actions. I call the thoughts that cling to the land imprints, or impressions, or (land) memories.

Similarly our thoughts and actions attach to nearby objects such as furniture, carpets, rocks and the like; imprints even form on our organs. We see this vividly with organ recipients who have reported that the organs they received retained the memories and thoughts of their donors. They call these 'inherited memories,' or 'cellular memories.' One of the most famous is Claire Sylvia dancer, with a rare lung disease who was one of the first recipient's of a heart lung transplant in New England in 1988.

In her book *A Change of Heart* she chronicles several examples of how the organs of her eighteen-year old male donor, who had died in a motorcycle accident, influenced her. Immediately in a post-operative interview she tells a reporter she was "dying for a beer," something she did not like before her transplant. She also found herself drawn to other favorites of her donor, such as

Snickers bars, Reese's Peanut Butter Cups, green peppers and Chicken McNuggets all of which she did not care for before her transplant. She also found an increase in what she called male energy.

There are many other examples of transplanted organs retaining the cellular memories of their donors. Psychologists Dr. Paul Pearsall, Dr. Gary Schwartz and Dr. Linda Russek in an article extracted for Nexus magazine cite 10 of 74 cases where organ recipients did more than develop new preferences and exhibited personality changes associated with their donors.[14]

In one case a 29-year-old woman received the heart of a 19-year-old woman who was an avid vegetarian, and as her mother said of her, she was pretty wild and into "the free love thing." The recipient said that she used to be MacDonald's best customer, but now she is a vegan. Her brother tells how she used to be gay, militantly so. Now she was straight.

In another case a 17 year-old black male was accidentally killed in a drive by shooting on his way to violin class. The 47-year-old white male recipient was a foundry worker who his wife described him as close to being an Archie Bunker. The recipient said he used to hate classical music, but now loves it and plays it all the time because it calms his heart. He also began inviting his black co-workers to his home for the first time.

Imprints, or memories play an important role for Mother Earth and humankind. I will discuss them later in several places because they are so critical to the vibe of a sacred site.

Mother Earth's Emanations

There is another influence that Mother Earth has upon humankind, Her many emanations. One of which is the consciousness emanating from the Fields of Consciousness in North Star Country. We are not used to thinking that in another realm, or higher Plane of Existence, Mother Earth is nourishing us in some way, as She does in the Physical Plane with food and water.

The Tectonic Strain Theory of Dr. Michael Persinger postulates that when tectonic plates below the surface of the earth shift they release electromagnetic energy that influences humankind. Persinger has studied numerous UFO sightings and other paranormal activity and found that they occur close to areas with seismic shifts, or have other powerful Earth Energies. He believes that the mystical experiences were the result of an increased jolt of electromagnetic energy from Mother Earth.

Dr. Todd Murphy, a protégé of Dr. Persinger, in his book *Sacred Pathways: The Brain's Role in Religious and Mystic Experiences* details the many affects of increased electromagnetic energy may have upon us from OBE's (out of body experiences), to NDE's (near death experiences), to bizarre dreams, to hallucinations, to sleep paralysis. He is quick to point out that:

> "Sleep paralysis, or anything else that the earth's magnetic fields contributes to, isn't caused by geomagnetic storms. It's caused by factors at work inside the human brain…Changes in the Earth's magnetic field make many experiences more likely, but that's not the same thing as causing them."[15]

To make the point that mystical experiences are nothing more than brain activity Persinger constructed what he calls the God Helmet, a snowmobile helmet with solenoids attached to replicate the mystical experience. A subject dons the God Helmet and magnetic fields are delivered through the solenoids to stimulate their brain. People have had a variety of experiences; seeing things, feeling a sensed presence and even sensing, or seeing God or, Christ while wearing the God Helmet.

To say that the brain creates mystical experience is like saying a light switch creates light—it is a processing instrument. It is only through our intention when we flick the switch on, thereby completing the electrical circuit that the light bulb goes on. Similarly through our intention, both voluntarily and involuntarily, we attract a response from Mother Earth; which is a dose of energy, consciousness, or some other essence.

In other words, we attract them (energy, consciousness, or some other essence) just like an energy healer, such as a Reiki practitioner pulls in energy and transfers it into the patient. Similarly those practicing pranayama (breathing exercises) attract energy, or what Hindu's call prana. This gift from Mother Earth in response to our intention turns the light on.

To better understand how and why Mother Earth's essences, energies and consciousness interact with us think of the movie the Matrix. In it Trinity, Morpheus and Neo would enter another reality through computers. The computers were like a sophisticated video game, that allowed them to enter the matrix, a virtual reality. Well Mother Earth is like the computers in the Matrix, but instead of creating a virtual reality She creates our physical reality.

We play a video game through its controls. By our intention we decide how we are going to move the controls around to participate in the game. The controls respond by moving around the avatar in our video game. Similarly it is with Mother Earth, She responds to our intentions to create the reality we call the physical world: but instead of using controls like a video game She sends us energies, essences or consciousness in response.

Similarly when we don Persinger's God Helmet and are stimulated with magnetic energy we may have a mystical experience; but instead of attracting the magnetic energy through our intentions and efforts, it is forced upon us.

Interestingly Todd Murphy has been able to create different types of God Helmets with various results by changing the pattern of the magnetic waves, or how they are applied. The Shakti Helmet is designed to enhance your mood and your meditation. The Shiva Helmet, is fashioned after the original God Helmet and simulates the mystical experience.

31

So by changing the pattern of magnetic energy the God Helmet can create a variety of experiences. Similarly Mother Earth creates our physical reality in response to our intentions, by altering what she sends us and where: only there is infinitely more that Mother Earth can send us and how and where She applies it compared to the God Helmet.

Mother Earth's essences and energies have a profound influence upon us—WE NEED THEM TO SURVIVE AND GROW.

Dr. Robert Becker who broke ground with his study of electromedicine and was nominated for the Nobel prize in medicine said that "the relationship between the external energies in the Earth's geomagnetic field and living organism has revealed that living things are intimately related to this field and derive vital, basic information from it."[16] Becker felt that living organisms have been tied to the Earth's natural magnetic field since life began.[17]

Dr. Richard Gerber who wrote one of the definitive books on energy medicine, *Vibrational Medicine*, believes that during energy healing "healers may be tapping into the geomagnetic field."[18] So energy healers are drawing energy from the same geomagnetic field that creates mystical experiences; two very different experiences. What distinguishes them is the intention and one has to assume different variations, or types of energy because the results are so dramatic; just as Murphy's Shiva and Shakti helmets. So intention determines what we attract, and in so doing, what we experience and what affect it has upon us.

For example, an energy healer attracts a particular type of prana during a healing that they funnel into the person receiving the healing. I call the energy they attract Earth Prana and it nourishes our Energy Body. Conversely when we meditate we attract a particular type of energy that I call Cosmic Prana. While it is energy, it also has a consciousness component that nourishes our soul. Two different activities attract two different types of energy.

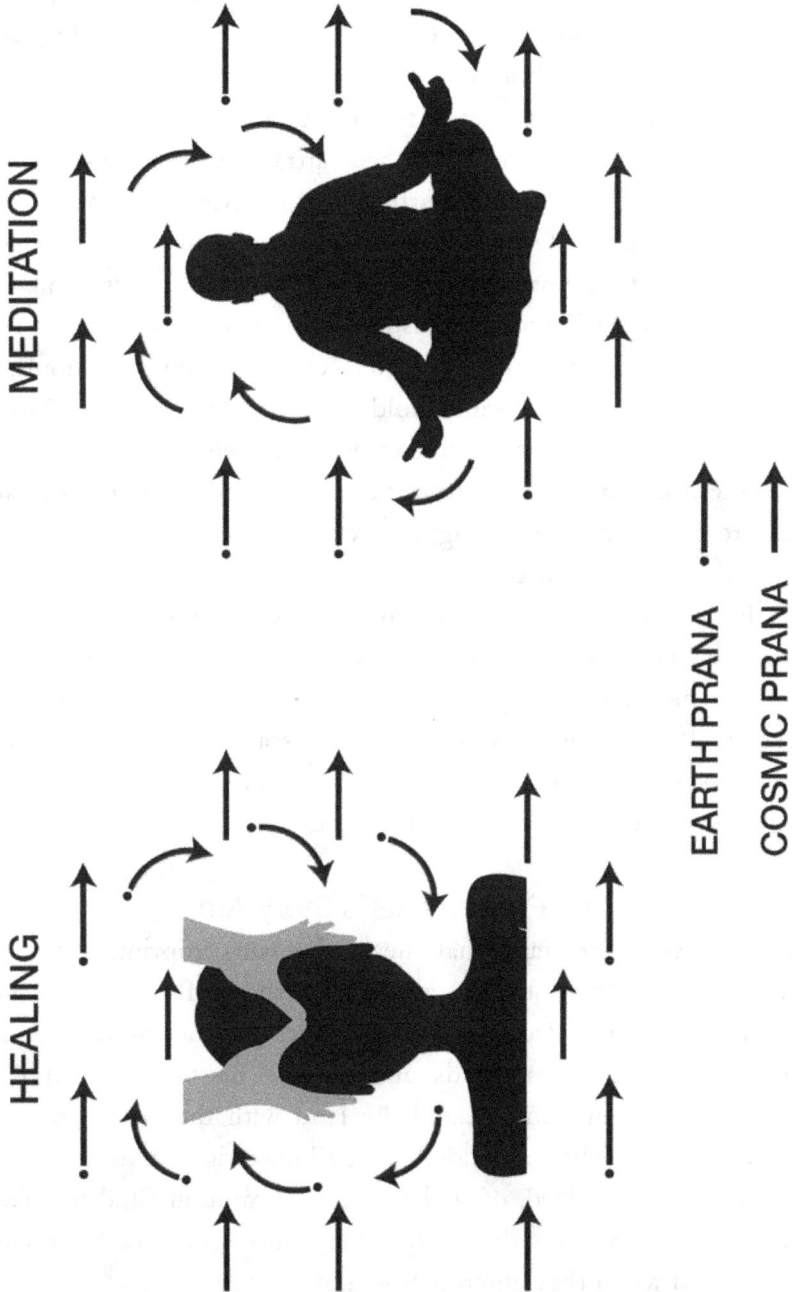

Exhibit 2.1. How Intention Influences the Flow of Prana. Image by Linda Donaldson of Imagine Design.

33

A person being healed by an energy healer will attract Earth Prana, but not Cosmic Prana. Conversely a person meditating will attract Cosmic Prana, but not Earth Prana. Exhibit 2.1 shows how our different activities attract different pranas.

To better understand why we attract energies/essences/consciousness from Mother Earth and their effects upon us let's turn to a classic Hermetic principle—"as above, so below." Which means that what goes on in the Physical Plane is similarly occurring in other Planes of Existence. So we eat food to nourish our physical body, we similarly need to consume energy to nourish our Energy Body. The same holds true for the soul. But soul needs to consume consciousness to nourish itself.[19]

There is much more to Mother Earth beyond what science can measure such as electromagnetic energy. She has a host of energies, essences and consciousness that is unknown to science, but that we experience every day. One of Her emanations of particular interest to our discussion is consciousness. The consciousness emanating from FOC is very potent compared to Cosmic Prana and nourishes your soul and raises your consciousness—make you more loving, compassionate, forgiving—as we shall learn in the next chapter.

The Peacemaker's Story Arc

Now that we understand that the land retains imprints that can shape us, we can better appreciate the influence of the Peacemaker beyond the literal to the unconscious mind of early America. Through his words and actions he transformed the Haudenosaunee and intoxicated the land with the wishes of the Creator—the equality of genders, that all have rights and that their opinions be recognized, of social justice, community and the like. It is this consciousness that early settlers and America's Founders experienced when they entered North Star Country.

A country's heroes and their stories define it. The mythologist Joseph Campbell, who's Hero's Story Arc serves as a model for

Hollywood's storytellers, said that myths are a "living inspiration... Religions, philosophies, arts, the social forms of primitive and historic man, prime discoveries in science and technology, the very dreams that blister sleep, build from the basic, magic ring of myth."[20]

The hero's journey of the Peacemaker is no myth; but a real life story like that of Jesus and Buddha, and just as powerful. It is a story of peace, reconciliation, of transformation and the melting pot. It teaches us to put our differences aside and bury the hatchet and shows how the human spirit can be transformed nonviolently. This is a story told repeatedly and endlessly by the Haudenosaunee at gatherings, to children during storytelling and passed on for generations. It reinforces the consciousness emanating from Fields of Consciousness—they are the same.

While the Peacemakers story has a variety of versions as Bruce Eliot Johansen notes in the *Encyclopedia of the Haudenosaunee*[21], all begin with the birth of the Peacemaker north of Lake Ontario. Upon reaching manhood he paddled a stone canoe across Lake Ontario to upstate New York where much violence and war was raging among people. There he begins his calling to bring about peace by turning hearts and minds.

The Peacemaker encounters a woman who is neutral but feeds the various warriors. When the Peacemaker tells her that the creator is upset with her actions she accepts his message of peace and offers to work with him. He gives the women a special duty— Clan Mother.

The Peacemaker gets Hiawatha to accept his message and work with him. There was an evil sorcerer, Adodarhoh, as evil as anyone who has ever lived; so evil that his body was twisted and snakes grew from his hair. He killed Hiawatha's daughters because he was upset that the message of peace was spreading. Hiawatha was so grief stricken that he could no longer work with the Peacemaker to spread the Creator's message of peace. But Hiawatha healed himself by finding words that would console others that were grief stricken. To remember the words, he strung together white and purple clamshells, creating wampum.

With his mind clear, Hiawatha got together with the Peacemaker again and confronted the Adodarhoh. By that time many had joined the cause of peace. They combed the snakes from his hair and got him to accept the Creator's message of peace. In this process they transformed him from a very evil and violent man into a spiritual leader. He was no longer the Adodarhoh, but the Tadodaho, a great spiritual leader, the greatest chief.

To symbolize the peace, the Peacemaker uprooted a white pine tree and had all the people throw their weapons into the stream that manifest below—bury the hatchet. The Peacemaker replanted the Tree of Peace and gave the people the Great Law of Peace.

He said: "These are the Great White Roots, and their nature is Peace and Strength. If any man or any nation shall obey the Laws of Peace … they may trace back the roots of the Tree … They shall be welcomed to take shelter beneath the Great Evergreen Tree." (Great Law of Peace, The Binding Law, 2.)

The message of the Peacemaker's story is a powerful one:

Peace/reconciliation—People were able to cast their differences aside and unite in peace.

Forgiveness—Everyone had to forgive, especially Hiawatha who had his daughters killed. A powerful message seldom seen in 'story arcs', or stories, whether they are religious, or nonreligious.

Transformation—America is the story of second acts, supposedly from immigrants finding a new home in a distant land. But the story of Peacemaker tells of one of the most dramatic transformations ever, the rebirth of the Adodarhoh into the Tadodaho. Imagine the most violent and evil person being transformed into a spiritual leader. Wow. What a transformation!

Melting pot/uniting—A universal theme especially of the world today—anthem of the New Age Movement, Theosophy and Hinduism. Before the USA became a melting pot of various cultures and races there was the uniting of the five tribes that became the Haudenosaunee.

Spiritual—the Creator through the Peacemaker brought about peace.

Women—were given an elevated status of clan mothers.

The story of the Peacemaker is the universal message of the Creator, as well as exhibiting the same effects of the consciousness exuded by FOC, as you will shortly learn.

Intoxicating the Founders with Peace and Freedom

When Europeans first came to the shores of America, and entered North Star Country, they came under the influence of two powerful forces—FOC and the land which contained the imprints and archetypes of the Haudenosaunee and other Native people. It was those forces that would shape the Founders and early Americans. That is at the core of what America is and what it can be. So while the Great Law of Peace appealed to the conscious mind of the Founders, an even greater influence from the land molded their unconscious mind; the imprints and archetypes buried in the land and the Fields of Consciousness.

It is hard to imagine that the land helped shape the Founders and early Americans, but we need to remember the land is much different today. Its inhabitants, both for the good and for the bad, are continually shaping the land. Unfortunately, we have sullied North Star Country since then; through the practice of slavery, the slaughter of Native Americans, a violent Civil War, degradation of the environment, a culture of war and violence focused on profit and plunder. We have failed to embrace a communal and matrilineal society, and spirituality that is at the core of the Haudenosaunee and the Great Law. In Jung's mythical house we have added floor upon floor each more polluted than the last. Yet in the floors below lies the consciousness and archetype of the Peacemaker and probably other such great prophets and those that lived by the Great Law.

In other words, that Consciousness, that Spirit, which intoxicated the Founders and the reformers of the nineteenth century is much more subdued and hidden. Yet at the core, in the lower floors Jung spoke about, the beauty of freedom and love still exists looking to sprout forth. Space can be cleaned; land can be made whole.

References and Recommended Reading

1. Phillips, Kevin, *The Emerging Republican Party, Doubleday*, New York, NY; 1969; Page 40.

2. Ibid. Page 186.

3. Jung, C. G. & Sabini, Meredith, *The Earth has a Soul, C. G. Jun on Nature, Technology & Modern, Life*, North Atlantic Books, Berkley, Calif, 2202, 2005, 2008; (Sabini page 207..DA,p.142.0

4. Jung, C.G., "Mind and Earth", Civilization in Transition, volume 10, No.49. Page29.

5. Interestingly professor David Tacey ("Mind and Earth: Psychic Influence Beneath the Surface" in Jung Journal: Culture & Psyche, Volume 3, No.2,) says that Jung means Upstate New York, not the Middle West, which is the heart of North Star Country.

6. Jung, C.G., "Mind and Earth", Civilization in Transition, volume 10, No.94. Page 46.

7. Sabini notes that Jung said such in a letter. *The Earth has a Soul, C. G. Jun on Nature, Technology & Modern, Life.* Page 14.

8. Ibid Page 73; Zarathustra Seminar P. 1541.

9. C. G. Jung. "Man and Earth", No. 103, Page 49.

10. Ibid. No. 54, Page 31.

11. Robins Lee N., Helzer, John E., Hesselbrock, Michie, and Wish, Eric; "Vietnam Veterans Three Years after Vietnam: How Our Study Changed Our View of Heroin", The American Journal on Addictions, Volume 19, Issue 3, pages 203–211, May-June 2010;
http//:onlinelibrary.wiley.com/doi/10.1111/j.1521-0391.2010.00046.x/abstract

12. Alex Spiegel What Heroin Addiction Tells Us About Changing Bad Habits, NPR, January 5, 2015;

www.npr.org/sections/health-shots/2015/01/05/371894919/what-heroin-addiction-tells-us-about-changing-bad-habits

13. Sylvia, Claire with Novak, William. *A Change of Heart, A Memoir.* Little, Brown and Company: New York, 1997, 84, 104, 107. 184-187.

14. Pearsall, Paul; Schwartz, Gary E.; Russek, Linda G. Extracted from Nexus Magazine, (Volume 12, Number 3 (April - May 2005)Organ Transplants and Cellular Memories; This article was originally published under the title "Changes in Heart Transplant Recipients that Parallel the Personalities of their Donors" in the Journal of Near-Death Studies, vol. 20, no. 3, Spring 2002. http://www.paulpearsall.com/info/press/3.html

15. Murphy, Todd *Sacred Pathways: The Brain's Role in Religious and Mystic Experiences*, CreateSpace, 2015, Page 380.

16. Becker, Robert, *Cross Currents; the Promise of Electromedicine, the Perils of Electropollution*, Jeremy Tarcher, LA, 1990. Page 80.

17. Ibid. Page 229.

18. Gerber, Richard, *Vibrational Medicine*, Bear & Co., Rochester Vermont. 2001 Third Edition, Page 531.

19. This is a very simplistic explanation. We attract consciousness in a variety of ways, through our good deeds and actions and more. I just want to make the point that soul needs to be nourished to develop.

20. Campbell, Joseph; *The Hero With a Thousand Faces*, New World Library, Novato, Calif, 2008. Page 1.

21. Johansen, Bruce Eliot, *Encyclopedia of the Haudenosaunee*, Greenwood Press, Westport Conn., 2000. Pages 265-282.
https://shaktitechnology.com/shiva/god%20helmet/index.htm
https: // shaktitechnology. Com/winshakti/rotating/
Email correspondence with Todd Murphy

Onondaga Nation website, history http://www.onondaganation.org/history/.

Chapter 3

Fields of Consciousness--How Mother Earth Helps Elevate Our Consciousness

Fields of Consciousness are part of Mother Earth's unseen architecture and are meant to transform and elevate human consciousness. They emanate God's highest aspirations for humankind—love, compassion, selflessness, generosity, altruism and... What some call Christ Consciousness, for Jesus' spiritual embodiment of love, selflessness and compassion. They are the sweetest of nectars that we can consume and absorb; like food they nourish us, only they feed our soul. In other words when in a FOC its emanations elevate your consciousness. Like food its effects, how much you absorb and retain will vary depending upon a number of variables.

Design and Function

When Ley Lines, or what I call Spirit Lines, or Lines of Consciousness (LOC's) pass over a FOC they absorb the consciousness emanating from it. They then carry their precious cargo of Christ Consciousness to the farthest corners of the world. In doing so they create a network of consciousness for Mother Earth, connecting all of humankind, and underscoring the Hindu Vedanta belief that we are all one and connected to each other.

When fully operational and in peak order, FOC and their network of Spirit Lines create a divine spiritual vibe, a proverbial Heaven on Earth; permeating the world with a spiritual and altruistic consciousness that envelops all of creation within it.

Understanding Consciousness

Hindu Vedanta holds that world is nothing but pure consciousness. Sri Aurobindo, the Indian activist and great mystic of the twentieth century, teaches *"Consciousness is a fundamental thing, the fundamental thing in existence—it is the energy, the motion, the movement of consciousness that creates the universe and all that is in it – not only the macrocosm but the microcosm is nothing but consciousness arranging itself."*[1]

But what is consciousness? One way of looking at it is to say that it is spirit versus matter. Matter is energy. Hinduism holds that to create the material world Shiva (consciousness), sends Shakti (energy) forth to manifest physical reality. So energy, or matter, is subordinate to consciousness. It is important not to confuse consciousness with energy, which is the material world.

Some define consciousness as our awareness, or being aware that we exist. I would add not so much that we are aware, but what we are focused on, or our intention. As I noted earlier our intentions and actions attract a particular energy, or essence from Mother Earth.

Consciousness has a morality to it, running the continuum from the divine to the demonic (Bhagavad Gita Chapter 16.) With divine consciousness being love, compassion, selflessness, altruism and the like; while demonic consciousness is violence, selfishness, etc. All consciousness lies somewhere along this continuum between the divine to the demonic. The consciousness emanating from FOC is divine consciousness—love, selflessness, generosity, altruism, etc.

So in a way consciousness is at the core of our being. Are we loving, or are we selfish?

One of the features of consciousness is that it interacts with the consciousness it comes in contact with. To conceptually understand this, visualize hot air being vented outside into the cold air through a duct. The temperature of the cold air outside near the duct will merge with the hot air and create a small pocket of warm air. In other words they will balance out. The farther you get from the duct the colder the air will be; until at some point the hot air has no influence on the temperature outside. Similarly consciousness will interact with the consciousness it comes in contact with and balance out differences, as the hot and cold air did. Generally they will not totally balance out, as the cold and hot air did by the duct. How much they influence each other will vary.

Living in a sea of consciousness we are constantly being shaped by the consciousness we come in contact with—our location, our friends, our job etc. All this matters because it affects our spiritual transformation—OUR SOUL. Our intention has a big influence on the evolution, or devolution of our consciousness/soul. Think and act out of love you and you will bring in the divine, think and act selfishly, or act out violently, you bring in negative consciousness and your soul devolves.

It is said we are what we eat; if we eat nutritious food it makes us healthy, if we eat junk food lacking nutrition it hurts our body and longer term can make us sick. Similarly in the unseen world we are what we absorb, if we consume divine consciousness it nourishes our soul and we spiritually evolve, if we consume demonic consciousness it depletes our soul and we spiritually devolve. Do a good act, give of yourself and your soul will be nourished.

We are constantly absorbing consciousness 24/7 through a variety of means. At our core we are consumers of consciousness (as well as creators of consciousness.)

So we need to consume as much divine consciousness, or as close to divine as possible, if we are to spiritually evolve. We can do this through a variety of way (our thoughts (divine), good deeds—which has Mother Earth nourish us and through our relationships, affiliations...)

The environment is a key variable. Again think of the hot air being released outside through a duct into the cold air outside. Think how temperature outside influences your physical body.

Similarly the consciousness of your environment, its imprints, influences your consciousness and spiritual being.

That is why it is so critical to have Mother Earth's architecture for the transportation of consciousness in proper working order; otherwise our soul will be in constant contact with a less than divine consciousness, which will diminish our consciousness, thereby making it more difficult to elevate our consciousness and transform our soul.[2]

Basic Architecture

While a FOC has several components there are basically two parts to it; The Field emanating the consciousness and the Spirit Lines that originate from it. The Spirit Lines pass over the Field and absorb the consciousness. From there they go in different directions and carry the consciousness they have absorbed around the world through their straight tracks.

There appears to be other aspects of FOC, which I do not have a total grasp of at this time. One feature is an even higher dose of consciousness as I note in my review of Swami Vivekananda's Cottage in the Thousand Islands (listed in Part II.) After visiting the cottage for several years it was only as I approached higher meditative states that I was able to sense that there was something of a greater, or higher order there; and most likely it was this that propelled this great soul to the highest meditative states.

FOC can come as single Fields, or several Fields together. I call multiple Fields linked to each other stacked Fields, because the Fields are stacked upon each other. Stacked Fields can range from 2 to 12 FOC stacked upon each other. The higher the number of stacked Fields, the stronger the Field is, and more is better. I abbreviate stacked FOC as S#. For example, a stacked Field of 8 would be S8, a stacked Field of 4 is an S4.

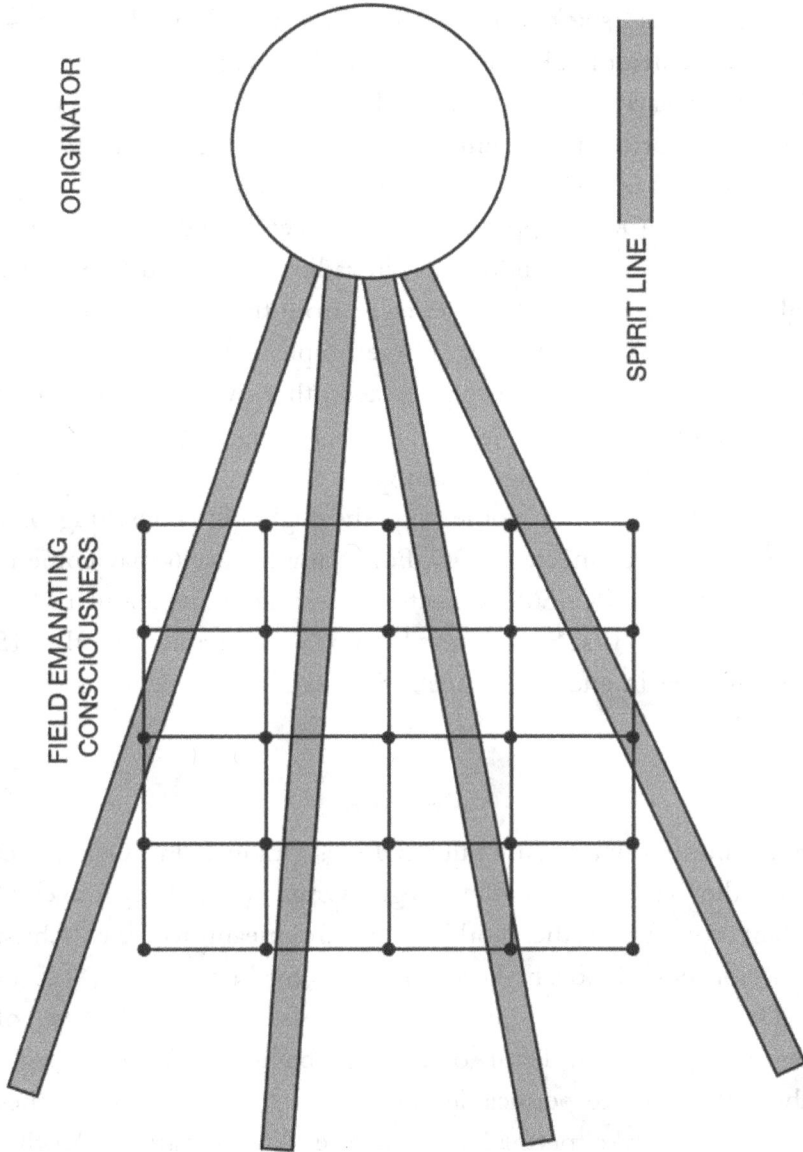

ORIGINATOR

SPIRIT LINE

FIELD EMANATING CONSCIOUSNESS

Exhibit 3.1. The Architecture of a FOC. Spirit Lines originate from an Originator. They pass over a grid emanating Christ Consciousness and absorb it. They then carry that Christ Consciousness to distant corners of the world.

The highest stacked FOC (S12) are found in the Utica—Rochester corridor. The most stacked 12 FOC are in the Syracuse area, particularly at Onondaga Lake. As you fan out from the center of North Star Country, Onondaga Lake, the number of Fields stacked upon each other begins to diminish.

A single FOC is approximately 15 feet in radius. A stacked Field can be several hundred feet in radius. A stacked FOC has a highpoint and as you get farther away from the center the number of stacked Fields diminishes. For example, a stacked FOC of 8 begins with 8 Fields stacked upon each other. As you fan out from the center the number of stacked Fields begins to diminish, 6, 5, 4, 3…How the numbers digress can vary.

Stacked FOC often come with the highpoint consisting of a series of three connected FOC. For example, an S6 may come in series of three FOC (S6) connected in a straight line about 15 feet apart. After the first S6 the next S6 would be in about another 15 feet, the next in another 15 feet. See Exhibit 3.2, A Series (3) of S6's.

Spirit Lines

Spirit Lines, or what many call Ley Lines, originate in FOC; in fact I call the places where they begin Originators. They travel to distant corners of the world. They are meant to carry Christ Consciousness, God's highest aspirations for humankind.

They are carriers of consciousness, not made up of consciousness itself. Think of them as being like a long straight tube only they are permeable and exude the consciousness they carry. They are a permanent structure that is part of Mother Earth's architecture. As such they can serve other functions such as being a system of transport for beings in other realms.

They are approximately 15-20 feet wide. Their reach and influence is well beyond their form, and they can exude the consciousness they carry several hundred yards beyond their structure, or more.

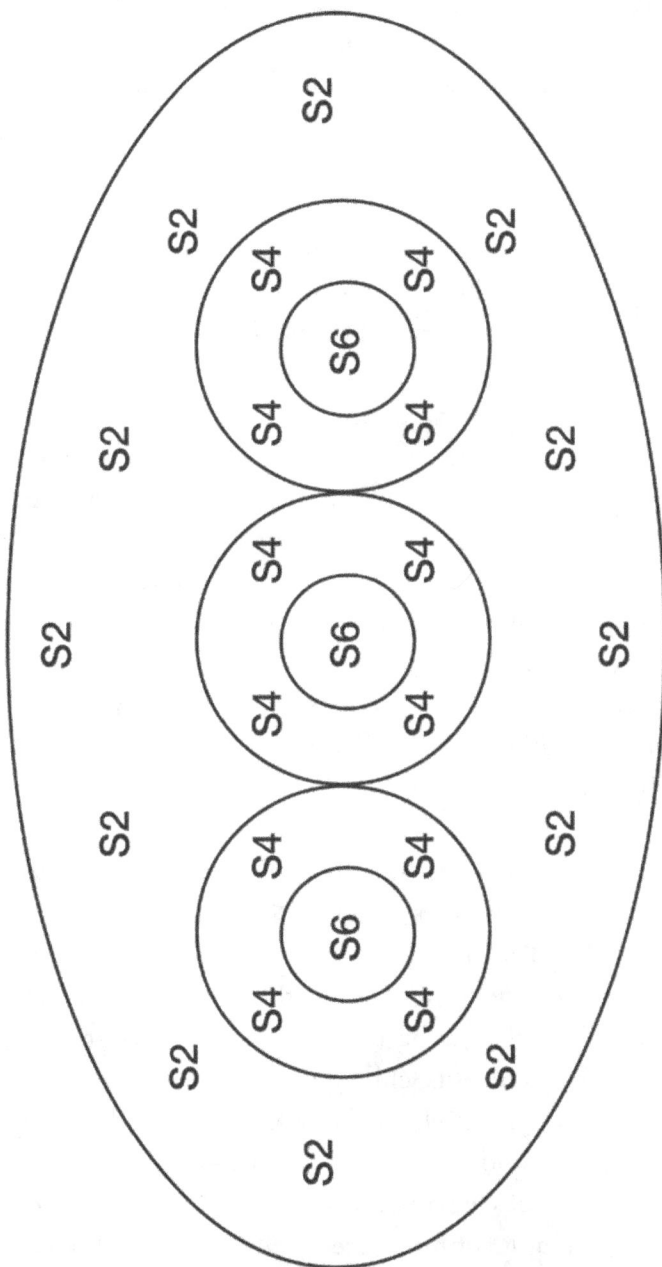

Exhibit 3.2 A series of (3) S6's. Notice how the number of stacked FOC diminishes the farther you get from the highest stacked FOC. But they all combine to make a large FOC.

For example, if a street were placed on Spirit Line the influence of the Spirit Line would extend several blocks on either side of it. Their cargo (consciousness) is the strongest within its channel; the influence of the consciousness it carries diminishes the farther you get from the conduit of the Spirit Line that carries the consciousness.

Spirit Lines exude consciousness and influence the space they travel through. Ideally they are meant to cover the world with divine consciousness, making a proverbial Heaven on Earth.

We absorb the consciousness exuded from a Spirit Line through contact. In other words, our consciousness will be influenced by the consciousness of a Spirit Line. How much will be contingent upon a variety of factors. Our contact with the consciousness of a Spirit Line is involuntary; compared to an act such as meditation, which like energy healing draws a particular energy/prana based upon our intention and is voluntary. We can also call it direct (Mother Earth responds to our intention,) or indirect (to absorb it we have to come in contact with it, as with a Spirit Line.) Again think of it (the consciousness carried by a Spirit Line) like the air temperature and how it affects your physical body.

When John Michell wrote his classic *The View Over Atlantis* he rekindled interest in Ley Lines begun with Alfred Watkins and his straight tracks. He also initiated interest in Earth Mysteries and became a New Age phenomenon. In the revision of his classic, *The New View Over Atlantis* he talks about "Ley Consciousness" implying it is what connects churches, monuments and the like and was recognized as such consciously, or unconsciously by poets, artists and common folk who never heard of them.[3]

Because Spirit Lines emanate divine consciousness places of worship and spiritual institutions are often located on them, or at the intersection of several Spirit Lines that is more of a power point. But Spirit Lines attract a variety of consciousness. For example, Joe Smith a beloved dowser and past trustee of the

American Society of Dowsers told me in an email he felt that Ley Lines connected places of higher learning and government offices. Michell tells of a line of hilltop shrines dedicated to St. Michael and other dragon killing saints in southwest England many miles in length. [4]

The consciousness carried by a Spirit Line is constantly interacting with the consciousness it traverses through. So the consciousness a Spirit Line is transporting in one location can be dramatically different in another. Spirit Lines will often take on a life of their own and vary dramatically with the intention, or consciousness they carry.

Their cargo of consciousness will, as the Law of Attraction (like attracts like) teaches, begin to attract similar sorts of consciousness to it. This helps explain why you can see Ley Lines focused on a specific type of consciousness or activity: there are Ley lines connecting prisons, hospitals, libraries, people involved with animal rescue, violent people or places of violence, advertising agencies, stamp collectors, etc. In other words they attract like-minded, or similar consciousness.

Because Spirit Lines travel great distances, exude consciousness well beyond their boundaries and dynamically interact with consciousness along their path, they have a profound influence in linking and shaping human consciousness. This may be one of the reasons so many places of worship are located on Spirit Lines.

A Spirit Line can expand the consciousness it traverses through. For example, if the path of a Spirit Line goes through a very negative area contaminated with selfishness it will absorb that consciousness. That consciousness will then spread in both directions that the Spirit Line goes. Conversely, a Spirit Line that traverses a place of divine consciousness will be enlightened with that consciousness and spread its influence much farther. All who come in contact with consciousness of a Spirit Line will in some degree, large or small, be influenced by it. In other words, Spirit

Lines shape our consciousness; they can contribute to making us more selfish, or more loving.

As noted earlier consciousness runs the gamut from the divine to the demonic. There are examples of such all over the world. In my hometown of Syracuse, New York, I know of examples at either extreme. I am loathe to mention the Shackham, or Fayetteville Ley, the violent one, because I fear it will attract all sorts of thrill seekers, the malevolently motivated, ghost hunters and the like who will only fuel the fires of negativity carried by the Fayetteville Ley.

Let me digress a little to explain why this is important. As I will go into detail in the next chapter, a space will retain the thoughts, or consciousness, of the people that traverse it; when people come seeking the ghoulish and fiendish, aka Ghost Hunters, they pollute the land with that consciousness. In other words, they spray the area with their pursuit of the fiendish and the ghoulish; a once Native American sacred site, or healing place with lots of earth energy where visionquesters had visions can mutate into a spectacle. If a place has problems, visiting ghost hunters and their ilk will effectively be pouring gasoline on it.

The divine would be "The Prophetic Ley" so called because it unites the places of worship with the strongest advocacy for the poor and social justice, as well as some of my community's (Syracuse, NY) most passionate peace and social justice advocates. The Prophetic Ley was revealed to me while I was meditating on a bench, which at the time was situated on it, in the garden of Grace Episcopal Church.

For example, Grace Episcopal was the first integrated Episcopal Church in Syracuse The first Native American deacon came from Grace, as did one of the first women to be ordained in the Anglican faith. University United Methodist was once the home of Dr. Norman Vincent Peale. It was the birthplace of several social service programs as was Temple Concord. Many well known activists in the Syracuse area are members of the places of worship along the Prophetic Ley; most notable was St. Andrews the Apostle many miles from the University Area before it was closed. A few miles farther away was the home of Jerry Berrigan, one of the famous Berrigan Brothers and another well known activist Kathleen Rumpf.

The Fayetteville, or Shackham Ley carries demonic consciousness, very evil, and connects some of the most violent and cruelest acts seen in Central New York and beyond. I used to primarily call it the Shackham Ley because I first became aware of it for a violent murder on Shackham Road in Fabius NY (30 miles south of Syracuse.) The trailhead for one of my favorite hikes, Morgan Hill is on Shackham Road. In 2002 when I learned that a nine month Internet romance ended with the violent multiple stabbing and bludgeoning of a 14 year old by a 17 year old at their first meeting, I began to do some investigating. Over time I began to notice a pattern of violent behavior along the Shackham Ley's, or Fayetteville's Ley's path.

The Fayetteville Ley begins north of Fabius in Fayetteville, NY a suburb of Syracuse, NY. It is named for its place of origin and for one of the more the gruesome acts along its path. Fayetteville, NY was home to John Jamelske, the dungeon man; a rapist-kidnapper who kept and raped women in a concrete dungeon in his basement for fifteen years.

There are numerous murders, suicides and violent accidents along the path of the Fayetteville Ley—most notably south of Syracuse near Cortland (Truxton, 10 miles south of Fabius) where seven people, including four children and an engaged couple, died from a runaway trailer dislodged from a truck. It devastated our community.

Going south, it travels through Binghamton, NY (70 miles south of Syracuse.) On April 3, 2009 a shooter entered the American Civic Association Immigrant Center and killed 13 people and wounded 4 others. It focused national attention on Binghamton. Ninety miles to the south in Wilkes-Barre, PA in

September 25, 1982 a man shot 13 people to death, including seven children, five of his own, and four women who were their mothers, plus some of their relatives and one bystander. The Fayetteville Ley appears to extend into South America.

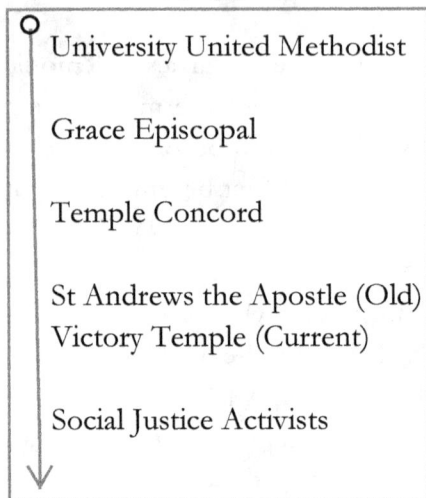

University United Methodist

Grace Episcopal

Temple Concord

St Andrews the Apostle (Old)
Victory Temple (Current)

Social Justice Activists

Exhibit 3.3 The Prophetic Ley.

I had always thought the Immigrant Center in Binghamton was on the Fayetteville Ley but never did any research on it until I began working on this book. A simple map dowsing, using a map and picture of the area, done from a distance indicates that it runs about 100-maybe 200/300 yards east of the Immigrant Center. I need to physically dowse the area, but I am fairly confidant that it is on the Spirit Line. Similarly a map dowsing of the location of the murders in Wilkes-Barre, finds that they are close to the Fayetteville Ley. [5]

I imagine that the Prophetic and Fayetteville Leys are hundreds, probably thousands of miles in length. Finding all the good deeds done and where people live along the Prophetic Ley was challenging because the media rarely reports on do-gooders and those that embrace the prophetic spirit. I have done only minimal work to clear the Fayetteville Ley; much more needs to be done. The Fayetteville Ley shows how critical it is to clear and keep Spirit Lines clean so that they can carry Christ Consciousness as the Prophetic Ley does.

It is important to reiterate that Spirit Lines are carriers of consciousness, not the consciousness itself. They are like a permeable pipe that interacts with the consciousness they encounter. They can also serve as a conduit, or path of transportation for beings in other realities. Portals that allow travelers entry are often found at the intersection of several Spirit Lines.

Fayetteville, NY
Women kept in dungeon as sex slaves.

Pompey Hills, NY
Trooper dies in crash pursuing speeder.

Fabius (Shackham Rd), NY
14 year old violently stabbed to death.
Teacher commits suicide.

Truxton, NY
7 die in minivan crash.

Binghamton, NY
13 murdered at Immigrant Center.

Wilkes Barre, PA
'American Spree Murderer." Man murders 13, including girlfriends, children.

Exhibit 3.4 The Fayetteville Ley

John Michell tells of fairy paths in Ireland that served as seasonal procession routes for fairies. He notes how one man whose house was on a fairie path would leave his front and back doors open on the day of the procession. There are many other stories of ghost lines, of funeral paths and more used by beings and spirits in other dimensions or realities.

Connectors/Artificial Leys

For geomancers and dowsers it is important to distinguish between a Spirit Line and a Connector, or what Scottish Dowser David Cowan calls an Artificial Ley. A Spirit Line originates from the heart of Mother Earth's Soul and is a permanent structure that is part of Mother Earth's architecture. A Connector, or Artificial Ley, is a structure that forms in response to human intention. For example, I had three sacred stone circles about 30 feet apart in my backyard in which I would meditate in. Over time (three) connectors formed connecting all three circles to each other.

I only mention this because there is much controversy amongst geomancers regarding what Spirit Lines (Ley Lines) are.

Heaven on Earth

In an ideal world the divine consciousness emanating from FOC would be carried unadulterated by Spirit Lines around the world. In the process the world would be blanketed with Christ consciousness. A Christ Consciousness that would envelop all of creation in its divinity and love and in the process elevate the consciousness of all of creation.

The ancients understood the transformative power of Spirit Lines to raise our consciousness. They would mark Spirit Lines with stones and charge them with the intention of prayer. The picture on the right is of a Charged Spirit Line; they can be quite powerful. Several sites listed have them.

The above picture is of a Charged Spirit Line at Brink Hill in HighTor. The rod marks one of the Spirit Lines going towards a stone in the distance. Both stones mark the intersection of three Spirit Lines.

Clearly Spirit Lines play a pivotal role in the spiritual well being of humankind. Many carry negative consciousness that reflects our selfish and violent culture. Fortunately, they can be cleaned up and again be carriers of divine consciousness and in the process help raise and elevate our collective consciousness. In the Appendix in the Earth Healers section I explain how Spirit Lines can be a valuable tool in cleaning space and elevating human consciousness.

References and Recommended Reading

1. Sri Aurobindo *Letters on Yoga*. Volume 22, Section Five, Planes and Parts of The Being, Page 236.
2. This is a very simplistic explanation of the process. Most certainly other factors such as our thoughts and deeds will influence our spiritual evolution. But our environment, the sea of consciousness we exist in, has a profound influence upon us; simply because we are constantly immersed in it and because it is a reflection of many of the other factors that influence us. Bottom line, in a perfect world we would have Heaven on Earth if we existed in a sea of love that nourished us 24/7.
3. Michell, John, *The New View Over Atlantis*, Thames and Hudson, New York, New York, 1983. Pages 104-105.
4. Ibid. Page 72-73.
5. I have not completely traced the route of either the Prophetic Ley, or the Fayetteville Ley, with my dowsing rods so I could be wrong. I have dowsed pictures and maps, as I have successfully done to find several of the sacred sites (FOC) listed in Part II.

I also looked at maps as best as I could using a ruler to connect places. The challenge here was that a minor slip by a few degrees over long distances results in large divergences. Perhaps using GPS would have given me further proof; but I refuse to use electronic devices that damage Mother Earth.

The question that both these Spirit Lines raise is, how far is the reach of the consciousness that Spirit Lines carry beyond their transport conduit? For example, Ryan Lawrence killed and burned his two old daughter, Baby Maddox, at Labrador Hollow (Tinker Falls) on Rt. 91 close to where it intersects Shackham Rd. Was his violent act of filicide so close to Shackham Rd. within the influence of the Fayetteville Ley?

If the reach of a Spirit Line is half a mile, a mile, or several miles on either side of its transport conduit then this horrific act was done on the Fayetteville Ley. The murder of Baby Maddox led the NYS Legislature to pass the Baby Maddox Law; making the murder of a child under thirteen automatically a charge of first degree murder. Similarly the death of the NYS Trooper chasing a speeding motorcyclist near the Fayetteville Ley led to the Todeschini Law (stiffer penalties for motorists fleeing police) after the deceased Trooper.

Chapter 4

Preparing For Your Visit

Making a journey to North Star Country and visiting a sacred site is a powerfully transformative experience. You can enhance the benefits of your pilgrimage with preparation—physically, mentally and spiritually. Preparation will better help you connect with a space, build enthusiasm and increase your focus for prayers and meditations when visiting a site. It is this intention of enthusiasm and interest and the solemnness that it builds, which will linger on the land after your visit and enhance it.

Planning

There are many places listed in this book and you need to plan where you want to go. North Star Country covers a large swath of land. The sites listed are miles apart and some sites require you to hike, or walk a distance.

Many of the places have educational programs, retreats, services, tours etc. that you may be interested in. This may determine the time of day, or year you visit. There are also related places close by you may wish to visit. For example, Peterboro, NY houses the Gerrit Smith Estate and the Abolitionist Hall of Fame.

Preparation will reduce problems, make for a more fluid trip and build enthusiasm. Reading about sites will acquaint you with them and help you select which ones to visit. Learning about sites will begin the process of building a bond that will help you connect with a site when you visit.

When I first backpacked through Europe and the Middle East I did a lot research in planning my trip. It was 1981 and I was doing ex-pat tax returns in Saudi Arabia. I spent as much time as I could learning about places to determine which sites to visit. I also got an idea of where things were located and the hours museums were open so I limited wasted time.

There are several things that you should consider in planning your trip:

Focus—are you interested in a specific theme such as Women's Rights, the Underground Railroad and abolitionism, Native American sites, peace, etc?

Outdoors/Indoors—many of the sites listed are outside and require hiking. If you visit one you will need gear.

Sensing Consciousness—are you interested in developing the ability to sense and feel Consciousness and gain sentience of it? If so you need to select places that would facilitate your chances. You should also try and work on developing your sentience.

Being able to sense and feel Consciousness when in a FOC is an incredibly rewarding experience that increases the benefits of meditating in a Field—it is no easy feat to accomplish this. Being able to sense and feel the Consciousness emanating from a FOC and focusing on it, means you will be absorbing more of it.

Potency—The potency, how strong the Fields of Consciousness are at a particular place varies. Generally the higher the number of stacked FOC, the more potent it is. But that is not always the case as the vibe can dramatically increase, or decrease the potency of a location.

The Vibe—I suggest visiting a place with a good vibe so that you can appreciate the power of human intention upon Mother Earth and how much it can enhance a FOC, or space.

Working on a Sacred Site—All of the sacred sites listed, no matter what their condition, can be further enhanced through prayer/meditation/ceremony. You should consider visiting places that have a neutral vibe and are not that potent; particularly places close to your home. In doing so you will help reinvigorate them strengthening Mother Earth's network of Spirit Lines and provide a refuge to raise the consciousness of those visiting a site.

Reading List

There is much more to the history and the people of North Star Country than mentioned in Chapter 1. Exhibit 4.1 is a listing of books you might want to read before your visit. This will give you a better appreciation of North Star Country as well as helping you better hone in on what places you would like to visit.

Many of the sacred sites listed have their own References and Recommended Reading List at the end of its survey. This is meant to give you the opportunity to learn more about a particular person, or place.

Get in Shape

It would help to exercise both your spiritual and physical selves before you come to North Star Country. You need to develop your endurance to able to spend a lot of time meditating and praying. While you may meditate daily at home you can end up meditating much more, possibly many hours each day.

You will also be meditating in powerful FOC. While you might not be able to sense and feel the Consciousness it will have a much more powerful effect upon you than you normally experience during your daily meditations. Much of what we draw into us during meditation is a blend of consciousness and energy. The consciousness emanating from a FOC is a higher blend, of consciousness; as such it will have a more powerful affect upon you.

Meditating in FOC can get your feel good chemicals humming and eventually have you plateau out, so that any more meditating has no affect upon you. A rigorous routine of meditating in advance of your visit will help, or least increase the time before you plateau out. Try and spend as much time as you can meditating, or praying before you visit North Star Country.

Exhibit 4.1 Reading List	
North Star Country	*The Crucible of Fervent, New York Psychic Highway,* by Emerson Klees. Provides an overview of North Star Country focusing on seven religious movements. *Upstate Cauldron—Eccentric Spiritual Movements in Early New York State,* by Joscelyn Godwin. An overview of the eclectic spiritual movements and their leaders. *The Burned-over District,* Whitney Cross. The classic on the Burned-over District.
Great Law, The Peacemaker	*White Roots of Peace, The Iroquois Book of Life,* by Paul Wallace. Tells the story of the Peacemaker. You can download the Great Law at: http:// www. iroquoisdemocracy.pdx.edu/html/greatlaw.html
Abolition UGRR	*North Star Country: Upstate New York and the Crusade for African American Freedom,* by Milton Sernett. The story of abolitionism in North Star Country. *Narrative of the life of Fredrick Douglass an American Slave,* by Fredrick Douglass. A searing biography that gives a first hand account of slavery. *Practical Dreamer, Gerrit Smith and the Crusade for Social Reform,* by Norman K. Dann. An excellent biography of the unsung hero who had his finger in just about every movement and cause in North Star Country, thereby telling the region's story.
Women's Rights	*Seneca Falls and the Origins of the Women's Rights Movement,* by Sally McMillen. Focuses on four leaders—Anthony, Stanton, Mott, Stone. *Matilda Joslyn Gage: She Who Holds the Sky,* by Sally Roesch Wagner. A telling story of the Women's Rights Movement and its most radical leader. *The Road to Seneca Falls, Elizabeth Cady Stanton and the First Women's Rights Convention,* Wellman, Judith. How the flame got started and that story of its leading voice

Exhibit 4.1 (continued) Reading List	
Mother Earth	*Vortices and Spirals—Unlocking the Mystery of Our Dynamic Relationship With Mother Earth*, by Madis Senner. Educates about vortices, imprints and our dynamic relationship with Mother Earth.
Regionalism	*Listen for the Lonesome Drum, A York State Chronicle*, by Carl Carmer. Stories and legends from early New York. Includes a section on seven key players in North Star Country.
Prayers and Inspiration	*Giving Thanks, A Native American Good Morning Message*, by Chief Jake Swamp. A short pictorial giving of thanks by the founder of the Tree of Peace Society. 11.75" x 7" His *Thanksgiving Address, Greetings to the Natural World*, is more compact (5" X 4") and can fit in your back pocket. *To Become a Human Being*, by Chief Leon Shenandoah; Wisdom from one of the Haudenosaunee's most beloved Tadodahos. *The Art of Pilgrimage, The Seekers Guide to Making Travel Sacred*, by Phil Cousineau. Advice and wonderful anecdotes on making a pilgrimage a 'bona fide spirit-renewing ritual.' *The World As It Is, Dispatches on the Myth of Human Progress*, by Chris Hedges, A collection of essays from one of the most strident and vocal progressives of our time. The church where is father served, Schoharie United Presbyterian, is listed.
Information, Sources	Places Where Women Made History, http:// www. nps. gov./nr/travel/pwwmh/womlist1. htm National Parks Services listing of 74 sites in MA and NY. Mother Earth Prayers, www. mother earthprayers. org a partial listing of sacred sites in New York and information on Mother Earth's cosmology. Free Thought Trail, www. freethought-trail. org locations important to Free Thought in upstate NY. My blog, http: //motherearthprayers. blogspot. com, has updates, listing of upcoming events and information on Mother Earth.

Create a Special Meditation or Prayer

Just because a place is a sacred site does not mean you will find it conducive to prayer, or meditation. You might feel awkward meditating in a public place, or out in nature. Developing and practicing a specific prayer, or meditation can help with this.

In many ways meditation is about creating a thought form, or what Hinduism calls a samskara, for meditating. Think of it like building strength, or a muscle, the more you work it the stronger it becomes. Similarly if you meditate on the same object, repeat the same mantra, or contemplate the same thought you are affectively building a muscle for a particular meditation.

I have certain mantra meditations (usually a story) that I have repeated countlessly to myself and led others in group meditation with. Just saying the mantra quickly quiets my mind and brings me into a meditative state. Similarly you can develop a particular meditation, or mantra, or prayer that you can call upon when visiting a sacred site in North Star Country. This will help reduce any barriers or inhibitions you may experience in a new place where you may feel uncomfortable.

I would also meditate beforehand on the sportsmen's cushion, or whatever you will be bringing with you to sit on when you pray, or meditate. We leave imprints of our thoughts and actions wherever we go on the land and on objects. Your meditation cushion will develop an imprint of your meditation, and improve your meditation each time you meditate on it, thereby facilitating your meditation. So bring it along.

Check with your doctor

You may want to check with your doctor before you come. Although FOC have a much higher consciousness component than the Cosmic Prana you attract during meditation, they still contain some energy, or electromagnetic energy. You need to make sure your heart and other organs are able to deal with the increased energy.

> **Exhibit 4-2   Learning to Feel and Sense Consciousness**
> (Learning to work with energy and connecting with Mother Earth before visiting a sacred site will help you to sense and feel Consciousness.)
>
> ➤ Take an energy healing course, better yet, practice energy healing. Try to feel the energy move through you during the healing.
> ➤ Work with your chakras to feel the energy move through your body.
> ➤ Practice pranayama and focus on trying to feel the energy in your body while performing exercises.
> ➤ Connect with Mother Earth. Developing a bond with Mother Earth will help you to better appreciate Her and possibly help you to sense and feel Consciousness. Simple things such as seeing Her, the trees and sky when you walk about and not the buildings and roads that make up our modern world.
> ➤ Visit a sacred site, or a place of power near . While there focus on trying to feel Mother Earth emanations going into your body; Whatever body part gives you a sensation, focus on it. If you don't feel anything, imagine Her energy coming to your body. Feel the energy radiating into your forehead or cheeks, even your hands.
> ➤ Give Thanks to Mother Earth.

Should you develop the ability to sense and feel Consciousness by focusing on that feeling, you can increase your draw (how much you attract or absorb) from Mother Earth. This can give you blissed out feeling and a spiritual high. Make sure it's okay.

Geomancy/Dowsing

You may wish to develop the ability to dowse before you come, to help you with finding features of Mother Earth. Finding Fields of Consciousness, places where the consciousness emanates from will be a challenge, but you should be able to develop the skill to find Spirit Lines (Ley Lines.)

There are numerous geomancy and dowsing organizations around the world, such as the American Society of Dowsers, or the British Society of Dowsers with local chapters that will teach you dowsing for free, or for a nominal sum.

Make Sure you Have the Right Gear

Have several water bottles that you can take with you, so that you will have plenty of water to drink while at a sacred site. As you pray and meditate your body's need for water will increase.

I strongly urge you to buy a sportsman's cushion to sit on when you meditate. This will give you something to sit down on when you pray and meditate, especially important if you are outside. Get a cheap clip so that you can attach it to your belt when you walk around.

If you plan on going into the woods make sure that you have the appropriate gear. Some of the things to consider having are a compass, hiking boots, a backpack, a rain jacket, a medical kit, bug spray... You should also consider a pair of low rise gaiters to keep the mud off your pants and make it more difficult for ticks to attach to you.

Chapter 5

Visiting Sites, Understanding Reviews

All of the sacred places listed in this book have FOC. Not all of them are conducive to spiritual practices. Many historic homes listed do not have prayer, or meditation rooms; in fact many are very un-conducive to prayer, or meditation. Other places listed are places of worship that have limited accessibility and availability only during services.

I have also included places far from the Utica—Rochester corridor, to not only show the scope of the FOC, but also to provide   places that might be closer to your home. While these places are not as potent, usually a single FOC and not in a series, their emanations can be greatly enhanced through human intention.

A description is provided where the FOC are located and often a picture is provided. Fields are large from 30 to 200 feet, or larger in diameter, so even if you do not find the high point, as long as you are close you will be fine. Generally the higher the number of FOC stacked upon each other the more potent the FOC is (they run from 2-12); the corollary of which is the more Fields that are stacked upon each other the wider the area they cover.

Other factors will also influence the quality of a location, particularly the vibe. A good vibe can greatly enhance the Fields, while a negative vibe detracts and is detrimental. A vortex is a very positive indicator that much prayer, good intentions and actions have occurred there. Vortices greatly enhance a place and I have noted places that have them.

A few of the place listed have other aspects of Mother Earth and are noted. There are also several places listed that have stone structures varying in size and condition.

Terminology

Fields of Consciousness (FOC, Fields). The Number Stacked S1, S2...S12—Are listed for the number of stacked Fields found at a location, the higher the better. For example, a FOC with three Fields stacked upon each other would be an S3, four Fields stacked upon each other S4...

Within the text I will note if they come in a series of 3, as a series (3), stacked Fields of Consciousness as most do.

Vibe—(0,1,2,3,4) The vibe of a space, how it feels—whether it is uplifting, or depressing, is the next most critical element after how many Fields are stacked upon each other in determining the quality of a space. A good vibe can greatly improve a space.

We leave imprints of our thoughts and actions wherever we go. The vibe of a place is the cumulative historical record of those thoughts and actions. Think of a scale; if we could put all the loving and selfless acts and thoughts on one side and all the selfish and violent ones on the other side, which way would the scale tip, and by how much?

Loving, selfless acts and thoughts (prayer, meditation) create a positive vibe that can greatly enhance a space. Mother Earth needs us to achieve Her fullest potential and we (all of creation) need Her to achieve ours. A positive vibe at a FOC bolsters its emanations, making them more potent. It is a virtuous circle, as the vibe rises the Fields increase in strength, and as the Fields increase in strength those in contact with it, or its Spirit Lines benefit from a more powerful blast of consciousness.

Vibe is very important. The purpose of this book is to fortify FOC and make them bright beacons of light radiating Christ consciousness by having people pray, or meditate on them. Human intention can greatly enhance FOC.

Wisdom's Golden Rod (Hector, NY) is a testament to the power of a positive vibe to empower and greatly enhances a space. Its highest FOC is an S3, most of the FOC are an S1 or S2, yet its vibe is very positive which greatly enhances the space. As a consequence the sensation created at the space is better than one would experience in a Field with a much higher number of stacked Fields with a neutral, or negative vibe.

Wisdom's Golden Rod demonstrates what is possible if people visit and pray at a sacred site. It is located in the heart of Mother Earth's Soul, yet it only has an S1 to S3, Fields you would expect to find at the fringe of Mother Earth's Soul; Ohio's Western Reserve, PS, MA, VT, CT, NJ.

None of the places listed as sacred sites have a negative vibe. I have however been generous at times saying that a place has a neutral vibe—I am not going to trash anyone's place of worship.

The vibe refers to the specific area of where the FOC are located. Often is the case that the vibe is much less once you get away from the FOC. In fact, it may not be very nice.

The vibe listed is for where the Fields are located:

Neutral –o
Slightly positive-1
Positive-2
Very positive-3
Extremely positive-4

Vortex, Vortex Ring— Indicates that a vortex, or vortex ring, is found there and is a very positive indicator. A vortex (a positive vortex) is a co-creation with Mother Earth that forms at a particular place with a very positive vibe where loving acts, or prayers have taken place regularly over a prolonged period. These activities significantly bolster Mother Earth at that location. A vortex is an indicator that a place has an extremely positive vibe.

A vortex draws in additional consciousness, or energy, to a particular spot and greatly enhances your spiritual experience there. Visualize a vortex, whirlpool or hurricane and how it sucks everything into its funnel. Similarly when you meditate in a vortex its funnel will be pulling extra consciousness into you.

A vortex ring is a precursor to the formation of a vortex.

Special Vibe— ☆ A few of the sacred sites have a special feel, or atmosphere to them, and will be noted. These places have a palpable layer above its vibe; that is a reflection of the activities that have taken place there. For example, Pumpkin Hollow where healers go and healing takes place has a very positive and therapeutic sense to it. Other places like the Peacemaker's Sanctuary and South Hill have powerful thoughts forms left by visionquesters and others over time that can grab you and provide insights, answers, or give you powerful visions.

Healing Area— ♡ Several of the places listed have healing areas, where you can nourish your energy body, or improve your health in other ways.

Sensing Consciousness— These are places that provide a better chance to develop the ability to sense and feel Consciousness. It takes effort and time to be able to sense and feel Consciousness, and there are no guarantees that you will ever be able to. Certain powerful places can improve your chances. I first learned to sense Consciousness within a vortex within a powerful FOC. Being able to sense and feel Consciousness greatly enhances your spiritual experience and your draw of consciousness.

Spirit Keeper Site— indicates that the remnants of a stone structure, and or a vortex, or vortex ring, created by Spirit Keepers is located on the sacred site.

I believe that the Spirit Keepers were an ancient culture that worked with FOC. I occasionally run into their stonework and they are a great inspiration to me. I believe that their focus was on working with FOC, and did this by working with stones. I have learned much from them.

A few places such as the Finger Lakes Trail in High Tor NYS DEC Forest have a vortex, or vortex ring, that I believe were created by Spirit Keepers. Meditating in such a vortex provides a rich consciousness-raising experience as you transcend time and connect with the consciousness of those that created it.

There is no historical record of the Spirit Keepers and they may well be a recognized Native American civilization, or a particular branch of their shamans, or holy people. My analysis is based upon the stonework that I have found and concluded that someone very knowledgeable of FOC created them. I have also experienced visions and heard voices while in solitude on long retreats meditating on FOC in the wilderness, in places that I believe were created by the Spirit Keepers.

Saying that a stone mound, or vortex, is attributed to the Spirit Keepers is a highly subjective decision; one that I base upon the location and placement of stones in a FOC.

Bathroom— , there is an indoor bathroom located there.

Indoor Prayer area with Fields— , indicates that there is either a meditation, or prayer area on a FOC indoors.

Hiking, Requires — , You will have to hike, or walk a short distance to access the FOC.

Contemplative Walk— , means that the grounds, or a trail, provide for a contemplative walk on FOC; or at least a large area with FOC where one can walk.

Retreat Center—🏠, indicates that the sacred site is a retreat center.

Classes— 🖼️, instruction, programs, lectures etc. offered.

Earth works— ☯, indicates that a labyrinth, stone circle or some other structure meant to connect with Mother Earth is found on the property.

Water— 〰️, Has a lake front, a pond, a river, or stream with a FOC close by.

History
Underground Railroad Site-- 🚂, was a stop on the Underground Railroad, or the home of a noted abolitionist.

Women's Rights— ♀ , the home of a prominent Women's Rights Advocate.

Native American— 🪶, a Native American Site, or a powerful connection to Native Americans.

Place of Reconciliation, Peace— 🕊️, a place where peace/reconciliation took place, the home of a noted peace advocate, an organization dedicated to peace.

Making an Impact With Your Visit

Your visit is going to have an impact upon a particular sacred space. As noted we leave imprints, spiritual imprints of our thoughts and actions wherever we go. If they are positive they enhance a space and fortify Mother Earth there. If they are negative they sully the space with negative consciousness and dampen Mother Earth at the location. Unfortunately, like most of the world many of the places listed having FOC don't have a great vibe.

Enhancing a space with your imprints begins with your preparation. Reading and thinking about your visit will strengthen your thoughts while there.

When visiting outdoor locations I suggest you approach your visit as if you were visiting someone's home. Consider bringing a gift to show your respect and intention. Something simple such as a flower, a piece of fruit, some tobacco; it is not so much what you bring, as an expression of your intention. You want to show interest and honor the space.

You can also show respect by asking permission before you physically enter a sacred site. Think of it like ringing a doorbell, or knocking on someone's door before you walk in. To do this ask permission, either mentally or verbally, before you enter the space. Wait a few moments before entering.

If you are visiting an outdoor sacred site bring an old plastic bag and pickup clutter. On your approach and once you are in the space pickup papers, beverage cans and other garbage and put it in you plastic bag to take out with you when you leave. By cleaning a space you are showing your concern for it and physically reinforcing your intention to spiritually enhance it.

Bringing a gift, asking permission to enter and cleaning up will not only help to lift the vibe of a location but can greatly enhance your experience at the site. A sacred space, particularly one in Nature is a neighborhood made of its vibe that can take on a life of its own, and Nature Spirits, or beings in other realms that may inhabit it. When you show respect and concern for a space the community may reveal things to you, or have you experience things that you would not have had if you had not shown respect. It will also help dampen the attitude of someone that does not want you there.

Act in a 'sacred manner' while visiting a sacred site. Keep your thoughts positive and focused on the divine. You are in very holy space, so act accordingly. Try to be as quiet as you can at a sacred site, particularly if you are outdoors. Visually acknowledge other pilgrims and let them be; unless of course it is clear you both wish to talk, then by all means do.

Technology

Please refrain from bringing technological devices with you on your visit such as cell phones, GPS's etc. as they are very damaging to Mother Earth. Electronic transmissions and WiFi disrupt Mother Earth's Energy Plane. In a world that is a sea of consciousness they are particularly pernicious and damaging.

Electromagnetic energy from Mother Earth could also damage your cell phone, digital watch, and digital camera. If you are looking to visit a place that is very charged be aware it could damage your devices.

You are looking to build a bond with Mother Earth. If you were a smoker would you smoke in front of friend who was suffering from a lung disease and challenged to breathe? Of course not. So please be judicious in what you bring with you when you visit your Mother.

Welcome Circle

A Welcome Circle for a sacred site is like the foyer of a home. It is where you greet your host, remove your coat, or boots if necessary and prepare for your entry. A Welcome Circle is meant to prepare you for your visit and help maintain the spiritual integrity of a space, and hopefully improve it.

Many of the reviews refer to a specific area that is to be treated like a Welcome Circle; a few have actually have one. Even if there is no designated area, you should still perform the actions of a Welcome Circle. If you are with a group, hug each other to show unity and friendship.

Cleansing. The first thing you should do in the Welcome Circle area is to smudge yourself. Smudging will help remove any negative thoughts or other spiritual debris you may have picked up recently. You may wish to carry a feather with you. If so, swirl it around your subtle body head to toe. You can also use your hands: either by flicking your subtle body as if you were removing lint or dirt from your clothing; or you scrub your subtle body as if you were washing your body with a wash cloth. I often say 'clean and protect' or just 'clean' while I smudge. Think of it like removing your dirty boots before you enter a home.

Under no circumstance should you light a fire, a stick of incense, or smudge stick for smudging. The risk of a starting a fire is too great.

The other thing you should do in the Welcome Circle area is to say a short prayer. A few words, whether be a blessing, thanks, or offer of hope, or a request. A prayer will help center you, prepare you and warm you up for your spiritual experience. Think of a foyer on how it acts as a medium from the outside to coming inside. Similarly with a Welcome Circle you are going from the profane to the sacred.

I ask that you please try and spend 5 to 10 minutes, or longer meditating in the Welcome Circle. This will help burn off any imprints (samskaras) that you may recently picked and give you a strong spiritual cleansing before you enter the holy area.

If you, or anyone else that is with you is hesitant to spend time in the Welcome Circle take it as strong warning that something is amiss. If this happens you should give strong consideration to not entering the sacred space.

By performing the rites of a Welcome Circle in the same space repeatedly you will give that intention to the space. Over time a strong imprint, or thought form, will develop increasing the potency of the ritual for subsequent pilgrims. Cleansing will become increasingly more effective and preparation for entering the space will become more, and more palpable.

Experiencing a Space

Try to find the FOC's listed in the review. You want to meditate, or pray in a Field and be as close as possible to the high point (the highest stacked Field); it is hotter closer to fire. This will help increase the consciousness you come in contact with and hopefully absorb. The closer you are will also help to cleanse (if necessary) and fortify the Fields. We need a strong and vibrant Mother Earth to achieve our fullest potential and She similarly needs us to achieve Hers. FOC are large (30 to 200, 300… feet in diameter) so even if you don't find the exact high point, as long as you are close to it you will be in it.

When we are in harmony with Mother Earth and work with Her, we improve Her and She us. Your efforts will strengthen the FOC and make it more potent.

Meditate, say a prayer, do a ceremony, visualize a beautiful image or hope for world peace. Do whatever you feel called to do. A few prayers and intentions are found in the Appendix.

Explore and look for other places within the sacred space that appeal to you. Often is the case that a specific location within a sacred site will appeal to certain people over others..

Read a book, be inspired, dream or just be. Enjoy. Just being in the space is going to lift up your consciousness.

If you are outside and have to go to the bathroom walk very far away, several hundred yards from the FOC. Bring a small shovel to bury and cover up any debris. You are looking to keep that intention outside of the sacred space and not sully the environment.

Try not to disturb the residents. Nature Spirits and beings in other realms often inhabit a sacred site, or places with a particular feature of Mother Earth. Sacred sites can also have a 'thin veil', where communication and awareness of other realms is greatly enhanced. You need to give respect to everyone, no matter what realm they inhabit.

Do not go to a sacred site looking for Nature Spirits, or try communicating with them. Think of how you would want someone to behave if they visited your neighborhood—would you want them to beep their car's horn to announce their arrival, and shout I am here? No, absolutely not.

Should you see or hear something take it as a blessing and let it be. Ditto with animals—Let them be. If you meditate for a long time and are very still you may encounter an animal. Ignore it and create some noise to make it aware of you. I am a big believer that a good day in the woods is a day when you don't see any animals.

If you are looking to sense and feel Consciousness and wish to enhance your draw of Consciousness, focus on the sensations you are experiencing while meditating. If you have a sensation in your legs, or arms, of head give strength to it by concentrating on that sensation.

People generally experience Consciousness in their forehead area, what Hindus call your Chidakasha; your mind screen, the seat of our consciousness.

If you don't sense anything visualize consciousness as rays coming into your body. See them coming into your heart center and nourishing your soul.

Several of the pictures in the reviews contain orbs. Many others would have contained orbs if I had been there at the right time. Miceal Ledwith and Klaus Heinemann in their book *The Orb Project* believe that orbs are either electromagnetic energy of some kind[1], a torsion field (a vortex)[2], or emanations from Spirit beings, not the spirit beings themselves[3]. Orbs are generally a good sign. The reason you see them may be because a space has been enhanced through positive human intentions such as prayer.

Neighborhoods, Soups and Layers

The sacred sites that you are visiting can be very complex and intricate. Several of the sacred sites with larger areas in nature have distinct neighborhoods, as I will note in the review. These are places within the larger sacred site that have a particular atmosphere to them, or places that are particularly friendly, or not. Vibe (imprints), locations can be very nuanced and differentiated.

Experiencing sacred sites can be like eating a soup, call it the 'soup theory of space.' A space like a soup is made up of its ingredients, or in this case imprints (soup can also mean aspects of Mother Earth found there.) It is the blend of the ingredients that make the soup; similarly it is the blend of the imprints that make up the vibe. At the same time when you eat let's say, a vegetable soup, you are eating various vegetables. Each one has the ability to stick out and dominate your eating experience. Similarly the individual imprints at a sacred site have the ability to grab you. For example, I have had incredible experiences at the Peacemaker's Sanctuary at Onondaga Lake where my prayers where once answered and at other times have had revelations, as well as gotten directional messages. Places with strong imprints, have parts of them that can jump out and grab you with the most wonderful of results.

At the same time a space is made up of layers. There are the deep layers; the archetypes that Jung talked about, that are built up by imprints over the centuries. Then there can be a special vibe—love, healing, questioning, etc—found at a place. There is also the immediate vibe, reflecting recent history—is it positive, or negative?

Like all of creation, sacred space and its imprints are a very complex thing.

Leaving a Sacred Space

Before you leave one of the sacred sites go to the Welcome Circle and say thanks. Express your gratitude with a prayer.

Make sure you can drive. Mother Earth can get your feel good chemicals going and give you a blissed out feeling, a spiritual high; like a good meditation, only more so. Most people will not feel much, but over time as you develop sentience of Mother Earth and consciousness you will start to get blissed out.

The consciousness you have absorbed is powerful and can have a dramatic affect upon you. Incredible levels of compassion, caring, love may manifest in you. You may get great insights, have an epiphany or even see other dimensions, or realities. I have had some incredible moments where I have been almost overwhelmed with love and compassion for others, even towards the most despicable and violent people.

Again you are absorbing Christ Consciousness and you will be affected accordingly. You are being transformed into a better person; it won't happen overnight but you will see small changes linger in who you are. Think of it like consuming food to build muscle mass. You consume lots of protein and other foods that nourish muscle; but not all of it will be converted to muscle. It takes time.

Electromagnetic energy can also affect your sense of balance and have other affects as well. Generally your thinking will be clear. But again make sure you can drive.

If need be, eating will help reduce your blissed out feeling; particularly eating root vegetables such as carrots or beets, or even potatoes. Just eat.

The Day After

Meditating in a FOC is a powerful experience that can have an equally powerfully transformative effect. You need to rest and not physically exert yourself too much the day after. Like an athletic after a major competition, or a workout that exceeds norms, you need to rest.

Some of you may crash, or have a minor let down the next day particularly if you absorbed a lot of energy. If so try meditating a little to get you over the hump.

I strongly suggest you don't smoke, or drink alcohol after leaving a sacred site. In fact I suggest that you wait several days before ingesting anything harmful to your body. Secondly, try to avoid being in negative spaces, spaces with a bad vibe. As noted earlier, consciousness interacts with consciousness. If you spend time in a negative space the consciousness you picked up will be dissipated as it interacts and looks to balance out to some degree with the negative space.

It will take several days for the consciousness you absorbed to work through your subtle body. Any initial blissed out feeling will be gone, but your body will still be processing what you consumed; the same way your body absorbs and digests food. Just like food, all the calories, or consciousness you absorbed will not be retained.

Bask in the love you have absorbed the day after. Feed on it, and nourish it. Read a religious text that inspires you, or brings out your best. Read and contemplate the, 'A prayer for the love of Mother Earth' in the Prayer section of the Appendix. Or, listen to music that inspires you, or wells up love, warmth, or compassion within you. Meditate on those feelings; this will give strength to them. You have been blessed with a powerful dose of Christ Consciousness, focusing on love, altruism and compassion will help you retain more of it—making you more loving and compassionate.

If you drink a lot of water, as you should, your body will retain water for a while as you purify yourself and raise your consciousness.

Sentience Warning

Developing the ability to sense and feel Consciousness will better help you connect with Mother Earth and make you more sensitive to Her many emanations and gifts. It can also make you very sensitive of the consciousness that permeates every speck of the earth, which unfortunately is mostly negative. As a consequence you will be sensing the vats of negativity we encounter each day; we experience these vats all the time, only now you will begin to feel them. You will experience this in your Chidakasha (your mind screen, seat of your consciousness) in the area of a forehead. Sensations can run from a slight headache or pain, to feeling as though someone is gripping you forehead with pliers around your forehead and gently squeezing. It's generally not that bad unless you are in an area of geopathic stress, or near a negative energy vortex, then it becomes very uncomfortable.

Gaining sentience of Mother Earth will greatly expand your aura. This can bring innumerable benefits, mostly health and spiritual gifts. An expanded aura will make you more sensitive to space; you may begin to feel hand movements close to you, or the movement of people as they slice through your aura.

An expanded aura means that you have a larger vessel to appreciate and absorb Mother Earth's Gift. As a consequence, activities such as drum circles, or sound therapy activities such as gongs, etc. can be too much for you; because you will be absorbing too much of the emanations from these activities.

You need to think about these things before you move forward with visiting FOC and trying to sense and feel Consciousness. This would not be a problem if we lived in the world we were meant to live in, and not one that is spiritually polluted.

The benefits are that you will be helping make a better world and helping heal Mother Earth. You will also be leapfrogging your spiritual development from the absorption of the consciousness emanating from FOC.

Stone Mounds and Other Structures

A few of the sacred sites listed will have stone mounds or other structures, most notably High Tor NYS DEC Forest. The inclination is that these places need to be physically preserved—they do. But they also need to be used and reinvigorated.

I have been visiting High Tor and meditating in its FOC and by its many stone mounds for over a decade. For years, I firmly believed that the stone mounds needed to be preserved and not walked on. I feared that telling people about them would bring treasure hunters on a futile effort looking for plunder. But over time, I came to realize that it was the vibe that made High Tor, particularly South Hill, special.

The vibe at South Hill in places is incredible. All the covered Earth Chakras and other energy formations electrify the air; but hiding beneath the charged ether are the powerful imprints of pilgrims that have come there on pilgrimages for centuries, if not millennia. It is those imprints, those collective thought forms that can grab you and give you a vision, a revelation, or lift you up into higher states of consciousness, or higher realities.

It is the vibe that makes South Hill. The stone mounds are only a vehicle, a catalyst of sorts, to help you achieve a mystical experience, or to connect with Great Spirit. The important thing is the vibe and it needs to be nourished, with prayer, ceremony, ritual or meditation to remain vibrant. While I still have an incredible admiration and appreciation of stonework it has taken a back seat to the imprints found there.

That said, I ask that you please contact the DEC and tell them to preserve the stone mounds and make High Tor a sacred site once again. The Appendix has information on who to contact and other efforts to preserve and reinvigorate sacred sites in North Star Country.

Several of the places you visit may have stones placed upon the FOC to serve as a marker. Look for large flat stones wherever you go. You should meditate on them, or close to them. **Please do not move, or add stones to a location.** There may be certain places that are more to your liking and you may feel compelled to mark it with stones—DON'T!

Call First, Donate, Get Involved

Please call before your visit, especially if such is noted in the review. Many of the places listed are small not-profits that don't have a large staff. They need to be notified before your visit. It helps you and helps them.

Also, places change their hours of operation. Or they may have closed, or changed into private hands. Over the years many incredible places have passed into private hands. So call before coming.

As noted many of the places listed are not-for-profits. Please make a generous donation so that they can continue their operation and offer their space for future pilgrims to visit. Reviews will note how to donate, or where the donations box is located. If you cannot find the donation box, please ask where it is. Remember your generosity and kindness will linger as sweet imprints.

Several of the places welcome volunteers to help with activities such as trail maintenance. Others such as the Fellowship of Reconciliation and the Peace Pagoda welcome you to join in their peace and justice activities. Please consider participating with them, or with others to keep the spirit of North Star Country blazing.

If you plan on visiting one of the sacred sites in Nature I suggest not doing this during (gun) hunting season for deer (particularly the first week) in the fall and turkey in the spring; both for your own safety and not to kick up deer for the hunters to shoot. Once I was climbing South Hill in High Tor NYS DEC Forest when I realized I was kicking up deer for the hunters higher up; I turned back. If you plan on going during gun season midday is the best time to go and wear orange/red. The appendix lists contact information for state hunting agencies.

Help Out and Participate

The Appendix contains a listing of activities you can help out with; such as the effort to make South Hill (High Tor) a sanctuary and bring about a total cleanup of Onondaga Lake. It also tells how we encourage you to spread the word and be very vocal about, 'you are in North Star Country on a spiritual pilgrimage.' Tourism helps the economy, which helps create jobs, which helps motivate politicians to pay attention. So definitely be very vocal with the people you encounter while visiting a place; explain that you are visiting sacred sites, Mother Earth's Soul, that you are on holy ground....

While I encourage you to visit and help local businesses I ask that you avoid those that may, should my work takeoff, offer to act as a guide and bring you to places and instruct you for money. That is problem that has befallen so many sacred sites—they have become commercialized; in the process they leave negative imprints and cast a pale over the site. By all means pay for transportation, rent a car, eat out, buy stuff, stay at a hotel; just don't pay for a guide.

Enjoy

Experiencing FOC is a wonderful experience, so enjoy it. You may notice a little more Christ Consciousness within yourself. Most people will see an improvement, sometimes a dramatic improvement after several visits, in their compassion, as well as in their meditations. This can be reflected in deeper meditations, going to higher states quicker, or in new and different experiences and insights. And while the initially powerful effects will diminish over time, a marked improvement will remain within you.

References and Recommended Reading
1. Heinemann, Klaus and Ledwith, Miceal; *The Orb Project*, Atria and Beyond Words Publishing, Hillsboro, Oregon, 2007; Page 44.
2. Ibid. Pages 53-59.
3. Ibid. Page 97.

Part II

Listing of Sacred Sites

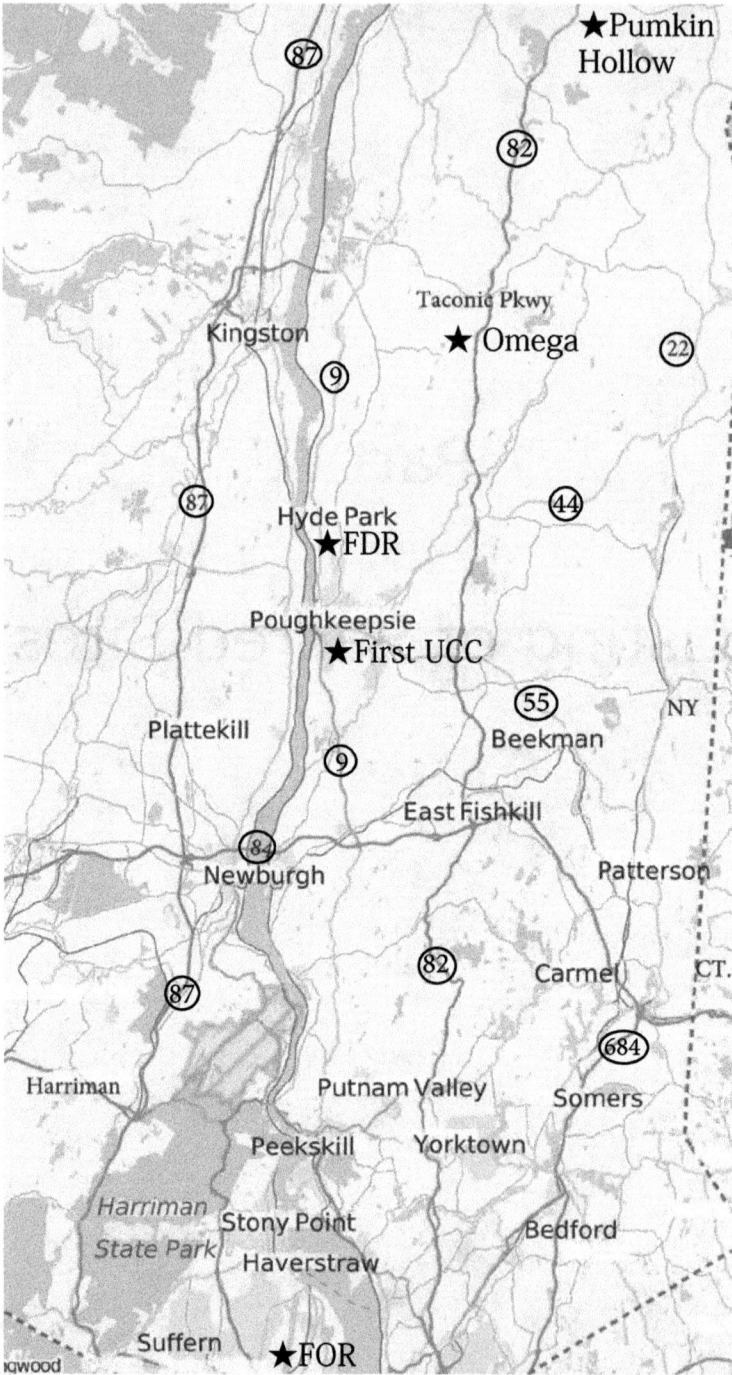

Map of Hudson Valley, Source www. openstreetmap. org.

Hudson Valley

The Hudson Valley was one of the main arteries of the Underground Railroad as Freedom Seekers traveled from the metro NY area to Albany and Troy. Many assisted the travelers, including the large Quaker population, particularly in Dutchess County. The First Congregational UCC of Poughkeepsie, one of the sacred sites listed in this section, had many conductors.

The Women's Rights advocate and abolitionist Lucretia Coffin Mott attended the Nine Partners School (Dutchess County.) Noted seer and healer, Andrew Jackson Davis, is from Poughkeepsie. To do his healings Jackson would go into a trance; as another famous healer, Edgar Cayce, would do fifty years later. As a clairvoyant Jackson predicted many things, including the advent of Spiritualism. Many consider him the "John the Baptist of Spiritualism."

The beautiful Hudson River inspired the Hudson River School (of Painting), which ran concurrent with Transcendentalism. As R. Todd Felton notes in his book on Transcendentalism; "Many key Transcendental themes—inspiration from the natural world, the spiritual unity are found in the works of the Hudson River School."[1]

Several large mansions—Vanderbilt, Roosevelt, Clermont, Montgomery Place...—are located on the banks of the Hudson River. Most offer tours; a little off the beaten path is the Mills Mansion (Staatsburg) and there is the majestic Olana (Hudson, NY), home to Fredric Church, a central figure in Hudson River School.

References and Recommend Reading
1. Felton, Todd R.; *A Journey into the Transcendentalists' New England*, Roaring Forties Press, Berkeley, California, 2006 Page 10.

Craryville, Columbia County, NY

Pumpkin Hollow Retreat Center
S2-4, V1-4, ▽ ☆ ♡ (↑) ⚄ 🚶 🏠 🖼 ☁ 〰

Pumpkin Hollow is where healers come to heal and learn. This intention of compassion and the desire to heal permeates the grounds, particularly on the building side of the stream. It is palpable, something very special beyond the vibe that is slightly positive, to extremely positive in places. A vortex is located in the meditation center.

A testimonial on its website by Ed Tick, Director of Soldier's Heart, (dedicated to healing war veterans) and author of *War and the Soul*, speaks to the Hollows' restorative power:

"Pumpkin Hollow offers an amazing space for holding and healing the devastating wounds of war. It's a magical place on the planet where Mother Earth holds the capacity to embrace and absorb the cries and heartache of raw pain, and where truth transforms brokenness into reconciliation, healing and home-coming.!"

Located on 134 acres there are nature trails, a meditation center, a labyrinth and more. Pumpkin Hollow offers workshops, yoga, and meditation and is a retreat center. Please call (518-325-3583) before you come and announce yourself upon arriving. Make sure to check the website before visiting to insure a retreat is not scheduled. Or sign up for a program.

History

During the height of the depression in 1936, clairvoyant and healer Dora Kunz, along with other Theosophists were driving around the Hudson Valley looking for a place to create a retreat center. Dora said "stop the car" when they got to Pumpkin Hollow, a farm at the time. Dora took a walk down to the waterfalls and said, "this is the place."

Kunz was a noted healer in twentieth century who along with Dolores Krieger, RN, started the Therapeutic Touch system of healing that is widely used by nurses in hospitals around the world. Dora could see people's auras and would often immediately see what was wrong with someone. It is said her Spirit visits when Therapeutic Touch classes take place. A friend and fellow Earth Healer can attest to Dora's Spirit; as it came to her and consoled her when she had an attack of appendicitis when visiting.

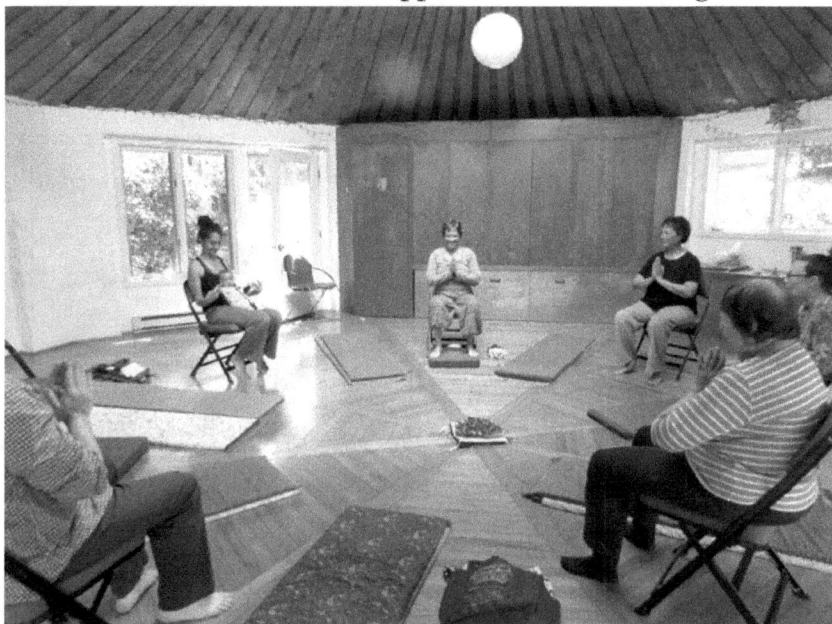

The Meditation Center. A faint orb is visible to the left of the light above the vortex in the center of the room

Madame Blavatsky, Henry Steel Olcott and William Quan Judge, founded Theosophy at the far edge of North Star Country in New York City in 1875. At the time it was very progressive, advocating the universality of all religions and saw no distinction between race, creed, sex, caste or color. Theosophy was early in the vanguard of studying comparative religions. It also recommends the study of the mysteries of nature and man's latent powers. Long before the world was focusing on metaphysics and esoteric knowledge Theosophists like Madame Blavatsky, Annie Besant, Charles Leadbeater were writing about it.

The grounds at Pumpkin Hollow were all pasture land before the Theosophical Society purchased it. They have intentionally let the land go fallow so that the woods could develop naturally.

Experiencing Pumpkin Hollow

There are numerous Fields throughout the grounds. A FOC (S2) covers much of the patio behind the Barn Meeting Hall.   There is another series of S2's on the hillside, or knoll, going towards the bridge.

There is FOC on the side of the hill on the way to the bridge. Papers mark the highpoints.

As you walk towards the bridge there will be a trail to your right. When the trail branches, go to your right. You will shortly come to some hemlock trees that are on a FOC (S4); where the trail crosses is the beginning of a series of (3) S4's. They break at an angle about 10 o'clock to the end of a stonewall. They are about 15 feet apart and the last one is right in front of the end of the stonewall. Anywhere in this area would be great to meditate in, as the whole area is on a FOC.

If you cross the bridge, shortly a herd path will break to your left, follow it. Stop at a knoll directly across from the meditation pavilion on the other side of the stream. It is on FOC (S4.) Notice the vibe is very nice but it does not embrace you as the other side of the stream does, where the activities take place. Use this as a reference to help you gain a sense of space. You might want to go back and forth to better help you gain that sense. The healing vibe on the other side of the stream speaks volumes to what the staff and visitors to Pumpkin Hollow have created. Definitely spend some time here meditating. It gives you some privacy and you are close to the water.

The grounds of Pumpkin Hollow are ideal for a contemplative walk, whether on the trails, or building side of the stream. FOC are located all around and the vibe is very nice.

The Facilities

Meditation Center—While it does not rest on FOC there is an energy vortex about 4 feet in diameter approximately in the center. This is a vortex of Cosmic Prana, which is the prana (energy) we normally attract when we meditate. Numerous Spirit Lines intersect in the center of the room. When I see so many Lines intersecting in the same place, I call it a nest.

The vibe in the meditation pavilion is sweet and it would be a great place to meditate, or take a class. When I was there last, local residents were taking a yoga class. A very informal, friendly and easy going group.

Nature Trail—The Nature Trail meanders through the grounds providing for a wonderful contemplative walk. It crosses several FOC and other divine aspects of Mother Earth. I suggest beginning north of the main house by the stream. Cross the footbridge and bear to your left after you cross the river. The trail is well marked. As you turn right and begin ascending you will be close to the neighboring property line marked with numerous "no trespassing" signs. Notice how distinctly different the vibe is near the property line. I believe that this has to do with the consciousness of control and exclusion on the neighboring property that is physically manifested by the posted signs. Continuing the trail will intersect and end at another trail marked with stones painted with silver triangles. To your left (north) is the labyrinth and to your right is toward the waterfall.

Plenty more— There is also a healing center, peace garden with a peace pole and other areas to explore and enjoy.

Reading room—If you are staying over, make sure to check out the library. It is full of classic Theosophical books.

Pumpkin Hollow is a not for profit and depends upon donations to help sustain itself. Please donate generously and help keep this divine space going. The donation box is currently located in the Main House. It has been moved about over the years so please ask if you cannot find it.

Don't be swept up by the physical beauty because you will miss out.

Address: 1184 Route 1, Craryville, NY 12521
Webpage: www.pumpkinhollow.org
Email: info@pumpkinhollow.org
Telephone: 518-325-3583
Fax: 518-325-5633
Donate, Volunteer: A donation box is located in the Main House. Please call if you are interested in helping with the garden, or the trails.
Hours: Pumpkin Hollow is open year round. There are daily meditations, regular yoga classes and various courses (check webpage.) You can even schedule a retreat. Make sure to check the events schedule before you come so as not to conflict with private retreats. Call before you visit.
Directions: From the Taconic State Pkwy take the Claverack/Hillsdale exit. Take a left if coming from the North or take a right if coming from the South onto Rt. 23 East. Continue

on Rt. 23 East to the first traffic light and turn right onto County Route 11A (Taconic Hills Central School sign). Continue .5 miles on County Route 11A to Stop Sign continue straight thru, you are now on County Route 11. Continue for 2 miles, Pumpkin Hollow will be on the left.

References and Recommended Reading
Pumpkin Hollow website, www.pumpkinhollow.org
Blavatsky, Helena P., *The Key to Theosophy*
"What Facilitators Say About Pumpkin Hollow Retreat Center,"http://pumpkinhollow.org/documents/testimonials_prep_website.pdf
Therapeutic Touch: http://therapeutictouch.org, http://therapeutic-touch.org

Hyde Park, Dutchess County, NY
Once was the home to the Vanderbilt's and Roosevelt's. The American Culinary School is located there.

Franklin Delano Roosevelt National Historic Site
S2, V0, 🕴🕴

The Springwood estate is the birthplace, lifelong home and burial place for Franklin Delano Roosevelt, the 32nd president of the United States of America. The FDR Presidential Library, the first presidential library, is located on the grounds. Both are part of the National Parks Service.

Experiencing the Roosevelt Grounds
There is a Field (S2) located near the side, or back of the Visitor Center, depending upon how you see it. Find the gravel path in front of the patio. When facing the patio, the center of the FOC

(S2) are located between two trees next to the gravel path and logistically are towards the western end of the patio.

Address: 4097 Albany Post Road, Hyde Park, NY, 12538
Webpage: http://www.nps.gov/hofr/index.htm
Telephone: Park Headquarters (Monday - Friday,) 845-229-9115 Ex. 2010
Henry A. Wallace Visitor Center (Everyday 9am - 5pm,) 845-229-5320
General Information, 1-800-FDR-VISIT
Donate, Volunteer: Several volunteer opportunities are listed on the webpage.
Hours: 9AM to 5PM seven days a week. Closed Thanksgiving, Christmas and New Years. Tours daily, limited schedule November to April. $18 for both the home and library. Children 15 and younger free. Top Cottage and $10 admission.
Close by: Eleanor Roosevelt National Historic Site, Vanderbilt Estate; Mills Mansion, NY State Historic Site, Staatsburg NY.
Directions: From the Thruway Exit 18 (New Paltz), take 299 East, to 9W South, follow the signs to Mid-Hudson Bridge. After crossing bridge follow overhead signs to Rt. 9 North. Home will be in 5 miles on your left.
Taconic-Northbound take Rt. 55 to Poughkeepsie to Rt. 9. Southbound take Rt. 199 exit Red Hook to Rt. 308. Follow for 10 miles until Rt. 9 south. Take Rt. 9 south.

Nyack, Rockland County, NY

Fellowship of Reconciliation—Peace and Justice
S4, V2, ♥☆♡

The struggle for peace and justice that was the hallmark of North Star Country in the nineteenth century continues at the Fellowship of Reconciliation (FOR), an ecumenical faith based peace and justice organization (nonprofit, 501c-3) that embraces nonviolence. It has a great vibe and FOC (S4) in the Metro New York City area. Very impressive, given how far it is from the heart of North Star Country. If you are looking to be uplifted and feel the compassion of peace and justice give it a visit. Better yet, get involved.

The national headquarters are located in Shadowcliff, a New York State registered historic home. Please call before coming and announce yourself when you arrive.

History

The FOR was founded in 1915 to bear witness to the horrors of WWI and work with Conscientious Objectors. Early on it helped organize the National Civil Liberties Bureau that would become the ACLU.

In the 1930's the FOR was involved with the labor movement. It was early on fighting the evils of racism. It held protests over the internment of Japanese Americans during WWII.

In 1943 with the Congress of Racial Equality (CORE) it coordinated the first interracial sit-in. It sponsored nonviolent training workshops throughout the South. It helped Dr. King plan the Montgomery bus boycott. One of its staff, Bayard Rustin, played a pivotal role in the March on Washington.

During the Viet Nam war, it made contact with the Buddhist pacifist movement and sponsored a speaking tour in the USA for Thich Nhat Hahn in 1968. In the 1990's it sent religious delegates to visit Iraq and worked to prevent war. It initiated the Bosnian Student Project to bring students out of war torn Yugoslavia to schools in the USA and found them homes.

Their prophetic voice and witness continues. The FOR was very helpful in an effort I was involved with to help an Iraqi American, Dr. Rafil Dhair, who was targeted as a terrorist during the second Iraqi war for his humanitarian work to help children in Iraq, devastated by the economic sanctions of the 1990's.

The dogs and backpack are in the area of the S4 outside.

Experiencing Shadowcliff

The vibe is positive on the grounds and in Shadowcliff; very few places have a positive vibe on all its grounds. Most of the south side of the building and its surrounding grounds sits on a FOC. The highpoint is a series (3) of S4's running from the outside to the inside. One S4 is located outside on the south side of the building. Looking from the stairs to the building one S4 is on a little knoll to the left, by the top of the stairs (see picture above.)

The other two in the series are located inside of the building. One S4 is located in the Peace Porch, the room closest to the outside. The sweetest Field is located in the Peace Room, almost in the center. This is where meetings are held, as well as group prayers and an occasional meditation.

The vibe in the Peace Room is very positive and has an uplifting feel to it. A vortex ring has formed, or is in the processing of forming; a precursor to the formation of a vortex. This speaks volumes on how not only prayer, but the action and intention of doing peace and justice work enhances a physical space.

The Peace Room.

Address: 521 North Broadway, Nyack, NY 10960
Webpage: www.forusa.org
Email: for@forusa.org
Telephone: 845-358-4601
Fax: 845-358-4924
Donate, Join: You can join the FOR, or donate to it online at their website, www.forusa.org.
Hours: Shadowcliff is open 9AM to 5PM, Monday to Friday. Please call, (845) 358-4601 before coming and announce yourself

when you arrive. Unless you join, or are a member, your visit should be confined to the outside.

Get Involved: The website, www.forusa.org, includes a blog and other sources listing actions and events the FOR is involved with.

Directions: From Upstate NY: Thruway (I-87) south to Exit 11. Turn left at the traffic light onto Rt. 59. At the next light, turn left onto 9W/Highland. Turn right on Fifth Street, left to Broadway. Continue on Broadway. From NYC, NJ: Take the Palisades Parkway to Exit 4. Turn left (north) on Rt. 9W, and follow this for 6 miles to Nyack. At Route 59/Main Street (light), turn right. At the third light, turn left onto Broadway. See above.

References and Recommended Reading

FOR website, www.forusa.org.

'Brother Outsider' (DVD), tells the story of Bayard Rustin, the unknown hero of the Civil Rights Movement.

Wink. Walter; *Peace is the Way: Writings on Nonviolence from the Fellowship of Reconciliation.*

Poughkeepsie, Dutchess County, NY

The county seat for Dutchess County and home to Vassar college.

First Congregational UCC Poughkeepsie
S4, V0-1,

An open and accepting church with a deep rooted passion for social justice. Founded as an anti-slave church it is a designated site on New York's Underground Railroad Heritage Trail. A FOC with a series (3) of S4's runs from inside of the church, to its outside. The vibe in the sanctuary is neutral, to slightly positive.

A Rich History

In 1837 eighty members of the First and Second Presbyterian churches of Poughkeepsie left their congregations to form the

96

First Congregational Church. They were disgruntled over theological differences and the refusal of their ministers to stand against slavery. Forty of the eighty were members of various anti-slavery societies.

In 1839 it extended membership to Samuel Ringgold Ward, an abolitionist, teacher and former slave. In 1851 when Fredrick Douglass was barred from speaking at city hall he was invited to the pulpit at First Congregational. It is believed that many of the church members were actively involved with the Underground Railroad.

Social reform and social justice have continued to be an advocacy for parishioners. In the 1960's and 1970's they fostered race relations, spoke out against the Viet Nam war and worked to help the needs of the city's children. The church has been an intake center to house the homeless for decades and has recently supported refugees from Viet Nam, Uganda and Kenya.

Experiencing UCC Poughkeepsie

Most of the sanctuary sits on a FOC. There are a series (3) of (S4)'s that runs from the right hand corner of the grounds next to the church (close to parking) when you face the church into the sanctuary. One S4 is located in the narthex (foyer) on the right hand side, about midpoint. The remaining S4 is located in the center back of the sanctuary.

Address: 269 Mill Street, Poughkeepsie, NY 12601
Webpage: www.opentogod.org
Email: fccoffice@gmail.com

Telephone: 845-454-2960
Hours: Sunday worship: 10:30 AM with Children's time, 10:45 AM Sunday school, 11:45 AM Fellowship Hour.
Directions: From Rt. 9 in Poughkeepsie exit onto Church Street, or the East West Arterial (one way), going east. Take a left onto Academy St. Take a left onto Mill St., East West Arterial (one way), going west. The church is a few blocks down on your right.

References and Recommended Reading

The Underground Railroad in New York Hudson Valley, Fergus M. Bordewich, http://www.fergusbordewich.com/blog/?p=38
'First Congregational Church UCC 175 years of Faith, Service and Justice: This is Our Story', Church pamphlet and website .

Rhinebeck, Dutchess County, NY

Omega Institute
S2-6, V0, 🧍 ⚡ 🚻 🏠 🖼️

Omega is a nonprofit center for lifelong learning offering workshops, professional training, and wellness vacations. It provides a forum for people to be exposed to new ideas from leading thinkers such as Al Gore, Gloria Steinem and Deepak Chopra. Omega consists of 250 acres and more than 100 buildings, including the Sanctuary, the Ram Dass Library, and the Omega Center for Sustainable Living (OCSL).

The woods behind the cottages are a delight. There are numerous FOC (the highest S6) throughout it. The vibe is neutral.

History

Eastern meditation teacher and scholar, Pir Vilayat Inayat Khan inspired the Omega founders, Stephan Rechtschaffen M.D. and Elizabeth Lesser to found a 'university of life.' They felt our society was ripe for exploring holistic ways of living and deeper spiritual reflection.

In 1981, Omega expanded from rented facilities in New York and Vermont to its current Rhinebeck home on the former grounds of Camp Boiberik, a popular Yiddish summer camp. Camp Boiberik operated from 1923 to 1979

In its first year (1977) Omega hosted a few hundred people: today over 23,000 visit (various locations worldwide) and another 2 million visit Omega online.

The name 'Omega' comes from French Jesuit Priest and philosopher Pierre Teilhard de Chardin, who famously said; "we are not human beings having a spiritual experience. We are spiritual beings having a human experience." De Chardin saw humanity undergoing an evolution of consciousness, reaching an "Omega Point" of greater unity.

My interest in Omega was piqued years ago when I read about a large and mysterious rock cairn located in the woods of Omega on the rock piles blog. I was interested not so much because the pile itself was anything mystical, but rather what the pile might be indicative of. Farmers clearing fields create most rock piles. Sometimes those stones were taken from the dismantling of Native American ceremonial circles, or prayer places. I have also found that stone piles are often subconsciously placed in a location because it is a natural power place; or was once a gathering place, or marks where several Native American trails once intersected. In other words, the rock pile may be on, or close to, a power place.

Experiencing Omega

Walk due north into the woods between cabins 17 and 18, you will see a stonewall on your right. Continue walking straight ahead, the land will rise a little. Keep the wall on your right as a general guide, but do not hug it, as it will have some movement and additions. After a few hundred yards you will see a large stone pile on your right (referred to previously.) There is a FOC (S6) to the left of the stone pile.

Looking at the large stone pile in the background standing in the FOC, the Nature Trail's bench is on the left, about 150 feet away.

The center of the FOC is on a little rise about 50-60 feet away from the midpoint of the large stone pile. A series (3) of S6's breaks from the FOC at 45° to the stone pile and are about 15 feet apart. In the picture above you are looking at the last S6. If you were to turn left, you would see the bench on the Nature Trail about 150 feet ahead. You could almost draw a straight line from where the trail bends to the S6. This FOC is quite large, so meditating anywhere in this general area will put you on it.

The next FOC (S6) is on a knoll to your left. Look for a pile of brush; the FOC is on the other side.

There are FOC's behind cabins 25-27, on the other side of the stone wall you will see some pine trees. Focus on how the trees have naturally created an opening forming a circle of sorts. It is before the wet area with the stone berm. The opening area is a very nice spot that sits on a FOC (S2.)

100

If you visit

A listing of workshops and programs are on he Omega Institute webpage; you can even have a catalogue sent to you.

If you are visiting for the day, you must call Guest Services in advance and check in at Main Office Registration (located near guest parking) when you arrive.

Address: 150 Lake Drive, Rhinebeck, NY 12572
Webpage: https://www.eomega.org
Email: registration@eomega.org
Telephone: 877-944-2002 (US) or 845-266-4444 (International)
Hours: Call when you wish to visit.
Donate, Volunteer: You can donate online at Omega's webpage. There are several opportunities for service at Omega listed on the webpage. You can become a steward, or volunteer.
Omega in Action (http://www.eomega.org/omega-in-action) is a blog focused on people and institutions making a difference, as well as providing ways you can give.
Directions: From the north take Taconic Pkwy south and exit Bulls Head Rd. Turn left (west) and go to Centre Rd (Rt. 18) about 2 miles and turn left. Continue (2.3 miles) and turn right onto Fiddlers Bridge Go 1.2 miles and turn right on Lake Dr.
From the south take Taconic Pkwy north to Pumpkin Lane and turn left onto the divider and stop. Carefully cross and continue, bear left and merge with Nine Partners Rd Continue straight onto Fiddler's Bridge Rd in Schultzville. Take a right onto Lake Dr.

References and Recommended Reading
Omega Institute website, https://www.eomega.org
'Cairn in Rhinebeck', http: //rockpiles.blogspot. com /2007/09/cairn-in-rhinebeck-ny.html
'Rhinebeck Cairns Experiential', Rock Piles blog, followup video of the stone cairns at Omega. http: //naturalwisdom. blogspot.com/2007/11/rhinebeck-cairns-experiential.html

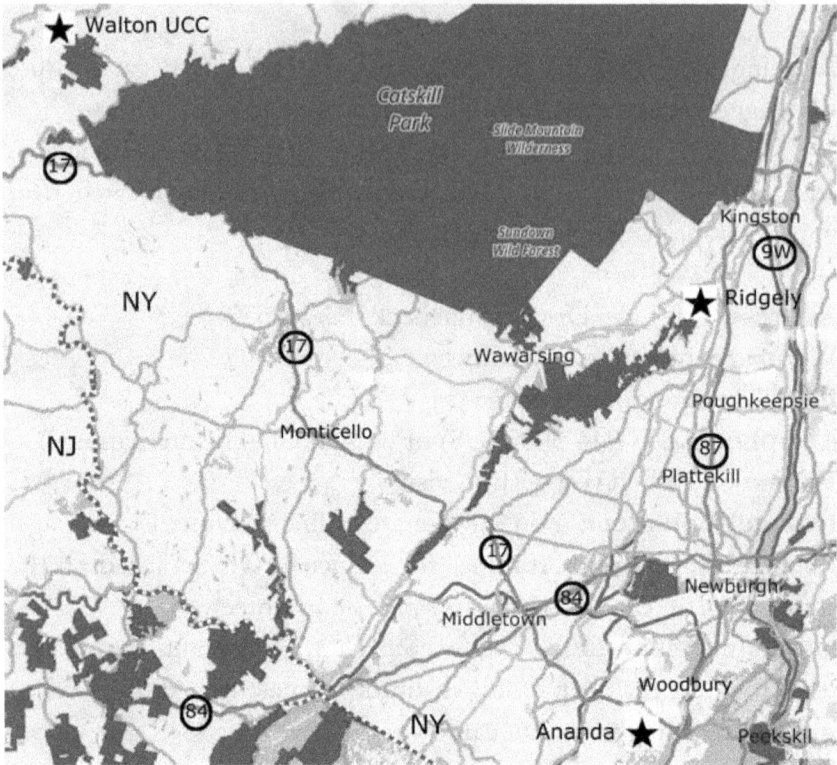

Sacred Sites in North Star Country

Map of the Catskills. Source-© OpenStreetMap contributors, www. openstreetmap. org.

Catskills

Located in southeastern New York, the Catskills is a mountain range. It was to the town of Catskill that seer and healer Andrew Jackson Davis was transported to. Jackson claimed a mysterious force overcame him and felt as though he were flying; and next remembered walking up in the Catskills.

The Catskills is also one of the places where the Hindu (Vedanta) mystic Swami Vivekananda spent time.

Monroe, Orange County, NY

Ananda Ashram
S4, V0, ⛹🧍🏠🖼

Ananda is a yoga retreat and spiritual educational and learning center. It offers daily meditation and yoga classes as well as a host of other classes and workshops. Many attend its Sanskrit classes and it has a yoga teachers training program. Guest and student accommodations are available.

There is a FOC with a series (3) of S4's on the grounds. The vibe is neutral.

Experiencing Ananda
A large FOC is located in front of the terrace in the back of the main building. The highpoint is a series (3) of S4's. Closest S4 is

about 40 feet in front of the center of the terrace, parallel to a small bush/tree on the right hand side.

Still facing the terrace the other two are to the right and about 15 feet apart. On the right hand side the section of the hedgerow closest to the house is indented compared to the rest of the hedgerow. Find the corner (right angle) where the hedgerow runs before the indentation is cut in. The remaining Fields run at an angle towards this corner.

Just plant yourself about 40 feet in front of the terrace and to the right and you cannot go wrong.

Address: 13 Sapphire Road, Monroe NY 10950
Webpage: http://www.anandaashram.org
Email: ananda@anandaashram.org
Telephone: 845-782-5575
Fax: 845-774-7368
Donate, volunteer: Ananda is a 501c-3. You can donate to several restoration projects online. There are a variety of volunteer programs, check the website; most are focused on helping out with chores to get a reduced rate for your stay.
Hours: Open year round. Activities begin with morning meditation and fire ceremony is at 9AM, and conclude with meditation/kirtan at 7:30 PM (Sat 7PM.) Suggested $10 donation (nonmembers.) Yoga daily classes check website. A vegetarian lunch and dinner is available to day guests.
Directions: In Harriman take Rt. 17 south. After going under the railway overpass (second overpass) take an immediate right onto Grove Street. Continue straight at traffic light onto Church St. Continue straight onto Harriman Heights Road past Sapphire Elementary School (right.) Take next left onto Sapphire Road. Ananda Ashram's is on the left.

Stone Ridge, Ulster County, NY

Vivekananda Retreat Center Ridgely
S3, V0-1,🏠 🖼

Ridgely is a 82 acre retreat center dedicated to preserving and continuing the universal teachings of the great Hindu mystic Swami Vivekananda. The Swami stayed at Ridgely on three occasions from 1895 to 1899, for a total of twelve weeks.

Experiencing Ridgely

There is FOC (S3) to the left of the retreat center (the smaller building, not the manor) when you face it. The vibe around the area of the FOC is neutral to slightly positive

Ridgely offers classes on a regular basis, as well as lectures and events by internationally known figures in Vedanta. Longer term stays and retreats are available. Please call at least one day in advance before visiting.

Address: 101 Leggett Rd, Stone Ridge, NY 12484
Webpage http: // ridgely. org
Telephone: 845-687-4574
Donate, Volunteer: Online
Hours: Open 9 AM to 7 PM daily. Please call at least one day in advance for visiting, five or more days to setup a retreat.
Close by: Close to the Hudson River (western side.)
Directions: Thruway (I-87) to exit 19 (Kingston.) Take Rt. 209 south, go 9 miles to Stone Ridge. Turn left onto Leggett Road.

References and Recommended Reading
'Vivekananda   at   Ridgely',
https://www.youtube.com/watch?v=1F6Uwf-UKQc

Walton, Delaware County, NY

The First Congregational UCC Walton
S6, V1-3, 👤👥🧘

The First Congregational Church has been part of the Walton community and helping those in need since 1793. Today it operates a Thrift Store (Elijah's closet), offers a medical equipment ministry where basic medical needs such as canes and walkers are shared, and a weekly luncheon program.

Experiencing the UCC Walton

All of the sanctuary and the outside area next to the church on Mead Street sits on a FOC that contains a series of 3 (S6); one inside the church, two outside.

The church has a nice air to it. The vibe runs from slightly positive to very positive. One of S6's is located in the pews a few feet from the center window.

The rest of the FOC is outside the church on the side of Mead Street and the series is perpendicular to the sanctuary. Facing the church with Mead Street to your back you will see that the sanctuary has 5 windows. The remaining of the two in the series of S6's is located in front of the center, or third window. The closest to the church S6 is located about 5 feet from the church. The remaining S6 is located about another 15 feet towards the sidewalk. Vibe is neutral outside.

Address: 4 Mead St, Walton, NY 13856
Webpage: http://uccwalton.com

Email: waltonucc@frontiernet.net

Telephone: 607-865-4066

Donate: Elijah's Closet Thrift Shops accepts donations and is open Friday and Saturday's 10AM to 4PM.

Hours: 10 AM Sundays.

Directions: From Rt. 88 take exit 8, Rt. 206 Bainbridge. Take Rt. 206 south (away from Bainbridge.) In Walton Rt. 205 will merge with Rt. 10. Take a left onto Townsend St. Take first right onto Mead St.

References and Recommended Reading.

Churches' website, http://uccwalton.com.

Thanks to Jeri Ogden and Judy Kipp for taking the time to speak to me about the church.

Sacred Sites in North Star Country

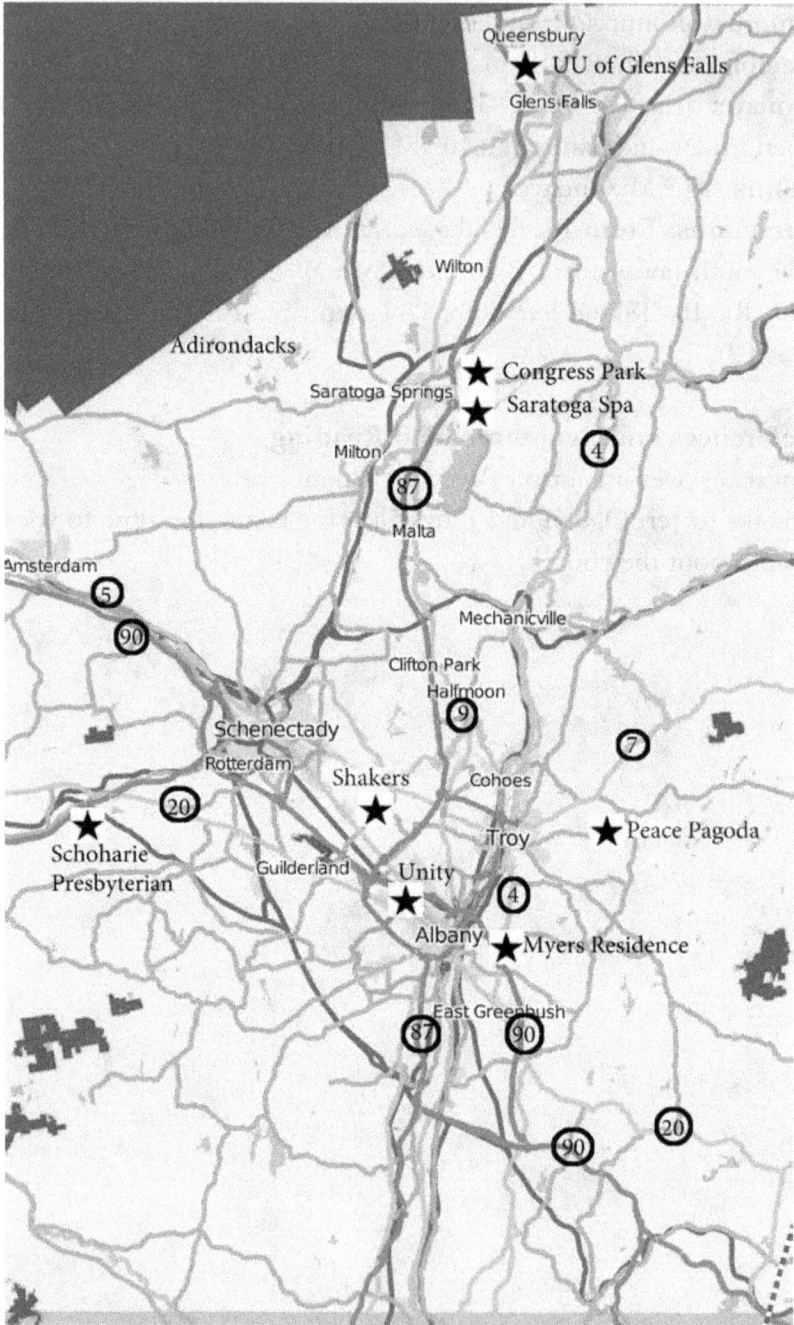

Map of the Capital District, Source--www. openstreetmap.org

Capital District

New York's capital, Albany, is a large metro area that includes the cities of Schenectady and Troy. This is where Mother Ann Lee and a few followers from England began what would be called the "Shakers" for their ecstatic dancing; they were a Utopian community. The Albany area was the home of the Mohawks and the far eastern door of the Haudenosaunee.

It was a major stop on the Underground Rail Road and several noted abolitionists, both black and white, lived in the area: Stephen Myers, Henry Highland Garnet, the Mott sisters (Abigail and Lydia), William Henry Johnson and Abel Brown.

References and Recommended Reading
Underground Railroad Project,
http://undergroundrailroadhistory.org

Albany, Albany County, NY
Albany is the capital of New York State and the county seat.

Stephen and Harriet Myers Residence
S4, V0,

Stephen and Harriet Myers were abolitionists and stationmasters on the Underground Railroad, whose Albany home served as a station stop. The Underground Railroad History Project of the Capital District purchased the home in 2004 and has been working since then to restore it.

Stephen was set free in 1818 and was active on the Underground Railroad by 1831. In the early 1840's he began publishing *Northern Star and Freemans Advocate* an abolitionist paper that later merged with another paper to become the *Impartial*

Citizen. By 1848 he was the leading spokesman for abolitionism in the capital district.

The entire house sits on a FOC (S4.) The center of which is just to the right of the house as you face it. The vibe is neutral.

While historic homes are not conducive to meditating there is a large couch in the parlor room and I am told people often sit on it for extended periods to take in the home and its rich history.

Address: 194 Livingston Ave, Albany, NY 12210
Webpage: http://undergroundrailroadhistory.org/the-stephen-and-harriet-myers-residence/
Telephone: 518-432-4432
Donate, Volunteer: You can donate and become a member online. Please call for volunteer and intern opportunities.
Hours: Please call in advance to insure someone is there when you visit. Open 12 PM to 8 PM M-F, 12 PM to 4 PM Sat. $10 adults, $8 seniors, $5 children 5 to 12, children under 5 free.
Directions: Going east on the Thruway (I-90) take exit 6, toward Henry Johnson Blvd. Keep right at the fork., follow signs for US 9S/Arbor Hill and merge onto US 9. In about ½ mile take a left onto Livingston Ave.

Unity Church in Albany
S8, V0,

110

All of the church's sanctuary rests on a FOC (S8); the vibe is neutral. The highpoint is a series (3) of S8s that begins just outside of the church on the left side of the entryway stairs to the church. The next in the series is located in the back of the church in the area of the center aisle. The remaining S8 is located in the pews on the right side of the church.

The nice thing about Albany Unity Church is that it provides several group meditation opportunities.

Address: 21 King Avenue Albany, NY 12206
Webpage: http://unityalbany.org
Email: unityalbany@yahoo.com
Telephone: 518-453-3603
Church Services: Sundays 9:00 and 11:00 AM, (Summers From 10:00 AM. Music/meditation/chanting, Sundays at 6PM.
Prayer and Meditation: Wednesday 6:30 to 7PM, Sundays between services (10:15-10:45 AM; Summer, 9:45 be early.)
Directions: Off of Rt. 90 in Albany take exit 5 onto Everett Rd extension going south until it deadends at Rt. 5, Central Ave. Turn left onto Rt. 5. Take first right onto King Ave.

Colonie, Albany County, NY

Colonie was once called Watervliet, it is a suburb of Albany and was home to the Shakers.

Watervliet Shaker Village
S6, V1, 👫 🖼

Watervliet was the first settlement of the Shakers, a Utopian community founded by Mother Ann Lee; so called because of their ecstatic shaking during worship. Shakers lived a simple life, practiced celibacy and believed in the mystical experience of a personal union with Christ. There is a FOC (S6) in the garden area. The vibe is slightly positive.

Shaker History

Shaker theology was forged by Mother Ann Lee's early life. Born in working class Manchester, England she was forced to marry by her father and had eight children, none of who reached adulthood (4 still birth and 4 infant deaths.) In 1758 she joined a group of religious dissenters called the "Shaking Quakers" for their ecstatic trembling dance.

Dissent brought arrest and imprisonment, so Mother Ann Lee and eight of her followers departed for America in 1774. They ended up in Watervliet in 1776. It is said that Mother Ann would lead her followers into the nearby woods for ecstatic dancing. The Shakers pacifism and British origin brought arrest and persecution during the Revolutionary war.

Mother Ann was one for revelations. The day after a solar eclipse on May 19, 1780 she announced the second coming of Christ. She died in 1784, a few months after her brother.

Within a few years of her passing, other settlements were established from New England to Ohio and Kentucky. A successful seed business led to other businesses such as the making of furniture, labor saving devices and vehicles.

Members would continue to have revelations and visions. After peaking in the first half of the nineteenth century their membership would begin to wane. Today there are almost no Shakers left; Sabbath Day Lake, in New Gloucester, ME being the exception. Many feel it was their celibacy and refusal to proselytize that was their undoing.

Experiencing the Shaker Village

In the picture the creamery is to your back, on the right is the far corner of picket fence that surrounds the garden. The first S6 is marked with a white tablet, Jaeda Bear (black dog) is on the next S6 and Pepper (white dog) is on the final S6. Notice the series runs parallel to the fence, but break slightly away.

The FOC can be found behind the garden between the garden and the woods. Cross the bridge to get to the garden. Go on the other side of the garden to the corner of the picket fence closest to the stream. Walk about 8-10 feet to your right away from the stream. The series (3) of S6's are about 35 feet in front you. They break at a slight angle away from the garden. The vibe is slightly positive giving it a nice air.

Located close to the airport noise can be a problem. The noise has greatly varied the two times I visited. The first time there was quite a bit of jet engine sounds. The last time there was almost no airplane noise. This could mean the level of sound will vary depending upon the day and time you visit as well as the flight patterns. Volunteers told me noise is not a problem.

There is much to explore on the grounds; a museum, a creamery and more. There are many events, fairs and workshops held throughout the year; some even teach the skills Shakers employed to make their products, such as basket weaving and chair taping. A calendar can be found on the website.

Address: 25 Meeting House Road, Albany, 12205.
Webpage: Shaker Heritage Society operates the facility.
http://shakerheritage.org
Telephone: 518-456-7890
Donate, Volunteer: Go the Shaker Heritage Society website to donate online and to join the society, or contact to volunteer.
Close by: National Parks has a Shaker Historic Trail that lists other Shaker villages, some are not too far away, . https:// www. nps. gov/Nr/travel/shaker/statichome.htm.
 Hours: open Tuesday-Saturday 9:30am to 4:00pm, Monday-Saturday 10 AM to 4 PM November to Christmas time; closed major holidays, and from around Christmas until February. Check the calendar on the website for specifics. Suggested donation, $5.
Directions: Take exit 4 off the Northway (I 87.) Follow signs for 155 (West) and Albany Airport. Remain left on Rt. 155 (Delessandro Blvd.) Take a left at second light in airport district onto Rt. 163/Heritage Lane.   Turn left at Shaker Heritage Museum sign.

References and Recommended Reading

Shaker Heritage Society, http://shakerheritage.org
"Watervliet Shaker Historic District", Shaker Historic Trail, http://www.nps.gov/nr/travel/shaker/wat.HTM
Godwin, Joscelyn, The Upstate Cauldron, State of New York Press 2015, pages 23-29.

Klees, Emerson, *The Crucible of Ferment*, Cameo Press, Rochester NY 2001, pages 139-157.

Petersburgh, Rensselaer County, NY

Grafton Peace Pagoda
S3, V0, ♀♂☺

Anyone in the northeast who has ever carried a placard, been to a peace vigil, or protested the war has heard of, or even met Jun Yasuda; or Jun-san, as she is affectionately called. This Japanese Buddhist Nun has walked all over America in the name of peace, and the Peace Pagoda in Grafton is her home.

Who cannot love such a tireless worker who gives of herself to the cause of peace and opens her home for all to visit? There is a nice FOC in front of the Pagoda that contains a series (3) of S3's. The vibe is neutral.

Peace Pagoda's History

Jun-san is a part of the Nipponzan Myohoji order founded in 1917 by Nichidatsu Fujii; it emerged from the Nichiren sect of Japanese Buddhism. They revere the Lotus Sutra. Their mission is to chant and walk for peace and nonviolence. Jun-san has walked five times across America and many other times in many other places, always beating her drum and chanting a prayer for peace, Na-Mu-Myo-Ho-Ren-Ge-Kyo.

Hank Hazelton, a long time Native American activist, donated land in Grafton to Walks Far Woman (as Jun-san is called by the Lakota) for a monument of peace in 1983. Volunteers began constructing the Peace Pagoda in 1985 and finished it by 1993.

The Grafton Peace Pagoda is hollow inside compared to most Peace Pagodas that are solid; historically they were built from stone and mud to serve as a monument rather than to be used for gatherings. Peace Pagodas have been symbol of non-violence for

2,000 years. A temple is located in another building where Jun-san lives.

Experiencing the Peace Pagoda

The grounds of the Grafton Peace Pagoda provide for a contemplative walk, although there is only one area that has Fields and that is an area in front of the Pagoda.

FOC on the rise in front the Pagoda. The cushion, paper and backpack mark the series (3) of S3's.

The whole small plateau in front of the Pagoda sits on a FOC. The highpoint is a series (3) of S3's. As shown above.

The vibe is neutral, but the atmosphere is hospitable warm and welcoming. I first visited the Peace Pagoda back in 2009 on my way to speak at the American Society of Dowsers annual convention. Jun-san was so warm and friendly and would not let me leave until I took a summer squash with me.

Address: Nipponzan Myohoji, Grafton Peace Pagoda
87 Crandall Road, Petersburgh, NY 12138

Webpage: http://www.graftonpeacepagoda.org
Telephone: 518-658-9301
Donate, Volunteer: A donation box can be found between the entry area and temple except in the wintertime. A plate for donations is always located on the altar in the temple.
Participate: Go to the website to see if there is a walk going on while you are visiting; or call the Pagoda if no walks are listed to join in an action, 518-658-9301.
Hours: Sunrise to sunset yearlong.
Directions: Take Rt. 7 East out of Troy, NY. Turn right (6 to 8 miles) onto Rt. 278, bear left and merge with Rt. 2. A few miles after Grafton Lake State Park take a right onto Crandall Rd. Pagoda is on the right a ways up. Park your car on Crandall Rd.

References and Recommended Reading
Peace Pagoda's website, http://www.graftonpeacepagoda.org. "People FOR Peace ~ Jun-san Yasuda", by Linda Kelly, FOR Blog, Friday, September 16, 2011

Queensbury, Saratoga County, NY

Unitarian Universalist Congregation of Glens Falls in Queensbury
S8, V0, 👥 🧘 👤

The mission of the church is to create beloved community, nurture the mind and spirit, inspire peace and justice, and serve with love and compassion. All of the church sits on a FOC (S8.) The vibe is neutral.

The high point of the FOC is a series (3) of S8's running from the entrance way to the outside on the right. The sanctuary ranges from S3 to S8. The higher stacked Fields are

located on the west side of the sanctuary. The vibe is neutral. There is a labyrinth on the grounds.

Address: 21 Weeks Rd, Queensbury, NY 12804
Webpage: www. glensfallsuu. com; http:// www. uua. org /directory/organizations/uu-congregation-glens-falls
Email: admin@glensfallsuu.com
Telephone: 518-793-1468
Hours: Sunday mornings 10 AM.
Directions: Take Exit 19 off I- 87. Go East on Aviation Road (Rt. 254) Go North on Route 9. Take left onto Weeks Rd.

Saratoga Springs, Saratoga County, NY

Called Saratoga. Known for its many healing mineral springs and summer time horse racing.

Congress Park
S4, V0

Congress Park is a 17-acre park in Saratoga Springs. There is a FOC (S4) at the northern end of the park along Spring St. Place yourself in the park about 10 feet from the cast iron fence on the grass anywhere between the carousel and Henry St. and you will be in the FOC.

Address: Spring and Henry Streets, Saratoga Springs, NY
Webpage: http://www.saratoga.com/hotspot_congress-park.cfm
Hours: There are no formal hours. The park is patrolled at night and there are cameras set up throughout the park.
Close by: The Congress Spring, one of many, is located in the Park. There is an antique carousel and the historic Canfield Casino (no longer operational) that houses the Saratoga Springs museum.
Directions: Spring St. is located off of Broadway south of Rt. 9 and Rt. 29.

Saratoga Spa State Park
S4, V-0, 👫

Saratoga Spa State Park is a 2,379 state park housing the Saratoga Performing Arts Center, the Spa Little Theater, the National Museum of Dance, the Saratoga Automobile Museum, the Gideon Putnam Resort and the Roosevelt Baths and Spa. There is a FOC (S4) on the grounds.

The FOC contains a series (3) of S4's that begins where the backpack is located, on the far right. The dogs mark the next two in the series. Sit in this general area to be in the FOC.

The FOC is located east of the automobile museum near Roosevelt Drive. It contains a series (3) of S4's that parallel Roosevelt Drive. Look for a path/walkway just west of Roosevelt Drive. The series begins 22 feet in front of the third light from Gideon Putnam Road and end approximately in front of a large oak tree. They run north south parallel to the path and are about 16-18 feet from the eastern edge of the path. Anywhere east of the walkway would put you in the FOC.

Address: 19 Roosevelt Drive, Saratoga Springs, NY 12866
Webpage: http://www.nysparks.com/parks/saratogaspa
Telephone: 518-584-2535

119

Hours: Sunrise to sundown. From memorial weekend to early October $8 per car.

Directions: The Park is located south of the city on Ballston Ave. From the city center take Rt. 50, Ballston Ave., south.

Schoharie, Schoharie County, NY

Schoharie is a distortion of the Mohawk word for the Schoharie Valley, "driftwood, or flood wood." The town has been flooded on several occasions.

Schoharie United Presbyterian Church
S5, V1-2, ☆ ⚦ 🧘

The church is a testament that the spirit of social justice and the desire to make a better world still blazes in North Star Country. Chris Hedges, a prominent figure in the Progressive Movement, spent his formative years at the church, from 1960 to 1971 when his father Thomas Hedges served as pastor.

What is nice about the church is that the vibe is slightly positive, to positive and there is a larger sense, or feel to it of acceptance and welcoming there. The sanctuary rests on a FOC (S5.)

History

Founded in 1734 the church is one of the oldest structures in Schoharie County. It is dedicated to community involvement and like many of the churches listed allows various organizations to use the church. It started and runs the town's food pantry. The congregation contributes to many causes.

120

In the 70's and 80's Bob, "Smitty" Smith, the pastor at the time, arranged with local farmers to allow various food coops and pantries to glean their fields after they had been picked. He also led the effort to prevent Schoharie valley from being flooded and converted to a larger reservoir for NYC, putting the town of Schoharie underwater. In 2011 the church, like much of the town was flooded.

Former parishioner Chris Hedges (father was minister) is a Pulitzer Prize winning journalist that has been a strident voice for progressive issues. His former employer the NY Times reprimanded him for publicly criticizing the paper's impartiality in covering the Iraq war. Chris authored what The New York Times described as "a call to arms" for the first issue of The Occupied Wall Street Journal, the newspaper that gave voice to the Occupy Wall Street protests in Zuccotti Park, New York City.

Experiencing the Church

All of the sanctuary sits on a FOC. The high point is an S5 on the middle right side of the church as you face the lectern. The center of the FOC is located outside and on the back side of the church.

The church has a very pleasant and warm feel to it; clearly there clearly is something special to it. It would be great to pray or meditate anywhere within the sanctuary.

Address: 314 Main Street Schoharie, NY 12157
Webpage: www.schohariepresbyterian.org
Email: SUPC09@Yahoo.com
Telephone: 518-295-8931
Donate, Volunteer: There are several volunteer programs online, an afterschool program and a food pantry.
Hours: Sunday Services 10:30 AM
Directions: Located in the center of town on Main St., Rt. 30.

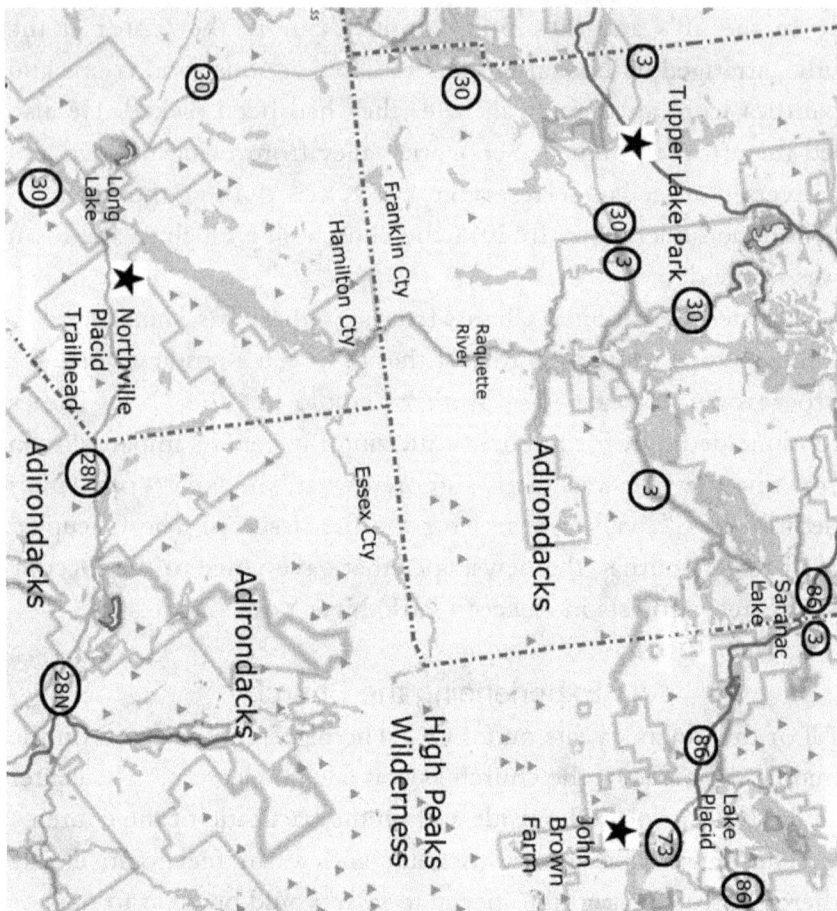

Map of the Adirondacks. Source-© OpenStreetMap contributors, www. openstreetmap. org

Adirondacks

The Adirondacks are New York's beautiful and majestic mountains where the winter Olympics has been held. In the interest of conservation the state created the Adirondack Park in 1892 and designated it to be 'forever wild' to limit development. It is 6 million acres in size, 2.6 million owned by New York State, the remaining 3.4 million is in private hands. It contains New York's highest peaks.

It is here that the black community, Timbukto, was created on land donated by Gerrit Smith to insure blacks could vote (they needed $250 in cash, or land to do so). Close to it is John Brown's farm and grave.

Long Lake, Hamilton County, NY

So called for its length, which can whip up some pretty strong head winds for canoeists, as I can personally attest to .

Northville Placid Trailhead at Long Lake
S3, V-0

The Northville-Placid Trail (NPT) is a 133 mile trail traversing south north through the heart of the Adirondacks. It was one of the first major trail constructions undertaken by the ADK (Adirondack Mountain Club) in 1922/23.

There is a FOC (S3) on the Northville Lake Placid trail. It is a short 150-200 walk from the Long Lake trailhead and is located 5 feet beyond the trail registry. The FOC is approximately 30-40 foot diameter. As long as you stay close to the trail registry you should be fine. The vibe is neutral.

Address: Tarbell Road. Long Lake NY.

Webpage: No formal site, however a internet search will show several groups with info on the NPT Trail.

Volunteer: The Adirondack Mountain Club (ADK) has an NPT chapter that works on the trail, www.nptrail.org

Directions: You can access the trailhead in Long Lake off of Rt. 28N east of the town. Turn north onto Tarbell Road.

Looking towards Tarbell Rd. The backpack next to the trail registry marks the center of the FOC.

North Elba/Lake Placid, Essex County

North Elba houses the Olympic Village; the winter Olympics were hosted by Lake Placid in 1932 and 1980.

John Brown Farm State Historic Site
S5, V-0, 🚻🚆

This is where the famous abolitionist, who led the Harper's Ferry rebellion that helped precipitate the Civil War, is buried. There is a FOC (S5) on the grounds, the vibe is neutral.

John Brown and his Farm

John Brown's passion for abolition started at the age of twelve when he saw a young slave beaten with iron shovels. Early on he embraced the pacifism of William Lloyd Garrison (a famous abolitionist who published The Liberator and demanded immediate emancipation) and admired Quakers. But things began turning in 1837; a proslavery mob in Illinois killed an abolitionist editor, Elijah Lovejoy, and the panic of 1837 brought hardship to Brown. He refused to vacate a property he lost and bore arms defending it with his sons.

In 1846 Gerrit Smith donated 40 acres of land in the Adirondacks to 3,000 black grantees so that they could vote. It was in response to the reenactment of the NYS legislature law requiring blacks to have $250 in land or own a home in order to vote. This became Timbukto, an experimental black community.

Brown purchased land from Gerrit Smith near the black colony Timbukto so that he could teach people how to farm. The majority of Smith's beneficiaries were literate city folk that were new to farming.

After his execution Browns' body was interred to North Elba for burial.

The FOC (S5) can be found on the trail in the woods not far from the farmhouse. It is near a large boulder; next to it is a pine tree, just on the other side of the pine tree is the FOC next to the trail. The vibe is neutral. Anywhere on the other side of the boulder, or close to it, would have you in the FOC; it is 50 to 60 feet in diameter.

Address: 115 John Brown Road, Lake Placid, NY 12946
Webpage: http://nysparks.com/historic-sites/29/details.aspx
Telephone: 518-523-3900
Donate, Volunteer: Friends of John Brown has a Facebook page.
Hours: The grounds are open year round for hiking and cross country skiing from sunrise to sunset. The farm house is open

May thru Oct., 10 AM to 5PM, everyday except Tuesday. Admission $2, seniors and children under 12 $1.

Close by: Lots of great hiking; Giant, one the Adirondacks 46 peaks over 4,000 feet, is near.

Directions: John Brown's Farm is located off of Rt. 73 between Lake Placid and Keene; closer to Placid. Turn off for John Brown near the airport.

References and Recommended Reading

Adirondack Journal — Timbukto: African American History in the Adirondacks,
http://www.adkmuseum.org/about_us/adirondack_journal/?id=63
John Brown Farm State Historic Site,
http://nysparks.com/historic-sites/29/details.aspx
Horowitz, Tony, *Midnight Rising, John Brown and the Raid That Sparked the Civil War*

Tupper Lake, Franklin County

Tupper Lake Town Park
S4, V-0,

In the town park on Rt. 3 going west out of the town center along the lake shore is a FOC (S4.) You can find it directly across from the Auto Parts store. Look for a two-sided bench and a low fence going towards the lake, close to the parking lot. The FOC is located in the middle area of the fence. A little past the fourth post in the ground; it extends about 20-25 feet around the post. Anywhere close to this area would place you in the FOC. The vibe is neutral.

Address: Rt. 3, Tupper Lake, NY
Webpage: http://www.tupperlake.com, Town Website.

Directions: The park is located on Rt. 3 west/north of Rt. 30 (Park St.), the town center.

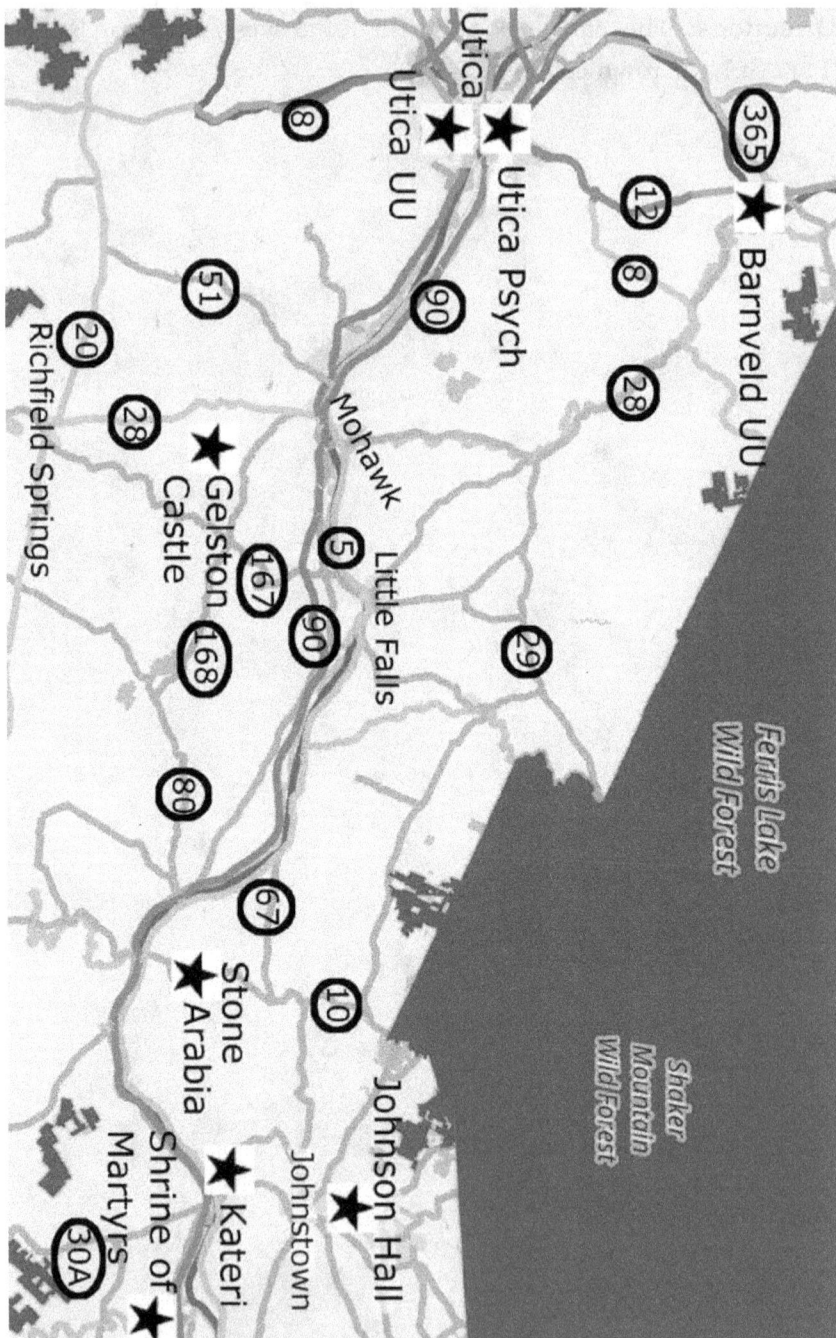

Map of the Mohawk Valley. Source- www. openstreetmap.org

Mohawk Valley

The Mohawk Valley surrounds the Mohawk River, which begins a little north of Rome, NY and empties into the Hudson River in the Albany area. It is a lowland sandwiched between the Adirondacks and the Catskills. Because of this it served as a pathway for the Underground Railroad and for frontier settlers. It is also the eastern door of the Iroquois Confederacy and home to the Mohawk Nation; while its western edge is the home to the Oneida Nation.

It is quaint, mostly rural and pastoral. If you have time take scenic route 20 through small towns rather than the NYS Thruway (Rt. 90.)

The western end Utica/Whitesboro lies at the edge of the heart of North Star Country, the Utica—Rochester corridor. The Oneida Institute in Whitesboro was the first college to educate black and white students on a equal basis. Its alumni includes several prominent black abolitionists, Jermain Loguen (Syracuse), Henry Highland Garnet.

There are a host of powerful and wonderful places to experience Consciousness such as Kateri and Gelston Castle, while Stone Arabia church affords a quiet pastoral setting.

Auriesville, Montgomery County, NY

Shrine of Our Lady of Martyrs
S6, V0, 🧍🧍

At a talk I gave on sacred sites at Beardslee Castle (Little Falls, NY) in April of 2010, I heard a testimonial from a woman who swore that she had been miraculously cured of macular degeneration, an incurable and eventually blinding eye disease by a laying on of hands by a priest there. I believe that she was telling me the truth, as there are several FOC's located around the coliseum area. The vibe is neutral.

History

The site of the Shrine of Our Lady of Martyrs was once a 17th century Mohawk village called Ossernenon where three Jesuit missionaries were martyred during the 1640s. Father Isaac Jogues, René Goupil, a Jesuit brother, and John Lalande, a lay missioner, are the only canonized American martyrs. Together with five Jesuit priests killed in the native missions of Canada, they are known as the North American Martyrs. The beatified "Lily of the Mohawks," Blessed Kateri Tekakwitha, was born here in 1656.

A lack of Jesuits forced the shrine to be closed in 2015. It reopened in 2016 thanks to volunteers and donations from several organizations. Masses are held on weekends and on holy days; check the webpage for times.

There are several FOC located on the grounds. The Coliseum, or the large chapel, is a popular place with the many tourists and bus tours that visit the shrine. A FOC (S6) is located in back of it.

Another place to tap into a FOC (S6) is at the outdoor shrine (statue) of Jesus located in front of the coliseum. It has memorial on it to the memory of Father Neil Poulin. It is located about 12-15 feet southeast of the monument if you face the monument and assume that you are facing north.

Address: 136 Shrine Road, Auriesville (Fultonville), NY 12072
Webpage: http://www.auriesvilleshrine.com
Email: friendsofauriesville@gmail.com
Telephone: 518-630-9922
Donate, Volunteer: Contact friendsofauriesville@gmail.com
Hours: Open daily April through October. Check website to see the schedule of masses for the Coliseum.

Directions: Take exit 28 off of the Thruway (I-90.) Take a left onto Riverside Dr (Rt. 920p) until it ends at Main St. Take a left onto Main St. Take a left onto Church St. (Rt. 5s.) Take a right onto Noelthner (Rt. 164.) Shrine Rd. will be on your left up the hill.

Barneveld, Oneida County, NY

Unitarian Church of Barneveld
S10, V0, 👫 🧘

Located on a side street in the town of Barneveld, the 200-year-old church has a calmness to it. All of the church sits on a FOC (S10.) The high point is a S10 on the right hand side toward the front of the sanctuary. The Field extends onto the grounds, outside of the church on the back right hand side as you face the church. The vibe is neutral.

Address: 100 Park Ave. Barneveld, NY. 13304
Webpage: www.uubarneveld.org
Telephone: 315-316-1330
Close by: Unity Hall in Barneveld is a community center that holds many art and music activities, www.unityhall.com.
Services: Sunday mornings at 10 AM.

Directions: Take Rt. 12 north out of Utica. It will merge with Rt. 28 just before Barneveld. Turn left onto Old Poland Rd, it will turn into Park Ave.

Fonda, Montgomery County, NY

Kateri Tekakwitha Shrine
S6, V4, ▽ ☆ (♦) ♦|♦ ⚘

Kateri Tekakwitha was the first Native American beatified and made a saint by the Roman Catholic Church. Many miracles have been attributed to her. The shrine in Fonda was created to honor her and other Native Americans.

The chapel is situated on a FOC (S6) and has one of the most positive vibes of any of the sacred sites listed in this book—it is out of this world. It also contains two vortices. This is a place to visit if you are looking to sense and feel Consciousness. The grounds are quite expansive.

History

Kateri was born in 1656 to an Algonquin mother and a Mohawk Chief in Ossernenon (modern day Auriesville) on the other side of the Mohawk River. Her whole family contracted small pox when she was 4 years old. She was the only one to survive, but it left her face badly scarred and her eyesight impaired. Because of her poor vision, Kateri was named 'Tekakwitha', which means 'she who bumps into things.'

Kateri's interest in Christianity began when she was 18 years of age. She was baptized on Easter Sunday April 5, 1676. It is said that the pockmarks on her face from smallpox completely disappeared within a few minutes of her death.

Be aware that Kateri can be a contentious issue to Native American traditionalists.

The picture is of the right aisle of the chapel. Notice the orb in the area of the vortex by rear pews on the right. All my pictures had numerous orbs. The chapel is filled with Native American artifacts such as the snowshoes in the upper center

Kateri has a long history of being a sacred site. Before Kateri was declared a Catholic Shrine, it was a sacred place for the Haudenosaunee, and before that it was a sacred place for a pre-

Haudenosaunee culture. On the grounds there is an archaeological display about the previous cultures from a dig done on the hill above the chapel.

The Miracles of Kateri

In 2006, eleven year old Jake Finkbonner in Seattle, Washington cracked his lip during a basketball game and ended up contracting a flesh eating bacteria. It spread quickly and required daily surgeries to remove parts of it. As it continued to progress doctors told his parents he was going to die. They had a priest perform last rites.

Based upon a recommendation from a priest with a Native background, his family, church and school began praying to Kateri to intercede. As Jake clung to life the Society of Blessed Kateri visited and gave him a pendant. The next day as he was preparing to go to surgery doctors noticed that the disease had stopped.

Experiencing Kateri

All of St. Peter's chapel sits on a FOC. The highpoint is a series (3) of (S6's) that run across the chapel; from the last pew on the left, the center of third pew from the back of the middle pews and the pew immediately behind the divider on the left.

Prayer permeates the air and has created a powerful imprint that can bring you to tears. It affords the opportunity for a strong connection to those that have been there before. Given such a strong vibe it is not surprisingly there is a vortex and a vortex ring in the chapel. The vortex covers the last two pews on the right side. The vortex ring is found on the left side in the area of the third pew from the front.

I would suggest spending time in either of the vortex areas; particularly the last two pews on right side. Try and feel the consciousness coming into your body. Explore other parts of the chapel as well because there might be an area that better suits you. Soak it up and enjoy.

Given the miracle healing associated with Kateri this would be s a great place to pray for your own health, or the health of others. Consider praying for healing the world and all of humankind.

The grounds are large enough to allow for a contemplative walk. There is a museum as well a picnic area.

Address: 3636 NY-5, Fonda, NY 12068, ¼ west of Fonda on Rte. 5. Mailing address: PO Box 627, Fonda, NY 12068
Webpage: www.katerishrine.com.
Email: Office @KateriShrine.com.
Telephone: 518-853-3646
Donate, Volunteer: online at website, www.katerishrine.com.
Hours: The chapel is open from May 1 to October 31, from 9 AM to 6 PM; and there are services on Saturdays and Sundays. The grounds are open year round. Check calendar on webpage for events.
Close by: Shrine of Martyrs is on the other side of the Mohawk River. Johnson Hall is up the road not more than a few miles.
Directions: Take exit 28 off of the NYS Thruway (I-90.) Follow signs to Rt. 5 west. Take a left onto Riverside Dr. Take a right onto Bridge St. and cross Mohawk River. Turn left onto Rt. 5 (E. Main St.) The shrine is located ¼ mile out of town on Rt. 5.

Johnstown, Fulton County, NY

Johnson Hall

S8, V2,☆

I have stopped at Johnson Hall NYS Historic Site on several occasions to rejuvenate myself on the way home after a long trip. There is something healing about the place, but ultimately it is a place of reconciliation. It must be the imprints left by the peace and healing Sir William Johnson achieved between settlers and

Native Americans. Several people have told me of having seen Spirits. A FOC (S8) with a positive vibe is on the grounds.

As Head of Indian Affairs for Britain before the Revolutionary War Johnson has been criticized for siding with the British. He also had several wives, numerous illegitimate children and owned slaves. Yet Johnson was adopted into the Mohawk Nation, had a Mohawk bride, Molly Brant, and fathered several children by her. He was respected and loved and got the Mohawks to side with Britain during the Revolutionary War. He learned the Mohawk language and earned their trust in negotiations. That is what gives life to the imprints on the grounds.

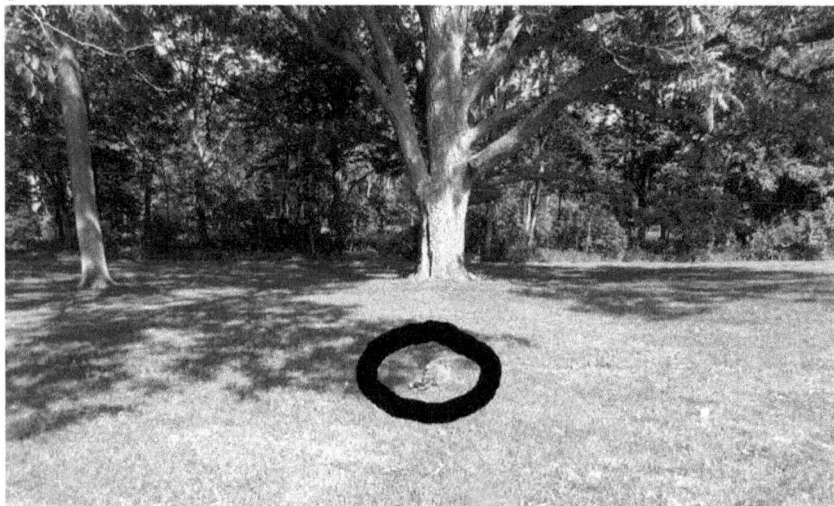

You are facing the honey locust tree. Johnson Hall is to your back, the carriage house to your left. My backpack, circled in black, is the first in a series (3) of S8's that break to the left and away.

Experiencing Johnson Hall

Look for a very large honey locust tree on the hill below Johnson Hall with a series of smaller trees, but still thick, in a line to its right if you face up hill. As you face up hill thirty feet in front of the large honey locust tree begins a series (3) of S8's. There are two more in the series. The last can be found 20-24 feet in front of the second tree from the bottom in the line of trees. The middle S8 is found between these two points.

This whole area in front of the honey locust tree and beyond is on a FOC. Pray or meditate anywhere in this area, or bring along a lawn chair and read a book. Fields are also located on the other side of the line of trees going towards the carriage house.

This is a powerful place of peace and reconciliation. If you are looking to mend a relationship pray for it, or visualize reconciling with the other person. This is an excellent place to pray for world peace and for people, groups, countries and religions casting aside their differences. Its positive vibe makes it a good place to sense and feel Consciousness.

Address: 139 Hall Ave., Johnstown, NY, 12095
Webpage: http://nysparks.com/historic-sites/10/details.aspx
Email: JohnsonHall@parks.ny.gov
Telephone: 518-762-8712
Hours: Guided Tours of The Hall, mid May to early October: Wed. to Sat., 10am to 5pm, Sun. 1pm to 5pm. Adults $4, seniors $3, children under 12 free. Grounds open year round, and are Free to walk on.
Directions: Take exit 28 off of the NYS Thruway (I-90.) Take a left onto Riverside Dr. A right onto Bridge St. and cross Mohawk River. Turn left onto Rt. 5. Take a right onto Rt. 30a (Broadway.) Continue for several miles. In Johnstown take a left onto S. Melcher St. and drive 1.1 miles to W. State (Rt. 29) and take a left onto W. State. In .3 miles take a slight right onto Hall St.

References and Recommended Reading

O'Toole, Fintan, *White Savage, William Johnson and the Invention of America*, Farrar, Strauss and Giroux

Jordanville, Herkimer County, NY

Jordanville is home to the Holy Trinity Monastery, a Russian Orthodox Church.

Gelston Castle
S10-12, V1-3, ▽ (♠) ♦♦ ⁊ ⅄

Gelston Castle is a piece of history with some mystery. There are majestic views, an old castle that is now in ruins, a palatial house, FOC's as high as S12, a vortex, a therapeutic energy grid and a great vibe. Given the vortex, one assumes that it once was a very sacred and revered space. For the pilgrim looking to walk around and explore, dream and imagine and raise their consciousness by meditating in FOC, then Gelston is for you. It is also a good place to try and sense and feel Consciousness. The grounds are 340 acres in size.

Gelston Castle is not open to the public, but the proprietors have kindly agreed to allow guests to visit this grand estate and enjoy its grounds. You must call (315-235-9988) two weeks in advance to schedule a visit. The cost will depend upon the number of people in your party, whether you want a guided tour and if you want access to the house. I suggest organizing a group of friends to go with you to help defray costs.

History

The Gelston Castle grounds had been in the Robinson family since the early 1700's. In the 1780's it became a summer residence and the first structure was erected. Harriet Cruger Douglas, the great granddaughter of Dr. James Henderson, the first landowner, had Gelston Castle built between 1834 to 1836. Constructed out of large limestones it was modeled after her uncle's stone castle in Scotland. Harriet is noted for having her bed sawed in half to be used as a sofa after she divorced her husband.

Harriet loved Gelston, or Henderson House as it is also called, and wanted to be buried there. When she died the family decided otherwise and buried her in the family plot in NYC instead. Many believe that this so upset Harriet that she refused to pass on and her ghost haunts the grounds.

The estate passed to Harriet's niece Fanny and her husband and then to their son Douglas Robinson and his wife Corrine, the sister of Theodore Roosevelt the 26th president of the United States of America. Their houseguests included Theodore Roosevelt, and Franklin Delano Roosevelt and his wife Eleanor. Eleanor personally planted the row of trees that line the road on the grounds that extends from the castle to the other side of the house; as well as a small apple grove on your left side as you approach the castle.

The estate stayed in the Robinson family until the Russian cellist Mstislav Rostropovich purchased it. He had fled to America after his native USSR curtailed his activities for his dissident support, particularly for housing Alexander Solzhenitsyn; a Nobel winning author that was an outspoken critic of the USSR for its totalitarianism and gulags.

By then the castle was in disrepair and falling apart. So instead of restoring the castle, Rostropovitch built a new 8,300 sq. ft. mansion. Fearing retribution from the KGB and wanting to protect his art collection from thieves, the home was constructed with extreme security measures in mind; the foundation has four foot thick walls, there is a concrete saferoom with a two ton vault, the window shutters are made of metal that can repel 50 caliber bullets, and there are extensive security cameras throughout the grounds.

Rostropovich's extreme security measures and fear of retribution from his Russian homeland is reminiscent of another refugee to North Star Country, Louis Muller. He fled Napoleon and France, built a secure mansion and led a reclusive and mysterious life in Georgetown, NY.

The current owner, the Safflyn Corporation, purchased Gelston Castle in 2007.

Experiencing The FOC at Gelston

There is a lot to do and explore at Gelston Castle, including several FOC on the grounds. Across from the castle and on the other side of the driveway in the garden area is a large FOC, with the highpoint being a series (3) of S10's. The first in the series is about 15 feet in front of the light pole going away from the castle. The next in the series of S10's can be found near the steps of the garden; to the right of the steps above the sunken area. The final in this series is

Trees planted by Eleanor Roosevelt line the road to the cemetery.

inaccessible, in a thicket on the other side of the garden. To find it visualize a straight line connecting the 2 S8's and continuing at that same angle across the garden into a thicket. Plant yourself anywhere near the steps and you will be in the FOC.

There is a large FOC by the trees that were planted by Eleanor Roosevelt, on the driveway going to the cemetery from the house and covers both sides of the driveway. The highpoint is a series (3) of 3 S10's; the first in this series can be found about 5 feet away from the driveway between the first two trees on the house side of the driveway. The next S10 is about 10-15 feet away from the first tree on the other side of the driveway. The remaining S10 is located about 10 feet away from the solar panel.

There is a large FOC that runs from inside the house to the outside in the back. One of series of S12's in the assembly meeting room of the house in front of the picture window looking out onto the property.

The deck behind the mansion sits on a FOC and provides beautiful views.

However if you ever have a chance to attend a program, or even put on a program at Gelston, that area is very sweet. The FOC includes the back deck and adjoining ground.

Other Interesting Features

Vortex—There is a vortex in a grass field across from the castle on the other side of the driveway. To benefit from a vortex you have to be in its whirlpool; this one is about three to four feet wide. So it can be best found with dowsing rods, or by your senses.

To try and visually find it, start in the grass field across from the castle. Going toward the entrance, look for not the closest, but the next closest tree to the house going toward the entrance. Now looking away from (opposite to) the entrance try and find a very large and tall maple tree several hundred feet away. If you were to draw an imaginary line where the tree in front of the castle and the large tree in the distance intersected at a right angle, that is where the vortex is.

It is a vortex of what I call Cosmic Prana (Energy), the energy we attract when we meditate and not the consciousness from a

FOC. Cosmic Prana has a lower consciousness component. If you can find the vortex I strongly recommend meditating in it.

Energy Grid—I first learned about Gelston Castle at a talk I gave on sacred sites. I was told that there had been several sightings of ghosts in the cemetery area and one was of a revolutionary solider. I believe that these sightings had more to do with the energy grid located on the driveway in front of the cemetery. It is often the case that areas of supposed hauntings are places with strong energy formations. Some of these places, such as this one, can be very therapeutic and healing. Years ago I wrote an article about this called 'Haunted to Health' that can be accessed online.

The dogs mark the beginning of the energy grid on the cemetery road that ends by my friends in the background.

Follow the driveway past the house through a wooded area. The grid begins about a 150 feet in front of the cemetery and ends about 75 feet in front of it. Facing the cemetery there are a series of 14 ducts on the left side of the driveway that are releasing prana (energy) that appears to be coming from the ground below. About 20 feet on the other side of the driveway (right side) is a series of chakras (whirlpools) that are pulling the prana(energy) into their funnels and then into the ground below. A chakra is a spinning wheel, or vortex that pulls in energy.

So there is a wave of energy sweeping from the left to the right across the driveway as you face the cemetery. The only image I can think of that is comparable would be what they call a force field in science fiction movies; although this apparatus is real and can be therapeutic.

I would plant myself in the driveway, about 100-125 feet from the cemetery to insure you are in the grid. Enjoy it, but make sure it makes you feel good, if not leave. See if you can feel the energy; if so focus on it and give it more strength. If you cannot feel anything try the same exercises you would do to try and sense and feel Consciousness.

The Grounds—The grounds of Gelston castle allow for a delightful walk and contain numerous FOC. All of the open areas have a positive to very positive vibe. The only area that is negative is some of the wooded areas, which may be because they have been contaminated with the intentions of hunters stalking their prey. We leave imprints wherever we go and if someone spends hours at one place focusing on killing and surprising, then the ground will be sullied with that intention.

Recently I was told of sounds, aka ghosts, in the house. Again the house sits on a powerful FOC (S12) with an extremely positive vibe in places, which can have a powerful influence upon your perceptions. Also in recent years, Gelston has been written up on several ghost, or haunted websites. Unfortunately, this has probably attracted a lot of similarly motivated thrill seekers that have left their morbid and ghoulish thoughts as imprints on the land. That said, a tape recorder left inside the house has recorded discernible voices and other sounds.

I think that there is a lot more to Gelston. It seems a little more is revealed with each subsequent visit, which is often the case. Having a vortex on the grounds tells me that this was once a sacred site. I encourage you to come and visit and add to the positive intentions at Gelston.

Please check the website to make sure there are no events (concerts, historic reenactments, outdoor plays, weddings…) going on at the time you wish to visit.

Address: 980 Robinson Rd, Mohawk, NY 13407
Webpage: www.safflyn.com/ChateauSafflyn/index.html
Email: billschmelcher@yahoo.com
Telephone: 315-235-9988
Hours: Gelston Castle is open from spring to late fall (approximately April 1st to November 30th) depending upon the snow melt. You must call Bill Schmelcher (315-235-9988, billschmelcher@yahoo.com) at least two weeks before your planned visit. The cost (cash payment) will vary depending upon the size of your party, whether you want a guided tour and access to the house.
Contact: Bill Schmelcher (315-325-9988, billschmelcher @yahoo.com
Directions: Take exit 30 off of the Thruway (I-90.) Take a left and cross the Mohawk River and bear right. Take a left onto Warren St., which will turn into Columbia St. Take a left onto Hammond St. (Rt. 168.) Go a few miles and take a right onto Mortz, Rd. Mortz Rd will deadend; take a left onto Robinson Rd. (Rt. 46.)

References and Recommended Reading
Gelston Castle webpage, www. safflyn. com/ ChateauSafflyn /index. html
HISTORIC BUILDINGS OF HERKIMER COUNTY JORDANVILLE AND THE ONCE FAMOUS CASTLE
http://herkimer.nygenweb.net/warren/gelstoncastle.html

Hopson, Caryl; 'The Garden in the Woods—the Cemetery at Gelston Castle', Herkimer County Historical Society, http://www.rootsweb.ancestry.com/~nyhchs/legacy.html,

Palatine/Fort Plain, Montgomery County, NY

Stone Arabia Church
S4, V1, 👭 🧘

A marvel to the eyes the church can be seen from a distance as one approaches Stone Arabia. This farming area has the feel of a bygone era. The Amish, who have been relocating to the area since the 1980's add to that feeling, as well as to the sense that, they like the Palatines before them, have come here in search of religious freedom.

If you are looking to spend some time in a quiet and peaceful setting with FOC (S4), then Stone Arabia is for you.

History

Stone Arabia Church is entwined with the Palatines who first came to the area upon receiving the Stone Arabia Patent in 1723.

This patent conveyed 12,700 acres to 28 families. Initially worshipping in each other's homes and barns, the Palatines where of the Reformed and Lutheran faiths.

The former Reformed Church was left in ashes following the October 19, 1780 raid of Col. Sir John Johnson. Col. Johnson was a son of Sir William Johnson. The cemetery located behind the church holds the remains of Col John Brown and others slain during Johnson's raid.

The present day graceful limestone edifice was built in 1788 and in 1978 placed on the National Register of Historic Places. The last service was held in 1990. Weddings, funerals and baptisms are held occasionally.

Experiencing The Church

The inside of the church provides a comfortable and peaceful setting. There are three sections of wooden pews that one can sit on. I have visited on several occasions over the years and each time I was the only one there. I imagine that you could spend a lot of time there and not be bothered.

All of the sanctuary rests on a FOC. The center of which is a series (3) of S4's that begins in the middle of the middle and goes towards the back of the church. The vibe is slightly positive. Pick a spot you like and enjoy.

The church is open from 8 AM to 5PM during the summer months of June, July and August. Several events are held at the church throughout the year. If you are going at some other time I suggest you contact Ken and Carol Edwards 518-993-4280 about access to the church, or holding an event.

Please make sure to sign the registry and leave your comments and donate if you go.

Address: 5371-, 5407 Ephratah Rd, Fort Plain, NY 13339
Telephone: 518-993-4280

Donate, Volunteer: You can join the Stone Arabia Preservation Society ($5 one, $8 family, $100 lifetime) or donate by mailing a check to; Stone Arabia Preservation Society, PO Box 692, Palatine Bridge, NY 13428

Hours: Summer (June, July, August) 8 AM to 5 PM.

Directions: Take exit 29 off of the Thruway (I-90.) follow signs to Palatine Bridge. Take Rt. 10, Lafayette St., the main street north. Continue on Lafayette, which will turn into Ephratah Rd outside of Palatine Bridge. A few sharp turns later the church will be on your left just before Hickory Hill Rd.

References and Recommended Reading
Conversations with Carol Edwards.
Church pamphlet.

Utica, Oneida County, NY

Utica and its neighboring Whitesboro are the eastern edge of the heart of Mother Earth's Soul, the Utica Rochester Corridor. The city was a major route on the Underground Railroad and hosted the New York Anti-slavery annual meetings from 1837 to 1840. The Utica Center has a walking tour of abolitionist and Underground Railroad sites in Utica (https://www.utica.edu /academic/institutes /ucsc/doc/ Utica%20Walking%20Tour%202%20Oct%202013.pdf.)

Utica Psychiatric Grounds
S10, V1

Referred to as 'Old Main' by local residents, Utica Psychiatric is listed on the National Register of Historic Places. The four story Greek revival portico with its tall columns is a formidable sight. The front grounds are open and spacious, providing a unique chance to experience FOC (S10) in a city environment that at the same time is very quiet and serene. The vibe is slightly positive.

History

Utica Psychiatric was the first institution in New York State to publicly care for the mentally ill, and one of the first nationally. Previously, the mentally ill were often kept in prison or locked away in an attic, closet or some other place; or just roamed the streets. Old Main began accepting patients in 1843 while it was still under construction.

Its first director Dr. Amariah Brigham helped found the Association of Medical Superintendents of American Institutions that later became the American Psychiatric Association (APA.) He created and was the first editor of The American Journal of Insanity, which became The American Journal of Psychiatry.

Because Dr. Brigham thought that mental illness was the result of a bad environment, Utica Psychiatric sought to provide patients with spacious rooms, good nutrition as well as physical exercise and mental stimulus. Patients worked the grounds and helped print Brigham's psychiatric journal. Patients had their own literary journal, 'The Opal', that they wrote and printed. Later in the nineteenth century the compassionate efforts of Dr. Brigham and others like him would be called the 'moral treatment' of the mentally ill.

Not all was good; Dr. Amariah's initiative the 'Utica Crib' has gained infamy over time. It was a restraining device modeled after a baby's crib with an overhead restraint of wooden slats and was used for the most disturbed patients.

Old Main closed in 1978. Part of the first floor was opened up in 2004 as a records archive for the NYS Office of Health.

Experiencing Utica Psychiatric

The right hand side of the driveway if you face the front of the building is basically one large FOC. I suggest meditating, or sitting on a portable chair and reading anywhere on the right hand side. I would focus on the other side of the first row of trees. The high points are a series (3) of S10's.

About 2/3's of the way up the driveway look for 2 large trees that are next to each other in a straight line perpendicular to the driveway. About 20 feet away from the trees and 5 feet towards Old Main is the first is a series (3) of S10', about fifteen feet apart, that break at 45° to the right towards Old Main.

The dogs are in the center of the FOC.

Accessibility

The asylum is closed, but the grounds are open year round. When I was there on a sunny weekday in the spring, the grounds were almost abandoned with only a few people periodically walking by and an occasional car passing by. While the neighborhood may have slipped in recent years the open and spacious grounds provide a nice sanctuary.

Address: 1213 Court Street, Utica, NY
Directions: Take exit 31 NYS Thruway (I-90.) Take Rt. 12 south. Exit onto Rt. 5a (Oriskany St. West) going west. Take a quick left onto Schyuler St. Go a few blocks and take a right onto Court St.

References and Recommended Reading
Czarnota, Lorna Macdonald; *Native American & Pioneer Sites of Upstate New York*, History Press, Charleston, SC, 2014

Botttini, Joseph P; Davis, James L.; *Utica, Then and Now*, Arcadia Publishing, Charleston SC, 2007

Grob, Gerald N., *The Mad Among Us, A History of the Care of the Mentally Ill*, The First Press, NYC 1994

Keene, Michael T., *Mad House, The Hidden History of Insane Asylums in 19th Century New York*, Willow Manor Publishing, Fredericksburg, Virginia, 2013

Roger, Luther, 'Utica State Hospital', http: // nysasylum .com/ utica/

Unitarian Universalist Church of Utica
S8, V0, 👫 🧘

The motto of Utica Unitarian Universalist is "A church where people with many different beliefs come together, in faith & pursuit of social justice. ~ All are welcome!" The church is located on a FOC (S8); the vibe is neutral.

The congregation is involved with a variety of activities. There are committees focused on social justice, climate change, among others.

The church and the immediate area of about 30 feet around it is on a large FOC. The highpoint is a series (3) of S8's that begins outside on the right side in back of the church if you face the front entrance. They extend through the church at a slight angle towards the front.

Address: 10 Higby Road, Utica, NY, 13501
Webpage: http://www.uuutica.org
Email: welcome@uuutica.org
Telephone: 315-724-3179.

Hours: Sunday morning services, 10:30 AM. Check the calendar as meditations are held several times each month.

Directions: Higby Rd. is located off of the southern end of Genesee St. the main street in Utica.

Map of Central New York. Source-www.openstreetmap.org

Central New York

The area around Syracuse and Onondaga Lake is the center of Mother Earth's Soul. There are more stacked FOC and more S12's than anyplace else. Not surprisingly it has born a bounty of fruit.

It was at the shores of Onondaga Lake that the Peacemaker planted the Tree of Peace and gave the Haudenosaunee the Great Law of Peace. Harriet Tubman, the Moses of her people lived here, as did Jermain Loguen, one of the most accomplished stationmasters of the Underground Railroad. Central New York was the home to the radical feminist Matilda Joslyn Gage, one of the key players in the Women's Movement. Then there was the famous social reformer Gerrit Smith, who through his finances and commitment was connected to many of the social changes in North Star Country.

The eastern edge of Central New York is home to the Oneida Nation; while greater Syracuse is home to the Onondaga nation.

Metropolitan Syracuse is the major urban area. There are many small towns and enchanted places like Madison County that has a very pastoral feel to it.

I have included Auburn in Central New York, close to Syracuse; it could have been included with the Finger Lakes. I have also included places just north of Syracuse in Oswego County, in the North Country section that immediately follows.

Auburn, Cayuga County

Auburn was home to noteworthy abolitionists Harriet Tubman and William Seward, who served as Secretary of State for President Abraham Lincoln. Auburn contains numerous FOC. Unfortunately, many of them are located in Fort Hill Cemetery that casts a pale over them.

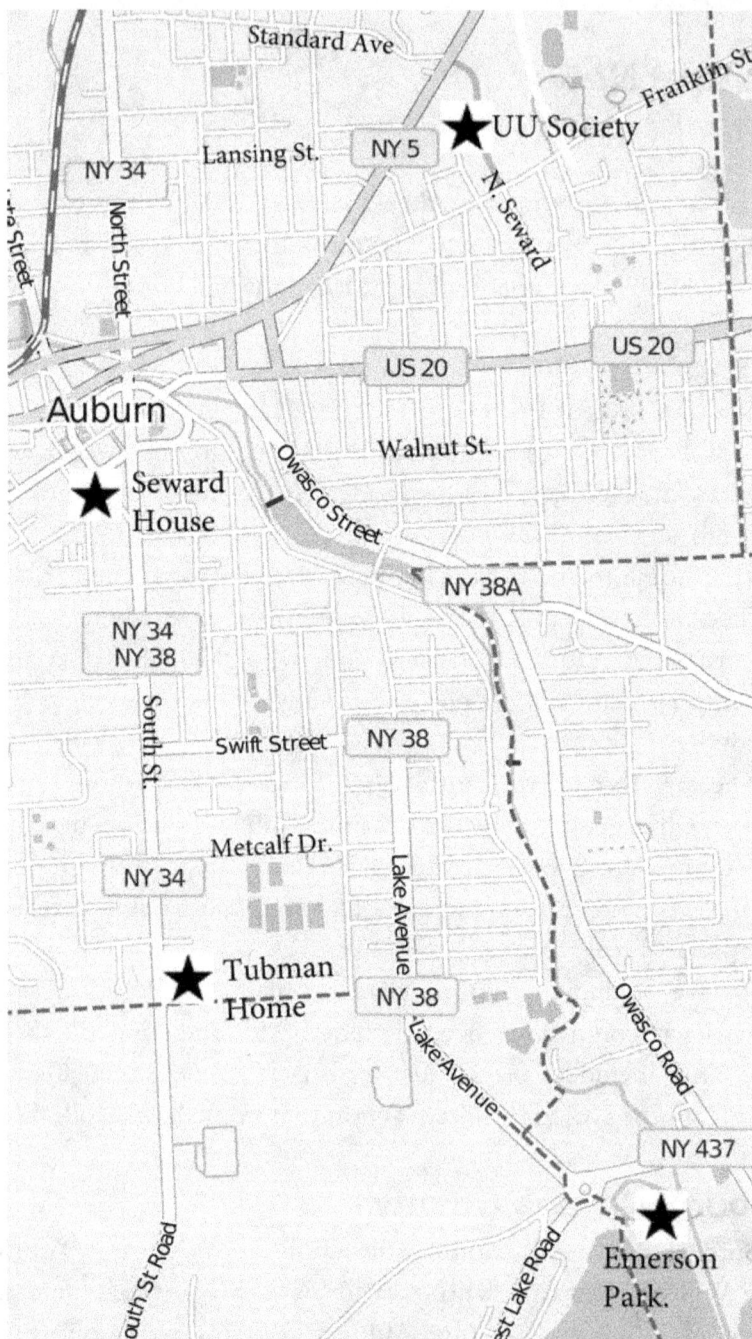

Map of Auburn. Source, www. openstreetmap. org.

For a driving tour of Underground Railroads Sites in Cayuga County: http://www.auburncayugafreedomtrail.com.

Auburn Unitarian Universalist Society
S10, V0, 👬 🧘

In its mission statement, the church says that it looks to "provide a safe haven for an intentionally diverse community that inspires, nurtures and empowers." The church and its property rest on a large FOC. The vibe is neutral.

Experiencing Auburn Unitarian

The highpoint in the FOC is a series (3) of S10's that begin on the lawn between the church and the parking lot in front of the third (middle) window. The remaining two S10's are in the church and run almost perpendicular to it. One is in the area to the side of the sanctuary. The other is in the sanctuary.

All of the backyard of the church sits on a Field. There is a series (3) of S8's located 15-20 feet behind the church parallel to the other series of Fields and parallel to the church. The first S8 is about 5 feet from the asphalt driveway. Second S8 is located about 15 away from the shed that is connected to the church. The final S8 is located about 5 feet from the children's roundabout.

Address: 607 North Seward Ave, Auburn, NY 13021
Webpage: www.auus.org
Telephone: 315-253-9029
Services: Sunday mornings 10:30 AM.

Directions: North Seward is off of Rt. 5 in the city of Auburn, east of the city center (where Rt. 5 intersects Rt.'s 34 and 38.)

Emerson Park
S1-5, V-0, 🚻 〰

Beautiful Emerson Park rests on the northern end of Owasco Lake. It consists of 135 acres, one mile of lakefront and two miles of river frontage. There are several Fields located at the western end of the park. The vibe is neutral.

One FOC is located just in front of a stand of trees just east of the parking area; it contains a series (3) of S5's. The other Field is located just west of the boat rental area. Look for a multi-limbed tree standing by itself close to shore. The Fields are just to the east of the tree, 20-30 feet from the tree; a series(3) of S 6's break away from the shoreline. Both are large FOC, so as long as you are close you will be within them.

Address: 6914 East Lake Road, Auburn, NY 13021
Webpage: http://www.cayugacounty.us/Community/Parks-and-Trails/Emerson-Park
Email: parks@cayugacounty.us
Telephone: 315-253-5611
Hours: The park is open dawn to dusk. The beach is seasonally open 11 AM to 7 PM. Free.
Directions: From Rt. 20 in Auburn take Rt. 38a south; which will turn into East Lake Rd. The Park is on your right.

Seward House — Historic Home
S3, V0, 👫🖼🛒 ♀

William Seward served as secretary of state during the Civil War. He was an ardent abolitionist, but a gradualist who advocated for the gradual emancipation of slaves. In 1849 he was elected NY state senator, one of the few abolitionist senators in the senate. The garden in the back sits on a FOC (S3.) The vibe is neutral.

The historian Doris Kearns Goodwin described the Seward home as "one of the most treasured museums in our country."

History

William Seward was the governor of New York, a state senator and Secretary of State for the Lincoln and Johnson administrations. As Secretary of State he made the Alaska Purchase from the Russians, known as "Seward's Folly." He was shot during the Lincoln assassination.

William Henry and Frances Seward were social reformers with a strong passion for abolitionism. They were conductors on the Underground Railroad as their home served as a station stop. They sold land to Harriet Tubman at attractive terms down the street so that she could relocate her parents in St. Catharine's and provide for a base of operations. They helped fund Fredrick Douglass' North Star newspaper and helped educate African American children. Frances was involved with Women's Rights.

Experiencing Seward House

The entire garden behind the house sits on a FOC. Looking from the parking lot the most potent area is to the right of the gravel path. Pick a place that you like and enjoy. This is the garden in which Seward waited in vain to hear that he was nominated as the Republican candidate for president in 1860.

There is a series (3) of (S3)'s next to the gravel path in the back. Looking from the parking area onto the garden the first S3 is located to the left of the bushes that are to the right of the gravel path. The next one is about 15 feet ahead and about 6-8 feet from after the gravel path divides and straightens out. The final S3 is to the left of the large tree on the right side of the gravel path. To see the trajectory of the Fields visualize drawing a line from the bushes to the tree.

Address: 33 South St, Auburn, NY 13021
Webpage: www. sewardhouse.org
Email: info@sewardhouse.org
Telephone: 315-252-1283
Donate, Volunteer: The Seward House is 501c-3 dependent upon donations, visitor admissions and programs to remain open, so please donate generously online. There are numerous volunteer programs available (see website.)
Close by: Harriet Tubman Home is down the street.
Hours: Tues-Sat, 10 AM to 5 PM; Sundays (summer) 1 PM to 5 PM. Closed major Holidays and the months of January and February. Admission: $10 Adults, $5 Students with ID, Children under 6 free.
Programs: Check the calendar on the website for upcoming events and educational programs. There is also an email list you can sign up for to get alerts.
Directions: Rt. 34 cuts through the heart of Auburn, going north/south. Above the Rt. 5 arterial it is called North St. To the south it is called South St. The Seward home is located on South St. across from Grove St.

References and Recommended Reading

http://sewardhouse.org

"Team of Rivals' author Goodwin tells stories of Lincoln, Seward at Auburn talk",aburnpub.com http://auburnpub.com /news/team-of-rivals-author-goodwin-tells-stories-of-lincoln-seward/article_3b93ea4c-3628-58ac-9d9e-02a70b737206.html

Harriet Tubman Home—Historic Home
S6, V0, 👫🚂 ♀

One cannot escape being in awe of Harriet Tubman, the most famous conductor on the Underground Railroad; called the 'Moses of her people.' She ferried more Freedom Seekers North to freedom than anyone else. Her generosity extended after the Civil War, when in her later life she built a home for the elderly and indigent.

Not surprisingly there is a FOC, with a high point of a series (3) of S(6) in the front yard. The vibe is neutral.

Harriet Tubman

Born into slavery in 1819, she was struck in the head by an overseer, causing an injury that would affect her for the rest of her life. After procuring her own liberty in 1849, she would return to the South thirteen times and free approximately fifty others. Using guile and a network of abolitionists, both black and white, she often disguised herself as an elderly woman, or man during her trips. Harriet was a woman of deep faith who prayed on her journeys, prayers that were often and mysteriously answered. She felt God spoke to her directly.

159

One of the many stories of her journeys was that once to prevent a frightened passenger from turning back she pulled out a gun and said to him, "you will be free, or die a slave." Anyone returning after leaving would have seriously jeopardized her and her passengers.

When abolitionist John Brown met Harriet, he called her "General Tubman." It is said if she had not been sick she would have been with Brown at Harper's Ferry.

She often found refuge for her passengers and herself at the home of Gerrit Smith in Peterboro, NY. By the time of the Civil War she had garnered notoriety and many feared she would be targeted, so Smith took her to Canada.

It was William Seward who lived up the street in Auburn (See Review) that wanted to reward Harriet for her valor, and offered her a home in Auburn on generous terms. It was thought that she needed a base of operations.

After the Civil War Harriet was involved with Women's Rights. Later in life she created a home for seniors on her property.

Objects mark the series (3) of S6's.

Experiencing the Tubman Home

The FOC is located on either side of the walkway going toward the road; it is 60-70 feet in diameter. The highpoint is a series (3) of (S6)'s that intersects the sidewalk.. The series breaks at angle towards the driveway favoring the house. The first in the series of 3 S(6) rests between the second and third tree (grass, not driveway side) from the house along the sidewalk (see the picture on the previous page.) driveway The second in the series is on the sidewalk. The final is close to the driveway.

Address: 180 South Street, Auburn, NY 13021
Webpage: www.harriethouse.org
Email: khill@harriethouse.org
Telephone: 315-282-2081
Donate, Volunteer: The African Methodist Episcopal Zion church oversees the Tubman home. You can donate online and join and become a member.
Hours: Tues. to Fri.: 10:00 AM – 4:00 PM, Sat.: 10:00 AM – 3:00 PM. Adults $4.50, Seniors (60+): $3 College students: $3 Children (6-17): $1.50 Children aged 5 and under: Free
Close by: Seward House is up the street.
Directions: Rt. 34 cuts through the heart of Auburn, going north/south. Above the Rt. 5 arterial it is called North St. To the south it is called South St. The Tubman home is located on South St. just south of Taber St.

References and Recommended Reading

Tubman Home website, www.harriethouse.org.
Larson, Kate Clifford; *Bound for the Promised land. Harriet Tubman Portrait of An American Hero*, Ballantine Books, New York, New York, 2004.
Clinton, Catherine; *Harriet Tubman, The Road to Freedom*, Little Brown & Co. New York, New York, 2004

Georgetown, Madison County, NY

Nestled in southern Madison County Georgetown seems like time has passed it by. Adding to that feeling is Spirit House, a nationally registered historic home that was once a Spiritualist's mecca. A marvel to the eyes, it looks like a giant wedding cake, its cornices seem like large icicles dripping from the roof. Nothing has been done to preserve the house in decades, so it is in need of serious repair.

I led an effort to buy Spirit House and turn it into a retreat center and museum until one of our members purchased it for themselves. So it is in private hands and you cannot walk the grounds, but you can certainly drive by.

I mention this because there is much mystery surrounding Spirit House and its builder Timothy Brown, who said Spirits guided him in its construction. Similarly Muller Hill, another place in Georgetown, is surrounded by mystery. If you are interested, Joscelyn Godwin's *Upstate Cauldron* contains a little write-up of Spirit House.

The town of Georgetown is a hotspot for FOC.

Muller Hill's Enchanted Forest
S12, V2-4, ▽ ☆ ♡ (♦) ▣ ⁊ ꝉ

There are parts of the NY state forest at Muller Hill that make you feel that you are in a mystical place. You expect that any moment you may encounter a hobbit, an elf or some other mythical creature. While some may wince about the existence of these fairy tale creatures, no one will escape the sense of something different, something unusual or something special about Muller Hill.

It could be the Amish and their buggies that have begun inhabiting the Georgetown area (40 Miles SE of Syracuse, NY) that gives Muller Hill the air of a bygone era. It could be Spirit House that drew thousands in the nineteenth century seeking communication with Spirits that creates this aura of mysticism. Or it may just be the mystery that surrounds its previous owner and his mansion that gives you the sense that there is something lying below the reality in the front of your eyes.

Muller Hill is for you, if you interested in a hike, or meditating in a beautiful natural environment with plenty of stacked Fields (several stacked Fields of 12) and vortices (which ones assumes were created by the Spirit Keepers.) Muller Hill would be a great place to try and sense and feel Consciousness.

History

A historical marker on Muller Hill Road marks the former site of the Muller Mansion. Constructed in 1808 all that remains are the foundations of buildings. Much mystery surrounds its builder Louis Muller. It is rumored that he was a general in the French army, loyal to the king and queen of France, who came to America to escape Napoleon, but no one knows for sure.

There is a sweet spot near the pond behind where the mansion once stood –tranquil, serene and a FOC (S10.)

In 1808 Muller purchased 2,700 acres in the then very remote area of southern Madison County. He constructed a large house, 70 feet by 30 feet; its foundation was 6 feet deep and 5 feet wide and the walls were cherry wood 1 foot thick. He brought several French servants with him and hired 150 laborers and created a small hamlet for them to live in the valley below. It is also said he clear cut much of his land.

All the stories surrounding Muller and his mansion, what some called a fortress, show him to be secretive, mysterious and very fearful that he would be found in America and be killed. It is rumored that there was an escape tunnel in the cellar, that he seldom left his estate and when riding around his land two armed guards always accompanied him.

I can attest first hand to mystery surrounding Muller Hill. Before I knew about the historic marker I dowsed to find the Muller mansion. I was led about a quarter mile south of where the Link trail crosses Muller Hill Road, on the west side of the dirt road, about 100 feet into the woods to an old foundation. State Forester Greg Owens tells me that an 1870 map confirms that a structure once stood there. Odd, because months later my dowsing rods would lead me to the woods behind the Mansion marker. Why was I drawn to a building in the middle of nowhere? Was it a secret hideaway house for Muller?

There are two main areas to explore in Muller Hill; the Link Trail area and the Mansion area. There are many other areas with FOC. When you visit Muller Hill State Forest make sure to come with an open mind and a yearning for a mystical connection, you will not be disappointed.

The Link Trail Area

The Link Trail
S3-6, V2-3, ⊂ 🚶

The Link Trail north of Muller Hill road makes for a wonderful contemplative walk in serene and majestic woods with FOC. The vibe is positive to extremely positive. It is also the path to get to other parts of Muller Hill.

History

The Link Trail was created to connect the Finger Lakes Trail System with the Erie Canal towpath and ultimately the North Country Scenic Trail. The section that goes north from Muller Hill Road passes through some beautiful woods and a good chunk of the beginning is on some powerful Fields. You can access the link trail just west of where Bundy Road intersects Muller Hill Road. You can park your car on Bundy Road off to the side near Muller Hill Road.

While the link trail passes through FOC and provides places to stop and meditate it is also a thoroughfare of sorts that provides access to other areas containing FOC; the Glen, the Holy Ridge and the Back Woods.

Please be advised that these three places are off of the link trail and you need to have a compass and sense of the woods; particularly for the Glen and the Back Woods. The Holy Ridge is close to the stream so it can act as a guidepost. All of these areas contain FOC, as well as other aspects of Fields. Again it would be helpful to have a compass if you decide to explore these areas.

Experiencing the Forest

Please use the beginning of the trail, the other side of the small berm, close to the road, as a Welcome Circle. This is definitely a place you want to announce yourself and indicate your intentions.

165

Consider an offering; some tobacco, or a flower. It is about a ten minute walk to the stream, assuming you don't stop.

You will immediately enter a beautiful pine woods and begin walking in a straight line northward. After a few minutes the trail will go to the right and then left and again assume its northward direction. You will be walking in a mixed forest of pines and mostly hardwoods. In about 40-50 feet you will be in a large continuous Field (S3-S4) with only a few small breaks until you reach the stream.

The Glen
S12, V3-4, ⬆

The cushion on the lower right marks the first FOC in the Glen. Notice the dogs in the background sitting on the roots of a downed tree.

The Glen is off of the Link Trail, about 50 yards from where the straight away through the hardwoods began. Look for a slight rise on the trail and an earthen mound 4-5 feet high to the right. The trail begins to slightly descend after entryway for the Glen. If you want to enter the Glen look for a herd path (it will be faint) on your left and go off trail walking perpendicular to the link trail.

This area can be soggy in the spring, so be prepared. You will be entering a hemlocked glen. The FOC's begin within a 100 feet and extend back another 200-300 feet.

Look for a overturned tree with its roots in the air to your right. The FOC is about 30-40 feet from the downed tree.

If you continue back and bear the left you will encounter another nice FOC on an elevated area. It is about a 100 feet to the right of another overturned tree with its roots in the air. There are numerous FOC's in the Glen so you need to explore.

Back to the Link Trail

Returning to where you turned off the link trail, get back on it and continue walking northward. You may want to stop to meditate, or do ceremony along this section of the trail. Years ago I placed flat stones and meditated on them at several locations along this part of the trail. Unfortunately hikers took those stones and placed them on wet areas; which is understandable.

When the trail turns left you are on a high embankment above the stream. On the other side of the stream you might be able to see another high embankment—that is the Holy Ridge you will ultimately end up on. As the trail turns left the FOC will increase to S5-S6.

As you get close to the stream you will see a herd path to your right that traverses backward as it descends to stream. Take the herd path to the streambed.

If you are visiting in late spring you may wish to continue on the trail crossing the stream. If you are lucky you may be able to see several large batches of marsh marigolds in bloom, near the trail and a service road on the other side. They are breath taking.

The Holy Ridge
S12, V3-4, ▽ ☆ ♡ (↑) ▣ ↗ ⅄ ≋

As you face upstream the hill that you saw as you turned left to walk down to the stream is ahead you on the left hand side. Look for a good place to cross the stream; it may be where two fingers of the stream come together. The water level will vary and it may be a challenge to cross in early spring.

For years I came to Muller Hill, and then one day I was directed to a vortex on the Holy Ridge; something that would clearly pique my interest and encourage me to come back. Mother Earth reveals Herself in many ways. Most often She does so gradually over time as our love and prayers give a glow to a place making things sparkle and revealing things previously unseen. Other times She has one of Her helpers, a kindred spirit of sorts, show you things. The latter was at work here. She wanted me to find this little Shangri-La.

Yet at the same time, as others and I have meditated and prayed in this divine forest over the years, other places have begun to glisten revealing more and more of Mother Earth divine aspects. As I have said Mother Earth needs us (humankind) to achieve Her fullest potential and we need Her to achieve ours.

I recommend meditating any place on the Holy Ridge, the area close to the stream. FOC are pretty much continuous for several hundred yards with several series (3) of S12's. The base near the stream is S6 and it goes to S12 on top. Pick a place that you like. Explore.

There are a few herd paths you can follow up the hill. The one in the middle at the base is recommended, it will shortly turn right and connect with the herd path close to the edge of the ridge. When on the ridge, stay to the right close to its edge, and follow the herd path. Downed trees, branches and other impediments may have you walking away from the ridge; after you go around any obstacle always return to the edge of the ridge. Stay on the right side close to the edge of the ridge following the herd path.

A Warm and Friendly Neighborhood

The first small plateau, or flattop, is maybe a 50-70-foot or so climb from the base by the stream. There is a series of S8's on it. Pick a place to meditate.

As you continue uphill, the forest will end on your left and become a large and continuous swath of raspberry bushes and other gnarl. This rabble on your left will continue and occasionally come close to the herd path and the ridge's edge.

After climbing 100-150 feet look for a three-limbed larger hemlock to your left; it is 15-20 feet from the ridge's edge. The first in a series (3) S12's is in front of the three-limbed hemlock; the other two are on the other side. The vortex is on the final S-12. It is in more of an open area on an incline.

As I noted earlier, large tracts of land, like large cities, have individual neighborhoods within them that are distinctive and different, yet at the same time combine with other areas to make a unique location. The neighborhood that comprises the Holy Ridge is divine and truly mystical. It is a warm and welcoming place that wants you to come pray, meditate and enjoy it. I was guided here to enlighten you about it and have you come and visit.

The vibe is extremely positive around the FOC, particularly this first series of S12's. The air is charged and the veil to the other side is thin. This is where you should dream, imagine, call for a vision, or ask for guidance and direction. Do so selflessly and with a big heart and you will be rewarded. Please consider some of the prayers in Part III such as the illusion of reality—the world is not real mantra; dream of a New Earth, or ask for divine inspiration. This truly is the place to dream, be inspired and connect with the divine.

FOC are pretty much continuous until you get to where the ridge dips near the Healing Area. Find an area you like and dream, imagine a better world where peace reigns and the lion lies down with the lamb. As you listen to water breaking against rocks in the stream come to understand that the world is truly mystical.

The first S12 on the Holy Ridge. Notice the three limbed hemlock tree. The first S12 is a little behind Jaeda (black dog). The next is by Pepper (white dog) and final S-12 is where my backpack is, it also is where the vortex is.

As you leave the first series (3) of S12's and walk on the herd path you will quickly come upon an earthen mound with a vortex upon it. This looks like an old downed tree, but it could be earth covering an old Spirit Keepers mound; whatever is, enjoy it and soak up the love. I expect other vortices to continue to form here.

The ridge that has been rising ever so slightly, will flatten out. To your left in the gnarl is a herd path to the Back Woods. You will be about 60-80 feet in front of a large downed tree that blocks the herd along the ridge. Turn here if you wish to go to the Back Woods. No guarantee on the condition of the path.

Continuing on the herd on the Holy Ridge the next series (3) of S12's on the other side of the downed tree; about 50 feet before the ridge begins to bend to the left. The series runs 10-30 feet on the other side of the tree and about 30 feet in front of large hemlock by the edge of the ridge. Again FOC's can be very large and there are some very sweet areas in front of the downed tree.

Continuing on the herd path you will find another potent spot about 200-300 feet ahead where the gnarl of raspberry bushes and briars almost touches the ridge and the trees diminish. Find a place to pause and enjoy this very sweet spot.

As you continue walking upstream along the ridge the herd path will get closer to the streambed. You will reach a point where it will become noticeable that you are as close as you can get to the streambed. There is a series of terraces or ledges that will allow access to the streambed. This is where you can access the Healing Area by the streambed below.

The Healing Area.

Before you begin the descent to the Healing Area there is another aspect of a FOC along the Holy Ridge. Pause here and see how it suits you. This area was activated through our praying and meditating along the Holy Ridge and from visiting the healing area. Again love, positive intentions and prayer enhance Mother Earth and make Her glisten and reveal more of Her and enhance Her. I mention this because the Holy Ridge has so much to offer and there may be places along it that are better suited to you than the ones mentioned.

You can access the healing area by walking down to the streambed. It is located on the right side near the creek bed. Pray for healing loved ones, or the world at large.

About 100-150 feet downstream from the Healing Area in the creek bed is a very sweet FOC. You may wish to walk upstream from the last S12 to experience it; or just walk downstream and see if you can sense it.

The Back Woods
S4-8, V1-3, ⬆ ⵒ ⵣ

The Back Woods is located on the other side of the gnarl from the Holy Ridge. You can access a herd path that cuts through it where the Holy Ridge flattens out; about 60-80 feet before the downed tree that blocks the herd path along the Holy Ridge.

As you traverse through the gnarl the first FOC's is close to a small stand of pine trees. There are several more FOC's until you come to a creek bed, which will be dry most of the year.

The bulk of FOC's in the Back Woods are on the other side of the creek bed. You need to be careful because there are many young trees that will block your vision and path. Explore and find a place you like. The FOC's extend a couple of hundred yards beyond the creek bed. Several of them will be in stands of pines.

Enjoy and make sure you have a compass so you won't get lost.

The Mansion Area
S6-10, V2-3, ☆ ⬆ ⌇ 🧍 〰️

The remnants of the Muller Mansion are located on Muller Hill Rd. about ¾ mile west of Chapin Rd and are marked by a blue sign. Follow the path going north a few hundred yards and you will come upon the foundations for some outbuildings. The mansion was located on the west side of the path.

Continue to follow the trail. Just after it turns to the right, there will be a FOC with an S6 on your left in front of some white pine trees. You will be entering an area with FOC that are continuous, with one small break until the pond.

The trail continues with a slight decline. It will go to the right and then breaks to the left before it shortly reaches a 30- acre man made pond (1955). This area is bogey and can be wet, very wet at times, so make sure to wear some boots and protect yourself from bugs.

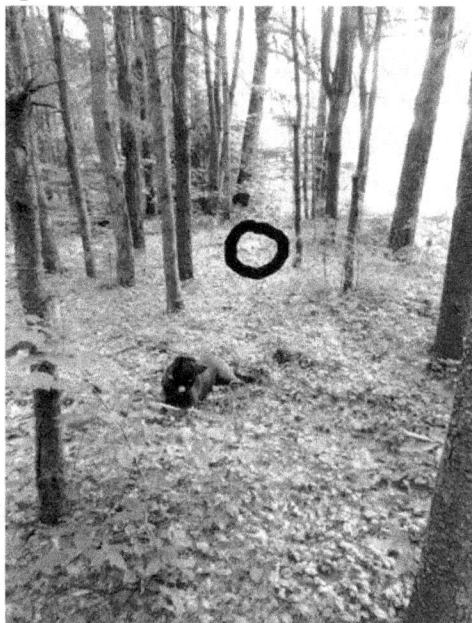

While much of this area is covered with FOC there is a series (3) of S10's in the pine woods to the left. It runs parallel to the path about 15 feet to the left of it as you face the lake. Very nice.

See the picture on the right above. The series (3) S10's are about 15 feet apart. I am standing on one of the S10's as I am photographing. Jaeda Bear (black dog) is sitting on the middle S10. Pepper (white dog) circled in black is on the last S10. It is in

173

an area just before the wooded area ends and the land dips a couple of feet. The pond is in the background.

The vibe in the pinewoods is positive to very positive, and it's wonderful to meditate next to a tranquil and serene body of water. That said there can be considerable challenges such as moisture and bugs, particularly in the spring. Also there are occasional visitors to view the mansion remains and a possible fisherman; but I am told the fishing is nonexistent.

There is much more for Mother Earth to reveal to us at Muller Hill. There are many more FOC and other divine aspects of Mother Earth. Please come and visit and help make Muller Hill sparkle even more, so that more is revealed.

Address: Muller Hill Road, Georgetown, NY
Webpage: http://www.dec.ny.gov/lands/8156.html
Email: info.r7@dec.ny.gov
Telephone: DEC Region 7 Sherburne Office: (607) 674-4017 M-F 8 am - 4 pm; Emergency, Law Enforcement & Rangers: (518) 408-5850 or 911
Directions: From Georgetown take Rt. 80 north. Muller Hill Rd. will quickly appear on your left. Go uphill and continue. The DEC State Forest begins after you cross Chapin Rd. From Deruyter take Albany St. east, which will turn into Crumb Hill Rd. About a mile out of town take a left onto Carpenter Rd; the turnoff is at a bend in Crumb Hill to the right. Be careful as Carpenter has several sharp turns. The turnoff (right) for Muller Hill Rd. is at a sharp left bend in the road. Follow Muller Hill (dirt road) to the state land.

References and Recommended Reading
Keefe, Anna F. "The Muller Mansion; Some Facts, Some Fiction." Urtz, Matthew, "Lewis Anathe Muller, Who Was This Mysterious Frenchman of Madison County???"

Conversations with current Madison County Historian Matthew Urtz and former Madison County Historian Sarah Davies Hasegawa

Hamilton, Madison County, NY

Hamilton is home to Colgate University; much of the college is located on FOC's. There are plenty of restaurants in this charming town, as well as things to do.

Chapel House
S4, V2-3, ▽ ⊛ ⫯⫯ ⛩ ⸆ ⅄

Chapel House is an ecumenical retreat center where pilgrims come to seek solitude and spiritual exploration. It offers an opportunity to heal, replenish and learn in a unique setting and of course, experience Mother Earth and Her FOC. Its library contains sacred texts and scholarly works from various world's religions. It has an audio room and chapel.

Located atop Colgate University's rolling hills, its woods and hiking trails provide for a contemplative walk. All are welcome

whether you are staying over night, or just coming to spend a few hours. Accommodations are $40 a night including three meals (2 night minimum); What a bargain.

The Spirit of Chapel House

Chapel house was designed to accept all faith traditions, or as its brochure says "none". It goes out of its way to teach and accommodate. For example, Muslims can find arrows pointing to the east to assist them with salat. The library contains over 5,000 religious texts of all faiths. It has welcomed visitors from all over the world, of different traditions and backgrounds.

Chapel House is run as a retreat for people questing and silence is asked for. Please try to remain quiet while there, or walking its grounds. I would suggest taking your shoes off when entering.

Chapel House was created in 1959 and funded by a benefactor who asked to remain anonymous. The intention was also to make it an ecumenical place for all. Per the brochure, "Chapel House belongs to and is administered by Colgate University. It operates on an endowment funds which must cover expenses without requiring any help from University funds."

The walls of Chapel House are filled with art representing a variety of traditions.

Experiencing Chapel House

The chapel is the place for serious prayer and meditation. It rests on a FOC (S4.) The vibe is positive to very positive; so it would be a good place to try and

sense and feel Consciousness. Because Chapel House is dedicated to ecumenism it would be a great place to pray and meditate on the unity of people and religions. We are one.

There is a vortex ring in the front of Chapel House near the door, a few feet from the corner of the building on the right side.

There is an extensive library containing sacred texts from a variety of religions. There is a music room that allows for listening of a variety of religious classics from earliest times to more experimental modern day pieces.

You need to make reservations a few weeks in advance and must stay a minimum of two nights and includes three meals. The charge is so inexpensive that one must wonder whether the charge even covers the cost of the meals.

Address: 13 Oak Drive, Hamilton, NY 13346-1398
Webpage: http://www.colgate.edu/about/facilities-at-colgate/chapel-house/resources
Telephone: 315-228-6087
Reservations: Call 315-228-7675 or online at: www.colgate.edu/about/facilities-at-colgate/chapel-house/overnight-guests
Hours: Chapel House is open Mon-Sat 8:30 AM to 10 PM, Sundays 8:30 AM to 5 PM. The Chapel is open 24 hours. Please check hours online before visiting. www.colgate.edu/about/facilities-at-colgate/chapel-house
Close by: A network of hiking trails are located a short walk up the hill from Chapel House.
Directions: Heading south from the town park on Broad St. (Rt. 128) fork left onto Oak St., don't make a full left turn onto E. Kendrick Ave. As you begin to climb take a left onto Alumni Rd. Continue onto Alumni Rd it will turn into Chapel House Dr. Chapel House is located on top of the hill on your right. Parking will be on your left just before Chapel House.

Oneida, Madison County, NY

So named for the Oneida Nation and Oneida Lake. Known for its Oneida silverware that was created by the Oneida Community.

Oneida Mansion
S3-4, V1, 👫 🖼

Oneida Mansion was home to the Oneida Community, a Perfectionist Utopian community. It was a bold and radical social experiment in the mid nineteenth century that challenged gender roles, child rearing, and monogamous marriage. Members practiced complex marriage where everyone was free to have sex with others; men practiced male continence as a form of birth control. The 93,000 square foot mansion has guided tours and offers overnight accommodation.

Two FOC's (S3, S4) are located in the garden areas of the 160 acre estate; giving the opportunity to meditate in a visually appealing environment. The vibe is slightly positive in those areas.

The view of the Oneida Mansion from the garden in the front. A FOC (S3) is located in the center part (urn) of the garden.

History

John Humphrey Noyes, the founder of the Oneida community, was a religious Perfectionist who believed human perfection was possible and that the Perfectionist doctrine made the case for establishing the kingdom of Heaven on Earth. Communalism flowed from individual perfection, because the individual had to abandon the ego and self-interest, and instead work for the greater good of the community.

The community was born in 1848 and all members had to give their assets to the community and rely on it for support. To fund itself the community turned to building animal traps and canning, which became so profitable that outsiders were brought in to do the work. By the 1860's profits helped build the mansion house.

By the 1870's, religious Perfectionism had faded to social Perfectionism and the sense of community was dissipating. In 1875 Noyes attempted to turn the reins over to his unwilling son Theodore and left in 1879. In 1880 the Oneida community dissolved into Oneida Ltd. and members were given joint stock (shares) based upon their original contribution and tenure. Many members continued to live in the mansion. The silverware company came about in 1893 to support the community.

Experiencing the Mansion grounds

There are two places to experience FOC at the Oneida Mansion. One is the garden area in front of the mansion that rests on a FOC (S3.) It encompasses an area of twenty feet plus around the urn in the center, with a slightly larger area going towards the mansion. The vibe is slightly positive. This is a quiet and serene location. When I was there one summer day I had the garden all to myself.

There is a FOC with a series (3) of S4's in the garden in the back near the Terrace; marked by the papers and backpack in the picture on the next page. They run parallel to the gravel path, and to its left if facing the mansion. The center of the series is located

20 feet in front of the garden terrace; the other two are located 15 feet either side of it. The FOC extends (length) approximately 50 feet on either side of the center in the series and 40 feet on either side of the series (width.) The vibe is slightly positive.

The objects mark the series (30 of S4

There are courses and talks given regularly at the mansion; check the webpage. I have attended several interesting talks there. The grounds provide for a delightful walk. Overnight stays are offered, check website for rates and availability.

Address: 170 Kenwood Avenue, Oneida, NY 13421
Webpage: http://www.oneidacommunity.org
Email: ocmh@oneidacommunity.org
Telephone: 315-363-0745
Donate, Volunteer: Oneida Community Mansion is a nonprofit (501c-3), you can donate on their webpage, or become a member. There are numerous volunteer opportunities from being a gardener, to a tour guide..
Hours: Guided tours Wed. to -Sat (10:00AM, 2:00PM) Sun. at 2:00PM. Tours last about 90 minutes. Self guided tours Mon. to Sat 9:00AM to 4:00PM, and Sun. 12:00PM to 3:00PM. Admission includes guided tour: Adults $5, Students $3 and children under 12 are free. Closed holidays.

Directions: Exit 33 off of the Thruway (I-90.) Take a left onto Rt. 365W. Continue on Rt. 365 to Rt. 5 and take a left onto Rt. 5 east. At the first traffic light left onto West Hamilton Ave. Right at the next light onto Sherrill Rd, it will turn into Kenwood Ave.

References and Recommended Reading

Carden, Maren Lockwood. *Oneida: Utopian Community to Modern Corporation,* Harper Torchbooks, New York, New York, 1971.
Godwin, Joscelyn; *Upstate Cauldron, Eccentric Spiritual Movements in Early New York State,* , Pages 106-117.

Peterboro, Madison County, NY

Gerrit Smith Estate—Historic Place
S12, V0, 👫 🖼 🛖 ♀ 🕊

"There are yet two places slaveholders cannot come, Heaven and Peterboro."
So wrote black antislavery radical Henry Highland Garner in a letter to Fredrick Douglass, which Douglass printed on the front page of his 'North Star' newspaper December 8, 1848. Garnet was referring to the deeds of Gerrit Smith who had made the hamlet of Peterboro (25 miles south east of Syracuse) a refuge for Freedom Seekers on the Underground Railroad and a well- spring for other social reforms during the nineteenth century.

While the vibe has diminished (neutral today) there are numerous stacked Fields (12.) Several of us continue to work to polish up this National Historic Landmark and make it glow and become the bright beacon it must have been to attract and motivate such a great soul. Please visit.

He Lived the Life He Believed

Smith was an ardent abolitionist and social reformer involved with issues such as Women's Rights, land reform, temperance, dietary

181

changes, to name a few. He took the poor and needy of all colors into his home and helped them financially. He embodied Jesus' teaching to love your enemies and visited Ku Klux Khan Prisoners in Albany, NY who were diametrically opposed to him. He posted bail for Jefferson Davis who was arrested for treason after the Civil War.

He was not only generous, but also compassionate, establishing an orphanage for poor children in Peterboro and taking great joy in bringing them apples. Once when a business acquaintance feared he would lose five acres of land because he failed to make payments, Smith gave him the land and wrote. " Learn, then, to pity the broken-hearted slave who has lost it all—lost it, too, by no fault of his own."[1]

Smith was a strong believer that abolitionists and social reformers should take a hands on approach and be involved in politics. He ran for President in 1848, 1856 and 1860 and served in the United States Congress; one of the few avowed abolitionist to do so.

Born the son of a wealthy landowner, he felt it was his duty to put his money to good use and help those in need. He bought and freed slaves, although some such as Lucretia Mott thought that he was doing nothing more than feathering the nest of slave owners. In 1846 Smith divided 120,000 acres into 40-acre land grants for 3,000 black Americans to meet the property requirement for voting. In 1850 Smith gave five hundred "white inhabitants of the State of New York," who were landless and poor, forty acres each plus ten dollars.

The deeds and actions of Gerrit Smith that benefited mankind are too numerous to mention. The New York Times summed it up when it said:

"The history of the most important half century of our national life will be imperfectly written if it fails to place Gerrit Smith in the front rank of the men whose influence was most felt in the accomplishment of its results."[2]

Sadly, Smith remains virtually unknown in history.

Experiencing the Property

While the mansion burned down in 1936, the Land Office where Gerrit Smith used to hide Freedom Seekers still stands. Most of the grounds, particularly close to the land office, are on FOC. Find an area you like and sit down. What is so impressive about this space is that that there are two sets of a series (3) of (S12)'s on the property and another one in the town square.

We have been using an area behind the wrought iron fence on Peterboro Rd (County Rd 32) as a Welcome Circle. Facing the land office with Peterboro Rd and the town square to your back, the area of the Welcome Circle is just behind the fence on your right.

One of the series (3) of S12's is located a few feet away from the wrought iron fence. The first in the series is located 3 feet to the left of the fence and 5 feet towards the land office. The series heads straight towards the land office, perpendicular to the road, and the highpoints are 15 feet apart and are marked in the picture above.

The other series (3) of S12's is located to the east of the Land Office and a series of signs and runs north south. The first S12 is about 10 feet to the right (east) of the closest sign to the street. The series parallels the signs, 10 feet from them, and moves away from the street and are spaced 15 feet apart.

Events and lectures are held throughout the year, particularly during the summer season when the estate is open. For specifics check the events calendar or signup for the email mailing. The Abolitionist Hall of Fame, down the street, has a gala each fall with a dinner to induct new members to its Hall of Fame.

The series (3) of S12's next to the signs, series moves away from the street.

During its hours of operation you can watch a short video on the life of Gerrit Smith. The Gerrit Smith Estate is run by volunteers, so please donate generously.

Address: The Visitor Center is located at 5304 Oxbow Rd., Peterboro NY 13134. The Land Office is located around the corner on Peterboro road (Main Street), Peterboro, NY.
Webpage: http://www.gerritsmith.org

Telephone: 315-280-8828

Donate, Volunteer: A donation box is located in the Lodge. You can also donate online.

Hours: The Visitor Center traditionally opens around Memorial Day and closes a little before Labor Day, Saturdays and Sundays 1 to 5PM. Admission is $3. Please check website before coming. The grounds are open year round from dawn to dusk.

There is a robust program of events and talks, check website.

Close by: The Abolitionists Hall of Fame http://www.nationalabolitionhalloffameandmuseum.org is a few hundred yards away at 5255 Pleasant Valley Rd.

Directions: From Syracuse (I-481, Exit 3E), follow Rt. 92 east. In Cazenovia left onto Rt. 20. Just past the Sunoco gas station bear left onto Fenner Rd. and drive 9 miles until it ends. Make a left onto Pleasant Valley north, go past the village green and onto Oxbow Rd.

From Thruway (I-90) get off at Exit 34 (Canastota). Make a left and follow Peterboro street south through Canastota. Cross Route 5 and continue south on Oxbow Rd. (Rt. 25) for 10 miles.

References and Recommended Reading

1. Dann, Norman K.; *Practical Dreamer, Gerrit Smith and the Crusade for Social Reform*, Log Cabin Books, Hamilton , NY 2009. Page 45.
2. New York Times, Vol. XXIV No. 7265 December 29, 1874.
Webpage http://www.gerritsmith.org
Conversations with Dot Willsey over the years.

Sennett, Cayuga County, NY

Sennett Federated Church
S8, V-0, 🕴🕴 ⚱

Sennett Federated Church, a Presbyterian Church, is a union of the Sennett Baptist Church (1795) and the Sennett Presbyterian

Church (1809), and includes a few independent worshippers affiliated with neither religion. Reverend Charles Anderson, minister from 1843 to 1861, was an ardent abolitionist and stationmaster on the Underground Railroad who had one of his sermons printed in Fredrick Douglass' North Star. A FOC encompasses the church and the grounds. The vibe is neutral.

Experiencing Sennett Federated

The FOC is located in the back of the sanctuary near the Weedsport Sennett Road and covers most of the sanctuary. Within in it are a series (3) of S8's beginning on the lawn between the driveway and the church (Turnpike Rd side) about midpoint between windows 2 and 3. The remaining S8's in the series cuts almost perpendicular to the church, with a slight angle towards the Weedsport Sennett Road; corresponding to window 2 on the other side of the church. The vibe is neutral.

Address: 7777 Weedsport Sennett Rd. Auburn
Webpage: http://cayugasyracuse.org/churches/sennett-federated
Telephone: 315-252-4936
Donate, Volunteer:
Hours: Sunday services at 10 AM.
Directions: While the church has an Auburn address, it is in Sennett at the intersection of Weedsport Sennett Rd and Turnpike Rd in Sennett both of which originate from Rt. 5.

References and Recommended Reading
http://cayugasyracuse.org/churches/sennett-federated
Tucker, Sheila; 'Sennett Federated Church-Underground Railroad,'
http://www.cayugacounty.us/portals/0/history/church/sennett/index.html

Syracuse, Onondaga County, NY

The center of North Star Country and Mother Earth's Soul is located in the Syracuse area. It is home to the Onondaga Nation, the Fire Keepers. It was on the shores of Onondaga Lake that the Peacemaker planted the Tree of Peace and gave the Haudenosaunee the Great Law of Peace.

Because of Jermain Loguen, Syracuse became known as the most openly abolitionist city in America, with some even calling it America's Canada as noted earlier. Loguen was an A.M.E.Z. minister who had escaped slavery in Tennessee on a stolen horse. Dedicated to helping Freedom Seekers, he said "So long as God spares my life, it shall be spent to defy all slave laws."[1]

Loguen brazenly advertised in papers and handed out cards telling Freedom Seekers where they could find help. He was dubbed, the "Underground Railroad King" by The Weekly Anglo-African. His daughter Amelia married Fredrick Douglass' eldest son Lewis.

Douglass introduced Loguen to abolitionist Gerrit Smith. Smith sent a letter back to Douglass saying, "What a man you have sent me! I asked him to pray and he prayed so feelingly for his mother and sisters in slavery that we were all in tears."[2] Smith hired Loguen to assist him in the donation of 200,000 acres to the poor, no matter what color they were. Many claimed that the land was of poor quality. Loguen investigated and found this not to be the case, but rather unscrupulous men would hire themselves as 'pilots' and misdirect recipients to mountaintops and swamps and scarf up the land for themselves.

Loguen lived at the corner of Pine and Genesee Streets in Syracuse, in what is now the University section of the city, from 1848. Unfortunately, his home was torn down and replaced with a Rite Aid Pharmacy. It sits on a FOC containing a series (3) of S8's. Some may wish to visit.

Being the heart of North Star Country there are numerous FOC throughout the Syracuse area.

Armory Square is the refurbished and trendy part of the city of Syracuse, containing small boutiques and numerous restaurants. I was in one of those restaurants years ago when I sensed it was on a FOC. It runs approximately from W. Jefferson (the northern arm) to W. Fayette between S. Clinton and S. Franklin Streets.

Close by at Clinton Square, near the corner of Water and Clinton Streets, is the Jerry Rescue Monument. It honors the rescue of freedom seeker William Henry (Jerry) from slave catchers during the anti-slavery Liberty Party convention in Syracuse.

On the corner of E. Onondaga and Jefferson Streets is the Mission restaurant, the former home of Wesleyan Methodist Church (on a FOC), a stop on the Underground Railroad. In 1994, an archaeological dig revealed seven faces carved into the wall, presumably made by Freedom Seekers. Three of the faces were saved and are on display around the corner at the Onondaga County Historical Society (331 Jefferson Str. 315-428-1864) part of their permanent Exhibit, Freedom bound: Syracuse and the Underground Railroad.

References and Recommended Reading
1. Hunter, Carol; *To Set the Captives Free: Reverend Jermain Wesley Loguen and the Struggle for Freedom in Central New York*, 1835-182. Garland, NY, NY, 1993. Page 75
2. Ibid. Page 179.
Saving faces, saving history at Wesleyan Methodist Church, Clark, Cammi A., Syracuse Post Standard, Feb, 11, 2005 http://www.syracuse.com/news/index.ssf/2005/02/saving_faces_saving_history.html

Heath Park
S8, V0, ⊋

Also called Conifer Park, in the city of Syracuse's Valley section (south) near the city's border is a hidden gem with its regal pines. The park is 30 acres in size and contains a hiking trail. It is a short walk and climb, because you have to ascend to get to the FOC. The walk is on dirt roads, so hiking boots are not a necessity to experience the FOC (S8.) The vibe is neutral. Because you will be close to Rt. 81 there is car noise.

Experiencing Heath Park

Turn off of South Salina onto Richfield Ave and park your car towards the end of the street, near the walkway and creek on the left that intersects Heath Park. Walk north on the walkway and enter the park. On your right you will see a dirt road that butts up against the backyards of the houses on Richfield Ave. Take a right onto the dirt road.`

X marks the spot of the FOC. Notice the trail above going from left to right.

The road will veer left and begin to climb. It will straighten and continue rising. In about 100 yards the road will turn right. The

FOC are located near the elbow of the turn, about 30-40 feet to the right, on a mound, or rise; the road will continue and above the rise. The FOC is oblong in shape containing a series (3) of S8's that run east west. Look for two large trees next to each other, and the series begins in front of the second tree away from the road and moves directly west downhill.

If you continue climbing, the road will end at a fence along Route 81. The trail bisects into two parts. If you go right, it will eventually turn downhill and south, ending up on South Salina Street several blocks south of where you began. The trail to the left ends shortly. There is another FOC located in a stand of pine trees close to Rt. 81.

Address: 5559 South Salina St., Syracuse NY 13205
Webpage: http://www.syracuse.ny.us/parks/HeathPark.html
Telephone: Syracuse Parks Dept. 315-473-4330
Hours: Dawn to Dusk
Directions: From the North: I-81 southbound take exit 17 (Brighton Ave/S. Salina St.) Turn left at the traffic light and then go straight and turn right at the second traffic light. Turn left at the next traffic light (Salina St., Rt. 11), drive about 2 miles, Heath Park will be on your left.
From the South: I-81 northbound take exit 16 (Nedrow.) Turn left onto US-11 N. Heath Park on the right (2.5 mi.)

Matilda Joslyn Gage Home, Historic Home
S8, V0, ⛄⛄ 🚐 ♀ 🪶

The Gage home is located in Fayetteville, a suburb of Syracuse. Gage was a leader in the Women's Movement and it is not surprising that her home sits on a FOC (S8) The vibe is neutral. The home was also an Underground Railroad station.

History

Gage was a true maverick; one of the more radical Women's Rights leaders, as well as an abolitionist and friend to Native Americans. Unable to make the first Women's Rights Convention, she attended the third national convention in Syracuse in 1852 as a speaker.

It was Gage and Elizabeth Cady Stanton who penned the Women's Declaration of Rights that Susan Anthony read at the July 4, 1876 centennial celebration in Philadelphia before 150,000 people. Gage, Stanton and Anthony collaborated to write the *History of Woman's Suffrage*; which unfortunately Gage was never properly recognized for, especially as she did at least half, if not more of the writing. Anthony bought out the other two, and with the help of Ida Harper wrote another three volumes up to the passage of the Nineteenth Amendment. Unfortunately Gage was written out of the fourth volume and Anthony placed herself as the leader of the movement.

The divide between Anthony and Gage grew with the merger of National Woman Suffrage Association (NWSA) and American Woman Suffrage Association (AWSA) a much smaller organization. Gage was against the merger with conservative AWSA focused strictly on voting rights, and not freeing women from oppression at home, and by the church, state and capitalism. Anthony was able to push through the merger by seizing control of NWSA's executive committee when chairman Gage was absent. Gage would create the Woman's National Liberal Union.

In 1893, she was adopted into the Wolf Clan of the Mohawk Nation as Ka-ron-ien-ha-wi, or 'Sky Carrier', literally 'she who holds the sky.'

Gage, like Stanton, saw traditional religion as oppressing women as she expressed in *Woman, Church and State*. She was a spiritual person and a Theosophist, like her son-in-law L Frank Baum, the author of *The Wizard of Oz*.

While Gage died at her daughter and son in law's home in Chicago, there is a memorial stone in the Fayetteville, NY cemetery that reads, ""There is a word sweeter than Mother, Home or Heaven. That word is Liberty."

Experiencing the Gage Home

The FOC is located in the Family Parlor and the Oz room in the front of the house. The vibe is neutral.

Address: 210 E Genesee St, Fayetteville, NY 13066
Webpage: http://www.matildajoslyngage.org
Telephone: 615-637-9511
Donate, Volunteer: You can donate, become a member or get on the email list online on their webpage.
Hours: Mon & Sat: 10am – 2pm, Tues-Fri: Call in advance. Closed Sundays. Adults $6, Students (ID) $5, Preschoolers free.
Close by: Up the road in Chittenango (L. Frank Baum's home) are the All Things Oz Museum and the Chittenango library, which has a fun Oz themed room for kids.
Directions: From Syracuse take Rt. 5 east towards Fayetteville. After Wegmans bear left at the V. The Gage home will be on your right on the top of the hill in Fayetteville.

References and Recommended Reading

Wagner, Sally Roesch; *Matilda Joslyn Gage: She Who Holds the Sky*, Sky Carrier Press, Aberdeen SD 2002.
Savion, Susan; *Quoting Matilda, The Words of the Forgotten Suffragist*

Plymouth Congregational Church, UCC
S4, V0, 👫 🧘 ♿

Plymouth Congregation in downtown Syracuse on East Onondaga Street rests on the same FOC, or connected FOC's, with Columbus Circle and the old Wesleyan Methodist (Church Mission restaurant.) The vibe is neutral.

From its earliest days in 1853 the church was a stop on the Underground Railroad. Many of its founding members participated in the famous Jerry rescue in 1851. Its history is steeped in peace and justice.

Experiencing Plymouth

All of the sanctuary sits on a FOC. The high point is a series (3) of S4's located on the left hand side of the church as you face the front. The first in the series is located about 20 feet from the lectern close to the aisle; the series breaks horizontally towards East Onondaga. The vibe is neutral.

Address: 232 E. Onondaga Street, Syracuse, NY 13202
Webpage: http://plymouthuccsyracuse.org
Email: office@ plymouthsyr.org
Telephone: 315-474-4836
Hours: Sunday Services at 10 AM
Directions: Plymouth is located at the corner of E. Onondaga and Warren St.'s. From I-81 take exit 18 (Harrison St. /Adams St.) Turn west (towards the city center) onto Harrison St. Turn

right onto S. Warren St. The church will on your right in a few blocks.

References and Recommended Reading
Churches website http://plymouthuccsyracuse.org
Conversations with former pastor Craig Schaub

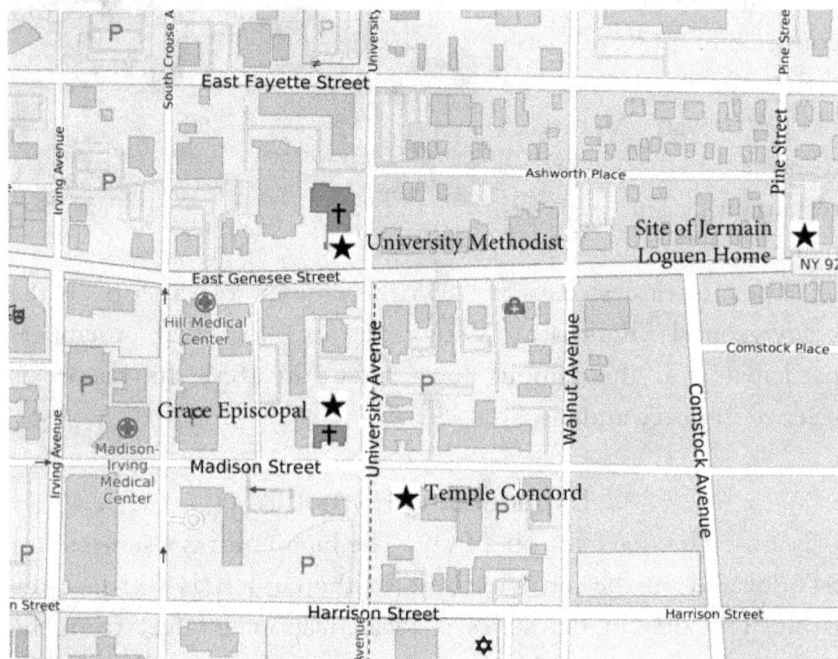

Are of the Prophetic Ley. Maps-© www. openstreetmap. org

The Prophetic Spirit Line (Prophetic Ley)

There is a Spirit Line in Syracuse NY that connects some of the most social justice and peace oriented churches and activists in the area. Interestingly this Spirit Line passes through, or close to, several other FOC beyond the one of its origin. In the map above it parallels University Ave slightly to the left, going down (south.)

The Prophetic Spirit Line was revealed to me in 2004 while I was meditating on the bench in the garden of Grace Episcopal Church. At the time, the bench was directly on the Spirit Line.

The Prophetic Spirit Line originates from University United Methodist. The three places of worship mentioned are all located on University Ave. or off of it just south of Genesee St. (Rt. 92) in the University section. Farther up Genesee St. is the former home of Jermain Loguen (FOC, S6), the famous stationmaster and abolitionist, now a Rite Aide store.

University United Methodist
S8, V0, 🚹🚺🧘

University United Methodist is a church that celebrates its diversity. Like the other prophetic places of worship, participants believe more in community than charity. From 1927 to 1932, Reverend Dr. Norman Vincent Peale served as minister. Housing Visions, a nonprofit organization that has helped restore and provide housing for low income people in Syracuse, was conceived at the church. Onondaga Pastoral Counseling Center (OPCC), a multi-faceted social services center also sprang from the strong social conscience of this church. Several of Syracuse's strongest peace and justice advocates are members.

All of the church is situated on a FOC (S8) with a series (3) of S8's in the back of the church close to the entrance. The series parallels Genesee Street. The vibe is neutral.

Address: 1085 East Genesee Street, Syracuse 13210
Webpage: http://uumcsyracuse.org
Telephone: 315-475-7277

Hours: Sunday Services, 10 AM Hot Topics (Contemporary Issues), 10 AM Adult Bible Study, 10 AM Sunday School, 11 AM Worship, 12:15 PM Fellowship, 12:30 Soup and Sermon Chat

References and Recommended Reading
Churches website past and present, http://uumcsyracuse.org. Conversations with congregants over the years.

Grace Episcopal Church
S3, V0, 🚻 🧘

Grace Episcopal Church has a long history of promoting social justice. Grace was one of the first Syracuse churches to racially integrate in the 1950's when it merged with St. Phillips, a primarily black church. David Pendleton Oakerhater, baptized at Grace, became the first Native American deacon in the Anglican Church in 1881. In his Cheyenne home in Oklahoma, he founded schools and missions, and continued to work among his people until his death on 31 August 1931. He was later canonized in the Anglican Church. Congregant Betty Bone Shiess was one of the first eleven women to be ordained in the Anglican Church in 1974 in Philadelphia.

Experiencing Grace Church
The sanctuary of the church rests on a Field. The highest is an S3. The vibe in the church is neutral. Most of the garden sits on a FOC (S1, S2), so you can visit and experience FOC on other days besides Sundays. The FOC ends near the sidewalk on University Ave.

Address: 819 Madison Street, Syracuse, NY 13210
Webpage: http://gracesyracuse.org
Email: gracesyracuse@gmail.com.
Telephone: 315-478-0901
Hours: Sunday Services 9:30 AM

References and Recommended Reading

Churches website past and present http://gracesyracuse.org.
Conversations with congregants over the years. I was a member of
Grace for the first years after returning to Syracuse.

Temple Society of Concord
S6, V0, 🧍🧍 🧘

Temple Concord, a
Reformed Synagogue,
was established in 1839
and is the ninth oldest
Jewish Congregation in
the USA. The temple
has a strong history of
social justice. InterFaith
Works an ecumenical
spiritual care organization that looks to build bridges between
various faith traditions and races came out of Temple Concord.

A large FOC encompasses the temple (S6), and the garden area
on the side (S2-S4.) The vibe is neutral.

There is an active program of speakers, films and cultural
events check the calendar on their webpage for more information.

Address: 910 Madison Ave., Syracuse, NY 13210
Webpage: http://www.templeconcord.org
Telephone: 315-475-9952
Fax: 315-475-9954

Hours: Shabbat Friday's 6:00 PM except for the first Friday of the month when it is held at 7:30 PM.

References and Recommended Reading
Conversations with Maggid Jim Brule

Continuing on the Prophetic Ley

Farther south, the Prophetic Spirit Line traverses the now closed (2009) St. Andrews church (124 Alden Street.) The back of the church and grounds sits on a FOC. The parishioners of this Roman Catholic were very active in peace and justice, as well as programs such as Jail Ministries and the Catholic Worker.

The Prophetic Spirit continues past where two well known activists lived; Jerry Berrigan, one of the Berrigan Brothers and Kathleen Rumpf, a well known Catholic Worker.

Unity of Syracuse
S6, V0, 🕴🕴 🧘

Unity Church in the Valley Section of Syracuse (south side) is a New Thought ministry. All of the church sits on a FOC (S6.) The vibe is neutral.

I first experienced Unity years ago when I took an Art of Living course on pranayama. I still remember to this day my herky-jerky movements as my upper body gyrated about during the group breathing that expunged the shaking that I was beginning to experience. So I have fond memories of Unity.

Unity of Syracuse is an accepting church that welcomes everyone and opens up its doors to many groups. There is a

vibrant calendar with weekly meditations, gentle yoga and more. Periodically they host well known speakers in Spirituality. If you live in Syracuse, or are visiting and looking for a place to meditate indoors on FOC, particularly in the winter, then Unity of Syracuse is the place.

Address: 300 W Seneca Turnpike, Syracuse, NY 13207
Webpage: http://www.unitysyracuse.org
Telephone: 315-492-0330
Hours: Sunday Services: Contemplative Service from 9:00-9:45 AM (quieter service), Celebration Service at 11:00 AM
*Fellowship after each service! Check the website for programs, meditation and yoga times.
Close by: Heath Park is not far away. The Zen Center of Syracuse (266 W Seneca Turnpike, zencenterofsyracuse.org, 315-492-9773) is one block away and offers several daily meditations.
Directions: From the North: I-81 south to exit 17 (Brighton Ave/S. Salina St.) Turn left at the traffic light and then go straight and turn right at the second traffic light. Turn left at the next traffic light (Salina St., Rt. 11) and continue to Seneca Tpk (Rt. 173.) Take a right onto Seneca Tpk. Unity Church will be on your right a little bit after you cross Onondaga Creek.
From the South: I-81 northbound take exit 16 (Nedrow.) Turn left onto US-11 N and continue to Seneca Tpk (Rt. 173.) Take a left onto Seneca Tpk. Unity Church will be on your right a little bit after you cross Onondaga Creek

.

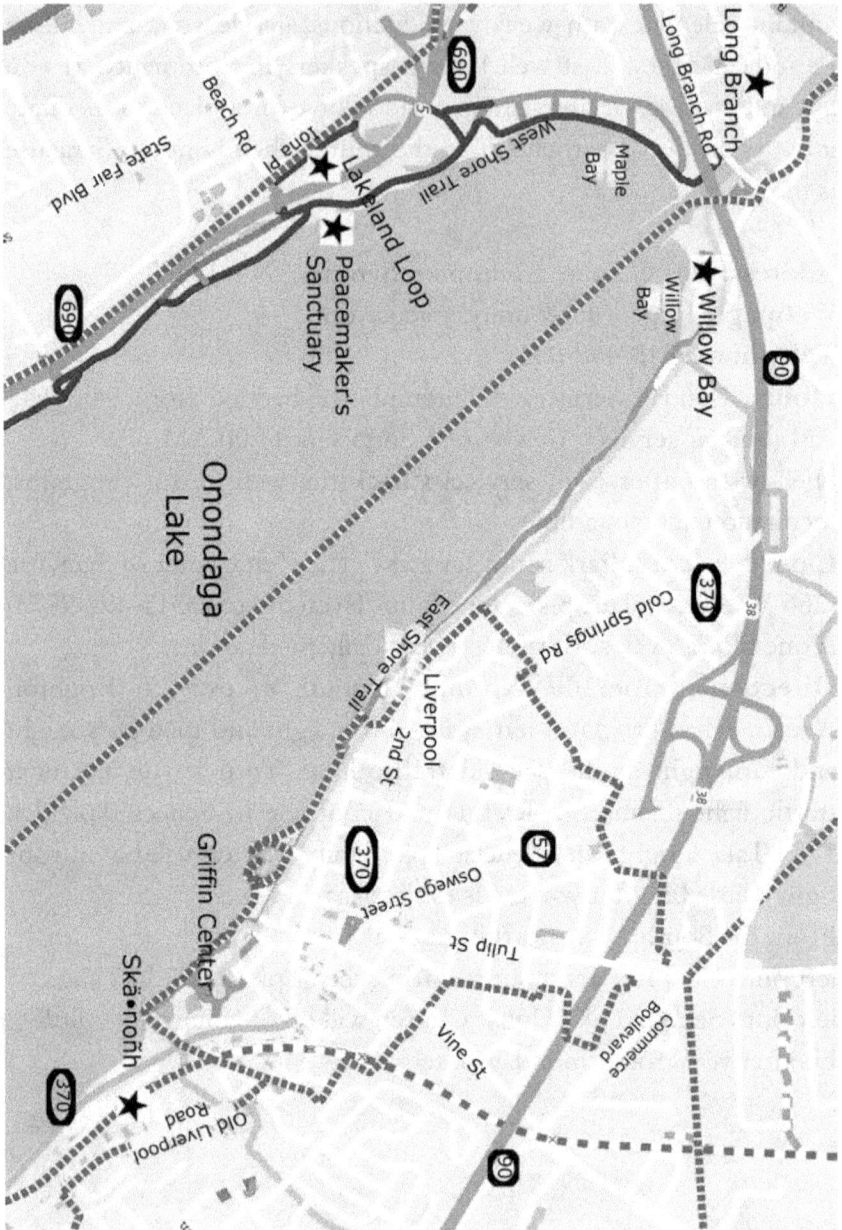

Map of Onondaga Lake. Source, © OpenStreetMap contributors, www. openstreetmap. org.

Onondaga Lake

Onondaga Lake is the heart of North Star Country and one of the holiest places in the world. It is here that the Peacemaker planted the tree of Peace and gave the Haudenosaunee The Great Law of Peace. There are numerous stacked 12's FOC around the lake.

Onondaga Lake is polluted. It was once the most polluted lake in America and even considered the most polluted lake in the world. For years Allied Chemical, which eventually became part of Honeywell, dumped industrial waste containing mercury into the lake. There were several other polluters. There are also waste beds of pollution around the lake.

This is problematic for many reasons. A polluted lake has devastating consequences for wildlife and plant life and for the ecosystem overall. Polluted water is not good for human consumption, or use. It is also disrespectful and insulting to the Onondagans and others to whom the lake is sacred.

Another problem with Onondaga Lakes' pollution is that it contaminates Spirit Lines. Hundreds, if not thousands of Spirit Lines originate from Onondaga Lake. Each one passes through the consciousness of pollution, of toxicity and of the total disregard for Mother Earth. They then carry that consciousness around the world. Is it any wonder that we have a global environmental crisis when the heart of Mother Earth's Soul instead of bearing the compassion, love and forgiveness taught by the Peacemaker, carries the consciousness of destruction and the exploitation of Mother Earth?

Honeywell began an initiative in 2005 to clean up the lake. Effort has been made to prevent the further release of pollutants into the lake and removing some of the pollutants. What toxins are not removed from the lake bottom are being capped to keep toxicity from bubbling up. Unfortunately, the caps have slid on several occasions contaminating even more of the lake. This is a partial effort that still has Spirit Lines passing through toxins and pollution.

The Onondaga Nation has always wanted the lake returned to its pristine nature and felt the Honeywell plan was inadequate. When it was reported that caps had slid on several occasions the Nation said it showed that the Honeywell plan was flawed. The Onondaga Nation has an informative webpage about Onondaga Lake, http://www.onondaganation.org/land-rights/onondaga-lake/. Please go to the How You Can Help section of the Appendix to see how you can help.

References and Recommended Reading
"Onondaga Lake—The Most Polluted Lake in America'; Onondaga Nation, People of the Hills website; http://www.onondaganation.org/land-rights/onondaga-lake/
Honeywell's cap to seal in Onondaga Lake toxins has broken loose three times" Coin, Glenn; Syracuse Post Standard, January 29, 2016,
'Onondaga Nation: Failures of Onondaga Lake cap prove Honeywell's 'cleanup' is flawed'; Coin, Glenn, Syracuse Post Standard, January 29, 2016,

Overview of Onondaga Lake
S2-12, V0-4, ▽ ☆ ♡ (♠) ⚕⚕ 🧘 🧍 ☁ 〰 ✎〜

Onondaga Lake Park surrounds much of Onondaga Lake and offers walking trails, recreational opportunities and picnic areas. There are many places to experience FOC around the lake. Not all places around the lake that have FOC are included. Some have a negative vibe and are contaminated with toxins, and others are not conducive for praying and meditating. Stick to the places listed.

The following areas around Onondaga Lake are reviewed:

Lakeland Loop Trail
Peacemaker's Sanctuary
Long Branch Park
Willow Bay
East Shore Trail
Skä•noñh – Great Law of Peace Center

Address: Main Entrance, (off of Rt. 370 (Onondaga Lake Parkway), Griffin Welcome Ctr., 106 Lake Drive, Liverpool, NY 13088
Webpage: http://www.onondagacountyparks.com/parks/onondaga -lake-park/
Email: olp@ongov.net
Telephone: 315-453-6712
Hours: April-October: 6am-sunset plus 1/2 hour. Free. November-March: 6am-sunset

The Lakeland Trail Loop
S2-10, V0-1, 🧍 〰️🍃🕊️

The Lakeland Trail beginning at the Beach Street access point provides for a nice contemplative walk in a continuous area of stacked FOC, as well as an access route to the Peacemaker's Sanctuary (a bit longer, but worth it.) There are plenty of places to stop and meditate/pray, especially if you bring a cushion with you. Because this area is not as well frequented as other parts of the park, it provides the chance for some solitude. It is also the only walk offered in this book that is totally on FOC.

When you get close to the lake you will be on the West Shore Trail that is asphalt covered. There you will run into bicyclists, skaters, runners and walkers. Unfortunately because it is much less congested than the other side of the lake, some of the bikers and skaters use it as an opportunity to let loose and accelerate. So be careful and remember pedestrians have the right of way.

You will be experiencing noise from the highway, Rt. 690, which you will constantly be close to and eventually crisscross.

Drive to Beach Street and park on the right hand side of Iona Street.

Stairway To Heaven

Cross the railroad tracks at the end of Beach Street going towards Onondaga Lake. Take the trail on your left; it is less than a minute after you cross the tracks. If you continue going straight you will cross the bridge.

Looking from the Welcome Circle at the Stairway to Heaven.

I call this first section of the trail 'Stairway to Heaven' because of the many Spirit Lines that cross its path. In 2003, before I knew about FOC I knew about and could dowse Spirit Lines. One Saturday that summer, my friend Zac Moore and a few others gathered to dowse for Spirit Lines. We found a bunch, close to a hundred traversing this first section of the Lakeland Trail if I recollect correctly.

Several of us have been doing Earth Healing on the Lakeland Trail and have been able to raise the vibe of the Stairway to Heaven to slightly positive, from neutral like the rest of the walk. I encourage you to stop along the way to perform ceremony/meditate/pray and elevate the vibe and keep it from slipping back.

Use the beginning of the trail (to the left) where it breaks off from the path to the bridge as a Welcome Circle. The Stairway to Heaven traverses through seasonal wetlands, so mosquitos can be a concern. As you continue and before the trail bends right there will be, two series (3) of S12's are on your right in the wetland woods. Numerous Spirit Lines crisscross the trail here. It is not exactly like a nest, where numerous Spirit Lines converge into a single point, or several points; It is just a mass of Spirit Lines intersecting the trail.

The trail will take a slight bend to the right towards the highway (Rt. 690) into an opening that appears to a path. The trail actually goes left. Feel free to stop and mediate at the beginning of this offshoot close to the trail. It sits on FOC (S8) and several have been meditating in this area.

As you continue, the FOC remain continuous, but drop to an S4 to S6. The trail then breaks sharply to the left, and the Fields go back into the range of S8 to S10.

The trail will begin to bend to the right as it approaches the Rt. 690 underpass. At about 150 feet from the underpass on the left hand side of the trail is a series (3) of S12's. The series begins 20 feet after a herd path into the woods on your left. It is about 120 to 130 feet from the underpass—tack on another 30 feet for the last in the series.

Find a place you like and sit down and meditate. Very nice. It will be noisy but you will not have many people walk, or run by while you are there.

After I felt called to get people to pray around Onondaga Lake, I would regularly go for contemplative walks on the West Shore and Lakeland Trails. It was in this area that my legs would often buckle, a sign that it was a holy and sacred space.

Twenty feet from the herd path into the woods my backpack rests on the first in a series (3) of S12's hugging the left side of the trail going towards the underpass.

West Shore Trail

Continue on the trail and walk through the underpass tunnel. You will come to a fork in the trail. Bear to the right. If you take the trail on the left, the FOC will end in less than 50 feet. Going right the FOC remain continuous, but drop to a range of S4 to S6.

The trail will end in a few hundred feet when it intersects the asphalt West Shore trail that follows the shoreline. Take a right and continue. If you go left, the Fields end in about 30-40 feet.

You are walking on FOC in a range of S4 to S6. They will pick up to a S6 to S8 after you cross a culvert with black handrails. Shortly you will see a clearing and a bench on your left side. The bench is dedicated to Lowell. C. Peckman. You may wish to stop and meditate here.

As you continue, the Fields will increase to a range of S8 to S10. In a few hundred feet there will be a grassy area on your left, you are getting close to the Peacemaker's Sanctuary. As the trail begins to bend towards the right, look for a path with slight opening going towards the water on your left with a bench on it. If you face the lake you will see a water duct to your right. This is the Peacemaker's Sanctuary. Spend some time here. Notice the difference in the vibe, it is very positive to extremely positive. Very, very nice.

Continue on the trail. In about 300 feet there is a fork in the trail. The asphalt trail turns left and a gravel path continues straight ahead. Continue straight on the gravel path. Take a right and walk across the bridge over Rt. 690. Shortly you will be back where you started.

Again use the beginning of the Stairway to Heaven section of the trail as a Welcome Circle. Give thanks and say a few prayers.

Directions: Exit Rt. 690 for Lakeland/State Fair Blvd. Take State Fair Blvd towards Syracuse/Lakeland. Take a left onto Beach St. across from Empower Federal Credit. Take a left and park on Iona Place.

Peacemaker's Sanctuary
S6-12, V3-4, ▽ ☆ ♡ ⚥ ⳤ ♨ ♨♨ ✐♡

The Peacemaker's Sanctuary at Onondaga Lake is one of the places I come to in search of answers. Powerful imprints formed long ago still cling to the land that can spiritually heal you, answer your prayers, give you insights, or provide mystical experiences. God once answered my prayers there about ending violence in the city of Syracuse. I mention this not to draw attention to me, but rather to a wonderful place that can help heal your and the world.

The Peacemaker's Sanctuary is the only place with a positive vibe on Onondaga Lake. Its imprints are the strongest of any

207

other sacred site in this book; not the vibe, per se, but something of a higher order between the vibe and the archetypes, that Jung says are embedded in the land. Years ago, a vortex formed to the right of the bench. Its embers in the form of vortex ring remain. I now realize that our efforts only rekindled an old flame, one of several vortices that blazed in this little Shangri-La. There is a vortex behind the bench and to the left as you face the lake.

The Peacemaker's Sanctuary would be an excellent place to try and sense and feel Consciousness; particularly in the vortex, or vortex ring.

Where My Prayers Were Once Answered

When I left Wall Street and returned to Syracuse in the fall of 2000, the level of violence in the city immediately struck me. I prayed and prayed asking God for guidance. In the fall of 2002, God answered my prayers and encouraged me to organize a prayer vigil in the area on the West Shore Trail that is now called the Peacemaker's Sanctuary. At the time, I had limited knowledge of sacred space and was questioning why this place?

On November 29, 2002, the Friday after Thanksgiving, twenty-five of us gathered for a prayer vigil and ceremony. After the ceremony I would continue to pray at the Peacemaker's Sanctuary every day for several months, except Christmas day when we received a foot of snow.

There were no murders in Syracuse until January 19, 2003. This was one of the longest periods in recent years without a murder in the city (November 14, 2002 was the last murder to January 19, 2003). For two months there were no murders in Syracuse after it had been averaging almost one every two weeks, even during the winter. The Syracuse Post Standard called 2002 "one of the bloodiest years ever in the county, with a record 25 filed in Syracuse alone."

For years, murders in Syracuse fell until 2008 when there were again 25. Unfortunately a new record was set in 2016.

While my prayers were answered many factors contributed to the decline from the efforts of the Syracuse Police Department, to groups such as Mother's Against Gun Violence and ACTS (Alliance of Communities Transforming Syracuse.)

I have had several spiritual insights and mystical experiences here.

Winter 2015/16, the spirit rekindled. The old wooden bench has been moved to the right and replaced with a newer bench made out of a composite material. The placard on the bench has the words "Peacemaker's Sanctuary" inscribed on it.

Experiencing the Peacemaker's Sanctuary

What this place will look like when you arrive can be dramatically different; in that there could be several more benches and the area may have a different look. I say this because the original bench was removed and the area became overrun. Fortunately, the Onondaga County Parks people put a bench back. We cleaned up the area and began meditating there. Then thanks to a generous donation we were able to add another bench, with a placard titled

"Peacemaker's Sanctuary." We are on a waiting list to add more benches.

When looking to relocate moving the old bench to a new area we found a FOC with an S12; not only that, but it had a positive vibe compared to neutral in the immediate area. The positive vibe was a clear indication that spiritual practices had gone on there. Then as we began meditating on the old bench in the new location we found other little pockets of a positive vibe.

With your back to the lake the chair marks the location of the vortex. The vortex ring is located in the lower left in front of and to the left of the plants.

These finds are a positive indication that this was once a very large holy area and helps explain why God led me to do a prayer ceremony here years ago. I surmise that these positive pockets may once have been where vortices once were, and that their strength has diminished over time from all the negativity and pollution heaped on Onondaga Lake and its environs. I expect that many of these areas will blossom into vortices. Again, when you visit there may be may be more benches, many more vortices, a thin veil to the other side and much, much more.

All of the Peacemaker's Sanctuary is situated on FOC (S6 to S12.) The vibe at the time of this writing runs from very positive to extremely positive. Find a place to sit down, whether it is a bench, seat cushion, or portable chair that you brought with you.

There are two paths, or entryways, off of the West Shore Trail you can use to access the sanctuary. Use either one as a Welcome Circle; preferably the area just before they flatten out.

This would be a great place for any type of spiritual practice; a ritual such as a water ceremony, meditation, or pray for others; or for a peaceful and loving world, or Mother Earth's need. Give Thanks. Dream, ask for guidance; this is a very holy and powerful place that is capable of much.

Make sure, I repeat make sure to quiet your mind part of the time and listen, because you may be told some wonderful things. Very old and powerful imprints are embedded in the land here and they can speak to you at times. Come with the purest of heart and the best of intentions and you will not be disappointed.

Directions: See the Lakeland Trail directions on how to get to Iona Streets. Walk across the railroad tracks. Shortly, the Lakeland Trail will break off to your left. Please treat the beginning of the Lakeland Trail as a Welcome Circle; as well as the area of two paths connecting the Sanctuary to the West Shore Trail.

You can follow the Lakeland Loop Trail, or bear right and cross the bridge. Take a left onto the gravel path. It will quickly merge with an asphalt path, the West Shore Trail. Continue in the same direction you were walking. The Peacemaker's Sanctuary is 200 to 300 feet ahead on your right. Look for a clearing, a bench and a water duct to the right of the bench. The words "Peacemaker's Sanctuary" will be on one of the benches.

Events: We hold events at the Peacemaker's Sanctuary so check my blog for listings, http:// motherearthprayers. blogspot.com

Long Branch Park
S4-8, V0-1, 🧍‍♂️🧍‍♂️ 🧍 ☁ 〰 ✒🕊

Long Branch Park is where people rent pavilions to hold major events. It also has FOC and two sacred mounds; ones that I believe may have been built by the Adena mound builders. They do not have the same electrified air as other places areas with sacred mounds such as High Tor. (See High Tor for a more detailed discussion.)

Experiencing Long Branch

The FOC are located near the parking lot fence at the far end away from the Seneca River, near the entrance. At the far corner of the parking lot where you enter to get to the mounds, there is a fence that intersects the fence you enter. Close by on that fence you will see a large gate. Facing the gate the FOC extend from the far right post for about 50 feet with a depth of 40 feet.

The two sacred mounds, or hills are located near the parking lot near the entrance. I have not been able to determine the origin of the mounds. I have heard they are natural formations, or that they are leftover sediment from the dredging of the nearby Seneca River, etc.; but I believe otherwise.

The first mound is close to the entryway and parking area. It is clearly a small hill and people sled down it during the winter. The other mound is behind it to the north and west. It looks more like a rise than a mound or hill. There are two pavilions and a restroom on top of it.

What is clear is that they both cover Earth Chakras, which is nothing special in itself. What is special is that the Earth Chakras surround the periphery of both mounds. In other words, if one where to construct two mounds that covered two areas of Earth Chakras that is what the structures would look like. It should be noted that there are no other Earth Chakras located within a half a mile of the two mounds.

The mound closest to the parking area.

The slightly positive vibe is a good indication that the mounds were once sacred. The vibe around the lake runs from neutral to awful, with some areas with severe geopathic stress; the only exception being he Peacemaker's Sanctuary. So there is something special to the mounds.

To say that they are Adena Ceremonial Mounds is a big leap of faith. I say that the mounds are Adena Ceremonial Mounds because I have found the same pattern of covered Earth Chakras at Serpent Mound (Peebles, Ohio); recognized as an Adena Ceremonial Site. High Tor, another sacred site listed, has several covered Earth Chakras as well. Covering Earth Chakras electrifies the atmosphere, although it is negligible here. Again I am making gross assumptions

Spend some time on the mounds. Spread some tobacco. Honor it with a ceremony, or some prayers. Meditate on it and see if you can feel the energy.

Address: 3813 Long Branch Road.
Telephone: 315-453-6712
Hours: Call to make sure no events are going on when you visit.

Directions: From Rt. 690 take the John Glenn Blvd. exit. Continue to first traffic light, Long Branch Rd. and take a right. The park will be on your left before the bridge.

Willow Bay
S6-12, V0, ⚥ 🚶 ♒ 🪶

In 2003, Chief Jake Swamp (Mohawk) of the Tree of Peace Society led a tree planting ceremony in Willow Bay near the mouth of the Seneca River, Unfortunately the tree died as did two other white pines we replaced it with.

Looking Syracuse. The dogs mark one of the series (3) of S12's. Meditating anywhere around here would have you in the FOC.

Much of Willow Bay rests on FOC, particularly as you head towards Salt Museum. There are several series (3) of S12's in the Willow Bay area.

From the public restroom walk directly towards the lake. As you get close to the lake look for a barbecue grill, the first of several. Between the grill and the lake begins a series (6) of S12's

214

that runs parallel to the lake; as the series ends, another series (3) of S12's breaks at about 30° away from the lake. Even you cannot find the highpoints, the FOC in the area is very powerful. So pick a place you like and sit down.

Address: 3813 Long Branch Rd, Liverpool, NY 13090
Directions: See directions for Long Branch—continue over bridge, entrance will be on your right.
Events: NOON (Neighbors of the Onondaga Nation) hold a Thanksgiving Day gathering. See www. peacecouncil. net /noon.

East Shore Trail
S4-8, V0, 👫 🚶 〰️ 🪶

The East Shore Trail extends from the Salt Museum to Willow Bay. There is a sidewalk as well as a road that is marked for roller skaters and bikes. This side of the lake gets much more use than the other side, so there will be people around most of the time. Lots of people walk this route. Most of this 1 ½ to 2 mile walk is on FOC that are almost continuous from about the Marina to Willow Bay. Begin in Willow Bay, or by the Griffin Visitor Center.

Skä·noñh – Great Law of Peace Center

The Peace center is a Haudenosaunee Heritage site that tells the story of Nature and Native People, told through the lens of the Onondagans.

Address: 6680 Onondaga Lake Parkway, Liverpool, New York 13088
Webpage: http://www.skanonhcenter.org
Telephone: 315-453-6767
Hours: Wed. to Fri. 10 AM to 4 PM, Sat & Sun. 11 AM to 4 PM. Adults, $5; Sr.'s (+62) & Students, $4, Children under 10, Free.

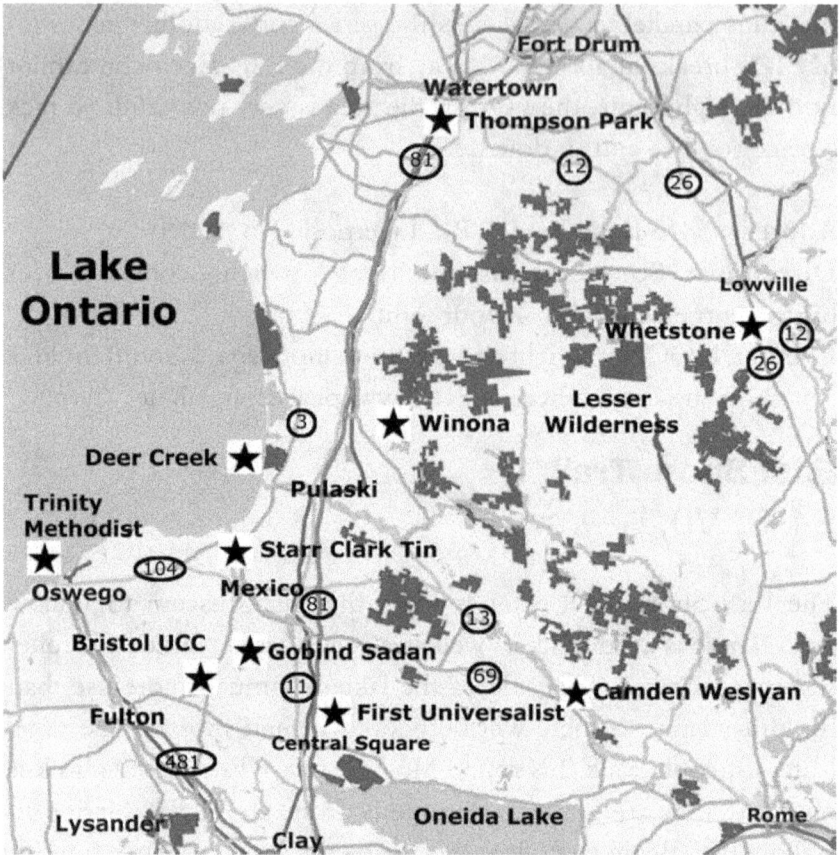

Map of the North Country. Source-© OpenStreetMap contributors, www. openstreetmap. org

North Country/Lesser Wilderness

The area west of the Adirondacks, 30 miles north of Syracuse to Watertown, is known for its snowy winters produced by the lake effect snow from Lake Ontario to the west. Producing some of the best cross country skiing in the east (Winona State Forest, reviewed in this section.) Parts are also called the Lesser Wilderness, after the Adirondacks, the Great Wilderness. It contains several gulfs, canyons produced by retreating glaciers.

It is here that Charles Grandison Finney, the great Congregational/Presbyterian minister, had his epiphany. He walked into the woods as a lawyer one evening and was called to work for God; he never returned to his office the next day. Instead he became a leading figure, if not the leading one in ushering in America's Second Great Awakening. He coined the term 'The Burned-over District.

Oswego was a force in the Underground Railroad primarily because of its location on Lake Ontario and its many abolitionists; Orson Ames, Asa Wing, James C. Jackson, Edwin Clarke and African American community leader Tudor E. Grant[1].

It is here that the Great Sikh spiritual leader Babaji gave his devotee Ralph Singh instructions from India exactly where to find a farm for sale, a place he called "one of the Holiest places in the world."

You can access a map of Oswego County's Underground Railroad driving tour at http://visitoswegocounty.com/wp-content/uploads/UGRR.pdf

References and Recommended Reading
1. Sernett, Milton C., *North Star Country, Upstate New York and The Crusade for African American Freedom*, Pages 173-174.

Camden, NY, Oneida County

Camden Wesleyan Church
S6, V0, 👫 🧘

Camden Wesleyan moved to its location in August of 2015 replacing Camden Presbyterian. It traces its roots back to 1842 when it began as the Wesleyan Methodist Abolitionist church.

A FOC (S6) runs from in front of the church near the Y in the sidewalk, slightly to the left, to back of the church. The first in a series (3) of S6's begins by the tree on the left hand side closest to the church, about a few feet toward the church. The remaining two break towards the church; the next is on the left hand side, in the church by the wall. The remaining one is a little left of center in the back of the sanctuary. The vibe is neutral.

Address: 101 Main St, Camden, NY 13316
Webpage: Facebook, https://www.facebook.com/Camden-Wesleyan-Church-179056002110251/
Telephone: 315-245-1987
Hours: Sunday Services at 8 AM and 10:15 AM
Directions: Take Rt. 69 out of Rome, NY. The church is at the intersection of Rt. 69 and Main St (Rt. 13.)

References and Recommended Reading
Devincenzo, Jen; 'Wesleyan Church marks 'historic change' in Camden's 'Spiritual Landscape'; Wesleyan Church website; https://www.wesleyan.org/4167/wesleyan-church-marks-historic-change-in-camdens-spiritual-landscape

218

Central Square, NY, Oswego County

The First Universalist Society of Central Square
S8, V0-1, 🚻 🧘

The church whose doctrine is love has a friendly and homey feel to it. It has been a strong advocate for the LGBT (Lesbian, Gay, Bisexual, Transgender) community and workers rights. It sits on a FOC (S8) with a neutral, to slightly positive vibe. We have held group meditations here and will continue, so I expect the vibe to improve.

Experiencing First Universalist Central Square

All of the church rests on FOC. A series (3) of S8's begin in the front of the church and the remaining two are in the sanctuary. Facing the front of the sanctuary they are at the end of the pews on the right side near the center aisle. One is by pews 2/3 and the other 8/9 counting from the front. You cannot go wrong sitting anywhere in the sanctuary because at its lowest it is an S4. The vibe is neutral to slightly positive.

Address: 3243 Fulton Ave. Mailing address, P.O. Box 429, Central Square, NY 13036. The church is located at the southwest corner of Routes 49 & 11 on Fulton Ave in Central Square.
Webpage: http://centralsquareuu.com
Email: andreaabbottuu @gmail.com
Telephone: 315-307-3400
Hours: Sunday Services 10:30 AM

Directions: Take exit 32 off of I-81 north of Syracuse. Turn west onto Rt.49 (East Ave.) towards Central Square. The church will be on your left after you cross Main St.

References and Recommended Reading
Churches Website: http://centralsquareuu.com
Conversations with congregant Tim Hart, husband of the former minister.

Gobind Sadan
S6-12, V3-4, ▽ ☆ ♡ ⬆ 𝑖 ⤸

Gobind Sadan is the USA headquarters for Baba Virsa Singh Ji, a Sikh mystic, who was fondly called "Babaji" by his devotees. He said Gobind Sadan (Central Square, NY) was "one of the holiest places in the world."

There are many mystical and magical stories surrounding this wonderful place, a few of which I will share with you. Its founder and leader Ralph Singh is well known in Central New York and across America for his educational work to break religious barriers and to educate children.

There are numerous FOC and vortices on this 270 acre property. The vibe is incredible, running from very positive to extremely positive. This is a great place, one of the best places, to try and experience and sense consciousness. Please call 315-676-2308 before visiting; leave a message if no one answers and come.

History
Babaji is noted for celebrating everyone's religions, saying all prophets come from the same place. His spiritual quest began at an early age. While helping on his family farm one day, he cut a plant and was overcome by the sight of the green sap oozing from it. He prayed for forgiveness and asked to be absolved from having to do such harmful work. He began meditating day and

220

night. Soon he developed healing powers and followed God's request and began visiting villages as a healer and teaching the eternal truths.

Here are a few of the mystical and miraculous stories surrounding Gobind Sadan (more can be found on their webpage.)

How Ralph Singh, founder of Gobind Sadan USA, met Babaji is a story in itself. It begins with Ralph sharing a cup of tea with a friend in his NYC apartment in August of 1970. To hear Ralph tell the story, "in a blink of an eye, the room suddenly vanished and there in front of him stood a great spiritual being with a diamond like light shining from his head and his eyes held the universe. He held up his hand and said, "don't be afraid.""

After that life changing experience, Ralph planned his quest. He flew to Europe, and traveled overland to India to be with the Tibetans in Dharamsala, but felt called by a 'different 'voice.' Arriving in Delhi in February 1971, he was brought face to face with the great being who had appeared to him in NY. It was the great Sikh saint, Baba Virsa Singh Ji.

Ralph adopted Sikhism and became Babaji's first foreign devotee and moved into the ashram. Five years later in 1976 it was time to return to the States as Babaji's representative in America; by then he was married to Joginder, a fellow devotee.

Before leaving for India, Babaji instructed Ralph and Joginder, to buy a farm north of Syracuse. Babaji simply said: "There is a widow 40 miles Northwest of you that wants to sell her farm, find her and buy it," and added that a real estate agent would help. Joginder visited many farms, but none fit the description.

With winter setting in she took a break. They were both sitting home in February when a call came from the realtor: "I have a client who is selling a farm and I understand you are interested." Neither of them had heard of this person. When Ralph asked the location, Hastings/Palermo (approx. 40 miles NW) and the seller was a widow, they drove up the next day, met the owner, walked

221

the land, and signed a purchase offer that evening. They called Babaji in India, who confirmed.

In the aftermath of 9/11 there was much hatred for Muslims and people that wore similar clothes such as Sikhs with turbans. A few high school students decided to set fire to Gobind Sadan; they said they thought the name of Babaji's retreat was "Go Bin Laden" not "Gobind Sadan." While battling the fire on the second floor of the temple a firemen heard a voice tell him to leave; he did and a few minutes later the floor collapsed. Everything in the ashram was burned except the religious texts.

The two backpacks mark the vortices on the wooden deck where the temple once stood.

The youth were caught. Ralph offered forgiveness and asked they be given leniency. He used the horrible and violent act to educate and build bridges between various people within the surrounding community. This touching and moving story was documented in a film 'North of 49.' So named because locals say that the lake effect snow bands from Lake Ontario are much stronger north of route 49.

Initially after the farm was purchased, the Gobind Sadan grounds were farmed for several years before they were allowed to go fallow and return to their original state. A new temple was constructed to replace the original one that was burned down. A concrete slab was placed over the foundation of the old temple, and a Sikh flag has been erected on the spot where the scriptures had survived.

The Old Temple
S6-8, V3-4, ▽ ☆ ♡ (⬆) ⚡ ♌

A wooden deck with handrails marks where the old temple used to be, located on the right hand side as you enter. It is directly across from the new temple. The FOC on the deck run from S6 to S8. The vibe is extremely positive.

Please use the area of the wooden platform closest to the concrete floor as a Welcome Circle. You may wish to give thanks for being here and for the positive intentions and prayers of those who were here before.

While at Gobind Sadan, consider asking for guidance and be open to hear the voice of God, as many have experienced it here. In other words make sure to quiet your mind at times so that you may hear. You may also wish to meditate on forgiveness, or give it, or ask for it. Forgiveness is a powerful part of the Gobind Sadan community. As Babaji said, "By forgiving our enemies we have the opportunity to create peace."

There are two vortices on the deck, both of which are made up of the consciousness emanating from the FOC there. As such they have a much higher consciousness component. They are about 4 to 5 feet in diameter and are very strong.

While on the deck, face the handrails. One vortex is slightly to the right of the third handrail from the left; to find its center count 17 planks of wood from the handrail. The other is slightly to the right of the fourth, or middle handrail. To find its center, count 22 planks. Because each respective vortex has a diameter of 4 to 5 feet it covers a large area, so even if you are not spot on, as long as you are within a few feet you will be in it. They will nourish your soul with a powerful dose of Consciousness and are a great place to try and experience and sense Consciousness. It was while meditating within a vortex in a FOC that I first sensed, or felt Consciousness. It was the increased dose of Consciousness from the vortex that made it easier for me to sense it.

Meditation Center: I strongly encourage you to attend an event at Gobind Sadan when the meditation center (a series (3) of S12's) is open. It has an extremely positive vibe, a vortex and powerful imprints that will uplift you and improve your meditative ability! Incense heaped on the sacred fire permeates the air.

Heaven's Gate
S6-12, V3-4, ▽ ☆ ♡ (⋔) 🧍 🕊

Much of the grounds of Gobind Sadan are situated on FOC. But since the property is in the process of returning to its natural form, parts of it are thick with growth and have not matured into older forests yet, limiting accessibility. There is however a very nice stand of trees towards the back of the property that is divine and easy to get to. We call it Heaven's Gate because it has a divine feel to it and can make your hair stand on end. The vibe is extremely positive.

Follow the driveways trajectory as you entered, past the old white barn with a red roof that has been converted to a museum. Continue straight on the dirt road. In about 250 yards you will see a pond on your left. Continue another 200-230 yards, a dirt road will enter from your left and merge with the one you are walking on. In about another 100-150 feet you will be entering Heaven's Gate; it begins about 50 feet before a path to your right.

You are now in a very large continuous area of FOC with lots of divine aspects. The wall to your left (about 50 feet) marks one boundary. The Fields continue for another 250 feet ahead of you. The path to the right has continuous FOC for another 400 to 500 feet.

You may wish to use the area where the trail branches to your left as a Welcome Circle; say a prayer, smudge yourself and ask for guidance from the divine.

Anyplace in-between the stonewall on your left and the dirt road, would be a good place to meditate, or pray. Within it is a series (3) of S10's. Look for a large dying old maple tree on your left; it has only a few leaves remaining on top of it. Walk 30 to 40 feet straight ahead. Then turn left and walk perpendicular to the road and look for two stones together that break back at an angle towards the stone wall and the dying tree. The last in the series is right next to the wall.

Jaeda (black dog) sits next to a large stone marking the first in a series (3) of S10's that break towards a multi-limbed maple tree. Pepper (white dog) sits next to stone marking the next S10.

Take the path to the right. Your left side is on large FOC (S10). A series (3) of S10's are 50 feet ahead to the left. Look for a very large maple tree with numerous branches on your left. The series breaks at about 60° to the tree; stones mark the series. See the picture on the previous page.

If you continue on the dirt road you will be walking in a FOC. Up ahead is an S12; 100 to 150 feet, or 150-200 feet from where the path began. Look for a stonewall. A series (3) of S12's breaks from the dirt road towards the stonewall. The first in the series is about 12-15 feet ahead of the stone wall close to the path, a large stone marks it. The next is 15 feet further at 50° towards the stone wall. The remaining S12 is on the other side of the stone wall. In the picture below backpacks mark two in the series.

The Fields continue for another 250 to 300 feet, although most of it is covered with thick weeds and dense growth.

It has an enchanted and very peaceful sense to it. Pick any place to meditate in the woods within the boundaries mentioned and you will be pleased. Look for flat stones on the ground that mark sweet spots. Most will have powerful imprints on them that will help your meditation. Some of the stones will be on higher aspects of FOC, so make sure a spot, or stone appeals to you. Do not remove stones from the stonewalls, or place stones on the ground as you please.

Heaven's Gate has a powerful sense of peace to it. It would be an excellent place to try and sense and feel Consciousness. It would also be a good place to meditate on peace, or focus on the mystical.

I expect that several vortices will shortly appear in Heaven's Gate. Before you leave, please return to the Welcome Circle area at the head of the path and say "thanks." We plan on putting in a donation box so look for one towards the front near one of the buildings.

Address: 105 Graves Road, Central Square, NY 13036
Webpage: http://www.gobindsadan.org
Email: gobindsadanusa@aol.com
Telephone: 315-668-9155
Hours: Please call 315-676-2308 before visiting to announce that you are coming; if no one answers leave a message to indicate that you will be coming. Please announce yourself upon arriving.
Directions: Take I-81 to exit 32 (Rt. 49/Central Square.) Turn west onto Rt. 49 to Central Square. Follow Rt. 49 to Rt. 11 and turn right. Follow Rt. 11 to Rt. 45 (Hastings-flashing yellow light) and turn left. Follow Rt. 45 for 2.8 miles to Graves Road (double road sign on left). Turn left on Graves Road for a short distance to Gobind Sadan.

References and Recommended Reading
Gobind Sadan's webpage, http://www.gobindsadan.org.
'North of 49' [videorecording] / W & P Productions presents a film by Richard Breyer and David Coryell.
Singh, Ralph; *A Path to Follow a Life to Lead: Reflections of a Student At Gobind Sadan*, Sterling Ltd. 2008.
Conversations with Ralph Singh over the years.
Wisdom thinkers webpage, http://www.wisdomthinkers.org.

Fulton/Volney, Oswego County, NY

Bristol Hill United Church of Christ
S3, V0, 👥 🧘 🚂

A church forged by blacks and whites in 1812. It was a stop on the Underground Railroad that is a nationally registered historic place, as well as listed on the National Parks Underground Railroad network.

All of the sanctuary rests on a FOC. As you face the church, a series (3) S3's begin outside by the signpost on the left hand side and cut diagonally across the back of the church.

Address: 3199 State Rt. 3, Fulton, NY 13069-4402

Webpage: www. ucc.org- see the directory, no church website

Telephone: Call the New York conference for more information and contact information, 315-446-3073

Hours: Sunday Services 10:15 AM

Directions: Rt. 481 north of Syracuse will turn into 4th St. and then into 2nd St. in Fulton. Take a right onto County Rd. 3 in Fulton, in a few miles the church will be on the left.

References and Recommended Reading
Churches website, http://www.bristolhillucc.com.
"Bristol Hill Church Beckoned to both blacks, whites", Mike McAndrew. Syracuse Post Standard, February 21, 2005

Lowville, Lewis County, NY

Whetstone Gulf State Park
S5, VO 2

Whetstone Gulf provides an opportunity to experience upstate NY's unique topography, a gulf (deep gorge), and a precious piece of Mother Earth's Soul. If you are looking for a hike with spectacular views along a rim trail with a Grand Canyon like feel with a stand of pines in which to experience FOC (S5), then Whetstone is for you.

Rim Trail

Whetstone Gulf is a 2,100-acre New York State Park with numerous campsites, a picnic area, a manmade swimming area and a creek at its basin. The north and south rim trails both begin from the basin and connect at the far end of the park making a 5 to 6 mile loop (trail.)

The rim trail affords spectacular views of the gulf below. At times, you will be walking precariously close to the canyon of several hundred feet. While the trail is well worn, you will find roots, wet areas and streams to cross that can add to the suspense. Caution is urged. Trees will block your view at times and you will be right at the edge.

Should you decide to take the rim trail to get to the sacred area it is located at the northwest end of the park, not too far from the midpoint where the trails intersect. It is in a large stand of pine trees. You will see a trail/opening to the north, which if you follow, will bring you to a large windmill.

North Rim's Sacred Site

If you are not going to hike to the rim trail to sacred area where the FOC are located take Corrigan Hill Road (dirt road), off West Rd (Rt. 29) out of Martinsburg just south of Lowville. A few miles in you will find a field of large windmills on your right hand side. Look for the pine woods on your left. You will see a trail going in with signs warning ATV's not to enter.

You are less than 100 yards from the rim. You will be walking south. The FOC is located on the right hand side; the center of which is located close to the rim trail. The highpoint is a series (3) of S5's, whose center is a few feet from an indentation of the gulf and extends 40-50 feet from the edge.

You will experience foot traffic in this area; both from hikers and ATV riders who hike in from the road. The views are spectacular. The vibe is neutral.

The white paper marks the center of the FOC near the edge of the cliff.

Address: 6065 West Rd., Lowville, NY 13367
Webpage: http://nysparks.com/parks/92/details.aspx
Telephone: 315-376-6630
Hours: The hours vary from season to season, generally the park is open from around Memorial Day weekend to around Labor

Day. The swimming area has a shorter season. Admission is $7. The park is open in the winter from December 15 to March 15. You are on your own if you enter by Corrigan Road.

Directions: Whetstone is located between Boonville and Lowville (just south of); West Rd. (Rt. 29) off of Rt. 26.

Mexico, Oswego County, NY

Starr Clark Tin Shop
S6, V1, 🚹🚻 ♿

Starr Clark and Harriet Loomis Clark were abolitionists whose business, the Tin Shop, and residence served as a station stop on the Underground Railroad. Because their Mexico, NY shop marked the intersection of three UGRR routes it served as a valuable asset for the UGRR. Clark organized the first antislavery society in Mexico.

The shop sits on a FOC (S6.) The vibe is slightly positive.

Address: 3250 Main Street, Mexico, NY
Webpage: https:// www. nps. gov/nr/travel/underground/ Starr_Clark_Tinshop.html
Telephone: 315-963-7868.
Hours: Fri, 4 PM to 7 PM, Sat 10AM to 1 PM.
Directions: I-81 exit 34 onto Rt. 104 going west, which will turn into Main St. The tin shop will be on your right.

Oswego, Oswego County, NY

Nestled on Lake Ontario, Oswego is considered the port city of Central New York. There are numerous FOC located throughout the city. Oswego was a strongly abolitionist city and it played a prominent role in Underground Railroad. The library sits on a Field (S4) and was a stop on the Underground Railroad.

In 1944 Oswego was the home to 982 Europeans, mostly Jews, escaping Nazism. To learn more you can visit the Safe Haven Holocaust Refugee Shelter Museum (http://safehavenmuseum.com) at 2 East Seventh Street.

Trinity Methodist Church
S7, V0-1, 👫 🧘

John Edwards, Gerrit Smith's business manager, was a member of Trinity Methodist. He assisted Freedom Seekers from Smith's Peterboro estate find passage to Canada, or helped them find employment in the area. The churches assistance today is focused on poverty and hunger.

The church sits a FOC (S7.) The vibe is neutral to slightly positive.

Experiencing the Sanctuary

All of the Sanctuary rests on a FOC that extends outside of the church. A series (3) of S7's runs from the center of the church to the outside. One of the S7's is found in the aisle around pew 63 and 64. Another is located on the left side of aisles 118 and 119. The vibe is neutral to slightly positive.

When I have taken pictures of the sanctuary I have seen orbs in them on several occasions. The first time in 2010/2011, several pictures contained smaller orbs. Unfortunately when I saved the pictures I reduced the resolution, thus making them unacceptable for a book. Then in 2015 I saw a large orb in my camera lens and thought it was dirt and did not snap the picture and instead wiped my lens. When I snapped the picture the orb was gone.

Address: 45 E Utica St Oswego, NY 13126-2617
Webpage: http://www.unyumc.org/resources/church/oswego-trinity-umc
Email: OswegotrinityUMC@gmail.com
Telephone: 315-343-1715
Hours: Sunday Services at 11AM.
Directions: Take 481 to Oswego. It will turn into East River Rd and then into East 1st St. In town take a right onto Utica Ave Utica Ave is just after East Albany St. and cross bridge.

Lacona, Oswego County, NY

Winona State Forest
S6, V0,

Winona is noted for its cross country skiing. Getting over 250 inches of snow annually, it is one of the snowiest places east of the Rockies. In 1980 New York State DEC officials and cross country skiing enthusiasts met to discuss creating a trail system through this 9,223 acre preserve.

Whether you are looking to hike, cross country ski or snowshoe, there are several FOC located in Winona State Forest. The most accessible can be found on the Bills Belly trail off of Wart Road close to the parking area of Wart Road, and Cty Rd 13.

Experiencing Winona

It is less than 100 yards from the Trailhead off of Wart Road to the FOC. The trail will turn right, rise and slightly dip and turn right. A series (3) of S6's are located on the right side of the trail. As a marker, the FOC begins about 30-40 feet before the series where there are no trees immediately to the right of the trail. The series begin with the trees. Also, just before the series there will be a dirt mound on your right; it is the remnants of the root system of a fallen tree. The series ends when you see tree stumps on the right. The FOC extends about 40 feet on either side of the series.

Looking back at the trailhead. An "X" marks the top of the trail before it descends. The dogs and paper mark the series.

Address: Lacona, NY 13803
Webpage: Winona NYS DEC
http://www.dec.ny.gov/lands/8072.html; Winona Forest

Recreation Association (cross country skiing)
http://www.winonaforest.com.
Email: DEC Region 6 Lowville Office:
information.r6@dec.ny.gov.
Telephone: DEC Region 6 Lowville Office: 315-376-3521
Hours: Open all year dawn to dusk. Free.
Directions: Take I-81 to the Sandy Creek, Exit #37. Go east on
Salisbury Rd. to the T and turn left onto Ridge Rd. (Cty. Rt.
22.) Make the next right onto Center Rd. Go a few miles and turn
left onto Wart Rd.

Pulaski, Oswego County, NY

Deer Creek Marsh
S3-6, V1, ≋

Deer Creek Wildlife Refuge on the eastern shore of Lake Ontario
offers a unique opportunity to connect with Mother Earth's Soul,
and at the same time experience the beauty of Lake Ontario. If
you are a water person looking for a seaside location to meditate,
or just gaze upon the western sunset in a FOC, this is the place. It
is close to the city of Oswego, whose sunset is rated one of the
best in the world.

The Refuge
Deer Creek consists of 1,195 acres on the eastern shore of Lake
Ontario. It has almost a mile of beachfront (mostly Lake Ontario
stones), sand dunes, a bird sanctuary, an estuary and lots of
woods. In 1979, the state of NY implemented the right of
imminent domain to rescue this land to protect the sand dunes
and provide a sanctuary for birds.

This is a wildlife refuge; there are no facilities on the grounds,
no place to barbecue, no place to pitch a tent, no place to start a
fire, no place to play ball. It is a place to take in Mother Nature.

Experiencing Deer Creek

Bear right as you leave the Rainbow Shores parking lot. You will not have to go more than 100 feet before you will be in a FOC (S3) in the area of where the path forks.

Continue bearing right; there is a small knoll just before you descend to the beach. Any of the beach area located from where you entered to 20 feet to the north (right) and 70 feet to the south (left) is part of the FOC (S6), as is the land behind it (up to and around the general area where the two paths fork.) The vibe is slightly positive in the area of the FOC.

The series of (3) of S6's begins by the backpack in the upper right, which is a few feet from the trail.

There is good potential for solitude, particularly after the swim season (there is no lifeguard.) I was there one day on a Memorial Day weekend when the only other party of people on the beach was far away. Other times there have been several groups. There can be foot traffic from nearby Rainbow Shores campground.

Address: Rt. 3, Pulaski NY
Webpage: http://www.dec.ny.gov/outdoor/68686.html
Email:
Telephone: DEC Region 7 (Cortland) 607-753-3095, ext. 247
Hours: Open year round.
Directions: Deer Creek Preserve is located off of Rt. 3 a little north of Port Ontario and a few miles northwest of Pulaski. There are several access points. To get to the beach you will have to turn west from Rt. 3 onto Rainbow Shores Road. Take a left onto a dirt road just before the road dead-ends at the water. Bear to the left on the dirt road. It will eventually dead-end at the parking lot.

References and Recommended Reading
Gateley, Susan Peterson, *The Edge Walker's Guide to Lake Ontario Beachcombing*, Whiskey Hill Press, Wolcott, NY, 2003.

Watertown, Jefferson County, NY

Thompson Park
S3, V0

John Olmstead, the nephew and adopted son of Fredrick Law Olmsted, designed Thompson Park. Years ago my interest in it was piqued when I was told it was haunted; particularly the area near the zoo. As noted previously I often find that such places have an abundance of energy, or electromagnetic energy, and that is what may be behind the visions. They merit investigation because it may indicate the presence of a FOC.

There are several FOC within the park. The vibe is neutral. Some of the viewpoints in the park offer spectacular views.

Accessing the Fields
You can access one of the FOC from Franklin St. going into the park. Take your first right heading away from the Overlook to

your left. Signs will be pointing to another Overlook area ahead, take your first left before you get to it. A series (3) of S3's that parallels the road is on your left hand side before a wooded area. See picture below.

There are several other FOC in Thompson Park, including the area in front of the zoo.

Address: Franklin St. and Thompson Blvd. Watertown, NY, 13601
Webpage: https://www.watertown-ny.gov/index.asp?NID=140
Telephone: Watertown Parks Dept. 315-785-7775
Hours: 7AM to 9PM daily.

Directions: From I-81 take exit 45 and turn east onto Rt. 3. Follow to the town square; halfway around turn right onto Franklin St.

References and Recommended Reading
Brauchle, Robert, 'IT HAS AN APPEAL TO EVERYONE'
Watertown Daily Times, Oct. 26, 2008
Thompson Park Vortex YouTube Video, https://www.youtube.com/watch?v=pl60vm7ngSE
'"New sign in Watertown park acknowledges area's paranormal vortex', CNY Central, http://cnycentral.com/news/local/new-sign-in-watertown-park-acknowledges-areas-paranormal-vortex?id=962276

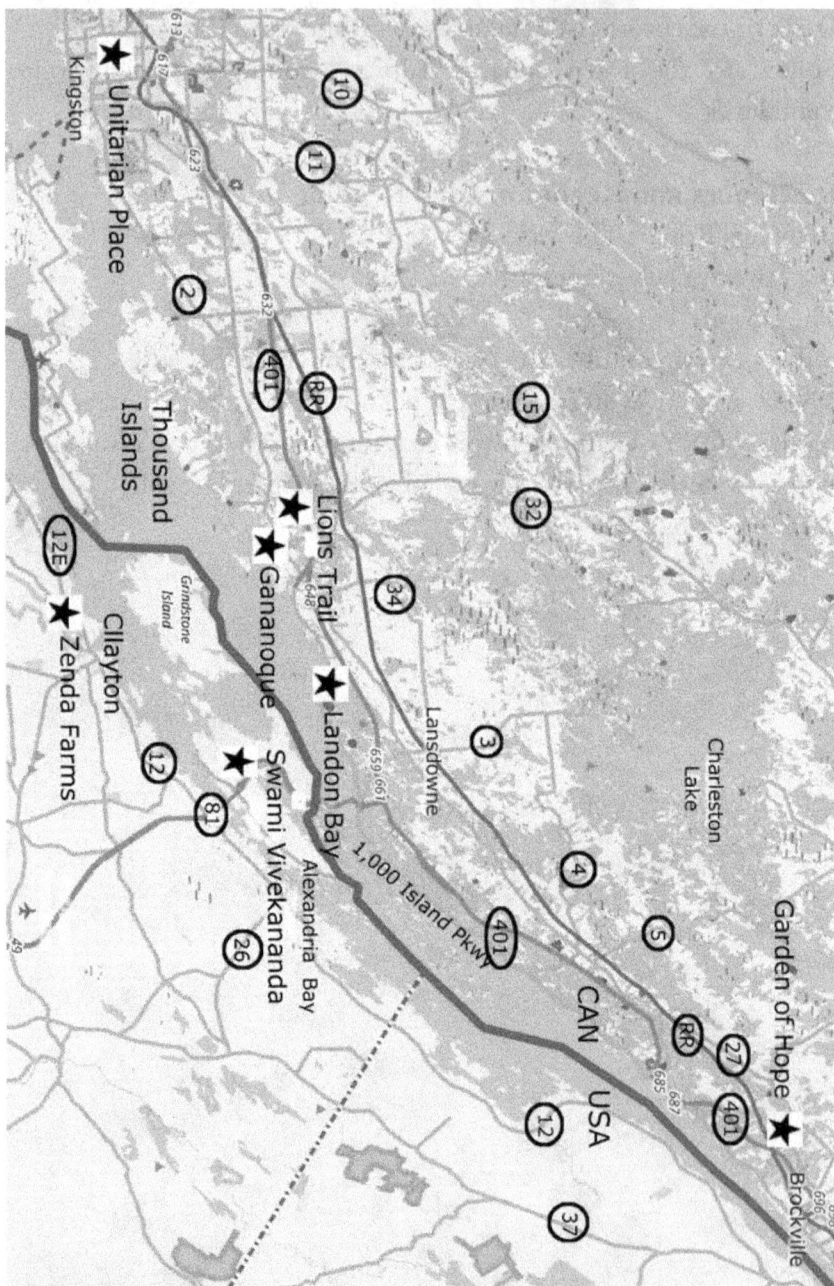

Map of the Thousand Islands. Source, ©OpenStreetMap contributors, www.openstreetmap.org

Thousand Islands, New York and Ontario, Canada

The beautiful and regal Thousand Islands are an archipelago on the St. Lawrence Seaway that straddles Canada and the USA. In many ways the region is a blend of the two countries. It is here that the Great Hindu mystic Swami Vivekananda achieved the highest meditative state of Samadhi, Nirvikalpa Samadhi.

USA
Clayton, Jefferson County, NY

Zenda Farms
S6, V1

Zenda Farms is a 400 acre preserve that was a working dairy farm until the 1950's. It is now part of the Thousand Islands Land Trust and open to the public. Its former pastures are now home to nesting grassland birds. The grass is not cut for hay until after August 1st; so you need to be aware that depending upon when you visit, the grass may be tall.

A FOC with a series (3) S6's can be found on a small knoll, or rise near the trailhead on Zenda Rd. The series is perpendicular to the trail and breaks away from it. The FOC is large extending from the trail to 70-80 feet away from it. In the picture on the next page the backpack marks the first in the series which aligns with the tree. The FOC extends to about 8-10 feet from the tree. A pond, or wet area is on the other side the knoll.

Address: 38973 Zenda Farm Rd. Clayton, NY 13624
Webpage: https:// tilandtrust.org/ explore/preserves-trails
/zenda-farms-preserve
Telephone: 315-686-5345 (Land Trust)
Donate, Volunteer: Call the Land Trust for more info.
Hours: Open dawn to dusk.
Directions: Take Rt. 12 to Clayton, either out of Watertown, or
the Alexandria Bay exit off of I-81. Turn onto Rt. 12E heading
south, Zenda Rd. will be on your right in about 1 mile.

Thousand Island Park, NY, Jefferson County

Thousand Island Park is a small charming hamlet located on the
southwest tip of Wellesley Island. It began as a Methodist (retreat)
camp.

Swami Vivekananda's Cottage
S3, V2-4, ▽ ☆ ♡ ⚲ ⚲ 🧘 ▣

In the summer of 1893, the great Hindu (Vedanta) mystic Swami
Vivekananda introduced yoga and Vedanta to the west when he
addressed the World's Parliament of Religions at the Chicago
World's Fair. His "sisters and brothers" introduction, instead of

ladies and gentlemen, led to a two minute standing ovation and a star was born. For the next four years, he would travel around the western world teaching seminars and educating people about Hinduism and the universality of all religions.

In the summer of 1895, he came to the Thousand Islands Park on Wellesley Island on the St. Lawrence Seaway to recuperate and teach for seven weeks. It is here that he blossomed, achieving the highest meditative state of Nirvikalpa Samadhi. The meditative state of Samadhi may be defined in several ways; one way is to say, it is when our awareness has transcended the physical world.

Each summer, I send out an email telling folks that the NY Ramakrishna Vivekananda center of NYC has opened Vivekananda's cottage for its summer stint and encourage them to visit. It is during the summer that the cottage is open.

I encourage you to visit this magnificent place as well. The vibe is divine (positive to extremely positive), there are FOC and there are vortices; one particularly powerful vortex whose embrace can intoxicate you almost instantaneously. This would be one of the better places to try and sense and feel Consciousness, particularly near the vortex in the shrine. It is truly a magical and special place.

Swami Vivekananda

Swami Vivekananda was the most noted devotee of Sri Ramakrishna, who advocated the universality of all religions and the necessity to experience God first hand, so that one could learn about God. He felt that all paths led to God and one just needed to select one and follow it. Many credit Ramakrishna for reviving Hinduism in the 19th century and he is considered by many of his devotees to have been an avatar, or incarnation of God. Both Ramakrishna and Vivekananda were mystics in the truest sense of the word.

Both were adherents of Vedanta; one of the oldest and most open and accepting of others, religions or belief systems. Its adherents believe in the divinity of the soul, our oneness with God and the universality of all religions.

Swami Nikhilananda, founder of the Ramakrishna Vivekananda Center of New York, in his book *Vivekananda a Biography* (1953) said that Swami Vivekananda's stay in the Thousand Islands proved to be, a "momentous period in his life."[1] Swami Vivekananda admitted that he was at his best there and the ideas developed there blossomed into institutions and movements both in India and the USA[2].

The Thousand Islands transformed the Swami;

"One cannot be but amazed at the manifestation of Swami Vivekananda's spiritual powers at the Thousand Islands…Thus one sees him at the Thousand Island Park reading the inmost soul of his followers before giving them initiation and foretelling their careers…At that time he experienced the power of changing a person's life by a touch, or clearly seeing things happening at a great distance."[3]

The Ramakrishna Vivekananda Center of New York acquired Miss Elizabeth Dutcher's (a student) cottage where Swami Vivekananda spent the seven weeks in 1946. Their members have been coming to the cottage each summer ever since.

Experiencing the Grounds

There are several opportunities to raise your consciousness, connect with the divine, or improve your meditative abilities at the Vivekananda cottage. The house is surrounded by numerous FOC (S1 to S3) and prayerful places. Choose a place you like and meditate or pray there. Make sure to bring a cushion to sit on because the house is situated on rock outcroppings.

The highest stacked Fields of Consciousness (S3) are on the driveway by the side of the house. The large rock in front of the house sits on a S1 and the FOC ends in front of it.

Backpack marks the vortex behind the house.

The single FOC in the back of the house ends a little beyond the house. There is a vortex behind the house, on the side away from the driveway, in a small clearing where there are no rocks. It is a vortex of what I call, Cosmic Prana, which is the prana that we draw when we meditate.

The Cottage

The cottage sits on a FOC. There are photographs of Swami Vivekananda and Sri Ramakrishna and his wife, as well as other interesting artifacts within it.

The real jewel is the shrine upstairs where Swami Vivekananda slept during his stay. A powerful vortex has formed in the center of the room. It is a vortex of the consciousness emanating from a

FOC; so it has a much higher consciousness component than Cosmic Prana, which you attract when you meditate.

While Swami Vivekananda planted the seed of intention that blossomed into a vortex, it was the devotion and intentions of the visiting pilgrims that fed it and created it. Years ago I came here for satsang (chanting and meditation.)

The shrine is a must experience event and a great place to meditate. I strongly encourage you to visit and nourish your soul there, and at the same time add to its incredible vibe.

The Tree in the Back

It is said that on August 7, 1895, his last day at the Thousand Islands, Swami Vivekananda went out back to meditate by a rock outcropping next to a oak tree. As he began to meditate his body froze solid in meditation, oblivious to torrential rain as he achieved Nirvikalpa Samadhi.

You can access this magical place by following the driveway and the red markers. You will be entering the Thousand Islands Park. If you follow the blue markers when leaving, they will bring you to the Tabernaacle.

For years I came and meditated at the cottage. I would walk in the back and wonder why did Swamji achieve the highest state of Samadhi here, as there where no FOC close by? It was only after my meditation progressed and I began to achieve some higher states that I realized that there was something else associated with FOC beyond the aspect, I have been cataloguing in this book. I suspect it is a higher form of consciousness, closer to pure consciousness. Because of this experience I came to realize that there are much more to FOC that I have mentioned.

The oak tree where Swamji experienced his ecstatic state has died, but its body remains. A monument was erected and dedicated in 2009 at this place. There is also a bench and a new oak tree has been planted.

Tree and memorial of where Swami attained Nirvikalpa Samadhi.

As his biographer would write "He had a unique experience of inner freedom at the Thousand Islands Park which he expressed eloquently in his poem 'The Song of Sannyasin". He wrote from there to a friend: "I am free, my bonds are cut, what do I care whether this body goes or does not go? I have a truth to teach—I am a child of God. And He that gave me truth will send me fellow workers from the earth's bravest and best."[4]

The mystical and transformative force that Swami Vivekananda experienced at his cottage on Wellesley Island still permeates the land. Go visit and be intoxicated with it. Namaste.

Address: VIVEKANANDA COTTAGE, 42822 St. Lawrence Ave., Unit # 74, Thousand Island Park, N.Y. 13692
Webpage:
http://www.ramakrishna.org/activities/TIP/visitors_info.htm;
Ramakrishna Vivekananda Center of New York,
http://www.ramakrishna.org.

Telephone: Cottage, 315-482-2189; NYC ashram, 212-534-9445.
Hours: Usually open from sometime the week after July 4th to the week before Labor Day. Dates will vary slightly each year. Daily visiting hours can also vary; recently 10:00 AM to 12:00 noon from 4:00 PM to 6:00 PM. You need to call to find out when the cottage is open. The grounds are open year round; I recommend calling the NYC ashram before visiting.

Lectures and classes are held during the summer; call for more information.

Directions: From I-81 north, just before crossing into Canada pay toll and cross the Thousand Island Bridge onto Wellesley Island and take first exit (Exit 51.)

Turn right and go to second stop sign. At second stop sign turn right, and proceed about 4 miles to the village of Thousand Island Park. In town proceed to stop sign (near Grocery, Ice Cream Parlor) and turn right onto St. Lawrence Avenue. Continue about 2 blocks until the T, the street ends at Tabernacle building.

At Tabernacle turn left, go about one block and park on the grass parking area on the left. Do not turn right up the small road marked with the arrow pointed to "Vivekananda Cottage."

References and Recommended Reading

1. Nikhilanda, Swami; VIVEKANANDA: A Biography, Ramakrishna—Vivekananda Center, NYC, NY 1953. Page 97.
2. Ibid Page 101.
3. Ibid. Page 102 -103.
4. Ibid. Page 105-106
Vivekananda, Swami; *Raja Yoga*, Ramakrishna-Vivekananda Center of New York, 1973
http://www.ramakrishna.org Ramakrishna-Vivekananda Center of New York.
Audio of Swami Vivekananda's 1893 speech to the Congress of World's Religions, there are several versions on YouTube, https://www.youtube.com/watch?v=ZQekcwOZ8FU

Canada

It is not surprising that North Star Country includes Canada. Many Freedom Seekers found freedom there, and the country has always had a benevolent and compassionate outlook for its citizenry through healthcare and other initiatives.

Gananoque, ONT, CAN

Less than ½ hour from Swami Vivekananda's cottage and 20 minutes from the Thousand Island Bridge, is Gananoque (pronounced - "Gan-A-Nock-wee") a Thousand Islands town. This warm and friendly place has public washrooms, several parks with walks, one of which is along the water. During the summer on Sunday's there is a nondenominational service held on Half Moon Bay, that you can paddle to, or take a boat to.

Gananoque Town Park
S8, V2, 👫

There is a town park located in front of the Municipal building, 30 King Street East, along King Street, bounded by Park and Adelaide Streets. All of the area in front the gazebo, or entertainment venue, is immersed in a lovely FOC (S8.) The vibe is positive, which is incredible because it is a public space; public spaces like parks usually don't have a positive vibe.

Within the FOC is a series (3) of S8's, marked by objects in the picture on the next page. Close to the corner on King Street is a sidewalk that takes you to the Town Hall. Walk about 20-30 feet until you are parallel to a tree on the left; the series is between the sidewalk and the tree. The center in the series is 25-28 feet from the Gazebo. Park yourself anywhere in the area of the FOC and enjoy.

When I was there, I ran into two women from Toronto that had come for a day trip and had just finished lunch. They offered to watch my dogs while I went to the washroom at the corner and took pictures. We had a good conversation, as I did with others in this lovely town. It is a very warm and welcoming place; perhaps that is why the vibe is positive.

Address: Adelaide and King Streets, Gananoque, Ontario
Webpage: http://www.gananoque.ca.
Telephone: Town 613-382-2149; Visitor Center, 10 King Street, (Open 8:30 AM to 4:30 PM) 613-382-8044, 844-382-8044.
Directions: From the Kings Highway (401) exit onto Rt. 2 (Exit 647 from the west, 648 from the east), or from the Thousand Islands Pkwy exit onto Rt 2 west. Rt. 2 will turn into King St East.

Landon Bay Centre
S8-10, V-2, 👫

The Landon Bay Centre is a 225 acre Ecological Reserve that was part of Frontenac Arch Biosphere Reserve and is being transitioned into Parks Canada. It is undergoing a facelift that is expected to be completed between 2019 to 2021, and may be closed for a season; so check with Parks Canada before visiting.

Remodeling may affect the entrance and the trailhead area where the FOC are located. That said Landon Bay Centre has the most potent FOC in Canada and a positive vibe.

A series (3) S10's are located at the entrance way and parallel the parkway. In the picture above the backpack marks the first in the series that ends by the sign. The FOC is large; be aware that there is lots of traffic noise.

A series (3) of S8's can be found near the beginning of the trail near the archway. Look for a series of large and old maple trees. In the picture on the following page the backpack marks the first in the series near an intersection of the trail starting from the archway (behind the two large maples) and entry on the right of the picture. Anywhere in this area would have you in the FOC.

Address: East of the intersection of Cross Center Rd. and the Thousand Islands Pkwy, Gananoque, Canada
Webpage: http://www.pc.gc.ca/eng/index.aspx
Telephone: 888-773-8888
Directions: From the Thousand Islands Bridge take the Thousand Pkwy west. Look for Cross Cemetery Rd. on your right. If you see River Rd. on your left you have gone too far.

Lions Trail
S3, V1

A section of the Lions Trail near Nalon Rd. (near town center) passes through an FOC (S3.) You can access the area by parking on Nalon Rd. and taking the connecting path to the Lions Trail.

The FOC is located at the intersection of the Lions Trail and the entry from Nalon Rd. In the picture below the backpack marks the center of the FOC that is 35-40 feet in diameter.

Address: Nalon Rd end, Gananoque, Canada.
Webpage: Trail map http:// www. gananoque. ca /community-services/parks-and-recreation/hiking-and-waterfront-trails
Telephone: 613-382-2149, 844-382-8044 (Toll Free)
Directions: From Kings St. W. right onto Victoria Ave and follow to the end. Turn left onto Fourth St. Right onto Crosby Rd. Crosby will turn left, go straight onto Nalon Rd., you will cross the Lions Trail; follow Nalon Rd. to the end.

Kingston, ONT, CAN

Unitarian Place
S6, V0, 🧍🧍 🧘

Two faith traditions meet at Unitarian Place in Kingston, Ontario;
the Kingston Unitarian Fellowship and the Thousand Islands
Meeting (Quaker.)

The Kingston
Unitarian Fellowship
is a Unitarian
Universalist church.
It is a caring
community where
diversity is
celebrated and
strives to make a better world. It is involved with Amnesty
International, Child Haven and Syrian Refuges.

Thousand Islands Meeting is a Religious Society of Friends,
Quaker. They have a strong social justice focus; current projects
are to save prison farms and to help the victims of crime.

All of the church sits on a FOC. The highpoint S6 is in the
meeting room. The vibe is neutral.

Kingston Unitarian Fellowship
Address: 206 Concession Street, Kingston, Ontario, K7K 2B5
Webpage: http://www.kuf.ca.
Email: info@kuf.ca
Telephone: 613-544-8777
Hours: Sunday Services at 10:30 AM.

Thousand Islands Meeting
Webpage: http://kingston.quaker.ca.
Email: timmclerk@gmail.com

Telephone: 613-634-9343

Hours: Sunday Services at 10:30 AM

Directions: From Hwy 401) take exit 617 onto Rt.10/Division St. south a few miles to Concession St. Turn right onto Concession St. Continue 8-10 blocks, church will be on your left.

Lyn, ONT, CAN

Garden of Hope and Faith
S2, V0

The Garden of Hope and Faith is a one acre Christian themed garden in Lyn, just north of Brockville. The goal of the garden is to be a place of reflection and healing, comfort and joy.

The FOC (S2) 30 feet in diameter is located in front of the statue and garden of hope near the entrance on the west side.

Address: 3545 Country Road 27, RR #2, Lyn, Ontario, KOE1MO

Webpage: http://www.gardenofhopeandfaithwalk.com

Telephone: 613-345-3424

Hours: May to October, from 8AM to a little before dusk. Call before hand to verify.

Directions: Take Cty Rd 29 north out of Brockville. Turn left onto Rt. 27.

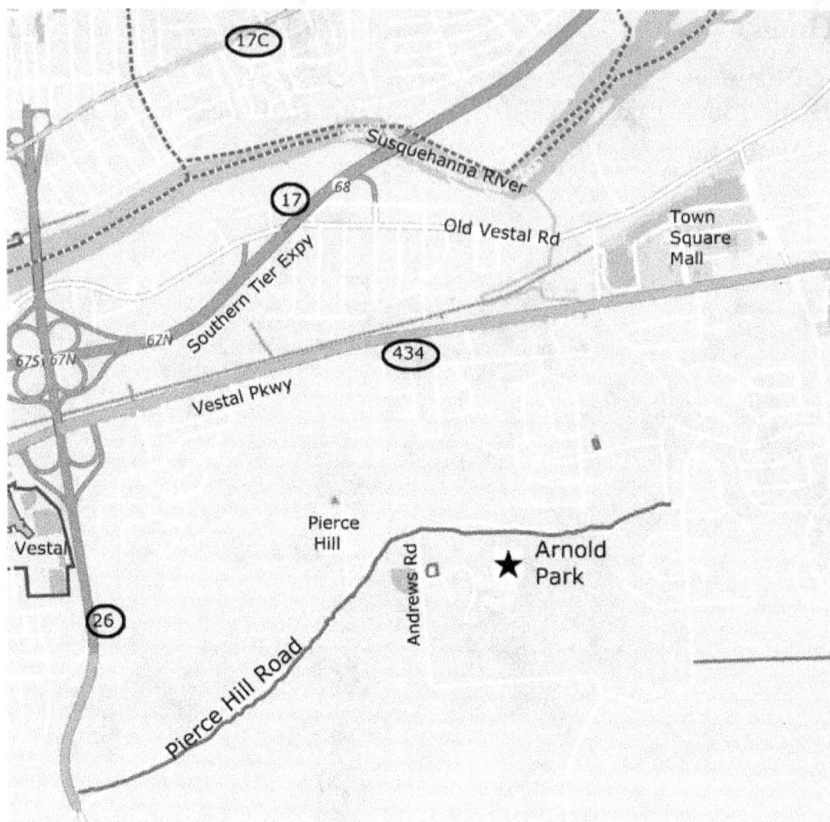

Map of the Southern Tier's Vestal area. Source, © OpenStreetMap contributors, www. openstreetmap. org.

Southern Tier

The Southern Tier is the southern part of NY (counties) that borders northern PA west of the Catskills. Arnold Park in Vestal is the only sacred site included. Other places that are formally part of the Southern Tier have been incorporated into Western NY.

Vestal, Broome County, NY

Arnold Park
S2-12, V2-3,☆

Arnold Park is a real gem, easy access, privacy, beautiful woods, a positive vibe and some powerful FOC (S12.) When I find places like this, I am awestruck and pleased. You will be as well.

The park has restrooms and areas for picnicking, sports fields, playgrounds, hiking and an Exercise or Fitness Trail—the Vita trail. You will be in the woods and at the times I have been there, activity was confined to the play and picnic areas, so there is solitude.

The vibe is positive to very positive throughout and is higher in the sacred areas where the FOC are located. This would be a good place to try and sense and feel Consciousness.

Experiencing Arnold Park

As you enter the park veer to the left side. Look for the signs and park in the Nature Trail area.

The woods on this side of the park are all positive (vibe) and the FOC are almost continuous from the woods to about 100-150 yards towards the other end of the park away from the nature trail parking area. For example, the woods immediately next to the parking area are from S2 to S4. Feel free to meditate in any part of the woods at this end of the park. Pick a spot and enjoy this little oasis; the vibe runs from positive to very positive.

The series (3) of S8' s along the Fitness Trail between stations 10 and 11 are marked. Notice sign in upper right corner.

The highest stacked FOC are found farther uphill. The Nature and Fitness (Vita) Trails will take you there. The Nature and

Fitness Trails is to your left as you face uphill from the Nature Trail Parking area.

Bear to the left and do not take the first trail to the right. Shortly on your left is the beginning of the Fitness Trail, stay to the right. In another few hundred feet the trail will divide again. Go to the left and you are on the Fitness Trail. Continue another few hundred feet until you come to stations 11 and 10. A series (3) of S's begins on the other side of the trail across from station 11. The vibe is very positive. Put your cushion down on the ground and enjoy.

Go back to where you turned left to get on the Fitness Trail and instead bear to the right. In a few hundred feet there will be several large oak trees. Look for an oak tree on the left that has a stump behind it and another stump directly across from it. The trail will bend slightly to the right around the oak tree. Ten feet ahead is another stump to your left. A few feet ahead will be another oak tree and the trail will bend left behind it.

Take a right between the stump on the left and oak tree, and go off trail. Continue about 40-60 feet until you come to a ridge and the land begins to decline downhill. A series (3) of S12's begins at the ridge and goes downhill. Even if you are not able to find the exact place, the FOC are all stacked very high so you will still be on a powerful place. The vibe is very positive.

There is a lot more to Arnold Park. Explore and find a place you like.

Address: Andrews Road off Pierce Hill Road, Vestal, NY 13850
Webpage: http://www.vestalny. com/ departments/ recreation/parks.php
Telephone: 607-748-1514
Directions: Take Exit 67 off of the Southern Tier Expressway (Rt. 17) onto Rt. 26 south. Continue until the traffic light for Pierce Hill Rd. Take a left onto Pierce Hill Rd, the park will be on your right.

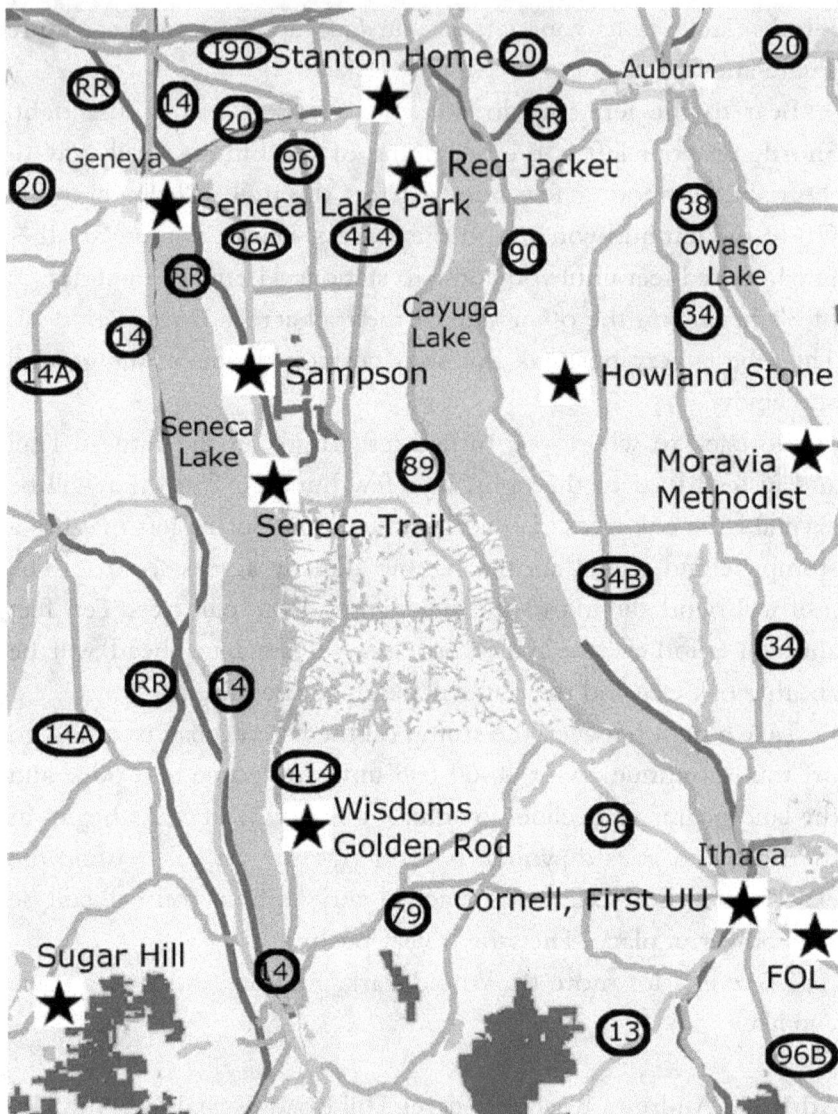

Map of the Finger Lakes. Source, © OpenStreetMap contributors, www. openstreetmap. org.

Finger Lakes Region

So called for its many lakes that look like fingers and stretch from Syracuse to Rochester. As such, it is in the heart of Mother Earth's Soul and contains numerous FOC. It is the home to the Cayuga and Seneca Nations. Recently it has gained notoriety for its vineyards and their wines.

There is the eclectic city of Ithaca with its waterfalls and gorges that seems more like San Francisco, than a town in upstate New York. If you have never been to Ithaca it is definitely worth a visit.

One of the more interesting phenomena in the area is the drums of Seneca Lake, or guns of Seneca. It is a popping, or booming sound often heard around Seneca Lake. Speculation on why these sounds occur range from natural gas released from fissures in the rocks in the lake, to military aircraft. No one knows for sure.

Emerson Klees of Rochester, who has written many books about the upstate New York region, says that the Seneca people interpret the sound as drums of their forefathers and an outward expression of evil spirits, or signals from the God of Thunder[1].

References and Recommended Reading
1. Klees, Emerson; *Legends and Stories of the Finger Lakes Region, The Heart of New York State*. Friends of Finger Lakes Publishing, Rochester, New York, 1995. Page 8.

Canoga, Seneca County, NY

Monument to Chief Red Jacket
S6, V0,🕊

Every year I make an effort to stop by here to say a prayer, to give thanks, and ask for the reconciliation of Native and non-Native people. If you are interested in the spirit of reconciliation, particularly in healing the wounds between non-Native and Native Americans, then please stop by.

A Spirit of Reconciliation

Red Jacket was a chief in the Wolf Clan of the Seneca nation, known for his oratory and negotiations as a peace maker. There is some controversy whether Red Jacket was born here or someplace else. His nickname 'Red Jacket' comes from the gift of a red coat from the British.

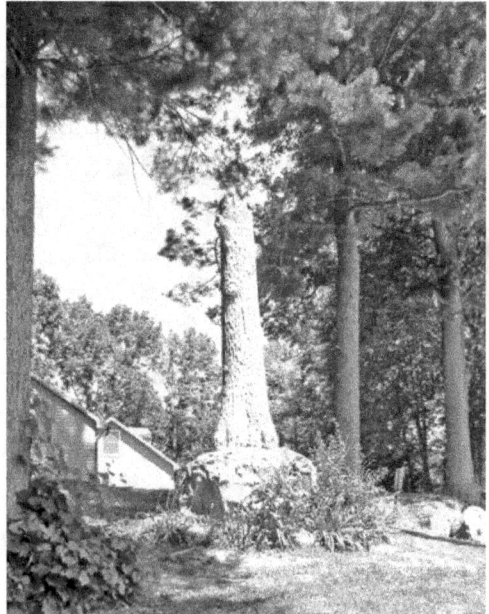

He played a prominent role in negotiating with the new republic around the time of the American Revolution. George Washington presented him with a peace medal that he proudly wore across his chest.

Red Jacket was a quick, witty and at times a sarcastic negotiator who kept his cool and took advantage of his opponent's failings.[1] He was an eloquent orator who commanded an audience's attention and defended and advocated for his people. One of his more famous speeches was in 1805 in defense of Native American religion against the assault to Christian missionaries. In it he said among other things, "Brother, we do not wish to destroy your religion, or take it from you; we only want to enjoy our own."[2] At the end of the speech Red Jacket

262

walked up to the missionary and extended his hand, which the missionary refused.

Experiencing Canoga

There is a large monument near the front of the cemetery. Years ago I met the caretaker and his wife on a visit and I could tell that they took great care and joy in tending to the monument and the grounds. I always say a prayer by the monument.

The FOC are located on the other side of the parking area and picnic benches. All of the grassy area up to about 60-70 feet from the picnic table is on a Field. Pick a place you like and sit down on the lawn.

Look for a large tree close to this area on your right as you face south away from the picnic table and monument. A series (3) of S6's begin 20 feet left of the tree towards the road and run at a slight angle away from the road, about 15 feet apart.

There is much to find fault with this little strip of land. It is too close to the road, passing cars make too much noise and it is part of a cemetery. I could go on and on about all that is wrong about where the great orator and peacemaker Chief Red Jacket was born, but I just love this place. Please visit and say a prayer and help heal the rift between non-Native and Native people.

Address: The monument is located just north of the intersection of Cemetery Road and Route 89 in Canoga, NY. It is on the Canoga Cemetery grounds on Route 89.

Directions: Take Exit 41 off of the Thruway (I-90.) Go south on Rt. 414. Take your first left onto Rt. 318. Continue until it ends at Rt. 20. Take a left east onto Rt. 20 and a quick right onto Rt. 89. The cemetery and monument are a few miles down on your left.

References and Recommended Reading

1. Densmore, Christopher; *Red Jacket, Iroquois Diplomat and Orator*, Syracuse University Press, Syracuse, NY 1999. Pg 36

2. Nerburn, Kent, editor; *The Wisdom of the Great Chiefs*, New World Library, San Rafael, Calif. 1994. Pg 5-11.

Geneva, Seneca/Ontario Counties, NY

Geneva straddles Seneca Ontario Counties at the northern end of Seneca Lake. Seneca Lake Park is in Seneca County.

Seneca Lake State Park
S6, V0, 👫

Seneca Lake State Park is a 141-acre park located along the shore of Seneca Lake providing beachfront walks and water activities. Several FOC located within the park. The vibe is neutral.

Experiencing the Park

There are primarily two sets of FOC at the eastern end near the marina. The first Field is on the western side of shelter 1 and covers a wide area. Within it is a series (3) of S6's that begins next to a tree about 25 feet from the shelter (front) on the western side and breaks away from the lake at almost a straight line (5°-10° to the northwest.) The dogs in the picture on the previous page mark the first 2 in the series.

The next FOC is by the bathroom at the far eastern edge of the park. The Field heads east from where two paths intersect on the eastern side of the bathroom.

Address: 1 Lakefront Drive, Geneva, NY 14456
Webpage: http://nysparks.com/parks/125/details.aspx
Telephone: 315-789-2331
Hours: Park open year-round. Vehicle entry fee collected from mid-May to mid-October. Restrooms available from May to October. 2015 Swimming Season: early June to early September, 11 AM - 6 PM, weekends & holidays only. Cars $7
Directions: The Park is located off of Rt. 20 in Geneva. Take Exit 42 off of the Thruway and head south on Rt. 14 towards Geneva. In Geneva take a left onto Lake St. (this will bring you to the city park.) Take your first left onto Lakefront Dr.

Hector, Schuyler County, NY

Native American paintings decorate the rock cliff on the shore of Seneca Lake near Hector. As writer Emerson Klees tells the Seneca were greatly outnumbered and being chased by General Sullivan during the Revolutionary War (they were one of the four tribes that sided with the British) and found themselves trapped along the cliffs. They escaped by using a narrow path and safely descended. Sullivan's men refused to follow and risk their lives on such a treacherous descent. The braves were so thankful that they went back and painted the Spirit Boatman, a Seneca warrior paddling his canoe.

References and Recommended Reading

Klees, Emerson; *Legends and Stories of the Finger Lakes Region, The Heart of New York State. Friends of Finger Lakes Publishing Rochester, New York,* 1995. Pg25-26

Wisdom's Golden Rod

S3, V3-4, ▽ ☆ (♠) ⚕ 🧘 🚶 🖼

Wisdom's Golden Rod is a spiritual retreat and learning center located on the east shore of Seneca Lake, a few miles north of Watkins Glen. While its highest FOC is only an S3, it has a powerful and welcoming vibe that runs from very positive, to extremely positive.

I make recommendations about going to particular places to try and sense and feel Consciousness, this is a place to visit to experience the transformative power that acceptance, love and devotion can have on a space. The meditation center has a huge vortex, the largest of any places listed. All are welcome.

About Wisdom's Golden Rod

The center was founded in 1972 by Anthony Damiani, a longtime student of Paul Brunton, and has been maintained by its members since his death in 1984. It is a not for profit (501c-3) that professes no particular tradition but explores a variety of spiritual alternatives. There are group meditations and a variety of courses are offered on some interesting topics.

The grounds sit high above Seneca Lake and provide scenic views. There are four buildings on the grounds, all constructed with hand-hewn logs that give them a very rustic feeling. At the same time, the buildings are of eastern design, creating a very visually appealing and yet homey feel. The library contains over 5,000 volumes. There is a central hall where group meditations and classes are held. There is an annex with guest rooms and a guest cottage that provides residence for long term stay. There is also a lovely garden.

Experiencing Wisdom's Golden Rod

Since the center holds meditations daily I would suggest trying to attend a group meditation. I would also suggest looking at their program of courses to see if something is going on for a weekend, or for a few days that you may be able to participate in.

Much of the grounds sit on FOC. They begin when you enter by the Japanese torii arch and end in front of the meditation building. The grounds are lovely and well maintained, so pick a spot you like and soak it up.

The Library sits on an S2 and would be great please to sit and read sacred texts, or just be.

The library, or learning center, sits on a FOC (S2.) Take one of the nearby meditation cushions and find a place within the floor design of the large circle. The Dalai Lama blessed this space in 1979. It has a very lovely feel well beyond what one would have expected to find with two Fields stacked upon each other. No doubt a lot of meditations and good thoughts have transpired there.

If you want the tranquility of a garden you will find a FOC located on the west side (lakeside) of the path about 30-50 feet before the footbridge.

While the central hall where meditation takes place does not rest on a FOC, it has a great feel to it and a huge vortex has formed in its center, 12-14 feet in radius, from all the meditating that has taken place there. Because it does not reside on a FOC the vortex draws in the same energy/consciousness mix, (what I call Cosmic Prana), that you normally do during meditation. While it has a lower consciousness component than a FOC, the amount you are pulling in because of the vortex makes up for it. Not only will you be getting a good dose of consciousness while meditating in the vortex, you will improve your meditative ability because you will be picking up the powerful imprint of meditation from the vortex. So if you are looking to develop your ability to meditate this would be a great place to go.

Please note that members can rent a cottage for a short, or longer term retreat (months); because of this Wisdom's Golden Rod has membership from around the world. I have met people from Sweden and Canada on the occasions I have visited.

The grounds are open year round from sunrise to sunset (longer if courses are going on.) You should call up before you come. Most classes (talks, discussions, gatherings take place almost daily) are based on donations; so please donate generously to insure this delightful place continues to sparkle for a long time.

Daily meditations are held at 8 AM and 5:30 PM, but if no members come the meditation center will not be open—so call first, at least a day before you come and leave a message.

Address: 5801 NYS Route 414, Hector, New York 14841.
Webpage: http://www.wisdomsgoldenrod.com.

Email: Questions about events and meditations: events@wisdomsgoldenrod.com
Questions about classes: classes@wisdomsgoldenrod.com
Telephone: 607-546-7777.
Donate, Volunteer: You can donate online, or send a check. There is a donation box in the front of the meditation center.
Membership: You can join online.
Hours: Sunrise to sunset. Call before visiting.
Other: You can register to receive an e-newsletter online.
Directions: you can take Rt. 414 north out of Watkins Glen. From the north you can take Rt. 96 south out of Waterloo. In Ovid continue south on Rt. 96a. You can catch Rt. 414 south in Lodi. From Ithaca take Rt. 79 west.

References and Recommended Reading
Wisdom Golden Rods Webpage, www. wisdomsgoldenrod. com
Godwin, Joscelyn, *The Upstate Cauldron*, State of New York Press 2015, Pages 294-297.
Conversations with Cindy Sittman.

Ithaca, NY, Tompkins County
Located at the southern tip of Cayuga Lake people say "Ithaca is gorges" because of the many gorges in the area and the three waterfalls within the city. It has a very distinctive feel to it, eclectic and experimental; no doubt fueled by its two colleges, Cornell and Ithaca. The Commons, a two block pedestrian mall in the center of town is its heart. Namgyal Monastery, the North American Seat of His Holiness the 14th Dalai Lama, is located on the outskirts of town.

Cornell University Campus
Within the campus there are two locations to experience FOC— the Azalea Garden and Sage Chapel.

Gardens Along Tower Road
S4-8, V0-2

Cornell's Plantation Program is a robust effort to promote horticultural diversity and provide natural areas for the education of such. It boasts a botanical garden, an arboretum and numerous nature preserves. One of its assets is a garden along Tower Ave.

Experiencing the Garden

There are two FOC in the park. The nicest one is located off the pathway in the woods in front the Red Barn. Enter the garden at western end close to Tower Ave and East Ave. Take the pathway up towards the Red Barn and bear right. Once you are on an elevated area look for an old fashioned street lamp on your on your right. There will be two series of numbers on it; S2 and directly below it N5. You are still west of the Red Barn.

'X' marks the entry path to the FOC (S8) in the woods across from the Red Barn.

A few feet after the street lamp you will see a herd path into the woods to your right. Take it. On your left will be several mountain laurels. Ahead to your right is a large hemlock tree. You are already in the FOC. Just to the left of the Hemlock tree are two flat stones on the ground, or at least they were when I was there. Farther ahead is a trail of stones that are covered and difficult to distinguish.

Clearly someone placed the stones to the left of the hemlock tree and nourished it with their prayers and meditations. The vibe is positive. Very Nice. And it sits on an S8. Whether the stones will be there when you arrive, students may move them, is unknowable. What will stay for some time is the great vibe.

The other FOC is located at the eastern end of the park close to Tower Ave close to Garden Ave. Walking west on Tower Ave to the main campus enter the Azalea Garden, the first path on your right with an open area with several benches. The FOC, an S4, is located in the mulched garden on your right as you enter. As soon as you walk off the path you will be in the FOC. The vibe is neutral.

Sage Chapel
S6, V0,

Sage Chapel is a nondenominational church located on Ho Plaza (which is a continuation of Tower Ave after it ends on East Ave. The Chapel will be on your left.) Since being built in 1875 it has more than doubled in size. Many of the stain glass windows commemorate those whose lives were cut short; the small pox of the late 19th century, Michael Schwerner (Cornell grad) who was one of three civil rights activists killed by the KKK in Philadelphia, Mississippi in 1961.

The FOC (S6) is located in the front half of the chapel; the center is a little left of center as you face the chapel. The vibe is neutral.

Address: Off of Rt. 366. Visitor Relations, Day Hall Lobby, Cornell University, Ithaca, NY 14853
Webpage: http://dos.cornell.edu/cornell-united-religious-work

Telephone: 607-254-4636

Hours: Sage Chapel is open Mon. to Fri., 8 AM to 11 PM; Sat. & Sun. 9 AM to 11 PM. Check the calendar of services on the webpage.

Directions: Enter on Tower road and ask at the entry Kiosk on your right after you pass Wing Drive where you can park. Or park at the Peterson lot at the corner of Tower and Judd Falls Road. The coin and credit card operated parking meter is near the entrance on Tower Ave.

References and Recommended Reading

The Essentials of Campus III: Sage Chapel
-https://brancra.wordpress.com/2009/05/29/the-essentials-of-campus-iii-sage-chapel/

Foundation of Light
S4-8, V2-3, ▽ ☆ ♡ (♦) ♦♦ ☖ ⋏ ⌂ ▦

The Foundation of Light (FOL) is an ecumenical spiritual and learning center located on the outskirts of the city of Ithaca. It provides a multitude of alternatives for pilgrims to connect with Spirit and experience Mother Earth's FOC. There is a meditation room, a healing room, various stone circles, a labyrinth, classes, a sweat lodge and much more. It is the only place listed that has seasonal celebrations: solstices, equinoxes, full moons, and New Years' Eve. And of course much of the grounds rest on FOC.

It is so 'Ithaca', blending new alternatives with traditional ways of exploring while not loosing grasp of God's universal message of love and the equality of all people.

It is a wonderful place with several FOC with great ways to connect with them and a vibe that runs from positive to very positive. The area in back of the labyrinth is a place you may wish to try and sense and feel Consciousness. There is a vortex ring, a precursor to the formation of a vortex, in the meditation room. It has so much to offer that you could spend the day there. Please visit and enjoy.

History

Kate Payne and Mabel Beggs founded the Foundation of Light in 1974 to provide a spiritual alternative to the Ithaca community and to reclaim what they felt was sacred space. Both came with the belief that there is an ancient timeless wisdom, a thread connecting all spiritual and religious teachings through the ages.

Mabel got involved with Theosophy in the 1950's and went on to study the ageless wisdom in the School of Esoteric Studies. Kate traveled widely in the 1960's visiting sacred sites around the world and studying with a variety of esoteric teachers. Both lived on the grounds.

In 1979 the main structure was erected. I was once told that many, many crystals were placed underneath the main assembly room to enhance it.

There have been various additions since. A Rudolph Steiner (Theosophy) Waldorf school, now the Lantern School that provides earth based mentoring to young children. Many prominent people involved with Earth Mysteries in the 1980's banded together to construct a stone circle made of stone pillars.

FOL members are a diverse group that has included people such as Dorothy Cotton, who was the top women in Dr. Martin Luther King's Southern Leadership conference in the 1960's.

There are no rigid rules or structure at the Foundation of Light. The only formalized program for the whole community is a group meditation on Sunday at the Gathering Room.

I used to come to the FOL to attend Finger Lakes Dowsers meetings. I remember Kate Payne asking me once if I was a lumberjack. I said no, but I cut down several overgrown trees on my property this past week. She acknowledged that was what she was picking up.

The pillared Stone Circle is towards the back of the property next to the labyrinth and close to Ellis Hollow Road.

Experiencing the Foundation of Light

There are a lot of options available at the Foundation of Light: a meditation room, a gathering room, a labyrinth, a stone circle, a peace pole, courses/programs and several acres of land to walk.

You will find numerous FOC and sweet places throughout the property. Here are some suggestions:

Gathering Room—Located in the Main Building. It is a great space with lots of light and a good place to meditate, particularly when it is cold outside. The Sunday morning gathering and meditation take place within it. A FOC (S2) covers more than half of the room in the back.

Meditation Room—Forget the directions and just follow the vibe; it will take you there. Powerful presence of prayer lingers. If you are trying to learn to meditate, or get better at it, spend some time there—the imprints of other meditators lingering there will assist you.

It sits on a FOC (S4.) A vortex ring, a precursor to the formation of an energy vortex, has formed and it should not be much longer until there is an actual vortex. Before the Dali Lama build his new monastery on the outskirts of Ithaca, and there was only the Namgyal Monastery downtown, the monks would occasionally come and meditate at the FOL.

Labyrinth—It sits on a FOC (S4.). I am not a big fan of labyrinths, primarily because of an insight I once got walking this labyrinth. The epiphany was that labyrinth walkers leave imprints that disturb the flow of energy/prana in the ether (Energy Plane), creating blockages that do not allow for the formation of a vortex. Interesting, a labyrinth is not the best thing for Mother Earth, yet at the same time I get this epiphany. Give it a walk and see what comes to you.

FOC (S8) Behind the labyrinth. The highpoint of the FOC (S8) is located behind the labyrinth. As you face the labyrinth the stone circle will be on your right. The first in a series (3) of S8's is about 5 feet behind the labyrinth, at 10 to 11 o'clock. The series breaks towards the right and away from the labyrinth. Don't worry if you cannot find the exact spot, the FOC behind the labyrinth is large. Very Nice. I placed several large flat stones flat to the ground and meditated on them several years ago; you might be able to find them.

Prayer Bench—I am told this is where people gather before a sweat lodge. It rests on a FOC (S6) and is located in the woods behind the Main Building. I believe that this is the general area where we constructed a small ceremonial circle in the woods once.

The grounds—This may be one of the best features of the FOL. Do a contemplative walk, find a place you connect with and meditate or just be with friends. While the grounds are pretty much an open field, they offer lots of love and insight. They have a great vibe and most of the land rests on stacked FOC.

Classes/Programs—
The FOL has lots going on so check out the calendar on their website to see if anything interests you.

The Foundation of Light is not the sophisticated and formal retreat center many urban dwellers may be used to. It is informal, unstructured and open

The prayer bench at the edge of the woods behind the Main Building.

to all. It is not a moneymaking institution, rather, they are like your local place of worship, which tries to make ends meet from congregant and visitor donations and small fees it collects from groups it is trying to help. Keep that in mind when you visit. They welcome you. Please say thank you in the way you feel called.

Address: 391 Turkey Hill Rd. Ithaca, NY 14850.
Webpage: http://folithaca.org.
Telephone: 607-273-9550, ext. 21
Donate, Volunteer: A donation box is located in the hallway of the main building. You can also donate and become a member online. Contact the FOL about helping out in the garden, on the newsletter or anything else. This is a small community of members.
Hours: Weekly meditation Sundays, 10:30 AM to 12 PM.

Directions: From the Ithaca Commons, Go East on Rt. 79 (State St.) 2.2 miles to a flashing yellow light. Take a left (North) onto Pine Tree Rd. At the first traffic light take a right (East) on Ellis Hollow Rd.. Drive 2.0 miles to the first 4-way intersection. At the 4-way intersection, go left (North) on Turkey Hill Rd. 0.1 mile to the 3rd driveway on right.

References and Recommended Reading

Kate Payne Obituary - Ithaca, NY, Ithaca Journal, July 19, 2008. http://www.legacy.com/obituaries/theithacajournal/obituary.asp x?n=kate-hopwood-payne&pid=113654828

Blavatsky, Madame; *Keys to Theosophy*

Mabel Beggs Obituary - Ithaca, NY, Ithaca Journal, November 20, 2005. http://www.legacy.com/obituaries/theithacajournal/obituary.asp x?n=mabel-chaffin-demotte-beggs&pid=87923869

Conversations with Melissa Hoffman and her predecessor Suzanne Cornell.

First Unitarian Society of Ithaca
S3, V0, 👫 🧘

The church has a storied past; Abolitionist Samuel May helped found the church and gave the first sermon. Ezra Cornell founder of Cornell University was an early congregant. It is said that one of the church minister's, Reverend Scott, invented the ice cream sundae. The church is very active in the community and has numerous programs and groups designed to help the community and the larger world.

All of the sanctuary sits on FOC (S3), the center of which is on the left side of the sanctuary. The vibe is neutral.

Address: 306 N Aurora St, Ithaca, NY 14850
Webpage: https://unitarian.ithaca.ny.us

Telephone: 607-273-7521
Hours: Sunday Services 10:30 AM.
Directions: You can access N. Aurora St. off of Rt. 79 (head north.) The church is at the corner near Buffalo St.

Moravia, Cayuga County, NY

Christ United Methodist Church of Locke and Moravia
S8, V0, ♟ ☗

Is a family and youth focused congregation. All of the sanctuary sits on a FOC (S8.) The vibe is neutral.

Address: 36 Church St. Moravia, NY 13118
Webpage: http://moraviaumc.org
Email: Christ_UMC@yahoo.com
Telephone: 315-497-2783
Hours: Sunday Services 8:30 and 10:30 AM.
Directions: Church St. is off of Main St., a few blocks south of Rt. 38a (W. Cayuga St.)

Romulus, Seneca County, NY
An old abandoned army depot along Rt.'s 96 and 96a contains a large herd of albino deer that can occasionally be seen. Effort is being made to save the deer, (http://senecawhitedeer.org) and create an ecotourism zone where the deer can be viewed. Please donate online to help

Sampson State Park
S4-6, V1-2, ♟ ☗ ☗ ≋

Sampson State Park is a 2,000 acre park located on the eastern shore of Seneca Lake. During WWII it served as a naval training base. In 1960 the land was transferred to New York State, and in 1963 Sampson opened. Many of the military buildings were taken down and others have decayed, as the state is allowing the land to return to its wild self.

There are several FOC located within the park, most are inaccessible, or difficult to get to. Below are two places that have FOC that you can access.

Seneca Lake Beach
S6, V2, 🧍🧍 ₂ 〰〰

Just south of the beach area at the northern end of the park is a FOC on a woodsy knoll by the shore. To access the location enter the park at the northern end and park your car close to the beach at southern end of the parking area. Begin walking south along the beach. Parts are overgrown with trees, but there are herd paths around any impediment. Look for a large gully to your left, it is less than a couple of hundred yards.

Walk up the right shoulder (with your back to the lake) of the gully this will bring you to a ridge above the shoreline. Walk south on the herd path along the ridge. Look for a cinder block fireplace in front of an oak tree, the first of three large oaks that are on their last legs. One has already lost a large limb. When I first started coming here they had not started to decay.

There is a FOC around the trees, but the highest FOC are located about 30 feet south of the third oak tree. Look for an old fire hydrant about 30 feet to your left as you face south. A pipe beginning from it extends out from the ridgeline about 3 feet below ground level.

Find a place you like in this general area. I have been meditating in this area for years and the vibe is positive. A friend told me she believes that a Seneca Village was once here.

Address: 6096 Route 96A,Romulus, NY 14541
Webpage: http://nysparks.com/parks/154/details.aspx
Telephone: 315-585-6392
Hours: The park is open year round. Daily operating hours are from dawn to dark. Visitors not registered to a campsite or boat slip must leave the park no later than 10pm. Restrooms may not be available in winter months; availability is limited in March-April and October-November.

Admission is $7 per car. Collected May 21- June 12, weekends and holidays only: 6 AM to 4 PM. June 18-Sept. 5, 8 AM to 4 PM Mon. – Thurs., 7 AM-4 PM Fri.-Sun.
Directions: Take Rt. 96a south out of Geneva.

The Seneca Lake Trail
S4-6, V1-2, ⚲⚲ ∠ 🏃 〰

At the southern end of Sampson State Park in the town of Ovid, there is a trail, a gravel path, that goes north along the shoreline. Much of the first part of the trail rests on FOC. It is a flat path that allows for a wonderful contemplative walk with several benches on FOC to stop and reflect, as well as look out on the lake. The vibe is slightly positive, to positive.

Experiencing The Seneca Trail

The FOC begin 10 feet after the gate and almost continuous for ¾'s to 1 mile. The highpoint of most of the FOC is on the left hand side, or lake side.

Here are a listing of some of the FOC and their respective signposts in order of progression going north:

First bench area on your left rests on a FOC (S3.)

Four large stones on your left area FOC (S6.)

A post, look for a post in the ground on your left FOC (S4.)

Five large stones forming a semicircle, FOC (S6.) There was gnarl and tall weeds around the stones, don't be fooled this is a sweet spot with a positive vibe.

Second bench on your left is on a FOC (S4.)

Six large rocks in the shape of semicircle; FOC (S6.) Nice.

The third Bench is on a FOC (S5.)

Seneca Lake Trail provides for a peaceful and contemplative walk. There are an occasional walker, runner and biker; Only once did a biker peddling too fast and endangering us bother me.

Directions: From Sampson entrance take Rt. 96A. Take a right, or bear right for the road to Willard. Take a right onto Cty. Rd. 132 and continue to bear right. Seneca Lake will be on your left. When the road ends, park in the lot on the right.

Seneca Falls, Seneca County, NY

Situated at the northern end of Cayuga Lake, Seneca Falls is the cradle of the Women's Movement where the first Women's Rights Convention was held. It is home to the Women's Rights National Park and the National Women's Hall of Fame.

For those interested in bird watching, Montezuma National Wildlife Refugee is near. Residents believe that the town served as an inspiration for Frank Capra's movie "It's a Wonderful Life"; a festival in its honor is held the second weekend of December.

Elizabeth Cady Stanton Home—Historic Home S6, V0, ♀

The home of Elizabeth Cady Stanton, one of the founders of the Women's Movement, is next to a FOC with a series (3) of S6's. There you have a chance to connect with the spirit and place she called "the center of the Rebellion." The vibe is neutral.

History

Before Elizabeth Cady Stanton was a Women's Rights activist and abolitionist. She met her husband to be, Henry Stanton, an ardent abolitionist, at her cousin Gerrit Smith's estate. They were married in 1840 in a ceremony where the word "to obey" was omitted, and for their honeymoon went to London for the World Anti-slavery conference of 1840. When Stanton, Lucretia Mott and other women from America were not allowed to take part in the convention and were forced to sit in the back, strong bonds and a network of women that would become the Women's Movement was created.[1]

The Stanton's moved to Seneca Falls in 1847. The next year, Stanton along with Mott and others organized the first Women's Rights Convention. Stanton helped draft the Declaration of Statements. A few years later she would hookup with Susan B. Anthony and Matilda Joslyn Gage.

She sold the property in 1862 and moved to New York City.

Stanton, like Gage, was more radical than others, especially when it came to religion. In 1898 she wrote the *Woman's Bible* and was censured by American Woman Suffrage Association.

The whole area of the back property and a little beyond is covered with FOC. Find a spot that suits you. The vibe of the property is neutral.

Address: 32 Washington St, Seneca Falls, NY 13148
Webpage: https: //www. nps. gov /wori/learn /historyculture /elizabeth-cady-stanton-house.htm
Telephone: 315-568-0024, Women's Rights Historical Park
Hours: Guided tours are offered daily (11:30 AM and 2:30 PM, historically, Wednesday-Sunday.) Closed for the winter, December-May. You can walk the grounds all year round.
Close by: The Seneca Falls Visitor's Center, 89 Fall Street, Seneca Falls, NY 1314, (315) 568-1510.
Directions: In Seneca Falls take Rt. 414 south and cross the river. Take your first left onto East Bayard. Take your second right onto Washington St. The house is at the end of the street.

References and Recommended Reading

1. Wellman, Judith; *The Road to Seneca Falls, Elizabeth Cady Stanton and the First Women's Rights Convention*, University of Illinois Press, Chicago, Illinois, 2004. Pages 60-64.

National Park Service, Women's Rights, National Historical Park, NY, Elizabeth Cady Stanton Home; http://www.nps.gov/wori/learn/historyculture/elizabeth-cady-stanton-house.htm

Sherwood, Cayuga County, NY

Howland Stone Store Museum
S6, V1, ♀

The Howland family was prominent in several reform movements. Their store was a station on the Underground Railroad. A few years ago it was converted to a museum. There is a lecture series. It sits on a FOC (S6); the vibe is slightly positive.

Address: Located on Rt. 34b in Sherwood. The formal address is 2956 State Route 34b, Aurora, NY 13026-9728. Questions—Box 124, Aurora, NY 13026. Sunday Social.; check calendar for topics.
Webpage: http://www.howlandstonestore.org.
Email: pwhite2299@aol.com
Telephone: 315-364-5587
Donate: You can donate, or join and become a member online.
Hours: Open June through September, Thursdays and Saturdays, from 1-4 pm. Or call for an appointment. See website for lecture series. Donation; Please donate generously to sustain this wonderful effort.
Directions: Located at Rt. 34b and Rt. 42a in Sherwood. Head south on Rt. 34 from Auburn. In Fleming turn right onto Rt. 34b.

References and Recommended Reading
YouTube video Slocum Howland and the museum, https://www.youtube.com/watch?v=kflGBwpr4HE
Conversations with Patricia White.

Watkins Glen, NY Schuyler County
So called for its glen with a descending stream between rocks that creates beautiful waterfalls and vistas. It is now a state park. Watkins Glen is also home to a famous auto race.

Sugar Hill State Forest
S12, V2-3, ☆ ♡ ⚲ ⦚

With hiking and horse trails on over 9,085 acres Sugar Hill offers the chance to roam around in the woods and meditate on FOC (S12) with a positive, to very positive vibe.

There is something to like about Sugar Hill; it has a warm feel to it. Whenever I have visited I felt as if I was being treated as a guest. It is a Friendly Neighborhood.

Experiencing Sugar Hill

Make sure to wear boots and gaiters if you have them because the trails can be muddy and horses walk all over.

Going west on Tower Hill Road, take a left onto Maple Rd. It most likely will not have a sign. It is the first road after the Tower Recreation Area. Go about ½ mile until you see a trail on your left with a gate and a dirt road on your right. That road turns into Aikens Road and declines precipitously. Park on the left—make sure not to block the road.

Walk due east on the trail. Take a right, going south onto the Mohawk trail. If you come to a lean to, you have gone too far. As soon as you turn onto the Mohawk trail the Finger Lakes Trail will cut across the Mohawk trail. If the trail you are walking on does not have the FLT cross immediately you know you are on the wrong trail.

The Mohawk trail is a multiple use trail. When I was there on a Memorial Day weekend, there had been a dry spell and the trail was muddy and had horse manure on it. So be prepared.

In a few hundred yards the trail will begin to descend. As the descent picks up you will cross a stream, it could be a dry streambed in the summer, and then the trail will rise quickly. Look for a clearing, almost like a parking area off to your left. You won't walk uphill more than 20-30 feet before the area appears on your left. The FOC begins on the other side of the stream before you cross it; so you can feel safe meditating anywhere in the area knowing you are on a FOC.

Toward the end of the pseudo parking spot, about 15-20 feet in is the first in a series (3) of S12's. Meditate on one of the flat stones or anywhere in the immediate area. The vibe is positive to very positive. The next in the series is 15 feet ahead of you going in the same perpendicular, and another 15 feet for the next.

As I was leaving I asked to see another FOC. I was directed to drive in the opposite direction to where I

The photo above shows the area of the trail dip and streambed before it rises. The dogs (circled) are on the left in the area that looks like a parking space.

walked in on the Onondaga Trail; to a narrow dirt road which descends dramatically and eventually turns into Aikens road. About ¾ of the way down the hill, I was shown an S8 in a little open area. Unfortunately the area was wet. But I was shown a FOC in an easily accessible place. Thank you.

Address: 3361 Tower Hill Rd, Watkins Glen, NY 14891.
Webpage: http://www.dec.ny.gov/lands/37446.html.
Telephone: 607-776-2165. DEC Region 8
Hours: Open year round. Free. Overnight camping allowed 3 night max, limit 10 people, campsite must be a minimum 150 feet away from water, road and trails; longer stays require approval.

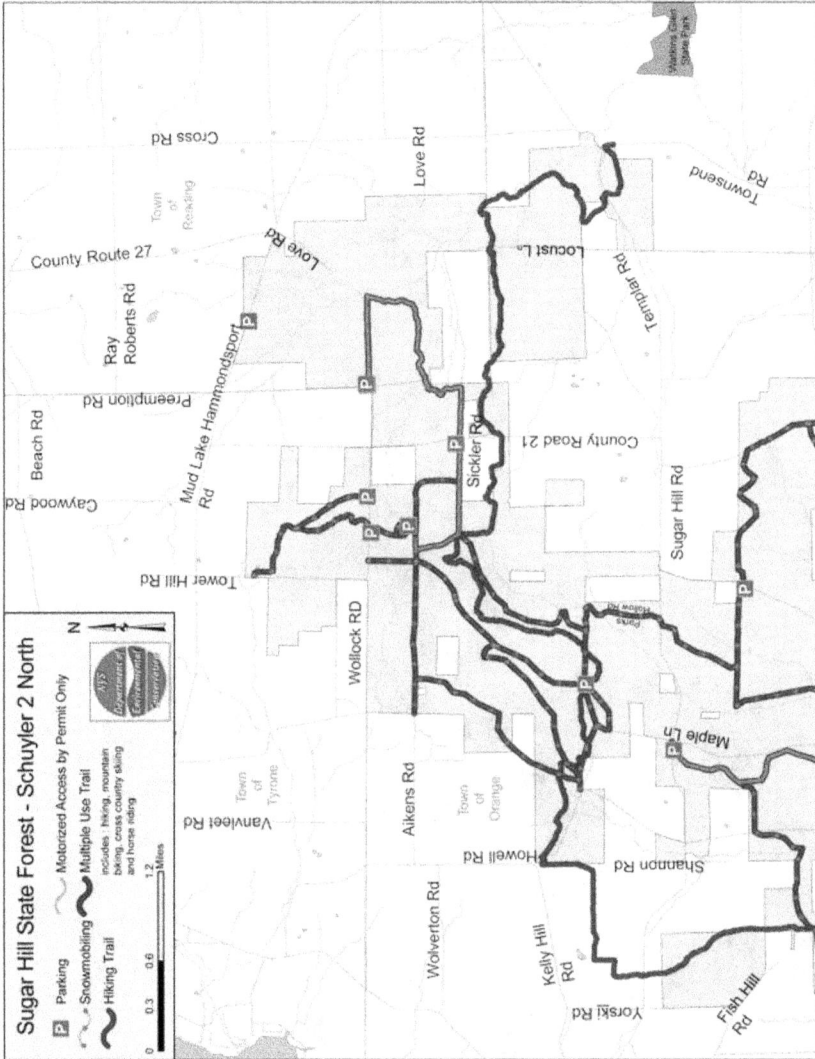

Sugar Hill State Forest - Schuyler 2 North

P Parking
Snowmobiling
Hiking Trail
Multiple Use Trail
includes: hiking, mountain
biking, cross country skiing
and horse riding
Motorized Access by Permit Only

NYS Department of Environmental Conservation

N

0 0.3 0.6 1.2 Miles

Directions: Take Rt. 14 north out of Watkins Glen. Take a left onto Bath St. Go a few blocks and turn right onto Rt. 28. Go a few miles and turn left onto Rt. 23. After several miles you will see markers for NYS DEC land. Take a left onto Rt. 21 and head south into the DEC forest. Take your first right onto Tower Hill Rd heading west. Take your first left onto Maple Lane (south.) Park across from Aikens Rd that begins on your right.

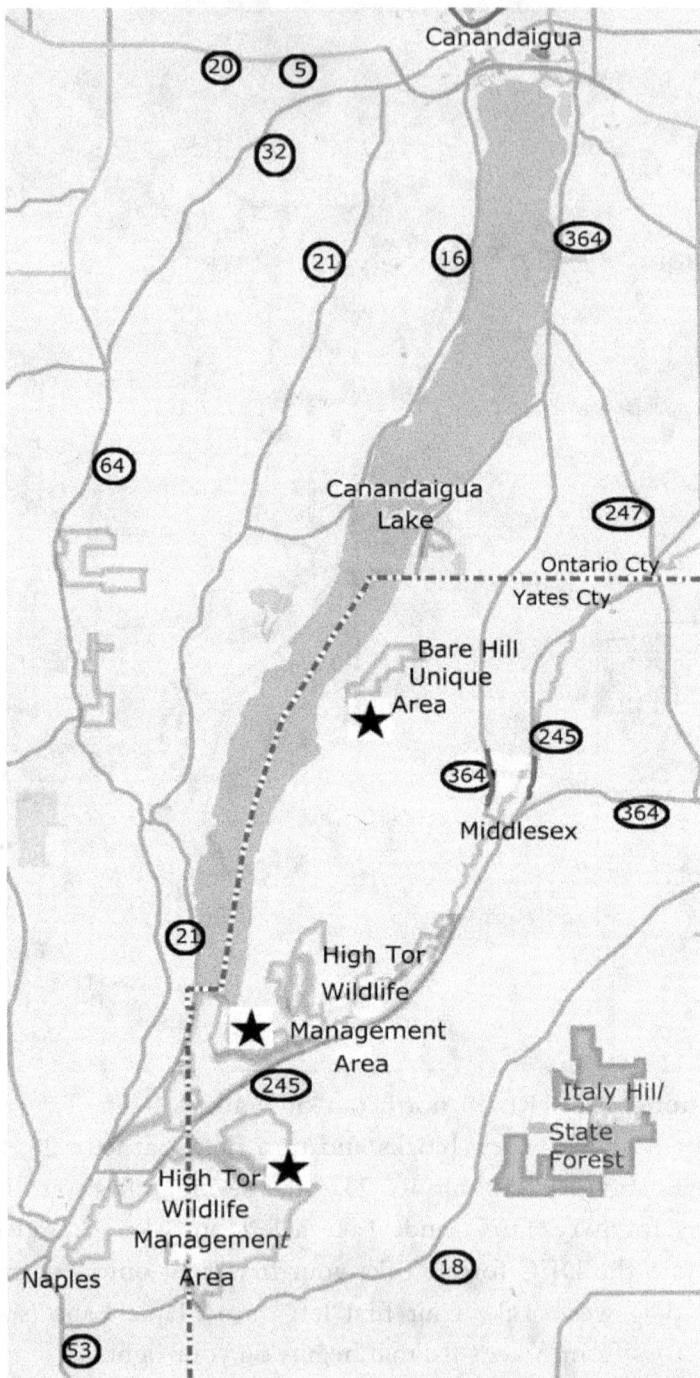

Map of Bare Hill and High Tor. © OpenStreetMap contributors.

Bare Hill and High Tor NYS DEC Forests

Both Bare Hill and High Tor NYS DEC lands located along Canandaigua Lake have a rich Native American background. Bare Hill is located in Middlesex (Yates County)/Gorham (Ontario County), while High Tor straddles Middlesex (Yates County) and Naples (Ontario County.) Each offers the pilgrim a unique opportunity to experience FOC and history.

Both places can lay claim to being where the Seneca people were born. I go with the state and list High Tor as the birthplace of the Seneca. High Tor contains numerous stone structures.

Middlesex, Yates County, NY

Bare Hill Unique Area

S6, V3,☆ ♡ 2 🍃

The Seneca Nation of the Haudenosaunee would hold their council meetings and offer prayers to Great Spirit at Bare Hill on the eastern shore of Canandaigua Lake. That spirit of peace and reconciliation that was involved with those prayers and council fires still lingers there today. The pilgrim looking to resolve an issue, needing a Big Answer to a question, or just looking to communicate with creator should spend some contemplative time on top of Bare Hill. There are FOC (S6); the vibe is very positive.

A Bare Hill

According to Seneca legend, Bare Hill was made barren (treeless) by a giant snake. The trees have grown back. The story goes that while canoeing one day a young boy found a colored snake in the water. He took it home and began to take care of it by feeding it insects and small reptiles. The snake turned out to have a ravenous appetite that made him grow and grow and grow. The snake grew so large that it had to be fed deer and other mammals.

Eventually he grew so enormous that the villagers feared for their lives. Before they could escape, the snake entwined itself around the village and killed everyone except a brother and sister. In a dream, the boy was told where to aim his arrow to kill the serpent. He was successful and the snake twisted and turned, destroying the trees at the top of Bare Hill before he fell into the lake. There are many variants of the story.

In the fall, to celebrate the harvest, a large council fire would be lit. Upon seeing this signal bonfires of tobacco would be lit around the shores of Seneca Lake.

The Ring of Fire was resumed on Labor Day weekend 1954. It is celebrated ever since on each Saturday of Labor Day weekend at dusk. Many homes along the shore of Canandaigua Lake join in with their own bonfire.

Finding the FOC

The FOC are located in a stand of pines next to a pond, A19 on the map at the kiosk. Unfortunately, the state cut DEC funding and the meadows on top of Bare Hill are no longer mowed that often. The place gets enough traffic so there will be herd paths, albeit in tall grass; how tall depending upon what time of the year you visit.

From the kiosk, bear right until the meadow ends. There will be a field (pathway) on the right going downhill—keep going straight forward. When the meadow ends, take a left uphill and walk through the woods for 100 feet. You will come upon a pond with a berm around it.

Head towards the stand of pines to the left of the pond. Within it is a clearing with a stone campfire.

The dogs mark the series (3) of S8's running along the edge of the trees. Notice the campfire on the right.

Experiencing Bare Hill

There is a FOC with a series (3) of S6's on the edge of the clearing in the stand of pines on the lake side. Even if you don't find the series all of the clearing rests on Fields.

The vibe in the clearing is very positive.

This is a pretty remote area and Bare Hill is not full of hikers. It affords you some privacy. You can build a campfire and meditate next to it, if you like. Nice. You can camp out and experience what it is like to sleep on a stacked Field with a very positive vibe. Primitive camping and camp fires allowed.

Address: Van Epps Rd, Middlesex, NY
Webpage: http://www.dec.ny.gov/lands/37438.html
Email: DEC Region 8 Bath Office: region8@dec.ny.gov
Telephone: 607-776-2165, DEC Region 8
Hours: Open year round. Free. Overnight camping allowed 3 night max, limit 10 people, campsite must be a minimum 150 feet away from water, road and trails; longer stays require approval.
Close by: High Tor NYS DEC Forest, Gossamer Wood Retreat.
Directions: From Canandaigua, take Rt. 364 south for several miles. Turn right onto Cty Rt. 10/North Vine Valley Rd. Right onto Bare Hill Rd and left onto Van Epps Rd.

References and Recommended Reading
Klees, Emerson; *Legends and Stories of the Finger Lakes Region, The Heart of New York State*. Friends of Finger Lakes Publishing Rochester, New York, 1995. Pg 22 sites South Hill as the birthplace of the Seneca.
Robinson, David D., 'Who build the "Old Fort" at Bare Hill, and other pre-Seneca Structures in Yates County, NY?", Crooked Lake Review, Spring 1997, http: //www. crookedlakereview .com/articles/101_135/103spring1997/103robinson.html.

Naples, Ontario County, NY

High Tor, The Holy Place
S4-12, V0-4, ▽☆♡(↑)▣ ⁊ ⚐ ☁✍ ☕

Imagine if you could go back in time 2,000, or even 3,000 years, or more, to when the mound builders inhabited much of the Eastern United States. Imagine if you could visit one of their sacred sites and feel the charged atmosphere of their spiritual practices as you sat next to one of their mounds. Can you feel the chills running up and down your spine as you cry for a vision and tap into the collective consciousness of the thousands that have been here centuries before you? Feel their thoughts, as they help elevate your consciousness, bring you closer to the Great Spirit, open up lines of communication to other worlds, and give you visions while healing you.

High Tor NYS DEC Forest (South Hill at the southern end of Canandaigua Lake in the Finger Lakes district of New York State is such a place. It consists of 6,100 acres and is part of the High Tor Fish and Wildlife Management Area. Aptly named as Tor, means craggy hill, or peak.

High Tor offers the pilgrim numerous FOC, stone mounds, powerful imprints, plenty to explore, hiking and much more. There are several areas with FOC that would be good to try and sense and feel Consciousness.

Elevated stone circle with Lucy (black dog) in the dimpled center. Ledges Area. Nice orb above her.

Sacred History

One of the appeals of High Tor are its stone structures. There are hundreds of stone and earthen mounds and other stone structures within it, particularly on South Hill. These structures were strategically placed to tap into Mother Earth to enhance the spiritual experience and/or facilitate healing. Many were built by the Adena and possibly the Hopewell; both Native American mound building cultures, as I will note shortly.

The thoughts of the many that have prayed, done ceremony, visionquested and performed other spiritual exercises there, still lingers on the land. The ether is a thick mixture of those thoughts and the essences of Mother Earth, which are enhanced by the stone structures.

The mound builders, the Hopewell and Adena, were not the only ones to hold South Hill in reverence. South Hill, or Nundawao, is where the Seneca people were born. According to legend it is at Nundawao that the earth divided and the Seneca people emerged. The Seneca refer to themselves as "Onodowaga," or "people of the great hill." The Seneca believe that they were born at "Kanandague," or the chosen spot. This is from where Canandaigua Lake gets its name.

There are also remnants of old Spirit Keeper stone structures, particularly in the Clarks Gulley, the base of South Hill. In other words, South Hill has a long history of being a sacred place and the area is covered with thoughts of the pilgrims that came there.

I don't believe that one culture created all the different stone structures on the various aspects of Mother Earth, but a variety of cultures and shamans did so over time. This analysis is based upon the knowledge I have gained over the years, plus some observations of the types of structures and aspects of Mother Earth that were, or were not, selected to have stone structures created on them. High Tor contains stone structures that were designed to tap into FOC, Earth Chakras, Energy Formations and

294

Spirit Lines. Further, I believe each structure is a representation of a particular culture. For example, Spirit Keepers focused on FOC, while others (possibly the Adena) worked with Earth Chakras. There is no proof, just my theory.

Brush Off the Dust

Years ago when I first wrote up South Hill for my listing of sacred sites for Mother Earth Prayers, I asked people not to pray, or walk on the stone structures, fearing that they would be damaged and lost for history. But my opinion about this has changed. South Hill is not a museum, but a holy area. It is the space, not the artifacts that matter most. And a holy place needs prayer and ceremony to remain vibrant; just like a muscle if it is not exercised it will atrophy. I discussed the importance of imprints in making a sacred space in Chapter 5.

You must look within yourself and ask how the stone structures should be treated. Should you decide to meditate, or pray on them understand that you will be influencing their structural integrity; so do so with the utmost care. Honor them, by using them as you see fit.

Please do not move around stones; or cut down trees, or bushes. What appears like an ordinary stone could have a purpose, or function. Be cautious. Act in a sacred manner.

Covered Earth Chakras

Most of the Earth Chakras on South Hill, and parts of Parish Hill and Brink Hill contained in High Tor, are covered with stones; a single stone, a pile of stones in a variety of shapes and forms. We have found many, into the hundreds (if you count single chakras, not the series they can come in), of covered Earth Chakras on South Hill. The only places that you do not find covered Earth Chakras are those that have been clearly farmed.

Placing stones over Earth Chakras blocks the movement of Earth Prana (energy) from properly circulating. The blocked prana lingers in the air and charges it up. Many people feel the energized air. It can give you an energy burst as if you drank an energy drink, or a cup of coffee. I notice it particularly in my dog's hyperactive behavior. If you cannot feel the energy directly, look for increases in the speed of your speech, or a rise in your endurance level.

Why do I believe the Adena constructed the stone mounds, or even placed stones covering Earth Chakras on South Hill and other parts of High Tor? Local historian and amateur archaeologist, David Robinson[1], notes that the NYS Dept. of Archeology determined that farmers did not create the stone mounds, in what we call

A covered Earth Chakra could be something as simple as one stone covering it, or a stone upon another stone to serve as a prayer seat, as pictured above. The staff to the right, in increments of 1' shows the structures size.

the Ledges area. Relying on the work of NY State Historians Parker and Ritchie, Robinson posits that the Hopewell and/or Adena created the mounds. In another article he refers to an aerial photograph taken in 1954 of the same area of South Hill that shows a large earthen mound, or ring that was deteriorating but would have been one half mile in diameter if in intact.[2]

I believe that it was probably the Adena that created stone structures that cover Earth Chakras at High Tor. I say this, partly because of Robinson's work, but mostly because Serpent Mound, the world's largest effigy mound (in the shape of a snake) in Peebles, Ohio, is strategically placed over Earth Chakras. Serpent Mound is considered to be an Adena Ceremonial site.

So, I believe that the Adena culture, through its shamans or others, were most likely the ones that placed the stones over Earth

Chakras. I don't see a contradiction that Serpent Mound consists primarily of earth, while the structures on High Tor are made out of stone. I believe that this is more of a function of available resources.[3]

I have been fortunate enough to have had some incredible experiences on South Hill. I have tapped into the thought forms of visionquestors that have caused me to cry for hours, as I asked God how I can better serve and help humanity. I have had visions on several occasions. I often gain insights and answers to questions that I have had. Feeling good, euphoria and spiritual highs are frequent. Having increased energy is a given.

I have also become melancholy, particularly the day after. I have had serious bouts of depression the day after as I crashed from my energy burst from the day before. I have found that meditating and spending time at places that emanate consciousness will help balance this feeling. The reviews of particular locations on South Hill will give you advice.

Please be advised that certain parts of High Tor, particularly South Hill, have a very charged atmosphere that can diminish your ability to sense FOC. In other words, you can become so energized that you don't feel anything else. Make sure your health and heart are up to it.

This is a holy place. Please treat the stone structures with respect and move in a sacred manner. Keep your thoughts and conversations focused on the divine. I expect my write-up will draw attention to this area, so if you see other people, remain silent unless they indicate they want to talk. Bow and show respect and don't hog a particular area, such as one with a vortex for very long. Remember we want to instill a vibe of giving, respect and community.

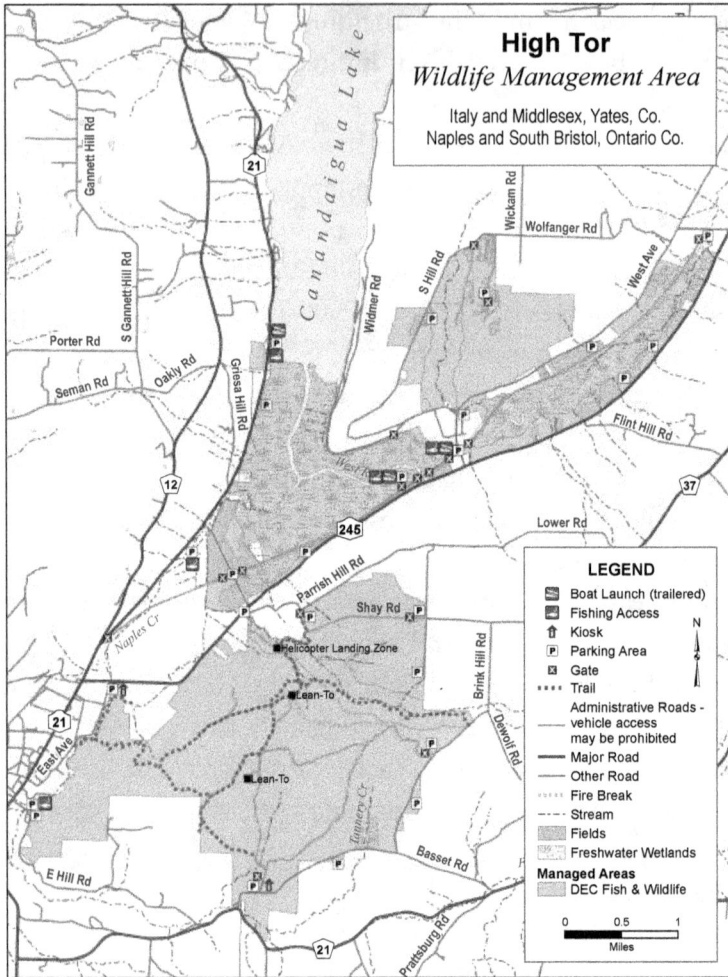

There are several places to experience Mother Earth and Her FOC and other aspects at High Tor:

Lower Clarks Gully
Upper Clarks Gully
The Ledges
The Hemlocked Glen
Keepers Area

Climbing the Gully/South Hill
Exploring South Hill
Brink Hill's Finger Lakes Trail
Exploring Parish and Brink Hills

Make sure to bring a compass with you, especially if go to the Keepers Area, or plan on exploring.

South Hill—Upper and Lower Clarks Gully

Clarks Gully is a deep gorge that has formed over time from water cascading down South Hill. It is a popular hike offering some spectacular views. The footing and steepness in parts are challenging.

What I call Upper and Lower Clarks Gully is the base of South Hill. The gully itself goes to the top of South Hill. The area I refer to is located on West Street near the intersection with Sunnyside.

Lower Clarks Gully
S6-8, V2-3, ☆ ⚕ 🔲 ♨ 〰 🪶

Has a great vibe, positive to very positive, and FOC throughout. There are numerous stone structures and lots to explore. The rush of water, which can alter the way things look, periodically floods this area.

You can access lower Clarks Gully from the parking area at the corner of Sunnyside and West Streets by taking the path on the left, the one closest to the stream. Or you could walk the stream from the parking area. Please be aware that the other side of the stream is private property.

Experiencing Lower Clarks Gully

Almost the entire lower gully area sits on a FOC. As soon as you enter you will pass several large stones, arguably boulders that mark the edge of the Fields. Look for a large protruding stone with a stone pile about 10 feet behind it. Use this area as a Welcome Circle. As you continue, there will be a stone mound on your right. It is on a stacked field of 6. Just pick a spot or spots you like, because you cannot go wrong.

Stay on this side of the stream. Ahead of you on the left you will see a fireplace where, by the beer cans I have picked up over years, indicates that partying goes on.

Look for a large triangular stone (see pic on the right) on the ground it rests on an S6. It is close to the lower elongated stone mound. I like this stone and have meditated on it several times because when I first found it I immediately thought that it was a Spirit Keeper's site.

You should be able to find two distinct wide and elongated piles of stones and a third one, a little above the other two (higher up.) They look like extremely wide stone walls that have fallen down, they are 1 to 2 feet high but are over 10 feet wide plus. Were they some sort of building, or a stone structure—or just created by the flow of water centuries ago when the stream may have twisted in a different direction? They are both powerful; the one farther up rests on an S8..

Again all of Lower Clarks Gully rests on FOC. Just find a place you like and enjoy.

Upper Clarks Gully
S2-8, V2-3, ☆ ⌇ 🪨 🍃

Upper Clarks Gully is located on the ridge above Lower Clarks Gully. It can be accessed by climbing the steep ridge on the right, as you face uphill; but it is granular and can be tricky. Instead you can begin at the trailhead at the intersection of West and Sunnyside roads. Take the trail on the right.

Experiencing Upper Clarks Gully

Less than a 100 yards up the trail, you will begin turning left and the ground will begin to flatten out. On your left side you will see a variety of stone structures from a stone wall, to flat stones, to small stone mounds on a variety of aspects of Mother Earth from FOC, to Earth Chakras to Spirit Lines.

There are several FOC on the left hand side in this first part of Upper Clarks Gully. Look for a large maple tree, with many branches, on your left hand side. In front of it is FOC with an S8. Spend some time exploring and meditating in this area. You may wish to use this area as a Welcome Circle.

Continue walking up the trail on the right side farther up and just before the trail turns right, you will see the remnants of what may have been a large stone circle. You should be able to see several large stones 2 to 3 feet high. Downhill, directly in front to the stones is a FOC (S8.)

Where the Trail Turns Right

If you turn left where the trail turns right, you will be going towards the herd path that hugs the rim above the gully that goes to the top. If you follow the trail to the right, it also goes to the top but way to the north of the Ledges and Keepers areas. Years ago I was guided to follow the trail and at a certain point to take a left and go uphill. I was eventually led to a very large three-tiered mound on the side of the hill on a steep part hidden in a briared

301

thicket. It consisted of three terraces each about 5 feet by 10-15 feet. Incredible. It shows how much there is to explore and find in High Tor.

The dogs are sitting in the area (circle) of large stones below where the trail turns right.

Climbing Clarks Gully
S?, V0-?, ⊇ 🖋

The climb up Clarks Gully is challenging, but doable. It is not a formal trail, but a hodgepodge of herd paths created by hikers, that hugs the edge of the gully. So there are no trail markers. I never attempted to climb the actual gully, the stream, itself.

Parts of the trail are very steep and covered with scree, or loose stones, that can cause you to slip, so you need to be careful. There are also numerous tree roots and scrub in places. To get a sense of what you will be facing in parts, try climbing the ridge from lower to upper Clarks Gully. You need to be in physical shape and have some experience hiking.

You can access the herd by climbing the ridge that separates upper and lower Clarks Gully; or by going to upper Clarks Gully and taking a left where the trail turns right and walking ahead until you get close to the edge of the ravine where you should find the herd path.

As you climb the gully will be to your left. In certain sections you will find several herd paths, many break to the left for people to get a better view. Some of these dead-end, or have you climbing steep scree covered areas. I suggest bearing to the right when you have a choice of herd paths. Most certainly explore and go to the left to get a better view, but remember to back track and bear right.

When you get closer to the top you will see a large downed tree and its exposed roots facing the gully. It offers some spectacular views. See picture above taken during the winter. The fall/winter/spring period when the leaves are down offer some of the best views. The also provide you better opportunities to see stone structures that may be hidden by flora.

One Labor Day weekend years ago I stopped and paused by this tree stump and saw what I thought were several large orbs. As I stared at them I realized that there were large swarms of monarch butterflies. Breathtaking.

Towards the top the trail will flatten and you will be walking in a pine woods. When you see a stream to your left, take the path to the left; this will bring you to the parking lot on South Hill Road. The trail will hug the side of a ravine for some distance bringing you closer and closer to the stream. Look for a place to cross the stream that allows you to get back up the other side. If you continue, the bank on the other side gets larger and larger.

When you cross the stream back track 20 feet or more and look for a herd path going up. This herd path will bring you to a trail on a ridge overlooking the Ledges area. If you turn to your left you can walk less than a 100 feet and get a spectacular view. To continue to the parking area take a right and walk until the trail flattens out and you see an opening in a pine woods to your right. Turn right into this area. The parking lot is on the other side of the grassy field in front of you. There should be a herd path through the field.

The Ledges
S12, V3, ▽ ☆ ♡ ⬆ ↋ ⛎ ✒️🕊

The Ledges area (South Hill) has the most charged atmosphere of anyplace in High Tor. Anyone that has ever visited an earthen mound and wants to experience what the energized vibe around them was like at their peak should go to the Ledges. The ether is electrified and the feeling is palpable. It is a hidden treasure.

The Ledges contains numerous stone mounds, most of which cover Earth Chakras. It has a very positive vibe and several FOC. It is easily accessible and does not require a lot of walking to get to and enjoy. It is located in a less remote area of the mountain where the woods are not so thick, so the chances of getting lost are less. It is at the Ledges that I first realized that the stone mounds there covered Earth Chakras. It can be accessed by a parking lot at the top of South Hill, off of (alongside) South Hill Rd.

The vibe at the Ledges is very positive. It is a great place to meditate at, do visionquesting, or perform ceremony. The spiritual embers remaining are very strong; there are several vortex rings indicating that vortices used to be there. Years ago there used to be at least one vortex, unfortunately it has dissipated. With a little love, intention and prayer, they will all come back to life. There is plenty to explore.

Please be advised that the ether of the Ledges area is highly charged, and it may impinge your ability to sense, or appreciate the FOC there; and possibly for the rest of the day.

The end of the rim trail above The Ledges provides views of the valley and gully.

Finding The Ledges Area

From the parking lot on the top of South Hill on South Hill Road follow the herd path through the grass to a pinewoods. Keep going. You will shortly come to a steep ridge with a trail along its rim. The Ledges area is directly below you. But you need to take a left onto the Rim Trail to access them. The trail has a slight decline to it that will eventually become rather steep for about 30 to 50 feet. You can avoid this steep bit by taking a loop to your left. Shortly the trail will begin to flatten out. You will see a trail to your left that goes into a lovely hemlock woods and stream (that is the trail up from the gully.) Five feet further ahead you will see a herd path to your right. Turn right on this path.

If the trail begins rising again you have gone too far. If you continue walking straight on the Rim Trail there will be a steep decline that will end at a spectacular view at a cliff's edge. Be careful, as South Hill is noted for steep inclines with scree that can rob you of traction and can act like ball bearings to move your feet without your permission.

The herd path to your right back tracks about 20 feet to bring you into the Ledges area. Immediately on your left you will see a stone mound that covers several earth chakras with a pond behind it.

Experiencing the Ledges Area

You are in FOC (which are found at either end of the Ledges area.) Walk about 20-40 feet and treat the area as a Welcome Circle. This is a very sacred place so please spend some time in the area of the Welcome Circle when you enter and leave. Please say a prayer and smudge yourself. Again spend time there, You will no doubt be taking pictures—that intention needs to be balanced.

There is a series (3) of S12's. The first in the general area of the Welcome Circle area; the other two are close to the base of the ridge above. Spend some time in this FOC. It is very sweet.

Ledges to your right

This section of South Hill (Ledges) is named after the series of embankments, or ledges that look like terraces at the base of the ridge above. They appear to be natural formations. Look for herd paths to help you traverse and climb the several ledges. There are no challenging sections to climb. The most interesting and best preserved stone formations are found on the higher ledges closest to the base of the large ridge above.

The Ledges area contains approximately two dozen stone circles/mounds, mostly covered earth Chakras. They are more like an oval/circle, 1 to 2 feet in height and 6 to 10 feet in diameter; often with an indented center. There are also several flat stones, ceremonial sites and other stone structures.

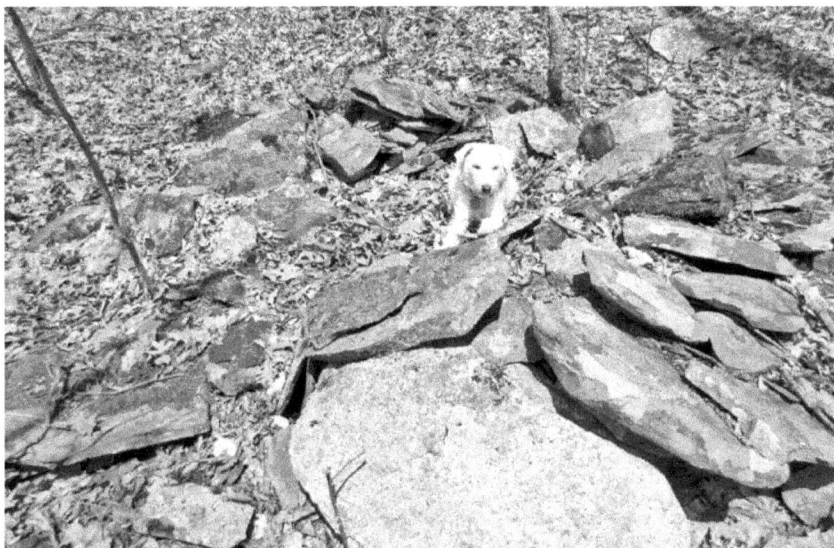

Pepper is in the dimpled center of one of the stone mounds in the Ledges.

I would recommend spending contemplative time close to the stone mounds. I believe that the dimple, or indented center, was intentional and this may have been where pilgrims sat for ceremony, or prayer.

FOC Ahead

At the farthest end away from where you entered is a pinewoods. At the northern part, or closest to the ridge, is a FOC that contains a series (3) of S12's. In the woods at the farther end of where you entered is another FOC with a series (3) of S12's.

You might want to spend some time here. Whenever I come I tend to get caught up with the stones mounds and forget that there are several FOC with S12's in the Ledges area. Meditating in consciousness will help balance out any edge or nervous energy you might have absorbed being on South Hill.

Healing Area

There is a very interesting stone structure that may have served as a healing place. It does not rest on Earth Chakras but another aspect of Mother Earth's energy apparati. It appears to be the three tiered elongated mound that David Robinson spoke about in one of his articles.

Looking downhill from where you entered, it is behind the pond and to the left. It is located on sort of a crest before the hill declines. To get to the healing stone structure, skirt the pond to the left. There is sort of a berm, or rise behind the pond. Below that is another rise, or crest upon which the healing stone structure is located on in a stand of pine trees.

The stone structure is about 25 to 30 feet long and about 3 to 4 feet wide. The lowest tier is a little over a foot high and is in the worst condition. The middle tier is about 2 to 3 feet high. The highest tier is 3 to 4 feet high and appears to have an indented center. That could be where pilgrims sat. Even though it looks a bit disheveled, given its age it is in remarkably good condition given that it is thousands of years old.

Meditating close to the lowest tier can be very therapeutic. Although near the upper tier ain't bad.

Earthen Mound?

Looking straight ahead from where you entered is an elevated area. It is below the ledges that are on the right side closer to the base of the ridge. Some people believe it is a manmade earthen mound.

There are also several vortex rings, Connectors/Artificial Leys, flat stones and more. Explore. Try to feel with your heart and not with your eyes and you will find plenty.

Looking lengthwise at the three tiered mound. Pepper is standing on the highest tier.

The Hemlocked Gully
V4, ▽ ☆ ✎

Next to the Ledges area is a beautiful forest of hemlocks by the gully that contains an energy vortex, or what I call a natural vortex. It is a vortex of Cosmic Prana, not the consciousness emanating from FOC. It is Very Sweet.

309

On the rim trail above the Ledges area, just before you turn right to enter the Ledges area, is a trail 5 feet ahead that goes to the left. That is the trail down the gully. Take it. You will find the vortex about 6-8 from where the herd path turns left before

descending to cross the stream. It is about 6-8 feet from an old stone camp fireplace. A large flat stone rests on it. There is no guarantee that the stone will be there when you visit.

The vortex underscores that there are many, many special and mystical places in High Tor that remain to be discovered.

The Keepers Area
S6-12, V0-4, ▽ ☆ ♡ (↑) ζ ♨ ✿

The Keepers Area contains dozens of stone structures, large mounds, sculpted structures, individual stones and more. There are some incredibly powerful FOC. It also contains a very nice healing area, similar to and related to the three-tiered mound in the Ledges area. Unfortunately all that remains of what was probably an intricate structure is a large circular stone pile.

The vibe in the Keepers is neutral to extremely positive. There are numerous vortices and vortex rings located in the area. One the vortices is located on what may have been a Spirit Keepers site—an elongated stone mound in the shape of a rectangle perfectly placed on a series of 3 S12's. It is a deteriorated stone wall that extends in both directions.

If you do not have experience walking in the woods with no trails or markers you should consider whether to visit the Keepers area. There is a dirt road that directs you there and that dissects the area. But many of the structures are located in heavily wooded areas with downed trees, so you need to bring a compass. Because the area is a little more secluded, it is less visited, so the chances of seeing someone are less. Should you get lost, go uphill and look for open fields. These fields ultimately connect to the parking area. In other words, if you go uphill you will eventually come to a road, or parking area.

That said, this is a great area to explore and connect with Spirit as well as try to sense and feel Consciousness. What is nice about the Keepers area is that it is not as highly charged with blocked Earth Prana from covered Earth Chakras the way the Ledges area is. I believe this is because the Ledges area is steep and close to the gully, so it was never farmed; and is not frequented as much by hunters, or hikers. Consequently, there are many more covered Earth Chakras, not only the larger mounds, but individual stones placed on an Earth Chakra that have never been moved.

While the vibe varies from neutral to extremely positive, it is evident that not all that has transpired in this area since the mounds were constructed was positive. So the imprints in several locations are less than desirable. This should not deter you from visiting. Praying and meditating in this area can help elevate it to its grandeur again as a sacred area.

Plan on giving yourself at least a full day to take in and appreciate all that the Keepers area has to offer.

Finding the Keepers Area

Finding the Keepers area can be a challenge. The quickest way is off of South Hill Road before it intersects Wolfanger Road. Turn into the Falls Gate parking area. Follow the road to the end and park at, or near, the roundabout. This path can be tricky!

Walk downhill through the field bearing to your right to an opening. Depending upon when you come the field may or may not be cut. The road traversing the fields is to your right (west.)

311

The opening may be overgrown. Walk a short distance, maybe 20-30 feet or so until you come unto a clearing. Follow the clearing downhill. Look for a path on your right in about 20-30 feet. This will bring you into a clearing that traverses the mountain perpendicularly. Walk right for 100 to 125 feet.

Look for a bird house (#63) downhill on your right. It is in a large field going downhill. Go the bottom far right of the field. You should be able to see a dirt road 20 feet in front of you. Go to the dirt road and take a left and head downhill; the Keepers area is about 100-125 yards downhill. Keep your eyes peeled for the posts of an old wooden gate on either site of the road.

This may sound confusing, but the herd paths will guide you. Basically bear to your right until you see birdhouse #63 and then go downhill. Be aware that the fields may be high. When I was there one fall the fields were recently cut and unfortunately, the cutting left stubble of stems and small trees 3-4 inches high that proved challenging. Walk slowly.

The second option, easier but longer, is to go to the top of South Hill Road and look for a service road on the south side just west of DEC Preserve Road that takes you to the Falls Creek Parking area. You will see two yellow gates and a stop sign. Make sure not to block the entrance to the service road when you park your car. Follow this road down about ¾'s to a mile, this is the longer route, but easier to find. It is the wide trail referred to in the previous paragraph.

Honoring the sacred area

The old gateposts mark the beginning of the Keepers area. We have used the center of the two posts as a make shift Welcome Circle. Please stop and say a prayer, do a cleansing/smudging, ask for permission to enter. If you bring an offering, leave it near the posts or by the large mound down below.

Upon leaving, please stop again at the Welcome Circle and give thanks and say a prayer. Remember to act in a sacred manner.

The bulk of the Keepers area ends when the dirt road ends.

You will see to your left a very large stone; there are two smaller, but still large stones in front of it forming a triangle of sorts. They mark the intersection of three Spirit Lines that forms a triangle. In the picture on the left Pepper is sitting on one the stones making up the triangle of stones at the end of the trail. This is a pattern of stone work you will see at other places such as Hipp Brook Preserve.

There are many more stone works, configurations of all sorts to be found in the Keepers Area.

The Keepers

The FOC begin on the dirt road about 60-80 feet down from the posts and continue to the left side of the large stone mound on your left. It is located just before the trail flattens; look for a large stone mound, 25-30 feet in diameter, on your left hand side, about 50 feet off the dirt road. In the fall it can be covered with leaves making it difficult to see. The mound covers seven Earth Chakras on two main energy lines. As you face it FOC extends from the left of the stone mound to behind it.

Years ago while I was meditating by this stone mound I heard a stern and mildly prideful voice within say, *"Four Keepers took care of this mound."* The implication was that it was a succession of four Keepers over a period of years that were responsible for the mound I was meditating on.

The Keeper would be a shaman, priest or some sort of other holy person. This was most likely a position of high honor. The

Keeper would be responsible for maintaining the spiritual and physical integrity of the mound. They would direct people where to sit, and would have lead ceremonies and other rites around the mound. They were also responsible for the physical maintenance of the mound.

Because of that vision I named this location the Keepers Area.

I ask that you please consider becoming a Keeper for a sacred site near your home. It does not need to be a recognized sacred site, only a place you hold dear, or wish to clear and keep clean. I am Keeper for several sacred sites.

Experiencing the Keepers Area

The left side of the dirt road has the most stone structures.. The last stone mound is located near the end by the corner of where the trail ends and another goes uphill. Just before the large stone that forms a triangle. It is a counterpart to the three-tiered mound in the Ledges area—a Healing Place. It is in poor condition and looks like rubble.

The Keepers Area is made up of stone mounds of varying shape, size and condition, a few are just rubble. The mounds also cover more than just earth chakras and include Spirit lines, FOC and other aspects of Mother Earth.

There is a FOC (S10) to the left of the stone mound that covers seven Earth Chakras, and extends behind it. The highpoint is about 30 feet behind the stone mound.

Several mounds are located behind the first large stone mound, or slightly to the right or left of it. Make sure to have a compass if you plan on exploring.

Spirit Keepers Mounds?

There is also a FOC (S12) farther behind the large stone mound. It can be a challenge to find. Continue walking perpendicularly away from the dirt road. Soon the land will rise slightly. When it begins to flatten out you will be in the area of the FOC. Look for a dilapidated stonewall that traverses almost parallel to the dirt road. Follow it to the right as it approaches a stand of pine trees ahead of you on your left. Notice how the stone wall is covered with smaller trees and brush; it is in a FOC.

The S12 with a vortex in the back area.

Within the Field is a series (3) of S12's. The first in that series contains a vortex. It is situated between 2 trees on two sides and two large stones on the other 2 sides. A gnarly old twisted tree is at the other end of the rectangular mound (stone wall.) LOOK FOR THE TREE IT IS A GOOD MARKER. It is pictured on the left side on the next page. Notice how its trunk is twisted and dying yet it extends a new limb into the sky. Spend as much time as you can meditating in the vortex and the area around it.

Spend lots of time in this area, particularly on the stone mounds (stone wall); it is one huge FOC. So even if you cannot find the specific spot you will be in a Field. The vibe is very positive to extremely positive. Soak it up.

The gnarled tree near the vortex.

While your inclination might be to max your time out in the vortex, I would suggest spending time in all of the FOC in this immediate area and the others in the Keepers area. Over the years I have come to believe that each FOC is unique in some way, because they can affect me in different ways. Often when I find a FOC for the first time and meditate in it I feel as though I have been nourished with something new, or something that previously I did not realize I was lacking.

This is an ideal place to try and sense and feel Consciousness. Try and visit several times and spend as much time as possible.

If you go back to the dirt path you entered on and continue going away from the area of the Welcome Circle you see a large area of Pine trees, what we call the Pines. As you continue close to the road is a vortex of Cosmic Prana that is not spot specific; in other words it is not on an aspect of Mother Earth, another indication that the Keepers area was a sacred site. You will need dowsing rods to find it, as it is in a nondescript area.

The rest of the Pines section contains several stone mounds and numerous stone piles, mounds that have fallen apart over the years, particularly close to the trail. Some of them cover some interesting aspects of Mother Earth and would be good to meditate on. Try to feel if a pile is special or not.

The West Side

The other side of the dirt road from the Pines is what we refer to as the West Side. It contains several mounds that cover Earth Chakras. The vibe is neutral.

Not far from the entry posts to the Keepers area as you descend downhill you will see a stone mound on your right about 75 feet off of the road. Someone has decided to stack a pile of flat stones creating a sort of monument upon it.

From the end of the dirt road that dissects the Keepers Area if you continue going downhill (Right) you may go a half mile or more and still find an occasional mound. There is a waterfall and spectacular gorges downhill to your left as well. But be careful, as downed trees and thickets in certain spots can get you lost.

Be Careful

It has been a long time since the stone mounds were constructed. Not everyone that has visited since has come there with the best of intentions, nor have they done the best things as is common with all cultures. Those thoughts can linger in places. This can create an atmosphere at many levels that does not bring out the best, or attract the best. These divergent attitudes are reflected in the vibe of the Keepers area, which is neutral to extremely positive, compare this to the very positive vibe in the Ledges area.

There are also parts where you may feel unwelcome in certain of its neighborhoods; or sense that a prankster is playing with you. It is all harmless, but can be disconcerting.

I say this not to discourage you from coming but to educate you about humankind's impact on Mother Earth. We can either enhance or make it foul and damage Mother Earth. All of the stone structures strategically placed on aspects of Mother Earth by a variety of civilizations indicate that the Keepers Area has been revered for thousands of years. Once the vibe was probably incredibly positive and vortices abounded throughout. It can be such again, Earth Healers are working on it. Please visit and help us resurrect this divine place to its former self through your prayers.

Come with the best of intentions. Bring an offering and spend time in the Welcome Circle and you will be fine.

Exploring South Hill
S?, V?, ☆ ⋜ 🐚 🖋

If you are an experienced hiker you may want to explore South Hill, there are hundreds of stones and stone structures marking aspects of Mother Earth located on it. As I noted I found a three-tiered mound up the hill from upper Clarks Gully. I have been coming to High Tor for over a decade, but it was only recently that I found the vortex near the rim trail by the Ledges area.

Exploring is also about finding a less traveled area where the thoughts of visionquesters and pilgrims linger powerfully in the air. Places that allow you tap into their imprints and catch a ride to higher states of consciousness, or other realities. While there is no guarantee of finding such a place, the effort needed should you find one, is certainly worth it.

Explore and enjoy and you might find something unique.

Finger Lakes Trail at Brink Hill
S12, V2-4, ▽ ☆ ♡ ⇑ 🔲 ⋜ 🐚 〰 🖋

Across from South Hill is Parish Hill and Brink Hill, part of the High Tor State Forest. It provides for a nice hike and some powerful FOC and some stone structures that once may have been a Spirit Keepers site.

318

The vibe runs from positive to extremely positive. If you are looking to experience and sense Consciousness, this would be a good place to visit. Very nice indeed!

Getting to the FOC

There are two routes to get to the trail.

Jones Road: It is a short 15-20 minute walk to the FOC (S12.) The hike is not strenuous or difficult, but there are some challenges—the trail to get to the Finger Lakes Trail (FLT), along which the FOC are located, is a herd path that is not maintained and I imagine crossing the stream to get to the FLT in the spring could be a challenge.

After you park your car, continue to follow Jones Road. It will take you 10-12 minutes to get to the stream. The herd path begins by going through an area of wild weeds, which if you come later in the summer can be quite tall. Within a few minutes you will be in a forested area and eventually you will be descending and walking on a streambed, which depending upon when you come, should be dry.

Toward the end, the streambed fragments into several little branches before it feeds into a larger stream. Look for a place to cross the stream. If you come in the spring, or after a torrential rain, bring along a pair of water shoes you can slip on to cross the stream.

Look for an FLT registry on the other side of the stream. Register. Take a right hand turn and get on the FLT, which follows the stream.

Brink Hill Road: You can access the Finger Lakes Trail directly from Brink Hill Road.

Park your car off to side of the road by the Finger Lakes Trail Marker on Brink Hill Road. Be aware that Brink Hill has a dog leg to it. It is about a 20-30 minute hike, or less, depending on how fast you walk.

From the Finger Lakes Trail Registry: Use the area in front of the Registry as a Welcome Circle. Follow the stream downhill. Within a few minutes you will be climbing a small embankment 8-10 feet high. You are entering a FOC. Continue on the trail. Shortly the trail will rise and then dips sharply within 5 feet. There will be small ridge on your left. There is a large stone on your right.

Experiencing the FOC

You are now in a big FOC. The vibe is very positive. Find a place you like; on the small ridge amongst the hemlocks, or perhaps closer to stream so you may hear the rush of water.

Closer to the stream there may be the remnants of an old Spirit Keeper site. Go to the large rock that was on your right when you first came to this area. See picture on the right. Looking from the large rock toward the stream, the series (3) of S12's are at 10 to 11 o'clock from you on your left. The first in the series is about 25 feet away and has a large flat stone placed upon it, in the picture on the right a backpack marks it. The next two are 15 feet apart and have a small pile of stones on them, very indistinct, but clearly a pile. The dogs mark them. The last in the series, closest to the stream (white dog, Pepper) has a vortex ring on it.

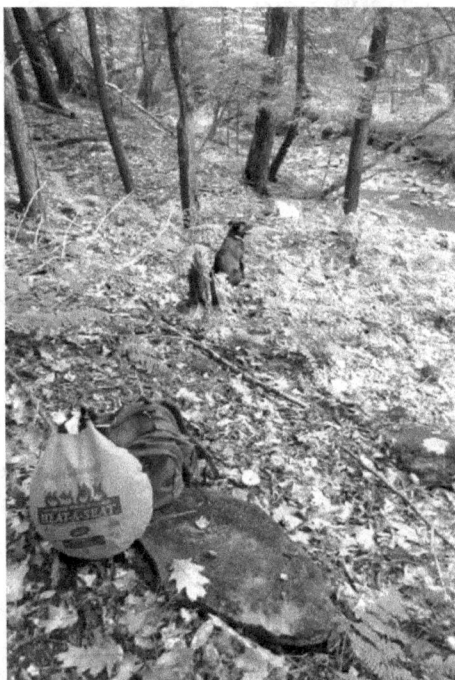

Because the stones were placed on the highest areas of stacked Fields (S12), I believe that they were placed there by Spirit

Keepers. Although I must admit that the stones are not extremely large, so it may well be that years ago they were carried there by the stream and runoff.

This is a very sweet FOC with a vibe running from very positive to extremely positive. Find a place you like and soak it up. Make sure to spend some time in the vortex ring.

Fields Ahead

There is another FOC containing a series (3) of S12's about a five minute walk ahead on the FLT. When the trail comes back towards the stream look for a little mini-peninsula to your right, a little before the trail breaks to left and narrows sharply.

The FOC is on the peninsula; the vibe is very positive. Two in the series (3) of S12's is on the peninsula; the other is below. In the picture above the first in the series is just in front of, and to the right a Manitou stone (upright stone in the ground.) My papers are next to the Manitou stone. The second in the series (S12) is located at the edge of the peninsula, where the backpack is.

Exploring Parish and Brink Hills
S?, V?,☆ ٤ 🝙 🪶

Like South Hill much of Parish and Brink Hills have a variety of Stone Structures. Consider exploring. Use the respective Trailheads as a Welcome Circle. I would suggest entering mid point such off of Parish Hill Rd., or Brink Hill Road. My personal experience so far is that the upper half of the mountain contains the stone mounds and sacred sites.

Charged Spirit Lines
The area along Brink Hill has numerous charged Spirit Lines, only a few remain potent. If you visit please consider charging them up by meditating on them, or by the stones that mark them.

The large rock in the picture above marks the intersection of several Spirit Lines. Notice the stone on the upper left it marks one Spirit Line. The other stone ahead the large stone marks another one. There are so many charged Spirit Lines on Brink Hill that you need to check out just about every stone you see. Please visit and help re-charge this divine area.

Address: High Tor Straddles Rte. 245 between Middlesex and Naples, NY. It is part of DEC Region 8, 6274 E. Avon-Lima Rd., Avon, NY, 14414-9519
Webpage: http://www.dec.ny.gov/outdoor/24439.html
Telephone:,585-226-2466, DEC Region 8
Hours: Dawn to dusk year round. **NO SEARCHING FOR HISTORICAL, OR ARCHEALOGICAL ARTIFACTS—IN OTHER WORDS DO NOT DIG, OR MOVE THINGS.**
Directions: From Canandaigua take Rt. 364 south. In Middlesex take Rt. 245 south.

References and Recommended Reading
1. Robinson, David D., 'Who build the "Old Fort" at Bare Hill, and other pre-Seneca Structures in Yates County, NY?', Crooked Lake Review, Spring 1997, http://www. crookedlakereview .com/articles/101_135/103spring1997/103robinson.html.
2. Robinson, David, 'Saint George the Serpent, and the Seneca Indians', Crooked Lake Review, February 1994. www. crooked lakereview.com/articles/67_100/71feb1994/71robinson.html.
3. I hope to write a book on Adena, or pre-Iroquois, Ceremonial Mounds that will go into greater detail about the use of covered Earth Chakras.
Klees, Emerson; *Legends and Stories of the Finger Lakes Region, The Heart of New York State. Friends of Finger Lakes Publishing Rochester, New York,* 1995. Pg 22 sites South Hill as the birthplace.
Quinn Barnard, Beth; 'Canandaigua Lake, N.Y.: Of Indian Legends and Sylvan Trails',; NY Times, October 1, 2006
High Tor Stone Monuments Blog, Has some great pictures, http://hi-torstone.blogspot.com.
Clarks Gully Blog, More pictures on the places mentioned, http://www.clarksgully.blogspot.com.

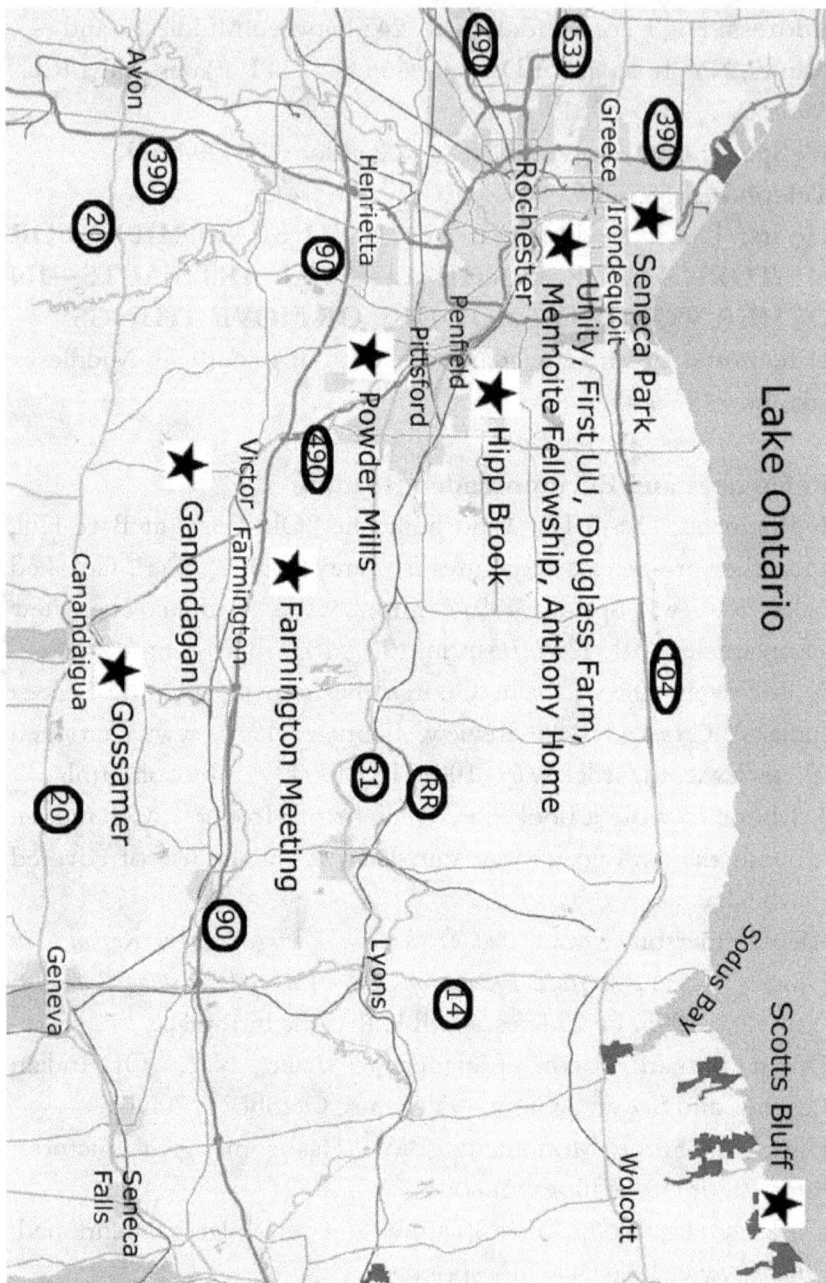

Map of Metro Rochester. Source, OpenStreetMap contributors, www. openstreetmap. org.

Metro Rochester, Genesee Valley

Metro Rochester lies at the western end of the heart of Mother Earth's Soul, the Utica—Rochester corridor. The area contains numerous FOC and places to experience them

Rochester was a hotbed of social reform and social justice, home to Susan B. Anthony and Fredrick Douglass. It was a major stop on the Underground Railroad with many boarding boats on the Genesee River to cross Lake Ontario into Canada.

East of Rochester along the shoreline of Lake Ontario are visually spectacular bluffs, most notably Chimney Bluffs State Park, and Scotts Bluff which contains FOC and is reviewed. The bluffs were created by retreating glaciers and are made up of a mix of rock, gravel, clay and sand that they dragged with them.

Canandaigua, Ontario County, NY

Located at the northern end of Canandaigua Lake, it was once a Seneca Village. Canandaigua in the Seneca language means the "chosen place." It contains numerous FOC.

Gossamer Wood Retreat and Healing Center
S4-12,V3-4, ▽ ☆ ♡ (↑) 回 ζ 𝍅 🖾 ♨

The grounds of Gossamer are dedicated to Mother Earth, particularly to FOC. The trail system meanders through FOC as high as S12, other divine aspects of Mother Earth, healing places, a Spirit Keeper's site and numerous vortices. Hundreds of flat stones and stone structures, where people have prayed, or meditated, are located on the grounds to guide you to the 'hot spots', for lack of a better world. The vibe runs from very positive, to extremely positive.

I have led several group meditations to connect with Mother Earth, and taught courses at Gossamer over the years; as well as worked with others to make this divine place sparkle even more. This would be a great place to learn to connect with Mother Earth, as well as one of the best places to try and sense and feel Consciousness.

The only caveat is that Gossamer rests on low ground so early spring, and after torrential rains, the grounds can be soggy and attract bugs. But the Tall Oaks area in the back, is elevated and always dry, and by the way is one the jewels of this lovely place. Please make sure to call before visiting.

PLEASE NOTE THAT AT THE TIME OF THIS REVIEW EFFORT HAD BEGUN TO CONVERT THE GROUNDS OF GOSSAMER INTO PUBLIC SPACE.

About Gossamer

Bill Dewey, owner and operator, is an energy healer who practices BodyTalk, Reiki, sound therapy and other healing modalities. He purchased Gossamer in 2001, a private residence nestled on 12 acres, so that he could focus on his healing practice. Bill took to remodeling the house and eventually put in a trail system. Bill and I connected in 2007; I helped refine the trail system by locating flat stones to highlight Mother Earth's divine aspects with a particular emphasis on FOC.

Classes and other activities are held at Gossamer.

Experiencing Gossamer

A series of trails traverse the grounds of Gossamer totaling 1+ miles in length. Most of them are on FOC, or higher aspects of FOC. They provide for a soul nourishing contemplative walk.

Numerous flat stones and stone circles are situated on FOC, on higher aspects of Mother Earth, in healing areas or in other special areas next to the trails. There are also little offshoots from the trails that give you access to divine, or healing areas. See the Trail map.

Owner Bill Dewey on the bridge to the 'Other Side.'

Bill had generously decided to donate his property to a land trust, but found no takers. He is still considering alternatives. Assuming that the property would end up being available to the public we had to put in a new trail system to accommodate a new access point and parking area. I also had to take a fresh look at the grounds, something I had not done in years. In the process we found lots of new FOC (S12), a Spirit Keeper site and much, much more. We have dubbed this new area the Ancient Area.

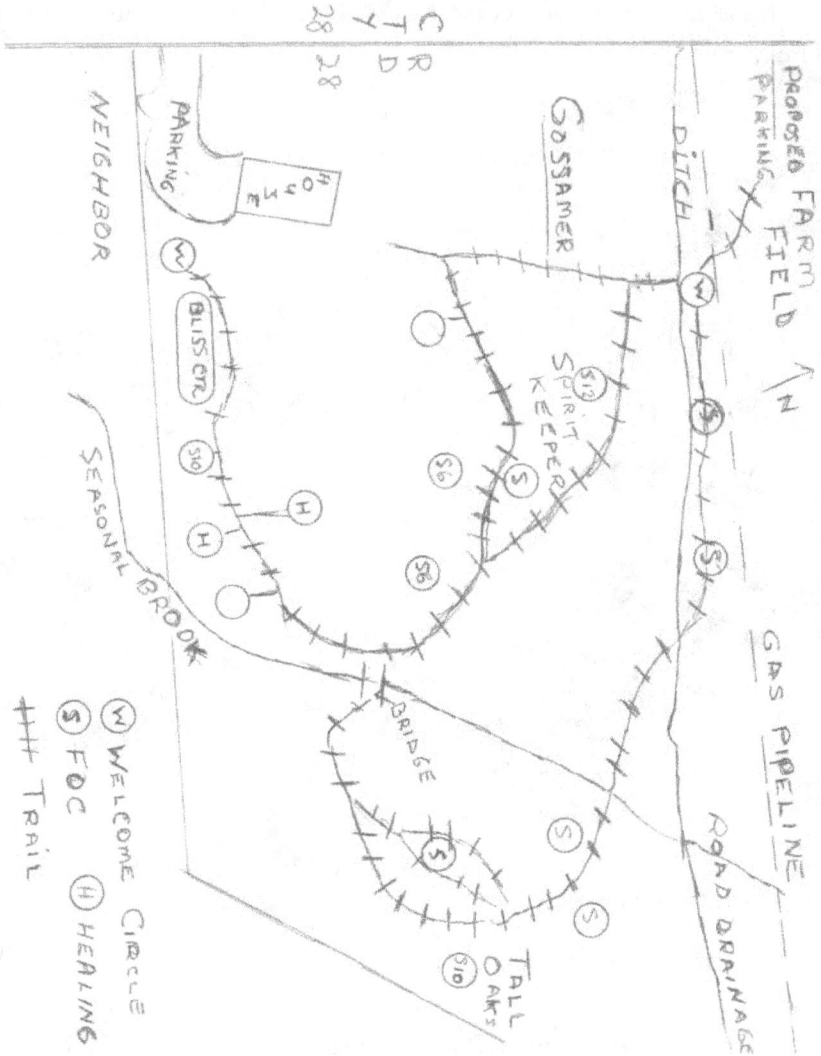

The Map above is an approximation of the Gossamer Trail System. It is not detailed, or exact, only meant to serve as a rough guide. How the trail system looks, or the status of the property when you arrive, could be dramatically different.

Since Gossamer is in the process of undergoing a transition I thought the best way to explain the trail system was to write separately about the original trail network and the new one (the Ancient Area.) Depending when you come for your pilgrimage

328

you may be parking behind the house, or just north of the driveway. This will affect how you approach your visit.

The Original Trail Network

The Welcome Circle is located on the right side of the parking lot. Please smudge yourself with a feather, or by hand. There may, or may not be a prayer on paper next to the Welcome Circle, so say a few words. Given that Bill is a healer and the focus of many of the programs is on healing, you might want to make that the focus of your intentions. The donation box is located next to the Welcome Circle. A vortex has formed in the center of the Welcome Circle so you may wish to meditate there.

The trail loops west/east from the front to the back of the property. I suggest starting at the northern end of the loop away from the parking area by the sweat lodge, and finishing by the Bliss Learning Center near the parking lot.

Beginning from the northern end of the loop, within a few feet you will see an indentation to your right with a stone circle. It is on an aspect of Mother Earth that can enhance your mood.

A few more steps and you will be in a FOC that will remain until the stream. The trail crosses a large stone Circle, the Spirit Keepers Circle. Most of the circle is on your left. It has the best vibe and highest stacked FOC at Gossamer.

Continuing there will be plenty of places to stop. Look for flat stones, or pick a spot that you like. The right side of the trail up to the bridge has several potent places. Be careful of poison ivy in spots.

Walk across the bridge to the 'Other Side.' As you cross the bridge you are entering another aspect of FOC that continues along the area around the path. See if you like it; if so stop and spend some time. This area was activated over the years by the prayers and meditations of visiting pilgrims.

As you continue walking look for an old woodpile on your left (about 100-150 feet) with a trail next to it. Turn left and take the trail. You will be in a large FOC with numerous flat stones on the ground. It is called 'Peace and Serenity' by the people that have felt such here.

The trail will split. To your left are more places to meditate; to your right is a more direct route to the Tall Oaks area.

The Tall Oaks is so called for its two tall oak trees. It contains a large FOC with a series (3) of S10's and a very positive vibe. Because it is elevated, you don't have to worry about ground water, so you can safely come here any time of the year. Even in snow the oaks provide a good marker and they are the center of a large FOC.

You may notice a line of stones between the two oak trees that continues towards the creek. It is a 'Line'; a replication of a Spirit Keeper technique I have found in places that is meant to link several FOC to enhance them, the same way you connect Christmas lights. Find a place you like and enjoy.

Circle of stones (S10) near the Bliss Learning Center.

To get back, you can follow the path by which you came or take the one closer to the distant oak tree. The two will eventually merge and take you to the creek. After you walk across the bridge take a left; FOC will be to your right. As you continue, you will see several indentations to your right and left. Most of these are healing places. Explore!

As you get closer to the house and the Bliss Learning Center look for a trail to your left. It is an indentation connecting three large circles marking a series (3) of S10's. This is a powerful place, the vibe is extremely positive and it is a great place to try and sense and feel Consciousness.

The Ancient Area

I call this area north of the old trail system and the Spirit Keepers the Ancient Area, because it has a very distinctive feel to it; A sense that it is old and has not been violated by the thoughts and imprints of humankind for sometime. I say this because the vibe is very positive, to extremely positive.

No one has prayed, or meditated in this area in decades, if not centuries, indicating it was once a sacred area. Why such a powerful vibe? I expect over time people will get insights, have questions answered and have other mystical experiences in the Ancient Area as they tap into the powerful imprints embedded in the land, whose form (the imprints) lies between archetypes and surface imprints.

The Ancient Area consists of the Spirit Keepers Loop and the new trail.

Spirit Keeper's Loop

The Spirit Keepers Loop runs through the Spirit Keeper's Circle from the house to the northern arm of the old trail system. It passes over the Spirit Keepers Circle that has the highest stacked FOC, a series (3) of S12's at Gossamer. It also contains what appears to be an ancient Spirit Keeper site—a large flat stone with a vortex on it. The location of the stone on an S12 and a vortex tells me this. Meditate on it, dream, tap into its imprints or try and sense and feel Consciousness there. It is powerful!

Spend some time in the Spirit Keeper's Circle. When we created the circle and consecrated it by meditating on flat stones within it, four/five separate flocks of geese flew overhead from different directions; some of them crossed paths. What a joy.

The Spirit Keeper's site, a stone with a vortex, in the Spirit Keepers Circle in the Ancient Area.

As you continue on the trail the short loop on the other side of the Spirit Keeper's Circle has plenty to explore and enjoy.

The Future Entry Trail

Enter the parking lot a few hundred feet north of 2235 County Rd. 28 and park your car (assuming the transition to public land is complete.) Look for a path in the woods that is the trailhead. Quickly there is a Welcome Circle. Say a prayer and smudge yourself. The Welcome Circle is the first of many FOC to follow.

Continuing, there will be FOC on both sides of the trail. Feel free to move 30-40 feet or more off of the trail to access places. Look for flat stones, or pink tap hanging over power places.

Eventually you will see a large ditch on your right which you will end up crossing and end up in the Tall Oaks area.

The open area along the trail on the other side of the ditch has numerous sacred areas and interesting places. It is a fairly open area. Please walk around and explore, there are some powerful areas a few hundred feet from the trail.

There are several Manitou Stones close to the trail. Most mark the intersection of Spirit Lines. It is difficult to tell if they are Charged Spirit Lines because the vibe at Gossamer is so powerful. Also I have not looked for connecting stones.

The above Manitou stone in the Ancient Area marks the intersection of 4 Spirit Lines.

Enjoy

Before leaving, please make sure to stop at the Welcome Circle and give thanks and say a prayer.

Until the land is turned into a public space enter and park in the parking area by the house and make sure to call before you come. Please donate generously to help Bill cover his costs and maintain the grounds. Periodically Bill asks for volunteers for trail work; so if you are interested email him.

Once the land converts to public use you should enter north of 2235 Cty. Rd. 28. There may, or may not be a donation box. You can also donate online at my blog (http:// motherearthprayers. blogspot.com.) Please become a Friend of Gossamer Wood and consider joining us for trail work and an Earth Healing at Gossamer. Again, check with my blog.

Address: 2235 County Rd 28, Canandaigua, NY 14424
Webpage: http://www.bodytalkrochester.com
Email: wdewey@rochester.rr.com.
Telephone: 585-394-9114.
Donate, Volunteer: A donation box is located next to the Welcome Circle near the SE end of the parking lot. You can also donate at the Gossamer webpage online. If you are interesting in

doing trail work, email Bill, wdewey@rochester.rr.com. Please join and volunteer for Friends of Gossamer Wood.

Hours: Gossamer Wood is open from May 1st to October 30th, 7 days a week from dawn to dusk. Please call Bill before coming, 585-394-9114. Should the land convert to public grounds it will be open year round (except the first week of gun season) from dawn to dusk.

Info: To learn more about Gossamer and upcoming events get on Bill's listserve by emailing him, wdewey@ rochester. rr. com, or on my blog (http:// motherearthprayers. blogspot.com.)

Directions: Gossamer is located just north of the city center. Out of Canandaigua take North Main St. (Rt. 332 north.) Turn left onto Macedon Rd (Rt. 28) and drive a few miles. From the Thruway (I-90) take exit 44 and Rt. 332 south. Turn left on Rt. 28.

Farmington, Ontario County, NY

Farmington Meetinghouse
S3-12, V2-3, ☆ ⛹ ⛹⛹ 🧘 🛝 ♀ 🪶🕊

The congregants of the Quaker Meetinghouse in Farmington played a vital role in bringing peace, healing and justice to America through its work with Native Americans, with Women's Rights and the abolitionist movement. The divinity and guiding spirit that inspired the Farmington Quakers to greatness is still there. There is a large FOC that encompasses the church, the grounds behind it and the old Meetinghouse across the street. The vibe is very positive both on the grounds and in the church.

A Rich Struggle for the Prophetic Spirit

Judith Wellman, professor emeritus Oswego State, in her nomination brief requesting National Historic Status for the Farmington Meetinghouse noted the significant role it played in North Star Country:

"[I]ndividuals who came to Farmington…influenced national policy completely out of proportion to their numbers through leadership roles in three nationally important reform movements: the movement to protect Native American sovereignty, the movement for Women's Rights, and abolitionism and the Underground Railroad…"

Spiritually attuned to ideals of equality, Farmington Quakers made this district a center for Quakers and reformers (both African Americans and European Americans) throughout the northeastern U.S. and Canada …"

Experiencing the Farmington Meetinghouse

The area of the Farmington Meetinghouse is a tranquil place with a powerful presence. The dedication to social justice, and attention focused on the divine, has created a very positive vibe.

The church and all of the grounds immediately surrounding it sit on FOC. The highest series (3) of S6's run from the outside to inside of the meetinghouse.

The area of picnic tables behind the meetinghouse on the other side of the driveway rests on an S3. So there are accessible FOC outside.

The old meetinghouse has been moved across from the current one. Work is being done to restore it and turn it into a museum. A series (3) of S12's are to its left hand side as you face it (with the meetinghouse to your back) and run parallel to it. The first one begins about 30 feet from the meetinghouse. In the picture on the next page the "X" marks the last in the series.

The vibe is positive in the FOC. Put down a blanket, read, meditate, or just be and soak up the grace of this space.

Address: 160 County Road 8 P. O. Box 25053 Farmington, New York 14425

Webpage: http:// www. nyym. org/farmington/; 1816 Meetinghouse, http: //farmingtonmeetinghouse. org

Telephone: 315-986-5559

Donate: Online at, http: //farmingtonmeetinghouse. org

Hours: Sunday mornings at 11 AM (informal service 8 AM)

Close by: Ganondagan, a Seneca village, Victor, NY.

Directions: Farmington Meeting House is located at the intersection of Rt. 8, and Sheldon and Allen-Padgham Rds. From Thruway (I-90) take exit 44 and Rt. 332 south. Take the first left onto Loomis Rd. At the T take a left onto Hook Rd.

Follow Hook Rd. until Allen-Padgham Rd. Turn right. The meetinghouse is at the next intersection.

References and Recommended Reading

National Historic Registration Filing (Website.) Correspondence with Judith Wellman.

Rochester, Monroe County, NY

Rochester is located at the southern shore of Lake Ontario and is nicknamed the 'Flour City,' for its many gristmills early in the nineteenth century.

It has a strong history of social justice and was a major stop on the Underground Railroad with several stationmasters; most notably Fredrick Douglas who published his North Star newspaper here. It was also home to Susan B. Anthony.

Rochester is the western door of the Utica—Rochester corridor that is the heart of Mother Earth's Soul. There are numerous FOC located throughout the city.

Unity Church of Greater Rochester
S8, V0, ⛹👤 🧘 🖼️

The New Thought movement started in Rochester in 1916. What would become Unity Church of Rochester began in 1930. Groundbreaking for the current church building began in 1969. The church is located on a FOC (S8) and the vibe is neutral.

Experiencing the Church

The church and its grounds are situated on a FOC. Within the sanctuary, the Field ranges from S6 to S8. A series (3) of S8's runs from the center of the church a little towards the back by the entrance, and continues to the parking lot outside.

One of the great things about Unity of Rochester is that there are several weekly meditations affording you the chance to meditate indoors on FOC regularly. There are other occasional meditations and healings, as well as several educational programs and gatherings.

Address: 55 Prince St. Rochester NY 14607

Webpage: http://www.unityrochester.org
Telephone: 585-473-0910
Donate, Volunteer: You can donate on the website
Hours: Sunday Services at 10 AM. Meditation (Wed. 12-12:30, Tues 7-8 PM.)
Directions: Unity church is located on Prince St. off of East Main St., near the Memorial Art Gallery in the city center.

First Unitarian Church of Rochester
S2-3, V0-4, ▽ ☆ ♡ ⛎ 🧘 🚶 🖼 ⛹ ♀ 🕊

The First Unitarian Universalist Church has a long history of social justice. Just about all of the church and its grounds sit on FOC. The garden in particular is a wonderful refuge with an incredible atmosphere. There is something more to its vibe beyond the positive to extremely positive reading. The church garden shows the power of human intention and love to elevate a space. As the churches website says about the garden, "its about wowing and welcoming." Not surprisingly, all this love in the garden has sprung forth a vortex ring, a precursor to a vortex. Well Done!

Church History

The Unitarian Universalist church in Rochester is one of the largest UU congregations in the nation. Formed in 1829, it has a long history of openness and activism. Two weeks after the first Women's Rights Convention was held in Seneca Falls in 1848, a follow-up meeting was held at the church, and the second Women's Rights Convention was held there. Its members have included people such as Susan B. Anthony.

At the end of the nineteenth century, its leader Reverend William Channing Gannett led a successful effort to end bringing the denomination to any creed. He also founded the Boys Evening Club as an alternative to young teens in the city of Rochester.

Ecumenical in spirit, James Zigler Tanner was ordained by two Jewish rabbis at the church.

Forced to move because of the construction of a midtown plaza in Rochester, the church hired Louis Kahn to design its current housing that was completed in 1962.

Experiencing First Unitarian

There are numerous FOC located throughout the property. I suggest a contemplative walk in the garden with stops to pray, or meditate at places that grab you. The garden encompasses much of the property and begins at the top of the hill south of the sanctuary (S2.) A sign refers to this as the upper woodlands. From there you can meander down the rest of the garden. What makes the garden so special is its vibe; while much of the grounds rest on FOC, the highest stacked Field is only an S3, but its vibe makes it feel so much more potent.

I would suggest bringing a meditation cushion and planting yourself somewhere along the path that meanders down. Pick a spot that you like and meditate there. You may prefer the bench on the right hand side.

You will come to a grassy area that divides the upper and lower woodlands. On the right is a memorial wall and to the left of it is a bench. This general area has a very positive, to extremely positive vibe that indicates it is bing used for contemplative purposes. A vortex is trying to form (there is a vortex ring), about 5 feet from the bench at a 45° angle going towards the memorial wall. See picture below. Again, the grassy area would be a great place to meditate, or pray.

The bench near the memorial wall. The dogs are in the vortex ring.

Another place with powerful imprints is in front of the three stone cairns. A sign in the area says:

"May this be a place of peace, reflection, healing and hope. May it remind us not only of the cost of war, but also our deep human hunger for a new day and a better way to solve conflict."

Continue to follow the path down and you will find additional FOC. They end when you reach a grassy area. To your right is an open area with a vegetable garden. Straight ahead is an area called "The Hollow." It has a very positive vibe, but no Fields. To your left are more FOC and a labyrinth. There are FOC (S2) on the other side of the labyrinth.

The church sanctuary sits on a FOC. The high points is an S3 on the right hand side. The vibe in the sanctuary is neutral to slightly positive.

Address: 220 Winton Road South, Rochester, New York 14610
Webpage: http://rochesterunitarian.org
Email: office@rochesterunitarian.org
Telephone: 585-271-9070
Hours: Services Saturday at 4:30 PM, Sunday at 9:30 AM and 11:15 AM
Other: The webpage provides opportunities to sign up for an assortment of email alerts about church activities, from social justice to music and art events. If you live in the area, you can sign up to join a variety of small groups, that range from courses to gatherings, some free or at a nominal cost. Here are a few; meditation, dream workshop, Qi Gong, Tai Chi, Labyrinth Questing, Discussion series, educational programs and more.
Directions: The church is located on S. Winton between East and Highland Aves. From I-490 take exit 20 and head south on S. Winton.

References and Recommended Reading
Church website, http://rochesterunitarian.org.
Calarco, Tom; The Search for the Underground Railroad in Upstate New York, the History Press, Charleston South Carolina 2014.

The Fredrick Douglass Farm, Highland Park
S12, V0-1, 🚜 ♀

Highland Park designed by Fredrick Law Olmstead consists of 150 acres of rolling hills in the heart of Rochester. There are numerous FOC with several series (3) of S12's at its northern end.

I call it Fredrick Douglass Farm because the northern end of the park, and possibly the FOC mentioned, were part of the farm. In 1852, Fredrick Douglass sold his home on Alexander St. and purchased a farm at 999 South Ave near the corner of Bellevue Drive. Today this property borders the northern end of Highland

Park. I was not able to find information as to how big the farm was and its layout relative to Highland Park.

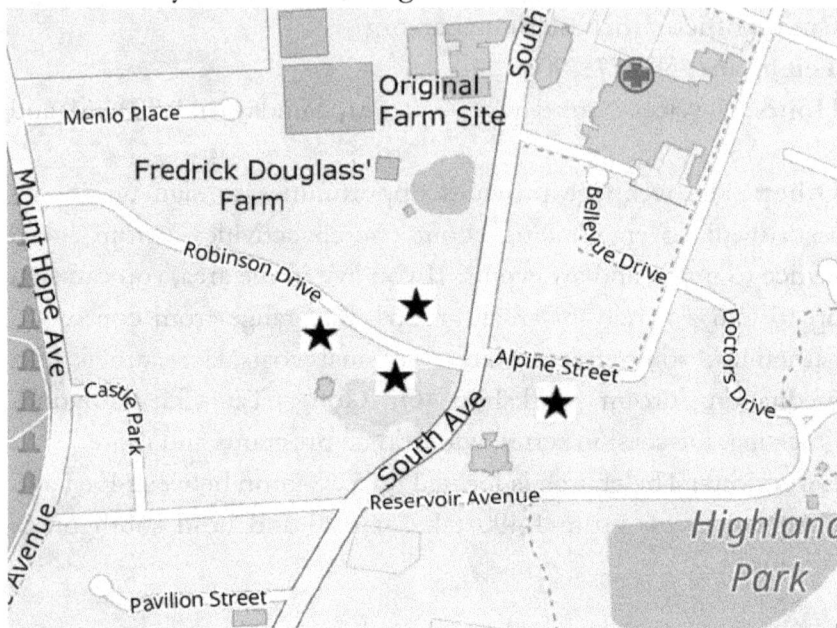

Fredrick Douglass' Farm, Highland Park, Rochester, NY. Source OpenStreetMap.org.

The building where the farm was (School # 12) rests on a FOC (S8). FOC are continuous from where Douglass house stood to a ¼ mile or more to the south to Robinson Drive. Basically, Douglass Farm was located on a large FOC.

I encourage you to please visit and help reinvigorate this space and elevate it to its potential; it has already shown you how lovely its fruit can be.

Fredrick Douglass

In his autobiography *The Narrative of Fredrick Douglass, An American Slave* Douglass tells of his upbringing as a slave in Maryland and in doing so exposed the horrors of slavery. He eventually escaped slavery and settled in New Bedford, MA with his wife. There he began attending abolitionist meetings and subscribing to William

Lloyd Garrison's Liberator. He also joined the African Methodist Episcopal Zion Church and eventually became a licensed minister.

A few years later while attending an abolitionist gathering he was asked to speak. Impressed by his story Garrison wrote about him in the Liberator, which led to Douglass making more lectures.

Garrison encouraged him to write his autobiography and it was published in 1845, which was the same year he parted for England. While there British supporters purchased his freedom.

Upon returning to the states in 1847 he settled in Rochester. There he began publishing his abolitionist newspaper, North Star, in the basement of the AMEZ church, whose motto was "Right is of no Sex – Truth is of no Color – God is the Father of us all, and we are all brethren."

In 1848 he attended the first Women's Rights Convention.

In 1851 North Star merged with Gerrit Smith's Liberty Party Paper to become the Fredrick Douglass' Paper.

Douglass was an ardent abolitionist and a stationmaster on the Underground Railroad. He would continue to speak on abolition and gained national notoriety. He publically advocated that blacks be allowed to join the military to fight for the Union. His son Lewis fought at the battle of Fort Wagner, immortalized in the film 'Glory' and miraculously was not killed.

After the war Douglass' star would continue to rise. He served as President of the Freedman's Bank and was the first black to be elected as a vice presidential candidate.

He had a split with Women's Rights advocates like Elizabeth Cady Stanton with the passage of the Fifteenth Amendment that gave black men and not black women the right to vote.

Rejuvenating Highland Park

Highland Park is loaded with FOC. There are several S12's within it. They need the positive intention of love, compassion and prayer to be activated. Please visit them. Here they are:

Highland Park Bowl
S12, V0, 🚂 ♀

The bowl is located on the south side of Robinson Drive, a little west of South Ave. It contains a monument to Fredrick Douglass and an amphitheater where summer concerts, Shakespeare in the park and free movies are held.

Sidney E. Edwards sculpted the statue of Fredrick Douglas. It was first housed and dedicated at the train station at Central Ave and St. Paul Street in 1899. It was moved to Highland Park and dedicated again September 4, 1941.

A giant FOC covers most of the bowl. A series (3) of S12's are located directly across from the Fredrick Douglas statue where the land begins to rise to form a ridge upon which Robinson Drive rests. If you were to draw a line straight across to the statue, there would be one S12 on the side towards the amphitheater; the other two would be on the other side. The vibe is neutral. See the picture on the previous page; the dogs and backpack mark the series.

The Robinson Drive Hilltop
S12, V1, 🏕 ♀

On the other side of Robinson Drive from the Highland Park Bowl is a hilltop with another large FOC that contains a series (3) of S12's. What is so nice about this area is that the vibe is slightly positive, compared to the rest of the park that is neutral to negative. It is a bit secluded and not as well traveled, so it gives you some privacy.

The backpack and dogs mark the series in the hilltop on Robinson Ave.

Climb the hilltop. Looking with South Ave to your back find the areas where the trees are clustered. With Robinson Drive to your left look for the outlier on the right side. The first S12 in the series is located approximately between the tree on the right and the next one over and extends back. The next one is 15 feet away, the final another 15 feet. The series parallels Robinson Drive. It is a large FOC so anywhere in the general area would place you in it.

Robinson Drive Near the Service Road
S12, V0, 🚂 ♀

Farther west down Robinson Drive is another FOC around the area of the service road. There is a series (3) of S12's on the south side of the street just east of the service road. Look for the service road on the south side of Robinson Drive; it goes to the amphitheater. One of the S12's is located in front of a large tree, the other two are about 15 feet apart going towards the service road and about 10 feet from the sidewalk. Anywhere within 100 feet south of the service road or 70 feet north of it would have you in the FOC.

Looking west on Robinson Dr. The service road is behind the two trees in the background.

The Hilltop Behind the Conservatory
S12, V0, 🚂 ♀

Another FOC with a series (3) of S12's is located near Alpine Street behind the conservatory. From Alpine Street the series is located between 40 and 56 Alpine street closer to 56. The series begins where the hilltop begins to descend. The FOC covers the whole hilltop, so bring a cushion, chair or blanket and enjoy. I imagine you won't see many people.

Many events take place in Highland Park, most notably a lilac festival.

Address: Administrative office, 171 Reservoir Avenue, Rochester, NY 14620. The FOC are located near the corner of South Ave and Robinson Dr.
Webpage: http://www2.monroecounty.gov/parks-highland.php
Telephone: 585 753-PARK (7275)
Hours: Open 6 AM to 11 PM.
Other: Movies in the park: www2. Monroescounty. Gov/parks-movies.php, Lilac Festival: rochesterevents. com/lilac-festival/
Directions: Highland Park is just east of Mt. Hope Cemetery. Going east on I-490 take exit 15 onto South Ave and head south. Take a right onto Robinson Dr. Going west on I-490 take exit 17. Take your first left onto S. Goodman St. A right onto Rockingham St which will end at South Ave. Take a left at the T and then a right onto Robinson Dr.

References and Recommended Reading
Douglass, Fredrick, *Narrative of the Life of Fredrick Douglass, An American Slave*.
Fredrick Douglass Rural home, Free Thought Trail 28. http: //www . freethought-trail.org /site.php? By= Person &Page =29&Site=45
Endya, " Frederick Douglass' South Avenue Home", http://www.gccschool.org/freedom/places/fdsouth.htm.
"Fredrick Douglas Biography", Bio.com, http:// www. biography.com/people/Fredrick-douglass-9278324.

Rochester Mennonite Fellowship
S8, V0, 👫 🧘

The Rochester Mennonite Fellowship is a gathering of people interested in the Mennonite vision. There is no minister, or paid staff. Members are active in a variety of social justice programs such as Christian Peacemakers and Partners in Restorative Initiatives. Visitors are welcome. All of the church is located on a FOC. A series(3) of S8's is located within the meeting room.

Address: 111 Hillside Ave, Rochester, NY 14610
Webpage: http://rochestermennonite.org
Email: contact@rochestermennonite.org
Telephone: 585-473-0220
Hours: Sunday morning worship begins at 10 AM.
Directions: Located near Cobbs Hill Park. Hillside Ave begins on the west side of Winton Rd. Take exit 20 off of I-490 and head south on Winton Rd. Take a left onto Hillside Ave.

Penfield, a suburb of Rochester

Hipp Brook Preserve
S2-6, V2-4, ▽ ☆ (♦) ⊡ ⅋ ↗ ⌒ ⬮

Hipp Brook is a 94 acre mostly wetland preserve in the middle of Rochester's upscale suburb of Penfield. Because it is a Class I wetland, it was able to avoid the fate of being covered with landfill and houses. The Genesee Land Trust began its rescue in 1990, and continued to buy parcels up until 1999. It was one of their first properties.

Hipp Brook is a hidden treasure containing powerful FOC (S6), a very positive vibe, vortices, Spirit Keeper sites, Manitou stones, charged Spirit Lines (charged Ley lines), intricate stone structures and more in a lovely and secluded setting.

This would be a great place to try and sense and feel Consciousness. An exciting place to explore and admire stone work. And of course a wonderful place to raise your consciousness.

There is a barely noticeable space underneath the large stone on top that allows you to see the other side, giving it the appearance of being a Dolmen; or a stone resting on other stones.

Where Did All Those Stones Come From?

When I first discovered Hipp Brook I was astonished and elated to find massive boulders, arguably mini megaliths, located on FOC. In all my years of surveying for sacred sites in the northeast I had never seen anything like this. What a find!

When I queried Gay Mills (President of the Genesee Land Trust) she told me that the boulders were the result of blasting to put in a sewer line that traverses the property and were left there by the contractors. You can see several drain caps on the property.

This made sense, but it was still odd to find massive boulders (2'-4' wide and long, and 2'-4' high) in a wetland. The stones seemed that they had been polished by the rain for centuries and not just a few decades. But then again, how could an ancient culture like the Spirit Keepers move them to a wetland?

When I revisited Hipp Brook, meditated on the grounds and resurveyed the property it became clear that all of the stones were

349

strategically placed (on FOC and Spirit Lines); by someone with great knowledge of Mother Earth, most likely the Spirit Keepers.

Here is why I believe this is so:

- Location, location... all of the FOC on the property are covered by large stones.
- Other large stones on the property, even the adjacent land, mark the intersection of several Spirit Lines, or are one of several stones placed on a Spirit Line.
- There are several Charged Spirit Lines (Charged Ley Lines); Spirit Lines marked by stones and have been charged with prayer. A few are quite palpable.
- The very positive vibe indicates someone has been praying and meditating there.
- There are vortices and a water dome. A water dome like a vortex forms in response to positive human intention (prayer/good deeds,) only it is below the surface.

Experiencing Hipp Brook

Please use the gate at the Phaeton Dr. Entrance for the Wild Iris Trail as a Welcome Circle. Please spend time in the Welcome Circle to cleanse yourself and prepare for the journey ahead.

This side of the preserve has the FOC. A simple rule of thumb to keep in mind; the FOC are covered with many large stones, single

The stones in front of a house by the entrance mark 3 Spirit Lines forming a triangle. Seen at High Tor's Keepers Area and other places.

stones, or a series of two or three stones mark a nest (intersection) of several Spirit Lines, or a single Spirit Line. Conclusion, find a boulder, you cannot go wrong.

There is much to explore and experience at Hipp Brook. I ask that you spend a multiple of the time you spend exploring, dowsing, or photographing—in prayer, or meditation. For example, if you spend ten minutes in these activities, spend twenty or thirty minutes meditating. Meditating and praying will help raise the vibe and make Hipp Brook sparkle even more, creating new vortices and revealing hidden aspects of Mother Earth. NICE!

Please be aware your view in the summertime may be impaired by brush that surrounds many of the piles of mini megaliths. You will also encounter lots of bugs when the weather is warm.

Immediately on your right upon entering you will see your first FOC covered by large stones. The highpoint is an S3. It will be followed by several more collections of small megaliths that range from S3 to S4. The vibe runs from positive to very positive.

Take a right when you get to the walkway. On your left will be collection of boulders covering a FOC (S4) with a positive, to very positive vibe.

The FOC (S6) behind the bench. Notice the two layers of stone and the oblong shape—it outlines the series (3) of S6's.

Continuing to your right you will come to a bench. Several large collections of mini megaliths are located behind it. Notice how there seems to be a base layer of earth and stone two to three feet high, with another collection of boulders on top of it. Notice also how the closest collection of mini megaliths seems to have an oblong, or rectangular shape (FOC, S6). And that there is another parallel oblong shaped collection behind it (FOC, S4) and another pile that seems to connect them.

The closest oblong collection marks a series (3) of S6's; in other words the oblong shape of the mini megaliths conforms to the series. At the end closest to the bench is a vortex ring, at the farther end is an actual vortex. The vibe runs from positive to extremely positive. Spend some time meditating here, especially in the vortex ring (precursor to the formation of a vortex) and the vortex. This would be an ideal place to sense and feel Consciousness. It is also a great place to transcend time and connect with the spirit of those that created the vortices.

Notice that the vortices are located at either end of the series. Why?—most likely because the creators wanted to fortify the FOC by surrounding it. Keep this in mind, because later in the Appendix I will discuss how to clean up a space by working from the outside in—the same as we look within to find God, or ourselves. These vortices and their placement is the work of Masters and I am always in awe and feel blessed when I find it. Homage to you Great Ones for the gift you created millennia ago and now bless us with.

Boulders mark a Charged Spirit Line. My staff shows its direction.

There are a few more FOC and several Charged Spirit Lines. Just after a wooden bench beyond the S6 is a particularly strong one.

Once you develop the ability to sense and feel Consciousness see if you can feel a charged Spirit Line. If you are focused on the vibe and come across one, it will hit you like, KABOOM; an appreciable pickup in Vibe. Very nice, very Sweet.

Enjoy Hipp Brook, it was an incredible blessing to find. I now share it with you. Honor it so that others may be blessed years from now.

Address: 100 Phaeton Dr., Penfield, NY
Webpage: www. geneseelandtrust. org/protected-places. aspx?id=4
Email: info@geneseelandtrust. org, for events, membership.
Telephone: 585-256-2130
Donate, Volunteer: Donations of land, money and time welcomed. There are several stewardship opportunities. Contact Kevin Ferrel (kfarrell@geneseelandtrust. org) if you are interested in being a Keeper (steward) for Hipp Brook.
Hours: Dawn to Dusk. No camping, hunting or fires. Be aware your view may be seasonally blocked by foliage and that warm weather can bring out swarms of bugs. Plan your visit accordingly.
Directions: From I-490 exit (23) onto Rt. 441 going east. Turn left onto Baird Rd. Right onto Whalen Rd. Left onto Jackson Rd. Ext. Left onto Brougham Dr. Your first left onto Phaeton Dr. Follow to the end and park in the circle.

References and Recommended Reading
Conversations with Gay Mills
Genesee Land Trust's webpage

Pittsford, a suburb of Rochester

Powder Mills Park
S6, V2,

This 380 acre Monroe County Park, with wetlands and steep hills, provides for a variety of activities: hiking, sand volleyball, trout fishing and downhill skiing in the winter.

There is one accessible FOC (S6) with a positive vibe. It is located around Trailhead marker #5 next to Corduroy Road on the right side, just north of Woolston Road.

There is a series (3) of S6's begins just left of the Trailhead marker 5 and it runs perpendicular to the trail through the trees and ends on the herd path on the other side. While a bit close to the road, the woods offer you some privacy. The appeal is that the vibe is positive.

Address: 154 Park Rd, Pittsford, NY 14534
Webpage: http://www2.monroecounty.gov/parks-powdermill.php
Telephone: 585-753-7275
Hours: 6 AM to 10:30 PM daily.
Directions: From the Pittsford Victor Rd (Rt. 96) Head west on Park Rd. (Rt. 25.) Take your first left south onto Corduroy Rd.

Seneca Park
S6, V0

Seneca Park is a 297 acre park designed by Fredrick Law Olmstead along the Genesee River. The FOC are located at the north end of the park near Seneca Park Drive. Park at the end of the street. Walk through the fence and follow the path to the right and you will shortly be in the FOC (S6.) A series (3) of S6's is located 60-80 feet off trail to your right.. The Vibe is neutral.
Address: Seneca Park Ave, Rochester, at the deadend.
Webpage: http://www2.monroecounty.gov/parks-seneca.php
Telephone: 585 753-PARK (7275)

Hours: Seneca Park is open daily 7:00 a.m. until 11:00 p.m. during the summer. The lower park is closed at dusk from October 15 through May 15.

Directions: Take St. Paul St. along Seneca Park going north. It will deadend at Cooper Rd. Take a left at the T. Go a short distance and turn left onto Seneca Park Ave.

Susan B. Anthony Home—Historic Home
S2, V0, ♦⛲🖼 ♀

Susan B. Anthony has become the face of Women's Rights. Her home, and her sister's home next door rest on the same FOC (S2.)

Susan B. Anthony

Susan B. Anthony was raised a Quaker in a family with a long tradition of activism. She was part of the triumvirate of Elizabeth Cady Stanton and Matilda Joslyn Gage that led the Women's Rights Movement; she was the less radical of the three. Like the other two, she was involved with a variety of causes besides Women's Rights: abolitionism, labor and temperance. Susan attended her first Women's Rights Convention in 1851.

355

Anthony was a tireless worker for Women's Rights who never married; instead she dedicated her life to many causes. In 1856 she became an agent for the American Anti-Slavery Society. In her newspaper, 'The Revolution,' in 1868 she advocated for an eight-hour workday and equal pay for equal work. She was elected president of the Workingwomen's Central Association in 1870.

In 1872, she famously registered to vote and actually voted, for which she was arrested. She used the opportunity before and during the trial to advocate for women voting. She was convicted and fined $100, which she never paid.

Gage, Stanton and Anthony collaborated to write the *History of Woman Suffrage*. Anthony bought out the other two, and with the help of Ida Harper wrote another three volumes, up to the passage nineteenth amendment and placed herself as the leader of the movement.

Her work continued until her death in 1906. In 1904 she presided over the Council of Women in Berlin.

Experiencing the Anthony Home

Not surprisingly Anthony's home and her sisters home rest on a FOC. Interestingly they are connected by a series (3) of S2's that run parallel to the street. The vibe is neutral.

Address: 17 Madison Street, Rochester, New York 14608, Visitor's Center 19 Madison Street.
Webpage: http://susanbanthonyhouse.org/index.php

Telephone: 585-235-6124
Donate: You join or donate online.
Hours: Open Tuesdays through Sundays 11:00 am - 5:00 pm. Closed Mondays, major holidays, and the day of our annual Birthday Luncheon (mid-February.) $15.00 per adult, $10.00 per senior citizen, 62 & over, & active military, $5.00 per student.
Events: Please check calendar on the website.
Directions: From the west, Thruway (I-90) to exit 47, I-490 east. Exit Plymouth Ave (exit 13.) Right onto North Plymouth Ave. Continue to Main St. and turn right. Take right onto Madison St. From the east, Thruway (I-90) west to I-490 west (exit 45.) Continue to Broad Street/Plymouth Avenue (exit 14.) Go straight to Main St. and turn left. Take right onto Madison St.

References and Recommended Reading

'Biography of Susan B. Anthony,' http:// susanbanthony house.org/ her-story/biography.php.
Linder, Doug; 'The Trial of Susan B. Anthony for Illegal Voting,' http://law2.umkc.edu/faculty/projects/ftrials/anthony/sbaaccount.html.
Wagner, Sally Roesch; *Matilda Joslyn Gage: She Who Holds the Sky*, Sky Carrier Press, Aberdeen SD 2002

Victor, Ontario County, NY

Ganondagan Town of Peace
S2-4, V0-2, ☆ ♡ 🕴 🖋🐚

Ganondagan (ga•NON•da•gan) State Historic Site in the town of Victor, 30 miles southeast of Rochester, NY sits on a hill where a once vibrant Native American community of the Seneca people stood. While the village where thousands lived is long gone, the spirit remains. That is what makes Ganondagan so unique, it's resonating spirit.

Ganondagan has a wonderful meditation garden and lots to do and explore—a replica of a bark long house, a cultural center, hiking trails and FOC (S4) with a positive vibe.

About Ganondagan

The Seneca's were Keepers of the western gate for the Haudenosaunee. Ganondagan is called a Town of Peace after the Peacemaker

The site consists of 300 primarily wooded acres with several hiking trails. There is a visitor's center with educational information and a video about Ganondagan. The newly constructed Seneca Art and Culture Center tells the 2,000 year history of Seneca. A replica of a bark longhouse allows visitors to experience first hand how life once was. There is also a garden conducive to meditation.

A strong sense of the positive and peace permeates the air. I first visited Ganondagan years ago before I knew about FOC. Back then I felt highly charged spots that made the hair on my arms stand on end. What makes this even more unique is that the New French wiped out the Seneca village that once stood here in 1687 over the fur trade.

Experiencing The Seneca Village

There are numerous FOC on the grounds. They begin just on the other side of the sign marking the "Trail of Peace" and extend to just before the bark long house.

The highest FOC (S4) can be found around the area of the monument for a Seneca family; on the path to the Long House and behind the statue. Across from the statue is a bench. A series (3) of S4's just to the right of the bench as you face it, and continue in a straight line, paralleling the cut grass for another 30 feet.

Meditation Garden near the Bark Long House.

The circular garden, what I call a meditation garden, near the bark house is arguably the jewel of the area. It sits on a S2 and has the best vibe, it is positive. Spend some time there and you will soon realize that others have already prayed, meditated or done ceremony there. Bring along a cushion and sit amongst the flowers. The sectioning of the garden is conducive for the meandering of a contemplative walk. Several people have told me how much they have enjoyed the garden.

Address: 7000 County Road 41 (Boughton Hill Road) Victor, NY 14564.
Webpage: NYS, State Historic http://nysparks.com/historic-sites/26/details.aspx; Friends of Ganondagan, http://www.ganondagan.org
Email: Friends of Ganondagan, info@ganondagan.org.
Telephone: 585-924-5848
Donate, Volunteer: Join/donate, Friends of Ganondagan, http://www.ganondagan.org/Support/Friends-Of-Ganondagan

Hours: Trails open 8 AM to dusk. Center Tues. to Sun., 9 AM to 4:30 PM. Closed Mon. and select holidays.

Admission (May to Oct), Adults - $8, Sr. – $4, Students (12 yrs. – College) - $4, Children (5 – 11 yrs.) - $2. Under 4- free.

Events: See calendar on the Friends of Ganondagan website.

Close by: Farmington Meeting House.

Directions: Thruway (I-90) to exit 44. Take Rt. 332 south. Go past Rt. 96 and turn right (west) onto Rt. 41 (Boughton Hill Rd.) Follow several miles, look for flashing light, close.

Wolcott, Wayne County, NY

Scotts Bluff
S6, V2, 〰️

Scotts Bluff located on the shores of Lake Ontario north of Wolcott (halfway between Rochester and Syracuse) offers the pilgrim great views, beach access and a sweet piece of Mother Earth's Soul (S6.) Rarely have I encountered people there. If you are looking for a serene location on a beach to meditate, and not be bothered, try Scotts Bluff.

The Bluffs

Scotts Bluff is located less than 10 miles east of the visually striking Chimney Bluffs State Park. It is the Red Creek part of the NY DEC's Black Creek Wildlife management area.

The area between Rochester and Oswego is noted for its drumlins, or rolling hills. There are also numerous spectacular bluffs near and on the shore. Fortunately, the DEC owns several strips of land just east of Sodus Bay on Lake Ontario.

The ridge above offers spectacular views of Lake Ontario and the Bluff. Be aware that the grass may not be mowed.

The entrance area and parking lot is situated on a plateau overlooking Lake Ontario. To the right you will get a nice view of Scotts Bluff. You may wish to spend some time above; be aware that the grassy area on the bluff may not be mowed.

To get to the beach, look for a herd path to your left in the woods. The herd path has a good pitch and there are lots of prickly wild rose bushes on either side. If this area is not maintained, the rose bushes can form a canopy and require crouching in parts to go down. However, when I was there last, the herd path had been groomed and no crouching or maneuvering was required to get down. The trail can also be wet. Bring along a thick shirt just in case to protect yourself, or wear a backpack to protect yourself for the path down.

The beach is about a mile in length and depending upon when you visit may have a few people or none at all on it. To your right (east) is Scotts bluff. To your left (west) are the FOC.

Looking east. Scotts bluff protrudes in the distance, as does the downed tree that blocks your path. Pepper (white dog), my backpack and Jaeda and I mark the S6's. Notice the downed trees parallel to the shoreline on the right. The water was high at the time.

The water can be high at times with 2-3 foot waves which can significantly reduce the beach area. Tides can also affect how things look. The temperature will also be more moderate; cooler in the summer, warmer in the winter. Expect a breeze.

Experiencing Scotts Bluff

As you walk west, in 100 to 150 feet you will run into an area where downed trees cover the beach and require some maneuvering to get past. Ahead, 120-150 feet you will see a large tree down at angle to the beach. The Fields begin 20 feet after the tree and are continuous for another 150-200 feet. The vibe in the area of the Fields is slightly positive.

Look for several large downed trees that are parallel to the beach. There is a series (3) of S6's in front of them. Look for a large American Willow. Very Nice. Another marker to guide you would be the inland marsh to your left. The highest stacked Fields are located in the area near the narrowest part of the barrier, a narrow sliver of land, which divides the Red Creek marsh from Lake Ontario. Stay close to and just west of the narrowest part, it widens the further you go west.

I am told that a heavy rain can overrun the barrier separating Red Creek Marsh from Lake Ontario. When this happens, a little waterway forms between the marsh and Lake Ontario at the center of the marsh, where the barrier is the thinnest. Such an overrun can dramatically alter the placement of the downed trees. So things may look much different when you visit.

Address: Broadway, Wolcott, NY at the deadend.
Webpage: Part of the Lake Shore Marshes Area (Black Creek Region) http://www.dec.ny.gov/outdoor/24441.html.
Telephone: 585-226-2466
Close by: Chimney Bluffs State Park.
Directions: From Wolcott head east on Mill St., turns into Oswego St.. Left onto Wadsworth Street Rd (Cty. 164.) Follow to end at T. Take a right onto Brown Rd. Take your next right onto Cemetery Rd and continue straight (will change names.) Take a left onto Broadway Rd. (Cty. 168.) Follow to the end.

References and Recommended Reading

Gateley, Susan Peterson, *The Edge Walker's Guide to Lake Ontario Beachcombing*, Whiskey Hill Press, Wolcott, NY, 2003.

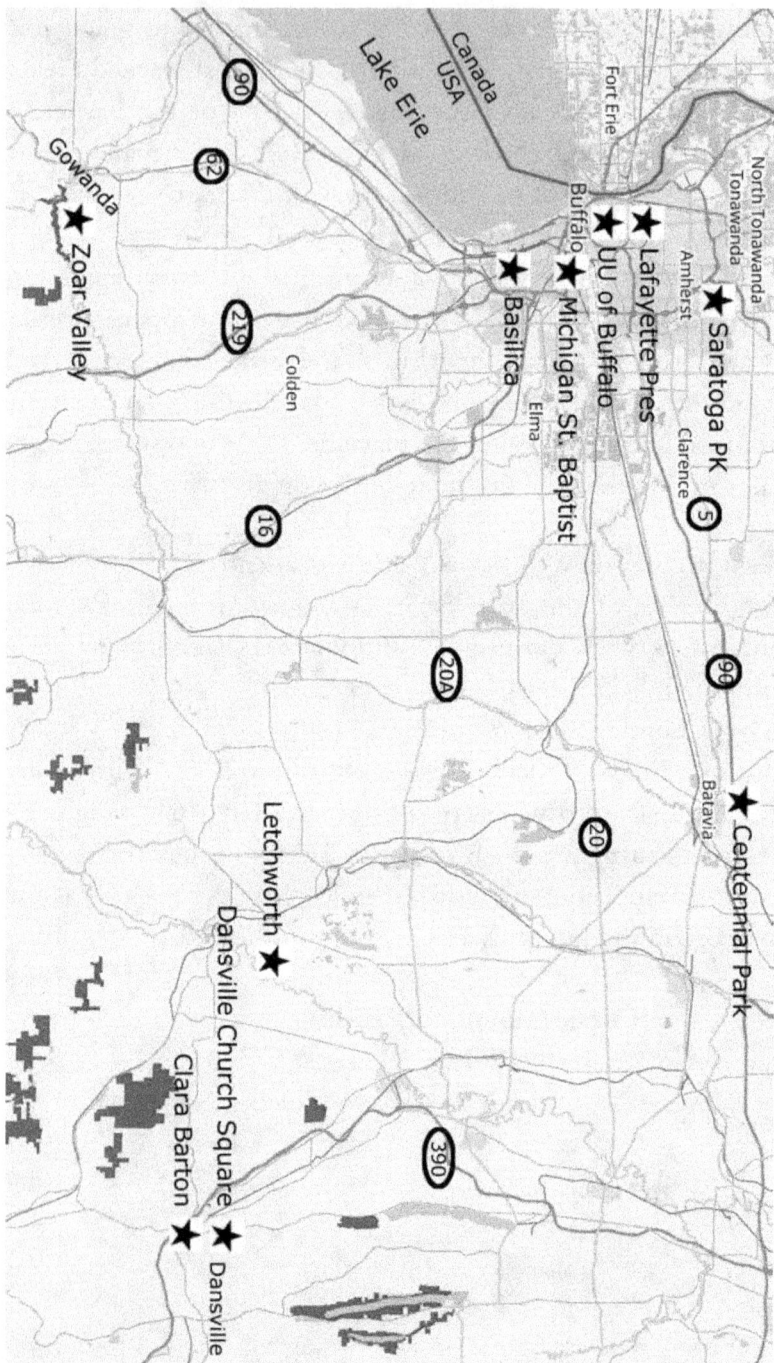

Map of Western NY. Source, Maps-© OpenStreetMap contributors, www. openstreetmap. org.

Western New York

The area west of Rochester and the Finger Lakes runs the gamut from the city life of Buffalo, to the splendid and awe-inspiring Niagara Falls to the remote and majestic Zoar Valley. There are some stimulating and interesting learning centers such as the Chautauqua Institute, a proverbial summer school for adults offering a myriad of programs, events and entertainment. Then there is Lily Dale, a mecca of Spiritualism where mediums, healers and the spiritually eclectic gather each summer to offer their services and instruction.

Here was born the predecessor of what was to become the NAACP. It was where the compassionate and beloved Father Baker built an orphanage, a home for unwed mothers and a magnificent basilica drawing pilgrims from all over the world.

Batavia, Genesee County, NY

Centennial Park
S4, V0-1

Located in front of the New York State School for the Blind, Centennial Park in the north central part of Batavia offers a quiet setting in a small town park. The park consists of 14 acres of grass lawn that is just about all covered with deciduous trees. There is a FOC (S4.) The vibe is neutral to slightly positive.

History
The genesis for Centennial Park began in 1866 when New York State selected the Village of Batavia to be the home for a school for the blind. Local residents purchased and donated 50 acres for

the school to the state. The cornerstone for the first of four buildings was laid on September 6, 1868.

The park was initially landscaped with shade trees. Since then, the park has undergone several changes such as a nine hole golf course and swimming pool, both of which no longer exist. In 1969 the state of New York donated the park back to the city.

Looking west from State Street between rows 2 and 3 of trees. Park Avenue and houses are on the left side. The series (3) of S4's are marked by Jaeda (black dog), Pepper (white dog) and my backpack; in the area in front of a large oak tree.

Experiencing Centennial Park

The FOC (S4) is located at the southeast section of the park along Park Ave near the corner of State Street. Place yourself anywhere within the second and third row of trees from Park Ave., beginning about 20 feet from State St. and going about 100-120 feet (note the first row is sparse.) Within it is a series (3) of S4's that run at a slight diagonal angle (almost parallel to Park Ave) in front of the third row of trees. Looking at Park Ave they run from 30 Park Ave to 32 Park Ave. Look for a large oak tree.

The vibe in the area of the Fields is neutral to slightly positive. Like any city park in a residential area, people will be milling about and events and picnics will be held, but generally it is fairly quiet.

Address: 151 State Street, Batavia, NY
Webpage: http://www.batavianewyork.com/for-residents/pages/parks
Telephone: 585-345-6300
Hours: 7 days a week, 7AM to Dusk. Free.
Directions: Thruway (I-90) take exit 48. Left onto Rt. 98 south. Take a left onto Richmond Ave. The Park will on your right in a few blocks.

References and Recommended Reading
Batavia Walking Tour, from the Genesee County website. http://www.co.genesee.ny.us/departments/history/batavia_walking_tour.html.

Buffalo (Metro), Erie County, NY

Buffalo was the western terminus of the Erie Canal. It was a stop on the Underground Railroad with several stations, most notably Michigan Street Baptist Church.

Amherst, NY, a Buffalo suburb

Saratoga Park
S8, V2

Most Buffalonians have probably never heard of Saratoga Park let alone know where it is. Yet it has a FOC (S8) which is pretty unusual (a high number) for a place so far from the Rochester, Syracuse, Utica corridor. It also has a positive vibe in the area of the FOC.

Saratoga Park is in Amherst New York, Buffalo's largest and most populated suburb. It is just south of the Amherst Middle School and Saratoga Road. While it may be off the beaten path, it does get traffic, because it is a precious gem to its residents.

Experiencing Saratoga Park

Park your car where Yorktown Road deadends just past Washington Highway. Continue west on Yorktown through the wooded entryway for maybe 100 feet. The whole area to the right is part of a large FOC, so pick a spot. A series (3) of S8's begins about 30 feet up the path on the right and 5 feet to the right.; the next two being 15 feet apart going north.

The FOC begins where the walkway curves to the right. The first in the series (3) of S8's is 30 feet beyond where the path that veers to the right at Yorktown Rd. entrance meets another path. The backpack marks the first S3 and the black dog and white dog about 15 feet a part mark the next two. Sit near that area and you will be fine.

Most of Saratoga Park consists of a mowed lawn, with the exception of its portion south of Yorktown Road. Much of it abuts the backyards of houses that border it. So while it is contained, you should expect to have people walking about and kids playing and riding their bikes.

If the traffic inhibits you from meditating or praying bring along a lawn chair to sit on, or put down a blanket. Read a sacred text to contemplate on, or some other book that inspires you and beckons your higher self. Enjoy.

Address: The deadend of Yorktown Road, Amherst, NY.
Directions: Yorktown Road is off of Rt. 240, Harlem Road. Just north of the intersection of Harlem Rd. and Kensington Ave.

Lafayette Avenue Presbyterian Church
S4, V0, 🚻 🧘

Located in the eclectic and funky Elmwood Village section of the city of Buffalo, is Lafayette Ave Presbyterian. It's sanctuary rests on a FOC (S4.)

The congregation traces its roots back to 1832. Ground for the new church was broken in 1894. To accommodate the church, the name of the street was changed from Bouck to Lafayette. It has served as a meeting place for the community; boy scout troop 2 constructed a log cabin in the basement of the church for meetings, it is still used today. The church was added to national registry of historic places in 2009.

At its peak, the congregation had 1500 members in a church that can accommodate 1200 -1400 people

Today the church houses the Elmwood Village association, a nursery school and a culinary school.

Experiencing the Church
The FOC covers most of the area of the pews; the strongest area is in the back area. There is a series (3) of S4's in the center area of

the sanctuary. They begin immediately behind the pews and extend into the open community area.

Address: 875 Elmwood Ave., Buffalo, NY 14222
Webpage: www. elmwoodjesus. org; http://www.pbywny.org
Email: patty@elmwoodjesus. org
Telephone: 716-886-6635
Hours: Sunday services 10 AM
Directions: The church is located in the Elmwood Village section of Buffalo, southwest of Delaware Park; at the corner of Lafayette Ave. and Elmwood Ave. It is just south of the intersection of Broadway Parkway and Elmwood Ave.

References and Recommended Reading
Napora, James, *Houses of Worship: A Guide to the Religious Architecture of Buffalo*, NY, Lafayette Presbyterian Church-1894; http://www.buffaloah.com/how/3/3.13/lafay.html
Elmwood Village Association: http://www.elmwoodvillage.org
Statement of Significance in the 2009 Nomination for Listing on the State and National Registers of Historic Places (Lafayette Presbyterian.)
http://www.buffaloah.com/a/elmwd/590/nom_signif.html

Unitarian Universalist Church of Buffalo
S2, V-0,

The garden area of the Unitarian Universalist Church in the Elmwood section of Buffalo sits on a FOC (S2.) It has a neutral vibe.

In 2015, the church was approved for the NYS Register of Historic Places. Its sanctuary has been called "one of the best Arts and Crafts spaces in Buffalo."

The garden space is pleasant, but can be noisy so close to Elmwood Ave. The FOC (S2) is located at the southwest corner of the front garden area near Elmwood Ave. The center is located between a large evergreen bush and tree.

Address: 692 Elmwood Ave
Website: http://www.buffalouu.org
Telephone: 716-885-2136
Hours: Sunday worship 10:30 AM
Directions: The church is located in the Elmwood Village section of Buffalo, Southwest of Delaware Park; at the corner Elmwood Ave and west Ferry Street

Michigan Street Baptist Church
S3, V1, ☆ 🚂 ♀

For the seeker looking for a divine connection and a chance to tap into the consciousness that drives the prophetic spirit, one would be well served by spending time on the grounds of Michigan Street Baptist Church. It was the bedrock of the black community in Buffalo during the nineteenth century and

played a pivotal role in American black history. One of its members, Mary Talbert, was inducted into the National Women's Hall of Fame in Seneca Falls. It is listed on the National Register of Historic Places. You can still feel its Spirit today.

There is a FOC (S3) in the garden area. The vibe is slightly positive and it is a great place to experience that spirit that motivated so many and helped shape our collective soul in the

371

struggle for freedom. It can be palpable, if you spend time and let it embrace you.

The Church's History

Michigan Avenue ran through the heart of Buffalo's African American community in the pre-Civil War period. The congregation that would become the Michigan Baptist Church began forming between 1832 to 1837. Construction of the church started in 1845 and was completed in 1846. As the sole Black institution at a time of slavery, the church served as a gathering place and a place to advocate reform. It was a sanctuary and a place of hope for many, particularly the numerous ex-slaves in the congregation. Religion and the church were the strongest sustaining force in their lives.

The church has a rich history of social justice. In 1842 it adopted a statement declaring slavery immoral and it was an Underground Railroad station. Although no formal physical proof has been provided, it has been widely accepted as being one. Its parishioners were similarly strong and vocal advocates of the prophetic spirit.

Dr. J. Edward Nash who became pastor of the church in the 1890s and remained there for 61 years helped found the Buffalo Urban League and the local branch of the NAACP.

Mary Talbert lived at 521 Michigan Avenue, two doors from the church (now demolished.) In 1905 W.E.B. Dubois and other prominent African American leaders met secretly at Mrs. Talbert's home and founded the Niagara Movement, the forerunner of the National Association for the Advancement of Colored People (NAACP.)

I have prayed and meditated on this bench behind the church on several occasions. It always brings me joy and I thank God for bringing me back.

Mrs. Talbert served as president of the National Association of Colored Women's Clubs from 1916 to 1920. She was a vice president of the National Association for the Advancement of

Colored People (NAACP) and was a delegate to the International Council of Women held in Norway. In 1922, Mary Talbert was the first woman to receive the NAACP Springarn Award for outstanding achievement. In 2005 she was elected to the National Women's Hall of Fame.

Experiencing the grounds

The strongest part of the FOC is the area of the series (3) of S3's that run from the bench behind the church towards it. In the picture on the previous page, the series begins from just behind the bench and ends in front of the window on the lower left. The second in the series is at the edge of the brick path.

You can meditate anywhere close to the bench, or pretty much anyplace else on the church property as much of it is on FOC. The vibe is slightly positive, which is very good considering that the church is in an urban area.

Address: 511 Michigan Ave, Buffalo, NY
Webpage: http://www.buffaloah.com/a/mich/511/hp.html
Close by: The Michigan Avenue African-American Corridor webpage http:// www. michiganstreetbuffalo.org/#!the-corridor/csgz has a listing of locations nearby focusing on the area's rich African-American history.
Directions: The church is located at 511 Michigan Street between Broadway and William Street in the southern end of Buffalo near Lake Erie. Niagara Thruway (I-190) take exit 6. Right onto Seneca St. Left onto Michigan Ave.

References and Recommended Reading

Fordham, Monroe, "Michigan Street Church" http://www.math.buffalo.edu/%7Esww/0history/hwny-michigan.st.church.html
Williams, Deirdre, "Proof of Church Claim is Lacking", The Buffalo News, April 4, 2013,

http://www.buffalonews.com/20130404/proof_of_church_claim
_is_lacking.html

Buffalo News, "Controversy Aside, Michigan Baptist Church Did Play a Critical Role in the Antii-Slavery Movement", April 12, 2013.

http://www.buffalonews.com/20130412/controversy_aside_mic
higan_street_baptist_church_did_play_a_key_role_in_the_anti_sl
avery_movement.html

'Mary Burnett Talbert', Women's national Hall of Fame
http://www.womenofthehall.org/inductee/mary-burnett-talbert/

BlackPast.org   on   Mary   Talbert
http://www.blackpast.org/aah/talbert-mary-b-1866-1923

University   of   Buffalo'   Talbert   Timeline
http://www.math.buffalo.edu/~sww/0history/hwny-talbert.html

Michigan   Street   African-American   Corridor
http://www.michiganstreetbuffalo.org/#!the-corridor/csgz

Castille, Wyoming County, NY

Castille is the listed home of Letchworth, although you will probably be entering from either Mt Morris, or Portageville. Access is also available at Perry and the parade grounds.

Letchworth State Park
S8, V2, ⚦ ⛁ 🖼

Known as the Grand Canyon of the east for its deep gorge that creates cliffs as high as 600 feet. In 2015, USA Today voted it the best state park in the United States.

If you are looking for majestic views, experience FOC in a beautiful hemlock woods and can deal with plenty of foot traffic passing by, then Letchworth is the place.

Letchworth State Park

Letchworth consists of 14,350 acres along the Genesee River.

The Seneca called it Sehgahunda, the "Vale of Three Falls", for the three major water falls within the park that are called, Upper, Middle and Lower Falls. It is estimated another 50 smaller falls are located on the tributaries.

The park is named after William Pryor Letchworth, who purchased 1,000 acres in 1856 and constructed the Glen Iris Estate. When he passed in 1910, the land was donated to New York State.

There are 66 miles of hiking trails ranging from ½ a mile to 20 miles in length. There is a swimming pool in the recreation area at the northern end of the park. Check the events calendar for festivals, guided tours and lectures. There is a restored Seneca Council house.

You can book a cabin or campsite with NYS Cabin/Camping Reservation System 1-800-456-CAMP (1-800-456-2267.)

Getting to the Fields

The FOC are located at the lower falls at the southern end of the park closer to the Portageville entrance. It may or may not be quicker to enter at Portageville over Mt. Morris, depending upon where you are coming from. It will be slow driving within the park but you will be provided with plenty of places to stop and take in some wonderful views.

Park your car in the lot. It is about a 6 to 8 minute descent on stairs to get to the Fields. The FOC are located in a Hemlock woods just above the lower falls. They will be to your right as you descend.

Experiencing the Fields

The woods consist of a stand of large hemlock trees, very pleasant and serene. The FOC begins a few feet from the trail down to the lower falls. There is a series (3) of S8's to the right of the trail approximately 50-75 feet from the trail on the other side of some downed trees. They break at a 45° to the left. It is a large FOC; so just get close and you will be in it.

My backpack, Jaeda (black dog) and Pepper (white dog) mark the series 3 0f S8's.

The vibe is positive around the FOC and are just far enough from the trail to give you some privacy, as a lot of people visit the lower falls, so there is much foot traffic.

When I was there last I was very saddened to see so many downed trees since I was there last in 2008/09. It appears that the Woolly Adelgid, a pest that has been making a march northward killing hemlocks in the Eastern United States is at fault. Sad.

Address: 1 Letchworth State Park, Castile, NY 14427
Webpage: http://nysparks.com/parks/79/details.aspx
Telephone: Phone: 585-493-3600
Hours: 6AM to 11PM
Directions: There are many entry points, here is one. Take Rt. 390 south and take exit 7 onto Rt. 408 west into Mount Morris. In Mount Morris turn left onto N. Main St. (Rt. 36.) The Park Rd entrance will be on your left.

References and Recommended Reading
New York State and Parks and Recreation, Letchworth http://nysparks.com/parks/79/details.aspx
Letchworth park.com http://www.letchworthpark.com

Dansville, Livingston County, NY
In the 19th century people flocked to Dansville for the water cure of Dr. James Caleb at the Our Home on the Hillside. He was a big proponent of hydropathy (using water to treat illness) that he credited with saving his life.

References and Recommended Reading
http://dansville.lib.ny.us/historyo.html#castle

Clara Barton Home-Chapter One American Red Cross
S8, V0, 👤🚻

After spending three years as a volunteer for the International Red Cross, Clara Barton came to Dansville in 1873 for the water cure and to recuperate. While in Dansville, she wrote Dr. Louis Appia in Geneva about starting a Red Cross in the United States.

All of the house sits on a FOC. There is a series (3) of S8's that cut diagonally from the left side of the house to the porch on the back right side.

Address: 57 Elizabeth Street, Dansville, NY 14437
Webpage: http://www.redcross.org/local/new-york/western-central-new-york/chapters/clara-barton
Telephone: 585-335-3500
Hours: Tours are available by appointment only, call 585-335-3500.
Directions: Exit 4 off of Rt. 390 to Clara Barton Rd. (Rt. 36) to Dansville. Cross Main St. At the T take a left onto Elizabeth St. The house is at the corner of Elizabeth and Ossian St.

References and Suggested Reading
"Clara Barton in Dansville, 1866 and 1876 to 1886"
http://www.dansville.lib.ny.us/clara.html

Church Square
S2-10, V0, 🚻 🧘

With a population less than 5,000, Dansville has a very nice small town feel to it. It also has a very interesting and divine connection to Mother Earth. There is a park in town, a square block that is surrounded by four churches.

Residents call it Church Square. Just about all of it is located on FOC. Church Square offers you a chance to experience Her Fields in the lovely setting of a small town park, or attend services at any of four churches. The vibe is neutral.

With Church Street to your back the paper and dogs mark the series (3) of S10's.

Experiencing Church Square

Church Square is located between School and Church Streets and bounded by Clara Barton Street on one end and West Liberty Street at the other end. Just about all of the square rests on FOC, with just north of the gazebo as the center. The gazebo rests on an S6 and is a nice place to pray or meditate.

The highest stacked Fields is a series (3) of S10's located near the Gazebo on the Church Street side. See the picture above.

Address: Between School and Church Streets and bounded by Clara Barton Street and West Liberty Street.
Webpage: Village, http://dansvilleny.us/content/.
Telephone: Village, 585-335-5330.
Directions: Take exit 4 off of Rt. 390. Take Clara Barton Rd. (Rt. 36) to Dansville. As you get into town Genesee Community College will be on your right. School St will be the next right.

The Churches in Church Square

Dansville Presbyterian Church—All of the sanctuary is on a FOC (S6.)
Address: 3 School Street, Dansville, NY 14437
Webpage:
http://gvalley.myworshiptimes.com/churches/dansville-presbyterian-church/
Email: danspresch@gmail.com
Telephone: 585-335-5363
Hours: Sunday Services at 10:30AM.

St. Peter's Episcopal Church—All of the Church sits on a FOC (S6.)
Address: 25 Clara Barton Street, Dansville, NY 14437
Webpage: http: // www. episcoplachurch. org/parish/st-peters-episcopal-church-dansville-ny
Email: stpete@grontier.net
Telephone: 585-335-5434
Hours: Sunday Services every other Sunday at 10 AM. Call or check website to verify; church currently sharing minister.

St. Paul's Lutheran— It is here where Clara Barton held the organizational meeting of the first chapter of the American Red Cross. The sanctuary sits on a FOC (S3.)
Address: 21 Clara Barton Street, Dansville, NY 14437.
Webpage: http://spdans.org
Email: spdans@frontiernet.net
Telephone: 585-335-5260
Hours: Sunday Services at 9:15 AM.

New Bread Ministries—All of the church sits on Fields, Highest Field is a S2.
Address: 6 West Liberty Street, Danville, NY 14437.
Webpage: www. facebook. com/pages/New-Bread-

Ministries/289866281137924
Telephone: 585-204-9042
Hours: Sunday Services at 11 AM. Bible Study Wednesday's at 6PM, Prayer Mondays at 10AM and 5PM.

Gowanda, Cattaraugus County/Erie County, NY

Zoar Valley
S1-6, V2-3, ▽ ☆ ⬆ 🔲 ⵒ 〰 ✒

Spectacular and awe-inspiring views, a sense of remoteness as if Mother Earth had not been tamed here; there are old growth trees, a river that can run wild at times and a dash of mystery all combine to make the vibe of this special and inspiring place. It is also home to one of the most powerful FOC in western NY.

The Preserve

Zoar Valley is a 3,014 acre conservation area located at the confluence of the main and south branches of the Cattaraugus Creek. It is an ecologically diverse area consisting of a river bed, plateaus with shear cliffs offering spectacular views of the creek and the canyons below, and numerous waterfalls. It was purchased by New York State and became part of the DEC in 1960; parts of it were protected from logging, mining and drilling in 2007.

As much as Zoar offers awe and excitement it presents many dangers. Parts of the cliffs above are compromised and do not offer firm footing, so people need to be careful not to walk too close to the edge. The Cattaraugus Creek can be flashy and swell up after rainstorms, or after winter melts creating a very fast torrent. If you plan on crossing the creek check water levels (see info that follows) beforehand and listen to the weather report; less than 2 ½ feet is preferred.

There is also mystery to Zoar Valley. As Algonquin healer and elder Michael Bastine and paranormal investigator Mason Winfield write in *Iroquois Supernatural*:

"The Origin story of the Seneca Dark Dance is set in Zoar Valley, long associated with the Little People and apparently all else paranormal. People say the valley hums at night, as if it breathes orenda or some other vital force. They talk about how hard it is to build roads that last through it. They talk about hunters and hikers who go missing in the valley, curiously and seriously lost."[1]

My last visit to Zoar Valley testifies to its mystery. A stray dog greeted me upon arriving. Fortunately, there was ranger there who escorted the dog back to the creek to find its owner. I met the owner later on my descent to the creek bed and she said that the dog just mysteriously bolted. My dog Jaeda Bear, the black dog in the pictures, is afraid of water and does not swim. When we got to the creek, within a few minutes she bolted to other side, crossing the creek in a high water spot where she had to jump several times to get across—it was the sound of the jumping that alerted me to

383

her escapade. A very large stone I remembered from my last visit had been swept away. When I went to Forty Road, a place I had only been to once before, I could not find the FOC I referred to in my write-up for Mother Earth Prayers. My dowsing rods kept pointing in different directions.

Valentine Flats
S1-3, V2-3, ☆ ⵑ 〰〰 🖋

While there is much to explore and appreciate in Zoar Valley, the FOC are found in the Valentine Flats area. The Flats plateau has great views that allows access to the river below.

Be aware that Valentine's Flat is a popular place so you will run into people.

The short walk to Overlook Point at the end of the plateau, where the lookout is, passes over several FOC. There are numerous places to stop and meditate in a beautiful hemlock forest with some great views and a positive vibe. Consider a contemplate walk stopping in places to appreciate the spectacular view and saying thanks to Mother Earth.

From the parking lot, follow the herd path to Overlook Point. After a few hundred feet, a trail will branch off to the right that takes you to the valley and river below. Continue bearing left. Shortly you will pass a stand of hemlock trees; on the left side of it is a grassy area that contains a single FOC.

I suggest using this grassy area as a Welcome Circle to enter Zoar Valley; say a prayer, offer some tobacco, ask permission to enter, use a feather or your hands to smudge yourself. Do something to declare your intention and purpose. It is as much about improving the vibe as it is reducing the mystery and possibly getting some guidance and inspiration. I also picked up some of the litter in the parking lot when I was there last.

FOC are pretty much continuous from the area of the green patch up to where the trail begins, increasingly rising as you approach Point Peter (Outlook Point.)

As you continue walking you will come upon a second hemlock stand that contains a FOC (S2.) Spend some time in this stand of pines.

Valentine Flats. Jaeda (black dog) is on the first of a series (3) of S3's located just right of the herd path going towards Overlook Point. Pepper (white dog) is 15 feet back on the next S3. My backpack is on the final S3 by a tree that is next to a tree with an elbow shaped trunk for its base.

As you continue walking the trail will begin to rise ever so slightly. Halfway up the rise on the right hand side is a series (3) of S3's. It is close to the cliff overlooking the stream below. There is a less well traveled herd path that passes over the area. I would spend some time meditating here. When meditating close to the cliff, be careful not to sit on un-secure overhangs created by trees that give you a false sense of security.

Look for the tree with a base that is shaped like an elbow, one of the S3's is just to the right of it. The others are 15 and 30 feet respectively in front of it. See the picture on the previous page.

Spirit Keepers Site in the Creek Bed (?)
S1-6, V2-3, ▽ ☆ (♦) ▣ ᒿ ﹌ ✐

There is a FOC with a series (3) S6's in the creek bed below that may have once been a Spirit Keeper site. The vibe is positive to very positive which enhances the Fields. Very nice.

To access the area, take the trail to the creek bed, the path that breaks to the right about 200 feet after the parking lot. The trail down has a few wet spots, so you might want to wear boots, although many people just wear sneakers. It is about ¾ mile to the creek and another ½ mile to the site.

Bear to the right as you descend towards the creek bed. The trail ends at the confluence of the Cattaraugus Creek and its south branch. The area is called 'Skinny Dip Beach' for a community of hippies that set up commune here one summer in the 1960's and would skinny dip in the water—which is still occasionally practiced.

Once you get to the creek bed, you will take a right and walk along the creek bed for a few hundred yards along a canyon wall. You are walking upstream of the south branch of the Cattaraugus Creek. Depending upon water levels, you may or may not get your feet wet. So bring along a pair of water shoes just in case. As previously noted many people just wear sneakers and get them wet.

As you continue walking, an embankment will appear on the right. Climb it and follow the herd path continuing upstream, that hugs the creek. When you see a patch of myrtle, one of several, you have arrived at the site. Another marker would be the canyon wall, cliff, on the other side of the creek. It begins rising right about where the FOC begins. The FOC extends to where the herd path reaches another embankment, or rise.

When I first discovered this place in 2008/2009, there were remnants of a vortex ring indicating that there may have once been a vortex there, which means it was a place where spiritual practices took place. You may also see several old stone piles, many covered with moss that could have been sacred mounds; but the myrtle indicates it was probably settled at some point. So one does not know for sure. The vibe is still good, being very positive; Again, another marker that good thoughts or actions transpired here. There is good reason to believe that this was once a Spirit Keepers site.

While I am always telling you to look for flat stones upon which to meditate on, you need to be judicious here. It seems since my last visit someone has taken to piling all sorts of large flat stones near the edge of the embankment and apparently scarfing up several from the various stone piles that were once there. It looks like someone is in the process of building something. There are also several campfires encircled by stones. So what this place looks like when you come may be much different.

Meditate, do ceremony anywhere between where the myrtle begins to the mini-ridge. I would not stray too far from the herd path; the right hand side of the herd path going upstream has a higher concentration of stacked Fields, although close to the creek bed is fine.

The picture is facing downstream, towards Valentine Flats. Pepper is sitting on an S6, in an area with several flat stones. The final S6 is in front of the multi limbed tree. The second one is in between the two.

The series (3) of S6's is located on the other side of a multiple limbed tree as you walk upstream on your right.

About thirty feet on the other side of the multi-limbed tree are several large flat stones marking the S6. This is a very sweet and intoxicating area, and if you are looking to try and feel Consciousness this is a good spot. Clearly people performing spiritual exercises here have enhanced the FOC.

Do some exploring and find some place that you like. See if you can find the remnants of some old stone mounds, or other flats stones that feel as if they have weathered time, and the love and aspirations to connect with the divine is still attached to them.

While this place is lovely, it can be so much more. All it needs is prayers and the loving intentions of a contemplative heart. The vortex ring might come back and may eventually blossom into a vortex. Clearly this once was a special place, help make it so again.

Leave some time for the walk back to the parking lot. Take your time walking back and don't exert yourself too much, you don't want to dissipate all that Mother Earth has showered you with.

Other Places

There is so much to do in Zoar Valley. Some of the possibilities are seeing waterfalls, visiting old growth forests and hiking trails. I suggest checking the References and Recommended Reading list and the web.

Bruce Kershner was an avid environmentalist, a renowned expert on old growth trees who even had a NYS environmental law named after him; the Bruce. S Kershner Old-Growth and Preservation Act. Unfortunately he passed too early in 2007. He wrote about the Gallery of Giants at Zoar Valley in the *Sierra Club, The Sierra Club Guide to the Ancient Forests of the Northeast.*

He tells that the Gallery of Giants can be found by crossing the southern branch of Cattaraugus Creek below Point Peter (Valentine Flats) and following the main branch up 500 feet until you reach wooded terrace. Enter it and bear to the right and you are in the Gallery of Giants. Continue walking this terrace and the next one upstream.

PS—The Cattaraugus Creek is notorious for washing out bridges, so make sure that your route has not been jeopardized, particularly if you plan on traveling to, or coming from the north side of the creek.

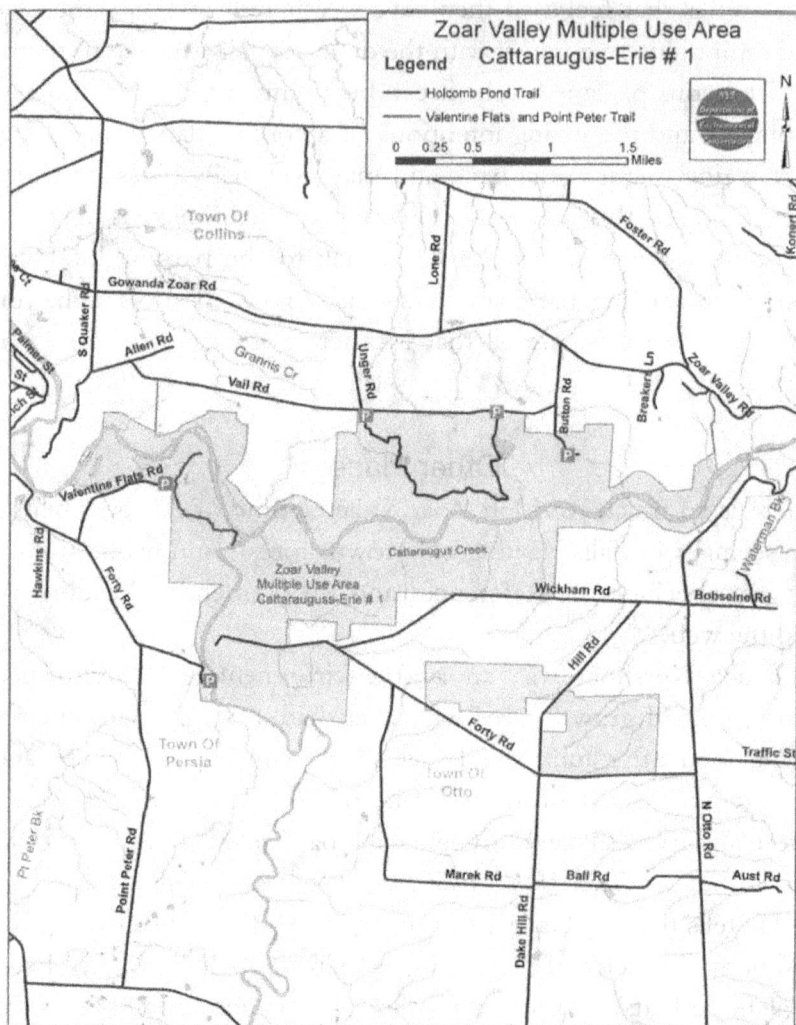

Address: Valentine Flats, Rd., Gowanda, NY
Webpage: http://www.dec.ny.gov/lands/36931.html
Email: DEC Region 9, Allegany Office: region9@dec.ny.gov
Telephone: 716-372-0645, DEC Region 9
Hours: Open year round, sunrise to sunset. No camping or fires. Free.

Check Water Levels: http:// waterdata. usgs. gov /usa/nwis/ uv?site_no=04213500

Close by: The Nature Conservancy has its Deer Lick Conservation area near Forty Rd.

Directions: From Gowanda take South Water St. South. Water St. intersects Main Street just south of the Cattaraugus Creek (bridge.) Continue on South Water and it will quickly turn into Commercial St. and then into Palmer St. Take a right onto Broadway Road (Rt. 4) and continue. Take a left onto Point Peter Rd. Take a left onto Valentine Flats Rd. and continue to the end.

References and Recommended Reading

1. Bastine, Michael and Winfield, Mason; *Iroquois Supernatural, Talking Animals and Medicine People*, Bear & Company, Rochester, Vermont 2011. Page 302.

DEC website, http://www.dec.ny.gov/lands/36931.html.

Frank Broughton's Zoar Valley Points of Interest Encyclopedia http://www.zoarvalley.us.

Wikipedia on Bruce Kershner https:// en. wikipedia. org/wiki/Bruce Kershner.

Kershner, Bruce S.; *The Sierra Club Guide to the Ancient Forests of the Northeast*, University of California Press, Berkeley, California, 2004

Bruce Kershner, Guide to Ancient Forests of Zoar Valley, Sponsored by Citizens Campaign for the Environment and Niagara Frontier Botanical Society, 2000

http://www.nature.org/ourinitiatives/regions/northamerica/unit edstates/newyork/places-preserves/central-deer-lick-conservation-area.xml

Lackawanna, Erie County, NY

Located just south of Buffalo.

Our Lady of Victory National Shrine and Basilica
S1-4, V0, ☆ ⚧ 🧘

The Basilica is home to the beloved Father Baker who helped the poor, unwed mothers and anyone else in need. It is a national shrine drawing pilgrims and visitors from around the world.

While I often complain about the vibe in spots within the Basilica, I love this place. Somehow the spirit of compassion and generosity as seen in Father Baker exists there, and it grabs you in places. Very powerful. I encourage you to visit. Most of the sanctuary rests on a FOC (S4.) I have led group meditations within it.

The History of the Basilica

The completion of the Erie Canal in 1825 brought an economic boom to the area. It also brought hardship over time as crime and poverty grew and many children were abandoned. In response, the Catholic Church constructed several orphanages in the 1850's, one of which was on Limestone Hill at St. Patrick's parish where the Basilica now stands.

When Father Nelson Baker took over St. Patrick's parish in 1882, it was facing financial collapse. Barraged by creditors, Father Baker reminded them that before he had entered the priesthood he had been a successful businessman that stood by his word, which he then pledged to fulfill the parish's debts. He emptied his personal savings to keep the creditors at bay.

A few weeks later his prayers were answered when an epiphany came to him to solicit all the Catholic women in the diocese into joining the Association of Our Lady of Victory for 25 cents a year, with the funds being used to help the orphanage. It worked. Within a few years the church was undergoing an expansion.

By the turn of the century the number of children living in the orphanage had almost quadrupled. A dredging of the Erie Canal found the bones of many babies that had been cast into it. To deal with the growing problem of infanticide from desperate and unwed mothers, Father Baker constructed an infant home in 1907. A decade later he had to expand it to meet the increased demand for services by constructing a maternity hospital.

In 1916 when the church burned down, the 74 year old Father Baker put forth a plan to construct a large Basilica that would rival anything in Europe. Father Baker consecrated the opening of the Basilica on May 25, 1926, and a few months later the Pope elevated it to the status of a minor Basilica.

During the depression Father Baker became known as the 'Padre for the Poor.' It was calculated that the church served 500,000 free meals from 1930 to 1933. When Father Baker, passed away on July 29, 1936 an estimated 300,000 to 500,000 people attended his funeral.

Experiencing the Basilica

FOC cover most of the sanctuary and are the most potent on the western side, right hand side if you face the front.

There is a series of Fields (S4) located in the western set of pews numbered 50 to 62 at one end and 142 to 160 at the other end. The area of pews 164-144 at the far end right hand side is very nice. As are the set of pews on the far right hand side in the picture (on the left.) The pews are off the beaten path and provide solitude.

On the west side of the church in front of the picture of the Infant Jesus towards the middle is a great place. If you were only going to pray/meditate/contemplate in one area, this would be it.

The prayer area in front of St. Patrick's towards the front on the west side is another nice place. The area in the middle a little away from the kneeling area is a good place to stand or put your cushion down.

These are only a few suggestions. There are Stations of the Cross, the Father Baker museum, lots of educational flyers, a gift shop and more.

Address: 767 /Ridge Rd., Lackawanna, NY 14218
Webpage: http://www.ourladyofvictory.org
Email: info@ourladyofvictory.org
Telephone: 716-828-9444
Hours: Open daily 7 AM to 9:00 PM. The hours have changed over the years so check first before visiting. Masses throughout the day—check the webpage. Guided tours Sunday 1 PM and 2 PM.
Directions: From Thruway (I-90) Exit 55. Take Rt. 219 to Ridge Rd. Take Ridge Rd. west. The Basilica is located at the intersection of Ridge Road and Route 62 (South Park Ave.) in Lackawanna.

Bibliography and Suggested Reading
Basilica's website-- http://www.ourladyofvictory.org
Various literature provided at the Basilica.
"The History of Father Baker", Erie College http://wnt.ecc.edu/cs215/HAWN/Spring2003/OLVBasilica/frbaker.htm
"The Servant of God, Father Nelson Baker", Catholism.org, http://catholicism.org/nelson-baker-sog.html.

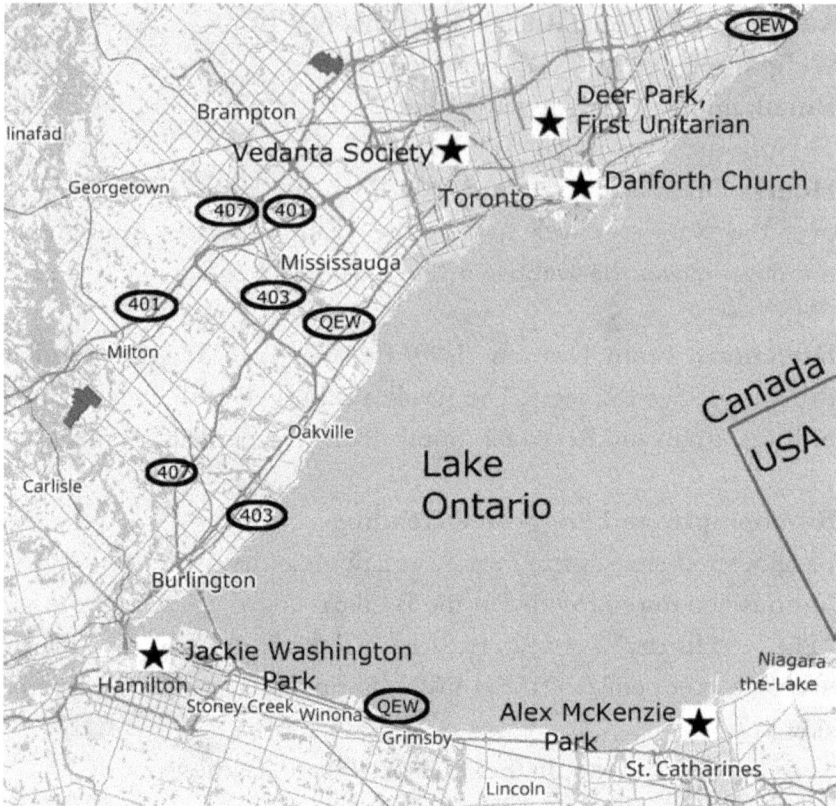

Map of Ontario's Golden Horseshoe. Source, © OpenStreetMap contributors, www. openstreetmap. org.

Ontario Canada's Golden Horseshoe

The area along Lake Ontario's north and western shores, southwestern Ontario, is not far from the heart of Mother Earth's Soul and contains numerous FOC.

Canada has a strong history of openness and acceptance. When slavery was fully abolished in Canada (1834) it became a refuge for multitudes of Freedom Seekers. Black communities sprang up in St. Catharine's, Hamilton, Fort Erie, London. Niagara Falls, Toronto... Black Settlements were formed in Buxton (Elgin), Canada West, Chatham and Little Africa. In recent years Canada has had one of the highest immigration rates in the world.

References and Recommended Reading
"Follow the North Star From Slavery to Freedom; Canada's Black Settlements"; http:// canadablkstlmnts. blogspot.com

Hamilton, ONT, CAN

Jackie Washington Park
S3, V0

Located near the bay area of Hamilton, Jackie Washington Park is an interesting mix. The park is dissected by a street and by railroad tracks. The park is named after its famous son, Jackie Washington (1919-2009) a beloved and noted jazz, blues and folk musician.

A FOC (S3) is located northeast of Simcoe St. near Wellington St. N. not far from the parking area along Simcoe St. It is also not far from the railroad tracks. In the picture on the next page the dogs mark the center of the FOC, about 40 feet in diameter. It is about 5 to 6 feet away from a metal grating that is marked by the backpack. The grating gives an excellent reference point.

The dogs mark the center of FOC, the backpack is on the metal grating. Wellington St. N is along the fence on the right.

Address: 371 Wellington St. N., Hamilton, Ontario
Webpage: https:// www. Hamilton. Ca/parks-recreation /parks-trails-and-beaches/parks-listing
Telephone: 905-546-3747
Hours: Open 24 hours a day.
Directions: From the QEW take exit 90, Burlington Ave. Burlington St. will undergo several name changes, Nicola Tesla Blvd, Industrial Dr. until it becomes Burlington again. Take a left onto Wellington and then a right onto Simcoe St. E.

St. Catharine's, ONT, CAN

St. Catharine's was the final resting stop for many Freedom Seekers that traveled with Harriet Tubman. She lived there briefly, as did her parents.

Alex McKenzie Park
S3, V0

Alex McKenzie Park is also referred to as the 'Haig Bowl.' A FOC (S3) about 40 feet in diameter is located near a tree close to baseball field. The vibe is neutral.

You are looking towards Haig St. Thomas St. is to your back and the Haig Bowl Bldg. on the left runs parallel to Pleasant Ave. The backpack and cushion mark the center of the FOC. Notice the bench in the distance; the baseball field is to the right.

Address: 17 Beech St., Haig, Beech and Thomas Streets, Catharines, ON L2R 2B6, Canada
Webpage: https:// www. stcatharines.ca/en/playin/ Alex McKenziePark.asp
Telephone: 905-688-5601
Hours: Dawn to Dusk
Directions: From the QEW take exit 46 Lake St. Go south on Lake St. away from Lake Ontario. Take a right onto Pleasant Ave.

Toronto, ONT, CAN

Toronto is the capital of Ontario province and has the fourth largest metropolitan population in North America. Considered one of the most multicultural cities in the world, nearly half of the city's residents are immigrants from another country.

There are numerous FOC in the city. What is nice is that several sanctuaries of the sacred sites listed are available for public use during the week.

Danforth Church
S4, V0, 🧘

Danforth church is located along Danforth Ave. in the Greektown section of Toronto. The church rests on a FOC (S4). The vibe is neutral.

Address: 60 Bowden St, Toronto, ON M4K 2X4, Canada
Telephone: 416-466-5658
Hours: Sunday services at 11AM

Directions: Take the Bayview Ave./Bloor St,/Danforth Ave. exit off of the Don Valley Pkwy. Take Bayview to Bloor St. and head east. Bloor St. will turn into Danforth Ave. Subway take Line 2 (Bloor/Danforth) to Broadview.

Calvin Presbyterian and Deer Park United Church
S3, V0, 🚻 🧘

Two churches worship at 26 Deslile St. When Deer Park United (United Church of Canada) sold its church on 129 St. Clair Ave it began worshipping at the Calvin Presbyterian's church. They have formed a distinctive yet united identity.

Per the Calvin Presbyterian Church website:

"Calvin Presbyterian Church and Deer Park United Church are joined together in an Ecumenical Shared Ministry Agreement.

We worship together, share in ministry and serve God together. We are two distinct congregations that share a history, a neighborhood, worship services and one Lord and Saviour whom we worship and trust."

Both Churches have a variety of community programs, outreaches and involvements. There is a community breakfast for anyone that wishes and a food bank. There are local programs, such as helping the homeless and International Aid Programs (Calvin Pres.) including helping aids victims in Africa and disaster relief.

Experiencing the Sanctuary

All are welcome to use the sanctuary for prayer and meditation as long as no programs are scheduled. Call and ask permission first and announce yourself upon arriving.

A FOC (S3) covers all of the pews on the right side of the sanctuary except the first 3 pews. The vibe is neutral

Address: 26 Delisle St., Toronto, Ontario, Canada M4V 1S5
Webpage: http:// pccweb. ca/calvinchurchtoronto/, http:// www. deerparkunitedchurch. org/index.html
Email: office@ calvinchurchtoronto. com
Telephone: 416-923-9030
Hours: Sunday worship at 10:30 AM. Call before visiting 9 AM to 5PM, Mon-Fri. to meditate in the sanctuary.

Directions: From Gardiner Expwy. take Bay St./York St. exit towards Yonge St. Delisle is on your left after St. Clair Ave. W. Subway take Line 1 (Yonge/University) to St. Clair.

First Unitarian Congregation of Toronto
S3, V0, 🚻 🧘

The First Unitarian Congregation of Toronto has a large and active membership. A FOC (S3) covers all of the sanctuary. The vibe is neutral.

The church has a long history of social justice. In 1846 it was the first church in Toronto to give equal rights and status to women. Today the church is involved in several activities: Aboriginal Awareness group, Central America Project, Green Sanctuary Group, Refugee Family Sponsorship and several Unitarian Universalists actions.

402

Experiencing the Sanctuary

First Unitarian Congregation of Toronto allows anyone to use the sanctuary for prayer or meditation weekdays (M-F, 9 AM to 5PM.) Make sure to check the calendar and call before you come, and announce yourself upon arriving; the sanctuary can be busy.

The backpack in the picture below marks the center of the FOC (S3) which is about 50 feet in diameter. It encompasses all the chairs on the left side and just about all on the right with the exception of the front and back corners on the right side.

Address: 175 St. Clair Ave. W, Toronto, Ont. Canada, M4V 1P7
Webpage: www. firstunitariantoronto.org
Telephone: 416-924-9654
Donate, Volunteer: Contact the office to get involved with one of their many activities.
Hours: Sunday worship 10:30 AM. The sanctuary is open for prayer and meditation Mon. to Fri., 9AM to 5 PM. Call first and check calendar before coming. Announce yourself once there.
Directions: From Gardiner Expwy. take Bay St./York St. exit towards Yonge St. Follow signs for York St. N. Turn left onto University Ave. Continue Queens Park Crescent. Continue on Avenue Rd. Turn left onto Clarendon Ave. Right onto poplar

Plains Rd. Right onto St. Clair Ave. W. Subway take Line 1 (Yonge/University) to St. Clair.

Vedanta Society of Toronto
S4, V1-3, (↑) ⭧⭨ ⚘ 🖼

The Vedanta Society in Toronto has some powerful FOC (S4) with a great vibe and a warm and welcoming environment. It is a real jewel in southern Ontario.

About the Vedanta Society of Toronto

The Vedanta Society of Toronto is a branch of the Ramakrishna Order of India; as is the Ramakrishna—Vivekananda Center of NY which overseas Swami Vivekananda's Cottage in the Thousand Islands, that is included as a sacred site in this book.

The Ramakrishna Order was founded on the beliefs of the great Indian saint Sri Ramakrishna and was started by his star disciple Swami Vivekananda in 1897. It has two purposes spiritual development (Ramakrishna Math) and social service (Ramakrishna mission.) Accordingly as the Vedanta Society of Toronto webpage notes the motto of the order is, "Liberation for oneself and service to mankind."

Experiencing the Place

A FOC (S4) covers all of the building. Within it is a series (3) S4's that cuts diagonally across the building from the left front to the back on the right side. When I visited for my review, the building was undergoing a remodeling so everything was in flux, there was lots of open space and dust in the air. Still the vibe was slightly positive, to positive throughout; very nice.

The shrine was open; and it is very delightful with a very positive vibe. The warm and friendly Swami Kripamayananda (the minister of the Society) happily showed us around and took us to the Shrine and told us to sit down and meditate for a while. It was a sweet respite that gave us a chance to burn off the many imprints (samskaras) that we had picked up from our travels during the day. Very, very therapeutic.

The Shrine. Vedanta honors and respects all religions and faith traditions and this is seen with the commemorative pictures in the Shrine above. In the center is Sri Ramakrishna who is flanked by the Divine Mother (his wife) and Swami Vivekananda. Jesus and Buddha in turn flank them.

Address: 120 Emmett Ave. Toronto, ON M6M 2E6 Canada
Webpage: www. vedantatoronto.ca
Email: info@ vedantatoronto.ca
Telephone: 416-240-7262
Hours: Call, check website for regular meditations.
Directions: From Rt. 401 take exit 348 and head towards downtown Toronto. Turn left onto Eglinton Ave. When you get to Raymore Park take a left onto Emmet Ave.

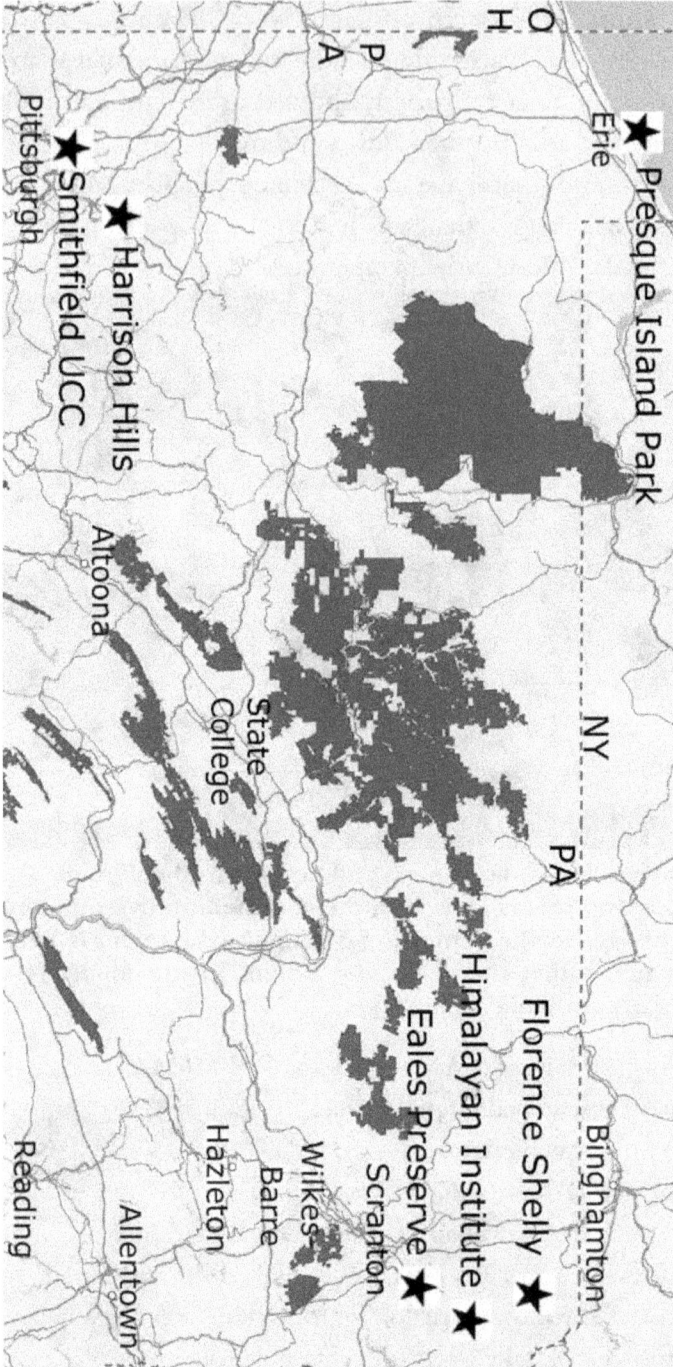

Map of Pennsylvania. Source, www. openstreetmap. org.

Pennsylvania

FOC cover much of Pennsylvania, although they are not as powerful as those found in New York. The Declaration of Independence and the United States of America Constitution were both signed at Independence Hall in Philadelphia, PA. Pennsylvania was one the first states to abolish slavery.

William Penn founded the colony of Pennsylvania calling it the "Holy Experiment." It has a strong and vibrant Quaker community, particularly in the southeastern part of the state, which was active in the Underground Railroad and other reforms.

Erie, Erie County, PA
Was home to the New Jerusalem free Black Community.

Presque Island Park
S1, V0, 👫

Presque Island Park is a 3,200 sandy peninsula along Lake Erie that offers sandy beaches, swimming, boating, fishing and great views of Lake Erie. There is a single FOC about 20 feet in radius near the park entrance on the east side. It is located near a group of trees close to the sidewalk on the bike trail near the entrance. The center of the FOC is 5 feet north and 5 feet east of the largest northern most tree of the clump of trees next to the entrance gate. The fringes of the FOC extend to the end of gate swing when it is fully open. The vibe is neutral.

Being so close to the entrance traffic noise is a concern, particularly during the summer. But the FOC is accessible, easily found and you can plant yourself off of the bike trail.

Address: 301 Peninsula Drive, Erie, PA 16505-2042 Official
Address; 10 Peninsula Drive is the Park Entrance.
Webpage: http://www.presqueisle.org,
http://www.dcnr.state.pa.us/stateparks/findapark/presqueisle/
Email: presqueislesp@pa.gov
Telephone: 814-833-7424
Hours: Open sunrise to sunset year round.
Directions: From I-79 take exit 182 and merge Rt. 20w/W. 26th.
Turn right Rt. 832 N (Peninsula Dr.) Follow to entrance.

Janice is standing in the middle of the FOC.

Bibliography and Suggested Reading
"Time Travel on the Underground Railroad," Goerie.com, http://
www. goerie.com/article/20130127/LEL02/301279996

Honesdale, Wayne County, PA

Himalayan Institute
S4, V2, ▽ 👫🏠🖼

The Himalayan Institute is a retreat center offering a variety of
programs in yoga, meditation and holistic health. A FOC (S6) is
located on the grounds and the vibe is positive in it.

Sri Swami Rama, a Hindu yogi from the Himalayas, formed the Himalayan Institute in 1971. It rests on 400 acres that includes several trails. There is a meditation center in the main building that has a very positive vibe and a vortex ring of Cosmic Prana in the middle back of the room.

The FOC (S4) is located in the field by the main parking lot next to the Havan Kunda (gazebo like pavilion.) With the main building behind you and the Havan Kunda on your right, look straight ahead towards the Forest Pavilion. You can find the center of FOC by drawing an imaginary right angle to where the Havan Kunda and Forest Pavilion intersect. The FOC is 75' to 80' in diameter.

The circle around my backpack marks the center of the FOC. Notice the gazebo on the right and the Forest Pavilion on the left. If you were to draw a line from the center of each they would meet at a right angle in the center of the FOC.

Address: 952 Bethany, Turnpike, Honesdale, PA 18431
Webpage: https: // www. himalayaninstitute.org
Telephone: 800-822-4547, 570-253-5551
Directions: I-81 take exit 187 to US-6 East (Carbondale.) Follow US-6 East approximately 30 miles to Honesdale. Turn left at PA-191 North (Main Street) and go approx. 1/2 mile to PA-670 North (Bethany.) Bear left to PA-670 North and go approximately 5 miles to the Institute on the right.

Jessup, Lackawanna County, PA

Dick and Nancy Eales Preserve at Moosic Mountain
S3, V0, 2

Dick and Nancy Eales preserve is located on top Moosic Mountain not far from Scranton. A short 15-20 minute hike will bring you to the FOC (S3.) The vibe is neutral.

About the Preserve

In 2001, the Nature Conservancy purchased 1,200 acres on Moosic Mountain, thereby saving it from becoming a business park. In 2009 the preserve was named after Dick and Nancy Eales, whose generosity enabled the preserve to expand to 2,250 acres.

It is a flat mountaintop with stunted pine and oak tress as well as various low-lying shrubs such as huckleberry, blueberry and rhodora (part of the rhododendron family.)

Experiencing the Preserve

The FOC is located on the Stonehenge trail. From the main parking lot walk straight ahead on the gravel road. Shortly Roman Road, another gravel road, will intersect the road you are walking. Take a left onto Roman Rd. Follow it a short distance until the trailhead for the Conglomerate Loop appears to your right. Take it. You will not walk far on Conglomerate Loop before it divides into two trails. Take the trail you prefer to follow. They will meet up again at the break off for Stonehenge.

Take Stonehenge. Within a few minutes you are in a woods. Continue walking a short distance. About 40 feet after the trail breaks out of the woods, look for a rock clearing created by a large flat rock, on your right hand side.

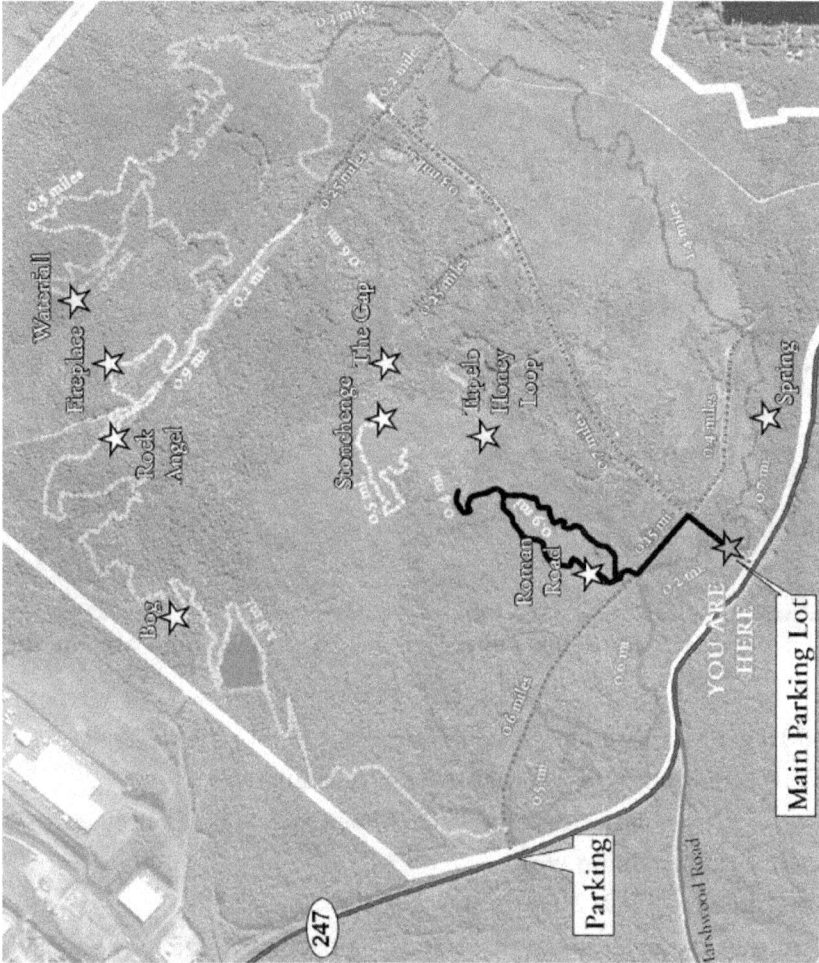

Trail Map of Moosic Mountain. The trail to the FOC is in black. Map courtesy of the Nature Conservancy.

The S3 is located in the center of the trail in front of the rock clearing. While the S3 is smack in the middle of the trail the remainder of the FOC (S1 And S2) extend about 15 in either direction from the center. Meditate on the S3 in the center of the trail, or anywhere within 15 feet of it. See the picture on the next page.

The backpack is in the center of the FOC, the dogs are on the large flat rock.

Address: Moosic Lake Road (Route 247), Jessup, PA
Webpage: http:// www. nature.org/ourinitiatives /regions/northamerica/unitedstates/pennsylvania/placesw:prote ct/moosic-mountain.xml
Telephone: 717-232-6001, 866-298-1267
Donate, Volunteer: Go the Nature Conservancy webpage, www. nature.org
Directions: The preserve is 8 miles northeast of Scranton. From I-81, take exit 187 for Carbondale/Rt. 6. Once on Route 6, go just over four miles. Take Exit 3 for Jessup, and travel south on Moosic Lake Road/Rt. 247 for about 2 miles.
Park at the Main Parking lot.

Pittsburgh, Allegheny County, PA

Smithfield United Church of Christ
S3, V0, 👫 🧘

Smithfield UCC is the oldest church in Pittsburgh organized in 1782. Its walk-in ministry food pantry has won praises from local leaders. Located in the "golden triangle" the heart of Pittsburgh's downtown Smithfield UCC provides the opportunity for those living in western PA and the surrounding area to experience FOC in a peaceful setting.

The church is situated on a FOC, an S3, which is pretty incredible given how far it is from the heart of Mother Earth's Soul. What makes it even more appealing is that the sanctuary is available for meditation daily (on your own); Monday to Friday, 9AM to 2:45 PM. Call first and announce yourself upon arriving.

The center of the FOC is located on the right side of the sanctuary as you face the lectern, approximately in the center area of the pews. It encompasses all the pews on the right side, and stretches to the far left side of the pews on the left. The vibe is neutral. Pick a place you like and soak it up.

I encourage everyone to visit Smithfield UCC and meditate in the sanctuary to help fortify the FOC at this wonderful church. It holds great potential; please visit and meditate if you can.

Address: 620 Smithfield St, Pittsburgh, PA 15222
Webpage: http://www.smithfieldchurch.org
Email: smithfield@verizon.net

Telephone: 412-281-1811, Fax: 412-434-0155
Hours: Services are held on the second floor sanctuary: Sunday - 11:00 a.m, Wednesday - 12:10 - 12:30 p.m. The sanctuary is open for meditation and prayer Monday through Friday, 9 AM to 2:45 PM. Please call first.
Directions: On I-376 take exit 71a and merge onto Grant St. Stay on Grant St. Turn left on Sixth Ave. Turn right on Smithfield St.

Natrona Heights (Pittsburgh), Allegheny County, PA

Harrison Hills Park is located in Natrona Heights, 25 miles northeast of Pittsburgh

Harrison Hills Park
S3, V0, 👫

Harrison Hills Park is 500 acre county park consisting of woods, ponds and fields. There is a FOC (S3) in the field next to the parking area for the Yakaon Pavilion which is close to the Environmental Learning Center.

Park at the farthest edge of the parking lot; on the side of the pavilion, away from the white maintenance building. Notice a tree on the pavilion side of the parking lot. From the tree the FOC is located a 45° angle towards the woods. The FOC begins 10 feet from the tree; the center is 30 feet from the tree. Picture follows.

Address: 5200 Freeport Rd, Natrona Heights, PA 15065
Webpage: http://www.alleghenycounty.us/parks/harrison-hills/index.aspx. Friends of Harrison Hills Park, http://www.friendsofharrisonhills.org
Email: Friends of Harrison Hills friendsofharrisonhills@gmail.com
Telephone: Park Office, 724-295-3570. Friends of Harrison Hills, 724-224-4102.

Donate, Volunteer: Go to Friends of Harrison Hills Park webpage: http://www.friendsofharrisonhills.org

Hours: 8AM to Sunset year round. Free.

Directions: Take Rt. 28 (Allegheny Valley Epwy) out of Pittsburgh. Take exit 16 and turn right onto Bakerstown Rd. Turn right onto Freeport Rd. Enter park by turning left onto Parks Lane Dr. and continue to Yakaon Pavilion. Or enter at Sportsman Park Dr. Take a left onto Cottontail Dr. Take a left onto Parks Lane Drive and continue to Yakaon Pavilion.

The backpack marks the center of the FOC. Notice the tree to the right referred to, and the administrative building in the background.

Thompson, Susquehanna County, PA

Florence Shelly Preserve
S3, V0

Florence Shelly Preserve has a FOC (S3) with easy access and a neutral vibe.

Its 357-acres consists of fields, woodlands, a stream, and a glacial pond surrounded by a floating bog. Named after Florence

Shelly, who organized a committee of citizen naturalists and volunteer professors from SUNY Binghamton to characterize and inventory the property. The Shelly family donated the land to The Nature Conservancy in the 1980s; the purchase of nearby Plew's Swamp completed the preserve.

Experiencing Shelly Preserve

From the parking lot across from Stack Street take the trail at the northern end of the parking lot. You will walk briefly close to the road and quickly begin a gentle descent. A FOC (S3) is located about 50-70 feet down the trail. Look for the following markers to indicate its location; an opening to your left (I could visibly see a little path up into the open area next to the preserve) and a 3 limbed beech tree. The FOC (S3) is located up a few feet from the beech tree on the other side of the trail, across from a small maple tree.

The radius of the FOC is about 15-20 feet. The dogs in the picture below are in the center of the FOC. The vibe is neutral.

Address: Rt. 171, Thompson, PA

Webpage: http:// www. nature .org/ ourinitiatives/ regions /northamerica/unitedstates/pennsylvania/placesweprotect/floren ce-shelly-preserve.xml

Telephone:717-232-6001

Donate, Volunteer: Contact the Florence Shelly Stewardship Committee about trail work, guiding and donations, 570-727-3362, 570-879-4244. Go the Nature Conservancy webpage, www. nature.org

Hours: Dawn to Dusk. For upcoming guided walks contact the Florence Shelly Preserve Committee, Andrew Gardner, or Trebbe Johnson at 570-727-3362, 570-879-4244.

Directions: From I-81 take exit 230 (Great Bend/Halstead.) Take Rt. 171 east and continue. In Oakland take a right onto Exchange St. and cross the river into to Susquehanna. Take a left onto Main St. Continue and take a right onto Rt. 171. Continue on Rt. 171, the preserve will be on your left. Park across from Stack St.

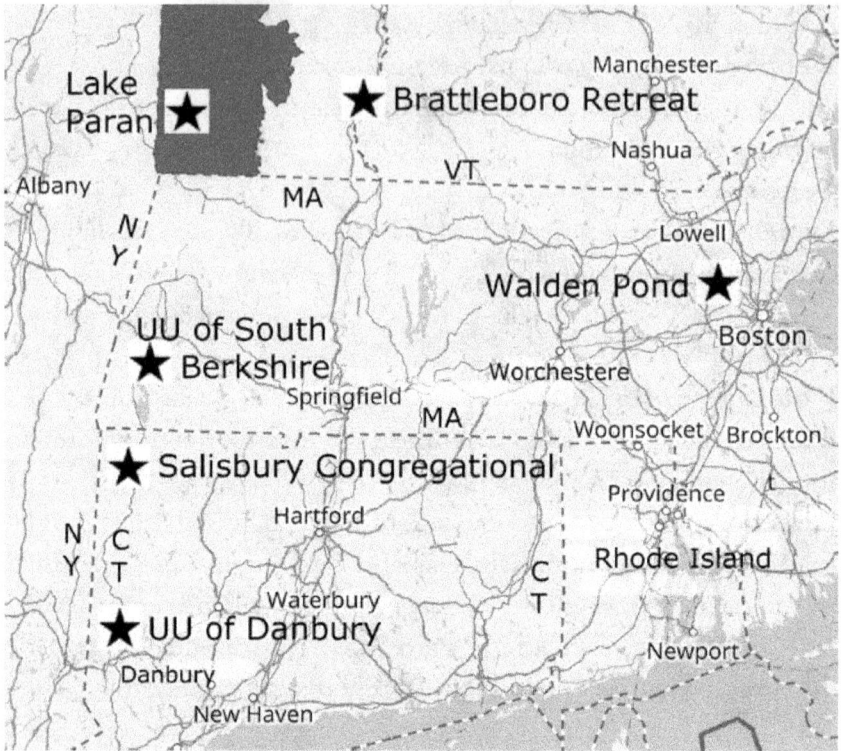

Map of New England. Source, © OpenStreetMap contributors, www. openstreetmap. org.

New England

Massachusetts

Massachusetts has played a prominent role in American history. The Pilgrims landed there. The Boston Tea Party and Paul Revere's ride are cherished stories synonymous with the American Revolution. It was the birthplace of America's First Great Awakening. Massachusetts Puritans would give rise to Congregationalists, the United Church of Christ and more.

Transcendentalism was born here and brought new awareness to the environment and eastern traditions. Abolitionism was strong. Prominent William Lloyd Garrison who published the Liberator hails from just outside of Boston. His home, Rockledge, in the Roxbury section of Boston appears to rest on a single FOC.

Concord, Middlesex County, MA

Walden Pond State Reservation
S3, V0, ♀♂ ⊇ 〰〰

Beginning in 1845 Henry David Thoreau spent two years at Walden Pond, owned by his friend and mentor Ralph Waldo Emerson. It was the inspiration for his classic *Walden*. Many consider it the birthplace of the Conservation Movement. The reservation consists of a 102-foot deep glacial kettle-hole pond and mostly undeveloped woods totaling 2680 acres, called 'Walden Woods', that surround the reservation.

There is a FOC (S1) besides the lake. The vibe is neutral.

Nature is Mother

Transcendentalists saw Nature as an inspiration that represented God and humanity; and believed much could be gleaned from studying and contemplating Her. In Walden Thoreau wrote:

"The earth is not a mere fragment of dead history…but living poetry like the leaves of a tree, which precede flowers and fruit—not a fossil earth, but a living earth; compared with whose great central life all animal and vegetable life is merely parasitic."[1]

Thoreau's retreat to Walden Pond is part of a long tradition whose roots go way back and is broad and diverse; from shamans, to Christian mystics and desert hermits who went into the wilderness, to Native Americans who would go off into the woods and 'cry for a vision,' to great Hindu and Buddhist sages who lived in solitude in caves and would meditate for days—such as the famous Tibetan Buddhist Milarepa. Their bounty was enormous.

Of his experience Thoreau would write:

"I went to the woods because I wished to live deliberately, to front only the essential facts of life, and see if I could not learn what it had to teach, and not, when I came to die, discover that I had not lived."[2]

Mother Earth is powerful. I like many others before me have had some of my most powerful mystical experiences in the wilderness. I strongly encourage you to take a retreat into the wilderness yourself.

There is an FOC (S1) about 30 feet in diameter on the south side of the pond; the left side as you face the pond from the entry point. It is in the area of the center of the first curve if you walk along the beach. About 60-70 feet from where the trail is closest to the beach at the curve. In the picture on the left on the previous page I am standing in the center of the FOC.

Address: 915 Walden St. Concord, Mass. 01742
Webpage: http: // www. mass. gov /eea/agencies /dcr /massparks/region-north/walden-pond-state-reservation.html
Telephone: 978 369-3254
Hours: Open year round, hours vary by season' call 978 369-3254 before visiting. $8 MA residents, $10 nonresidents
Directions: From Mass Pike Rt. I-90: Get on Rt. 95/128 North, take exit 29B onto Rt. 2 West at 3rd set of lights take left onto Rt. 126 South. Parking is ¼ of mile down on left.

References and Recommended Reading
1. Thoreau, Henry David; *Walden*, in *Walden and Civil Disobedience, Authoritative Texts Background Reviews and Essays in Criticism*, Edited by Owen Thomas, Norton & Co., NY, NY 1966. Page 204.
2. Ibid, Page 61.
Felton, Todd R.; *A Journey into the Transcendentalists' New England*, Roaring Forties Press, Berkeley, California, 2006
www. mass. Gov/eea/docs/ parks/pdf/walden-pond.pdf

Housatonic, Berkshire County, MA

Unitarian Universalist Meeting of South Berkshire
S2, V0, 🚻 🧘

Located in the lovely Berkshire Mountains, UU of South Berkshire sits on a FOC (S2.) The vibe is neutral. The church has a variety of programs such as the Human Rights Speaker Series and community walks in the woods.

As you face the church the FOC (S2) is on the right hand side of the sanctuary; the center of which is along the wall.

Address: 1089 Main St, Housatonic, Great Barrington, MA 01236
Webpage: http://www.uumsb.org
Telephone: 413-358-3877
Hours: Sunday Services 10:30 AM
Directions: Take exit 1 off of I-90 in MA. Take Stockbridge Rd (Rt. 102) towards Stockbridge. Take a right onto Glendale Rd (Rt. 183) as you approach Stockbridge. In Housatonic take a right onto Main St.

Vermont

Known as the independent state, Vermont is the least populated state after Wyoming. The original state constitution (1877) forbade slavery, making it the first state to outlaw it. It was the first state to recognize civil unions of the people of the same sex. It has a strong progressive and independent bent.

Brattleboro, Windham County, VT

Hogle Wildlife Sanctuary Trail (Brattleboro Retreat)
S4, V1-2

Located in downtown Brattleboro the Hogle Wildlife Sanctuary Trail passes through a FOC (S4) with a slightly positive, to positive vibe—pretty incredible. If you are not too far away and don't want to drive to far to experience FOC this would be a great place to visit and meditate at.

The backpack marks the center of the FOC (S4.)

Experiencing the Trail

Brattleboro Retreat is a not for profit mental health and addictions center that traces its roots back to 1834. The FOC is located at the northwest end of the grounds close to Linden street` on the Hogle Wildlife Sanctuary Trail. The center of the FOC (S4) is located 15 to 20 feet behind the entry gate.

Close to the road, traffic can be noisy. But the vibe, slightly positive, to positive, on a S4 makes this place shine and well worth a visit if you live in Vermont.

Address: Trailhead of the Wildlife Sanctuary Trail near Linden Street, Brattleboro Vermont.

Close by: There are numerous other trails close by.

Directions: Take exit 2 off of Rt. 91 in Brattleboro. Take Rt. 9 Western Ave east. Turn left onto Cedar. St. Follow until the T and turn right onto Linden St. Take a left onto Anna Marsh Lane and look for a safe and approved place to park.

North Bennington, Bennington County, VT

Lake Paran, State Fishing Access
S3, V0, 〰️

There is a FOC (S3) located at the Vermont State Fishing Access point on Lake Paran. The vibe is neutral.

From the parking lot the FOC is centered about 25-30 directly left of the park kiosk if you face the kiosk. In the picture below the dogs are in the center of the FOC.

Address: State Access point Lake Paran, North Bennington, VT 05257

Webpage: http:// northbennington. org/paran.html

Directions: Take Rt. 67a to North Bennington. It will turn to Main St. in the town center. Take a right onto Sage St. Another right onto North St. Turn left onto State Access point Lake Paran, follow to the end.

Connecticut

There are several FOC in the western part of the state. Connecticut had numerous Underground Railroad routes pass through it. Abolitionist John Brown hails from the state.

Danbury, Fairfield County, CT

Unitarian Universalist Congregation of Danbury
S3, V0, 👫 🧘

UU of Danbury traces its roots back to 1822. It has a vibrant outreach program. The sanctuary behind the house is centered on a FOC (S3). The vibe is neutral.

The congregation is involved with a variety of activities: Dorothy Day Soup Kitchen, volunteer assistance to teachers and several programs to assist immigrants.

Address: 24 Clapboard Ridge Rd., Danbury, CT 06811
Webpage: www. uudanbury.org
Telephone: 203-798-1994
Hours: Sunday service 10:30 AM
Directions: I-84 take exit 5 in CT. Get onto Main St. It will turn into Clapboard Ridge Rd (Rt. 39.)

Salisbury, Litchfield County, CT

Congregational Church of Salisbury
S5, V0 ♀♂ 🧘

The church traces its beginnings back to 1744, with the first Meetinghouse building in 1750. It has a vibrant Health Ministry assisting people as far away as Haiti. There is a Christian Action Committee involved with a variety of activities and a food pantry.

A FOC (S5) located in the center that encompasses all of the sanctuary. The vibe is neutral.

Address: 30 Main St., Salisbury, CT 06068

Webpage: www. Salisbury congregational.org
Telephone: 860-435-2442
Hours: Sunday services 10 AM

Directions: Main St. in Salisbury is Rt. 44 in Salisbury, you can catch off of the Taconic (NY) or eastern part of CT.

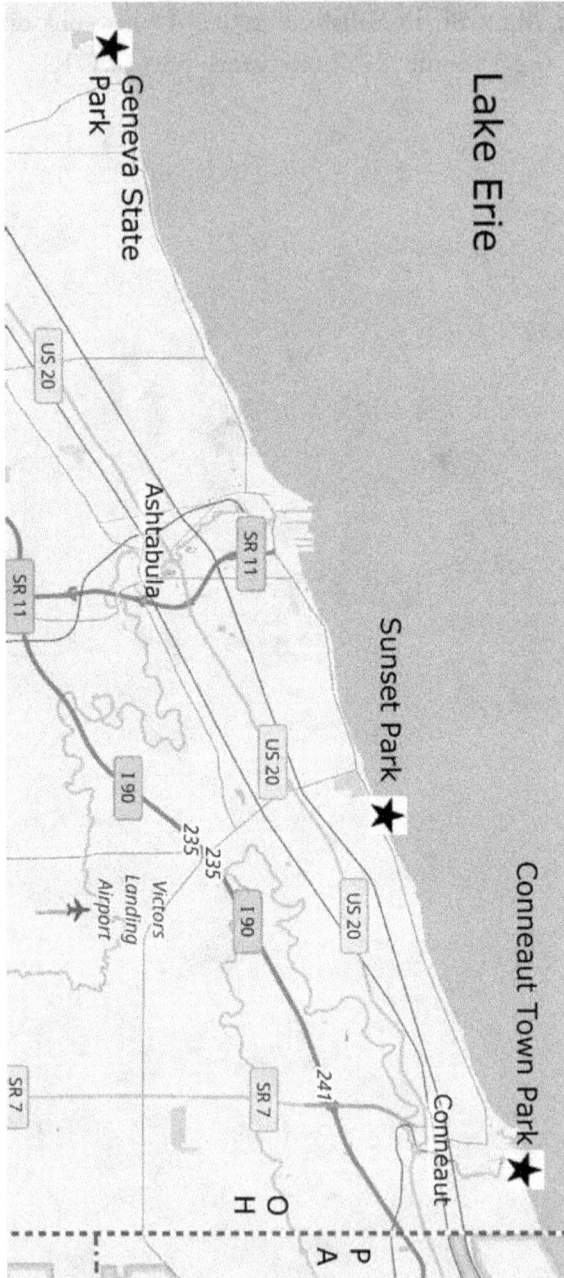

Map of Ohio. Source, © OpenStreetMap contributors, www. openstreetmap. org.

Ohio

The Western Reserve along Lake Erie is the western tip of Mother Earth's Soul. So called because the Colony of Connecticut once claimed it, as did state of Connecticut later; the claim was dropped after the American Revolution. It is also the western edge of the Burned-over-District. There was a vibrant Underground Railroad system supported by the state's many Quakers. Charles Grandison Finney, the leader of America's Second Great Awakening, would end up teaching at the progressive Oberlin College and become its second president.

While single FOC's emanate consciousness they are very difficult to sense. But do not be discouraged a little effort will definitely do them well.

Conneaut, Ashtabula County, OH

Conneaut Township Park
S1, V0, 🚻

Conneaut Township Park is a thirty-acre town park on the south shore of Lake Erie. The bluff above its sandy beach offers a spectacular view of Lake Erie. There is a single FOC (18-20 feet in radius) near the entrance way at the southeast corner of the park. Going west on Lake Road (Rt. 531) take your first left after Wright Ave to enter the park (Lake Erie Dr.) The FOC is located on your right side a little farther ahead just before you cross Pearl Street. Continue ahead to park your car and walk back.

The backpack marks the center of the FOC. Notice how it is directly in front of the chimney of the house on the corner of Pearl St.

The best marker for the FOC is the chimney of the house on the end of Pearl Street on the south side next to park, 401 Pearl St. As you face the house the center of the FOC is just right of the chimney. It is closer to the sidewalk (30 feet from) than the road you came in on (40 feet from.) It is 60 feet from where Pearl Street intersects the park. Since it is almost 40 feet in diameter even if you don't find the exact center, as long as you are close you will be fine. The vibe is neutral. Given it is a single FOC and the vibe is neutral you won't feel much, but it is there.

Dogs are not allowed in the park.

Address: 480 Lake Road, PO Box 373, Conneaut, Ohio 44030-0373.
Webpage: http://conneauttownshippark.com
Telephone: 440-599-7071
Hours: 7 AM to 7 PM, or dusk

Directions: Exit 241 off of I-90. Take Rt. 7 north through Conneaut. Turn left onto Rt. 531.

Geneva, Ashtabula County, OH

Geneva State Park
S1, V0, 🚻 〰️

Geneva State Park is a 698 acre state park located along the shore of Lake Erie providing a host of activities: swimming, boating, hiking, archery and winter activities such as cross country skiing.

Facing away from the shore the backpack marks the center of the FOC. Notice the metal box ahead and to the right.

A single FOC is located by a rocky beach near the marina. The vibe is neutral. As you enter the park follow the signs for the marina, but instead of turning left to enter the Marina bear right and cross the water way and park your car at the eastern end of the parking area. Follow the paved path through the reeds and bear right towards the Geneva Resort Lodge.

As you bear right on the walkway the FOC is located on your left. If you look back away from the beach to where you came from, you will see a utility box to the left of the paved path. The center of the FOC is about 50 feet from the metal box and 5 to its left as you face it.

Address: 4499 Padanarum Rd, Geneva, OH 44041
Webpage: http://parks.ohiodnr.gov/geneva
Telephone: 440-466-8400
Hours: Dawn to dusk year round.
Directions: Exit 218 off of I-90. Take Rt. 534 north to the park.

North Kingsville, Ashtabula County, OH

Al Cummings Sunset Park
S1, V0,〰️

Located on a bluff overlooking Lake Erie it has a less traveled and rustic feel to it. There is a single FOC at the western end of the park. Look for a stream, or dry creek bed that dissects the park at an angle.

Find an opening amongst a few trees, closer to the pavilion as there are woods at the western end of the park. It will appear as if the trees were planted to surround the FOC. Often trees will mark the boundary of an aspect of Mother Earth forming a natural circle of sorts. Another marker is a large group of big rocks a little south of the FOC towards the road. The vibe is neutral. When I was there on a sunny day in May no one was there. Enjoy.

Looking east, Lake Erie is on the left. The backpack marks the center of the FOC.

Address: Lake Road (Rt 531), North Kingsville, Ohio; 0.4 miles east of where Rt 193 intersects Rt 531.

Webpage: http://www.northkingsvilleohio.org/parks.htm

Telephone: 440-224-0091

Hours: Open daily from dawn to 10PM.

Directions: Take exit 235 off of I-90. Take Rt. 193 north. Turn right onto Rt. 531. The park will be on your left side.

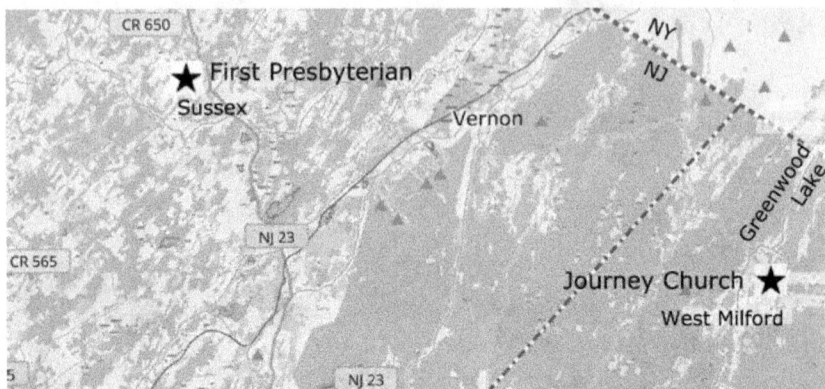

Map of New Jersey. Source, © OpenStreetMap contributors, www. openstreetmap. org.

New Jersey

FOC extend into northern New Jersey, with the strongest ones located in the northwest corner of the state. Several Underground Railroad routes cut through the state. The state briefly granted women the right to vote in 1797.

Sussex, Sussex County, NJ

First Presbyterian Church of Sussex
S3, V0, ♀♀ ⚱

The First Presbyterian Church of Sussex rests on a FOC (S3) that covers most of the sanctuary. The center is located on the left side. The vibe is neutral. There are a variety of ministries that people can get involved with.

Address: 21 Unionville Ave, Sussex, NJ 07461
Webpage: http:// www. sussexpresbyterian.org
Email: sussexpresbyterian @embarqmail.com
Telephone: 973-875-4760
Hours: Sunday services 9:30 AM
Directions: I-84 take exit 1 onto Rt 23 south to Sussex. In town turn left onto Newton Ave. Slight ride onto Unionville Ave. (go uphill), church is on your left.

West Milford, Passaic County, NJ

Journey Church of the Highlands
S2, V0 ♀|♂ 🧘

The center of a FOC (S2) is located in the center of the sanctuary. The vibe is neutral.

Address: 184 Marshall Rd., West Milford, NJ 07480
Webpage: www. awakenj. com
Telephone: 973-728-3479
Hours: Sunday services 10 AM to noon.
Directions: From West Milford town center take Marshall Hill Rd; the road will turn sharply left out of town. The church will be on your right.

Part III
Conclusion and Appendix

Conclusion--Transformation not Revolution

The cries of revolution have always echoed throughout history, but today they seem to have a greater urgency. But what is revolution and does it really bring about something new, or is it just a costume change of the consciousness that already exists in a place and within its people? In other words, is a revolution in a country like a person that dons a new outfit, only the country instead of changing outfits, changes leaders who have the same perspective on how to rule the country and how it treats its people.

Having a dictator forgo his military outfit for a business suit, or casual attire is not going to change how they rule or govern. Changing clothes is a phenomenon of the Physical Plane. It is a material change; it may become more, but at its core it is a material change. It is the same with a Revolution.

Real change requires a transformation of the soul; it is a consciousness raising experience that alters your very being. It is a spiritual experience where your soul evolves.

The Game Never Changes, Only the Players

When the Arab Spring burst forth in February of 2010 in Tunisia, it stirred the passions and hopes of many in the Arab world. The fires of change burned in several countries as dictators toppled. But the quality of life, the rights and freedoms for the vast majority has not improved, and has arguably deteriorated in many countries.

Consider Egypt. Protests erupted in January of 2011. A month later President Mubarak resigned. In May/June 2012 Mohamad Morisi became the first freely elected President in Egypt. But the freely and democratically elected Morisi chose not to bring about reforms to empower the Egyptian people and foster democracy; instead he cast an even stronger net over the Egyptian people and issued a temporary constitutional declaration that gave him unlimited power, and the power to legislate without judicial oversight. A few months later protests erupted. In July of 2013 Morisi was deposed by a military coup.

There were several leadership changes in Egypt, what I would call costume changes, but the underlying consciousness of those in power and how the people were treated did not change and arguably deteriorated. It could be argued that more time is needed, but when we examine other supposed revolutions and great political changes the underlying results are the same.

Many hold the Russian Revolution as an example of the possibility for change. Did anything change for the proletariat after they seized control from the Czar in 1917? No. While initially there were some gains and new freedoms for the people, it was not long before Russia was governed by what George Kennan called, a "dictatorship of the communist party."[1] When Stalin took over millions were killed, or sent off to gulags. Hope for reform appeared again when the Berlin wall came in 1989. Then ex-KGB officer Vladimir Putin was elected in 2000 and has served since, either directly or through surrogates, all the while stifling dissent and exerting his will over the Russian people.

Even the American Revolution inspired by the Great Law of Peace and the consciousness of North Star Country fell short. Yes, it certainly brought freedom to many, but it allowed slavery, and women were treated as second-class citizens. Capitalism weighed heavy on it and continues to grow and wrangle the people. Perhaps its biggest mistake was that it did not embrace a spiritual perspective.

Where we do see a dramatic transformation is with the Haudenosaunee. The Peacemaker ended the blood feuding and cannibalism. He created a matrilineal community where women were empowered. It was democratic, and while chiefs held power, they were the servants of the people. The Great Law was a spiritual document.

Transformation

Real radical wholesale change requires a change of heart, a transformation. It is a spiritual event that radically transforms, as what once was is no longer; it is a new birth. It is when hate becomes love, when anger becomes compassion, when violence becomes self-sacrifice, when selfishness becomes altruism. Mincing words with some vow of faith, or pledging to change conditions and offering hope are but words.

It is as Jesus said that we must be reborn. Accepting some principals, citing some words, following some practices are but a cosmetic costume change. Transformation means the spiritual death of your consciousness and a birth of the new. A dramatically new being. It is soul transforming.

The conversion of the evil Adodarhoh to the Tadodaho is such a change, when someone very despicable and truly evil becomes someone loving, caring and spiritually guided. That is transformation. And transformation, whether it be an individual, or a country, or society is a challenging near impossible feat.

Yet it once happened in North Star Country.

Lessons from North Star Country

There are many lessons to be learned about transformation and bringing about collective change from North Star Country.

Spirituality played a major role. Many movements and causes were intertwined with spirituality—you cannot separate the two. Change requires a spiritual change and the embracing of it. It requires a change of heart. Not surprisingly when we look at revolution you see the influence of intellectuals, the intelligentsia, the professorial class all focused on the mind and strategy; compared to transformation, that is a spiritual change of heart.

Spirituality does not necessarily mean embracing a traditional view of God. Although I accepted God's call in 1999 and left Wall Street, this is not the case with all spiritual people. Spirituality is about recognizing that there is something greater beyond ourselves, whether it is God or not; and that we are our brothers and sisters keeper, and intimately interconnected to all of creation, including Mother Earth. We are called to adhere to the golden rule, to do unto others as you wish others to do unto you, which is at the core of every faith tradition.

Many of the movements born in North Star Country had a mystical element, or focus to them. By focusing on the material world we give strength to it and bind ourselves to it. By understanding and focusing on the mystical world we give strength to it, and in the process begin to break the bonds that tether us to materialism and physical reality. Ultimately we are spiritual beings.

All of the great souls of North Star Country that helped transform the world lived on or close to, or in some other way were connected to FOC and their network of Spirit Lines. By living in North Star Country they were also influenced by the archetypes buried in the land. Ultimately it was the power of the land, the FOC and the archetypes that brought about change. We need to reinvigorate FOC and their network of Spirit Lines.

The logistics of Change

Those of us that advocate for wholesale and radical change are not used to thinking in terms of logistics; the support, nourishment and supplies critical for success. It is the military that embraces logistics. Wars have been won and lost over the ability to feed and provide munitions to troops. A common phrase by many is that "logistics win wars." Lt General Franks who helped lead the ground war during Desert Storm said "forget logistics, you lose."[2]

The logistics of transformation is that our souls need to be nourished with divine consciousness. FOC and Spirit Lines were meant to intoxicate the world with Christ Consciousness. To make every nook and cranny of the world awash in divine consciousness and the intention of giving, compassion, altruism, self-sacrifice....FOC and Spirit Lines are the equivalent of the military's supply lines.

What would the world look like if it were as God and Mother Earth intended and divine consciousness blanketed the world? Would peace reign?

As noted earlier, consciousness interacts with the consciousness it comes in contact with. It looks to balance out differences and find equilibrium, as it did with our example of hot air once released into the cold air by a duct. The degree of equilibrium achieved is not always so dramatic or complete—but there is an influence upon each to some degree.

So it is with the consciousness carried and emitted by Spirit Lines. It interacts with everything and everyone it comes in contact with; this is one of the laws of the universe.

Unfortunately the world is spiritually malnourished. It is not so much that we lack nutrition, but that we are enshrouded in negativity. The world is caked over with negative consciousness. It surrounds all of us 24/7, and is constantly interacting with us and dragging us down. It is as if we are running on a treadmill in a room filled with cigarette smoke and toxins; no matter how much we run our health does not improve, but deteriorates. Or its as if we get dressed up in a white suit and walk outside and roll in the mud; because the consciousness lingering around us is the mud— the negativity, the violence, and selfishness that shroud our being.

We need to return FOC and Spirit Lines to their intended pristine state so that the world will be again enveloped with divine, Christ Consciousness. This will help raise our collective consciousness and make for a better world.

Some may think it ridiculous that such a plan can help transform the world. The idea that our environment can raise our consciousness because we will be interacting with it, the same as drinking milk can help us build muscles may seem far fetched. But that is the premise of this book, and I have offered countless examples of people, places and movements that were transformed by North Star Country.

Faith will Deliver US

We are so used to thinking about strategies and plans, but it will be our faith and beliefs that will help herald changes.

As Jung taught us, the archetypes that help define who we are lie buried deep in the bowels of the earth. They are there beckoning us, driving us and manipulating us. North Star Country welled up great prophets and souls who radically altered their worlds to embody the prophetic spirit of love, selflessness and giving. I am sure that other great souls and prophets traversed North Star country long before the Haudenosaunee's Peacemaker did. Their imprints, their thoughts still linger in North Star Country.

When people come in contact with those archetypes and imprints they will be inspired. The consciousness emanating from FOC will contribute to their inspiration.

It is the land that will inspire folks with ways to make a better world. It is the land that will help foster the spirit of change and transformation.

We need to abandon control, and focus on creating a positive and loving environment. We can do this by fortifying FOC and their network of Spirit Lines, and have faith that we will be delivered.

North Star as America's and World's Regional Hub

America is a story of migration and population shifts; much of the movement was west. It started with the movement from the east coast to the Appalachia and North Star Country. Then it went to the Midwest and America's heartland. From there, to the prairies and farther west and to California and then to the Pacific Northwest.

Every shift was to a region of the country with its own identity, its own archetypes buried in the land, and often particular aspects of Mother Earth that distinguished it and made it unique. Like North Star Country and the Southern Regionalism that Phillips talked about, all had distinct influences upon people.

With each migration, a new region would become the hot area that would set the tone for the rest of America. In other words, not only did the region influence its inhabitants, but the rest of the country as well.

The dramatic social changes of the Antebellum period were greatly influenced by North Star Country that was America's hub in the early to mid nineteenth century. American values took hold when the Midwest became the hub. In the twentieth century California and its surroundings came to dominant American trends and tastes.

The idea that California and its Hollywood has been a trendsetter in clothing, lifestyles and trends in general is well recognized. National Journal reporter Neil R. Peirce in 1990 with a bit of conservative sarcasm says such in a LA Times editorial:

"For decades, people have been saying California's today is every other state's tomorrow. History says they're right--from suburban sprawl to anti-growth hysteria, Disneyland to fervid environmentalism, '60s student radicalism to drive-by shootings."[3]

Beginning in the latter part of the twentieth century there were two main migrations, to the South and the Pacific Northwest. I have already discussed the regional influences of the South— conservatism, NASCAR and country music. The Pacific Northwest gave us grunge/indie music, progressivism/ environmentalism.

North Star Country needs to reclaim the mantle as setting the focus and tone of America and the world. When North Star

Country was the hub, social justice, equality, spirituality and the mystical reined. North Star Country must again be the center of America's and the world's consciousness.

A New Age Movement

Historians grapple with larger social and cultural changes. Sometimes they can clearly see a precipitating event, such as an election, a tragedy, or economic hardship that led to a historical, or revolutionary change. Other times, change is gradually precipitated by events in the distant past, so minute, or disparate, that they seem to lack a coherent link.

The world changed when early Americans experienced the consciousness permeating North Star Country from archetypes to FOC. The land spoke to and influenced the Founders. It still does.

The seeds planted[4] in North Star Country in the nineteenth century continue to grow. It was not until the 1960's and 1970's that one of those seeds was recognized and named, 'The New Age Movement.'

It is so North Star Country: embracing social and spiritual experimentation, counterculture, emphasis on the esoteric and mystical, and spiritual practices such meditation. Yet it was conflicted; between the abolitionists and the proslavery advocates, Women's Rights and traditionalists. Similarly the New Age is conflicted, between the greed of capitalism and service to others, and between ego/power and community. But in North Star Country the greater good finally rose to occasion.

A new birth is upon us, we just don't see it yet. How it looks and what it is, we do not know, because it is still being forged as we are being transformed.

Come Visit

Please come visit and pray, or meditate at one of the sacred sites mentioned in this book. Perform a ceremony, or conduct a ritual. This will help clean and fortify the FOC. A fortified FOC is more potent and will emanate a more transforming dose of consciousness. Mother Earth needs us to achieve Her fullest potential, and we need Her to achieve ours.

I also ask that you please become an Earth Healer and begin cleansing, fortifying and charging Spirit Lines near your home and even on your travels. The appendix provides a simple technique for cleansing and fortifying Spirit Lines.

The process of cleansing Spirit Lines needs to be an ongoing process because what you cleanse will soon come in contact with negative consciousness. Your efforts will appear to evaporate and you may feel like Sisyphus pushing a large boulder up a hill only to have it come down again. But your efforts will bring small incremental changes and raise the vibe ever so slightly. The hill of consciousness you are pushing the boulder up will become ever so much smaller. Over time, the infinitesimal becomes large.

Fortifying FOC and cleansing Spirit Lines will not necessarily bring about a respect for all of creation, or herald a new democracy. What it will do is create an environment that can facilitate a new birth that will transform our collective soul. It will provide enough spiritual protein to help build strong souls.

The birth that will transform our collective soul will come from North Star Country. It has done so before in so many ways and will do so again. It will speak to someone, or to many, as it has done so many times before.

A new birth, a better and more just world for all of creation lies sleeping in North Star Country. Come and pray, meditate, or just dream and awaken it.

References and Recommended Reading

1. Kennan, George F. "The Russian Revolution Fifty Years Later" Foreign Affairs, October 1967, https://www.foreignaffairs.com/articles/russian-federation/1967-10-01/russian-revolution-fifty-years-after

2. Passion for Logistics, http://www.passionforlogistics.com/logistics-quotes/

3. Peirce, Neal; "California's Tarnished Reputation as a National Trend-Setter : Governance: Prop. 111 will double the gas tax? Big deal. The tax is now 47th-lowest in the U.S.; California ranks dead last in transportation spending." LA Times, May 20, 1990.

4. Seeds such as Theosophy with its emphasis on the occult, esoteric and equality, the introduction of Eastern traditions, the communication with other realms (Spiritualism), spiritual practices such as meditation introduced by Swami Vivekananda, the birth of the new (religions, sects) and a counterculture, or counter the status quo mood. (And of course social justice and democracy.)

Keeping Abreast, Updates

The following resources are available to learn about Mother Earth, Her FOC and keep abreast of goings on in North Star Country.

http: //motherearthprayers.blogspot.com—My blog is updated regularly with upcoming events, news about North Star County and Mother Earth. This is the place to go if you want to see if an event, or gathering is planned for in the future.

http:// clarksgullyblogspot.com—My blog about surveys done and activities in High Tor NYS DEC forest: Clarks Gully, South Hill, Parish Hill, Brink Hill…

www. motherearthprayers.org-- webpage on Mother Earth.

www. motherearthpress.net—Information on Mother Earth Press and my ongoing efforts.

YouTube Videos: MotherEarthPrayers

How you Can Help

The best thing you can do is to visit and meditate/pray/do ceremony on a FOC at a sacred site in North Star Country. You can also help by cleaning and charging Spirit Lines near your home. Here are some other things that you can do.

Attend an Earth Healers Gathering—Events are held throughout the year for group meditations, or to work on clearing a sacred site. Information will be listed on my blog (http://motherearthprayers.blogspot.com) about upcoming activities.

Become an Earth Healer--Please consider becoming an Earth Healer and begin by working to clean spaces and Spirit Lines near your home.

Become a Keeper—Take your Earth Healing to another level and become a Keeper for a sacred site, or place you wish to make sacred. A Keeper is part of an ancient tradition of watching over and taking care of a particular sacred site. Which means maintaining its spiritual integrity, and physical appearance, if applicable. It could also involve guiding visiting pilgrims and educational work.

Help Raise Awareness About North Star Country— While visiting North Star Country tell everyone you encounter why you are visiting. When you call a tourist bureau and ask for maps tell them that you are coming to visit sacred sites. The more people in the region that hear about it the more support it will garner towards our effort. Please also tell your friends and others in your hometown, some may wish to visit.

Donate—Please consider donating to our effort to improve sacred spaces and hopefully longer term acquire a sacred site. Thanks to a generous donation we were able to buy a bench for the Peacemaker's Sanctuary at Onondaga Lake. We would like to buy more benches for the Peacemaker's Sanctuary, and help some of the sacred sites listed; buy benches/donation boxes, etc.

Your money is tax deductible and will go to Jubilee Initiative a 501c-3, EIN 16-1609072.

You can donate online at either my blog, http://motherearthprayers.blogspot.com, or at my website, www.motherearthprayers.org.

Help on a Campaign—Here are some initiatives your help with would be appreciated:

Preserving the stone structures and Vibe at High Tor. We would like NYS to increase the protection and preservation of the stone structures, as well as the vibe and sacred space, at High Tor NYS DEC State Forest. What do I mean by protecting the vibe?

Reenactments of historical events are an accepted practice at historical places. We are asking for a reenactment of the intention that visiting pilgrims once brought to High Tor that made it so special. To retain and reinvigorate the vibe at High Tor we ask that effort be made to have visitors approach it in a 'sacred manner.' To be respectful, and honor it in the way that it deserves. Eliminate activities that diminish, or violate the sacred intent pilgrims once came with; no hunting, fishing, archaeological digs, etc.

We ask it be designated a protected area and special protection given to the stone structures. We understand you cannot be the thought police, but you can certainly educate and provide information on the intent visiting pilgrims once came with.

Please contact, call or write, officials about this:

Region 8 Director Paul D'Amato

NYS DEC Region 8 Director

6274 East Avon-Lima Rd. (Rtes. 5 and 20)

Avon, NY 14414-9516

585-226-2466

DEC Commissioner Basil Seggos

625 Broadway

Albany, NY 12233-1011

518-402-8545

To email the Commissioner go to: http:// www. dec. ny. gov/about/407.html

We plan on other initiatives such as a petition in the future. Updates will be posted on http:// clarksbullyblogspot.com, or http: //motherearthprayers.blogspot.com.

Cleaning Onondaga Lake: Go to the Onondaga Nation website (http:// www. onondaganation.org/land-rights/onondaga-lake /onondaga-lake-as-a-superfund-site/) and the NOON (Neighbors of the Onondaga Nation (http:// www. peacecouncil.net/ programs/neighbors-of-the-onondaga-nation/environmental- issues) for current actions. You can also sign a petition at: https:// www.change. org/p/andrew-cuomo-remove-the-toxic- black-goo-onondaga-lake-needs-a-better-future

Volunteer—Please consider volunteering at one of the not for profits listed as a sacred site

Bear Witness in the Spirit of North Star Country—Please join the FOR (http:// forusa. Org), get on their listserve and consider participating in an action.

Join Junsan http: //www. graftonpeacepagoda. org, 518-658-9301.

Earth Healing—Working with Spirit Lines

We need to return Mother Earth's network (FOC and Spirit Lines) for connecting us and blanketing with the world Christ Consciousness to its intended pristine state. Praying/meditating/doing ceremony at FOC will strengthen them. We also need to clean and charge our Mother's Spirit Lines.

As carriers of consciousness they are sensitive to and react with the consciousness that they come in contact with. They also magnify (carry) the consciousness that they come in contact with. So when you clear a Spirit Lines, or charge it with love, those intentions will be several fold greater than if you did the same in a normal space. Location, Location, Location—MATTERS.

You need to learn the basic geomancy technique of finding a Spirit Line. This means using a pair L-rods, or dowsing rods, to guide you. This takes some time and practice and most people are able to learn this fairly quickly.

Attending a local ASD (American Chapter of Dowsers) chapter meeting, or joining a local geomancy or dowsing group near your hometown. There are dowsing organizations around the world, in Britain, Canada…. Having experienced dowsers teach you will propel your progress. Our local Finger Lakes Chapter has a practice session before meetings to teach the basics. Go to the ASD website to find a chapter near you: http://dowsers.org.

Cleaning a Spirit Line—To clean a Spirit Lines you need to change and elevate the consciousness it carries. You do this by praying, meditating or performing a ceremony on it.

Step 1. Find a Spirit Line, or the intersection of several Spirit Lines. An intersection of several Spirit Lines provides the opportunity to clean several Spirit Lines simultaneously.

Step 2. Pray/meditate/ceremony on the Spirit Line. Spend some time doing this.

Step 3. Reinvigorate. Keep coming back and praying/meditating/ performing ceremony there.

Group Meditation on a Spirit Line—Meditating with a group of people on a Spirit Line is a powerful experience, as the Spirit Line acts as a conduit connecting the consciousness of the participants, thereby magnifying the intention and results. It can seriously step up your meditation by several levels.

A group meditation on a Spirit Line can dramatically raises its vibe and that of the immediate space around it. Negativity is burned off and the Spirit Line becomes charged. I say charged because afterwards when you are in the Spirit Line you say "Whoa." You may even think you are meditating in a FOC.

A group meditation is a great way to charge a Spirit Line.

Prayer Seat in a nest of Charged Spirit Lines at Italy Hill. The prayer seat is the flat rock in the middle on the right, the stone behind it is its back. My measuring staff and branches show a few of the Spirit Lines. Notice the stones (a few are visible) marking some of the Spirit Lines—appearing like spokes on a wheel. The vibe was very positive—incredible given that this area is hunted and there was a hunter's stand less than a 100' away (a negative influence.) Italy Hill was not included because it does not have FOC. I am always inspired and moved when I find such stonework.

Charging a Spirit Line—Tradition would be to mark a Spirit Line with stones and meditate on the stones and other locations on the Spirit Line. You effectively charge a Spirit Line whenever you meditate/pray/do ceremony on it.

If you want to follow tradition you can use very small stones, even pebbles, to mark a Spirit Line. The size of the stone is not going to impede a charge. I have prayer stones that are a ½" in diameter and have a vortex attached to them that is 3' in diameter.

Cleaning a larger area of a Spirit Line. You can clean a larger area of a Spirit Line by clearing two points on it. Clean one spot on a Spirit Line and then go and clear another spot not more than a few hundred feet away. If you want clean a larger segment start small and extend the distance from your original point over time. Remember to reinvigorate by coming back to the locations.

Cleaning an Area. You can also use Spirit Lines to clean a space. The key is to: Work from the Outside In. Just as we are supposed to look within for spiritual guidance, so it is with cleaning space. You can use this technique to clean, or enhance a place of worship, your home, a part of a forest, or anyplace else.

I use this technique to clean particular places at a sacred site; a bench, a stone circle or something similar within it. Unfortunately, many people leave their negative imprints at altars, or special places. It is amazing to see how often the vibe is negative at an altar compared to five feet away in a traditional place of worship. If you become a Keeper you have to regularly clean the holy places within it.

Start small. If you have a larger space you wish to clear, begin with a smaller center section and gradually extend out over time.

You will be basically looking to envelope a space in positive consciousness.

Step 1. Pick your location.

Step 2. Find all the Spirit Lines closest to the location.

Step 3. Clean all the Spirit Lines around the periphery of the property. Always work clockwise. Preferably there is not much space between Spirit Lines. If there are no Spirit Lines close by, or there is a large space between them, meditate between them. Try not to go more than 20-30 feet between cleaning areas.

Step 4. Reinvigorate. Do this regularly over time.

Step 5. If you want to clear a larger space, expand your circle and keep adding more circles until you are complete.

This is an incredibly powerful technique I have used many times effectively.

Sacred Site Recommendations

The following are some suggestions for visiting sites for a specific purpose or for tours:

Places to sense and feel Consciousness

Gobind Sadan, The Peacemaker's Sanctuary, Gossamer Wood, Muller Hill, Kateri Shrine, The vortex at Swami Vivekananda's Cottage, FLT Trail on Brink Hill (High Tor.) Places at the periphery: Vedanta Society of Toronto, FOR, Zoar Valley, Arnold Park, Saratoga Park Buffalo, Hogle Wildlife Sanctuary Trail.

Contemplative Walks

Gossamer Wood, The Link Trail at Muller Hill, The Lakeland Trail Loop at Onondaga Lake, Seneca Lake Trail, Hipp Brook.

Great Vibe

Any place with a vortex. Wisdom's Golden Rod, Pumpkin Hollow, Muller Hill, The Peacemaker's Sanctuary, High Tor in places, UU of Rochester's garden, Arnold Park, The Foundation of Light, Hipp Brook.

Underground Railroad

Michigan Avenue Baptist Church in Buffalo is without doubt has the best vibe and power of place than any other UGRR site listed in this book.

Mystical places

High Tor, Zoar Valley, Muller Hill, Gelston Castle, The Peacemaker's Sanctuary at Onondaga Lake

Where to Cry for a Vision, or places of Epiphany

High Tor, Muller Hill, The Peacemaker's Sanctuary .

Helpful Contact Information

Tourist Bureaus

Many tourist bureaus will send you promotional literature for free.

New York

I Love NY, http:// www. iloveny, 800-CALL-NYS, info@ iloveny.com

Visit NY, http:// www. visitnewyorkstate. Net

NYS Empire Pass http:// nysparks. com/admission/empire-passport/default.aspx, Buy yearlong access to all NYS Parks. $65.

Free Thought Trail, a listing of locations important to Free Thought in Upstate NY, http:// www. freethought-trail. org

Hudson Valley

Discover Hudson Valley, http:// www .travelhudsonvalley. com, 845-615-3860 or 800-232-478, Can also sign up to receive tourist information on individual counties.

Historic Hudson Valley. http: //www. hudsonvalley. org

Columbia County Tourism, www. columbiacountytourism. org, 518-828-3375, 800-724-1846info.cctourism @gmail. com

Dutchess County Tourism, www. dutchesstourism. com, 845-463-4000, 800- 445-3131,info@ DutchessTourism. com

Rockland County Tourism, www. rockland. org, 845- 708-7300, 800-295-5723, info@ rocktourism. com

Catskills

Discover the Catskills, http:/ /www. visitthecatskills. Com

Catskills Destinations, http:// www.t hecatskillregion. com/destinations-tourism.aspx

Delaware County Tourism, http:// www. greatwesterncatskills. com, 607 746 2281

Orange County Tourism, http: //orangetourism. org, 845-615-3860

Ulster County Tourism, http:// www. ulstercountyalive. com, 800-342-5826

Albany Capital District

Capital-Saratoga Region Tourism, www. nys captal district tourism. com, info @capital-saratoga. com

Albany County Tourism, www. albany .org, 800-258-3582, 518-434-1217

Albany (City) Tourism, http: //www. albany.org/things-to-do/ .org

Rensselaer County Tourism, www. renscotourism. com, 518-270-2900

Saratoga County Tourism, www. saratoga. org, 800-526-8970, 518-584-3255

Schoharie County Tourism, http:// visitschohariecounty. com, : 800-41-VISIT, 518-296-8991

Adirondacks

Visit Adirondacks, http:// visitadirondacks. com

Hamilton County Tourism, http:// www. adirondackexperience. com, 800-648-5239, 518-548-3076, info@ adirondackexperience. com

Lake Placid/Essex County Tourism, http:// www. lakeplacid. com, 518-523-2445

Tupper Lake/Franklin County Tourism, http:// www. tupperlake. com/region, 518-359-3328, contact@ tuuperlake. com

Mohawk Valley

Mohawk Valley History, http:// www. mohawkvalleyhistory. com

Fulton County Tourism, www. 44lakes. com 800-676-3858, 518-725-0641

Herkimer County (Visit), http:// www. visitherkimercounty. com

Montgomery County Tourism, www. visitmontgomerycounty ny. com, 800-743-7337, 518-725-0641

Oneida County Tourism, www. oneidacountytourism. com, 888-999-6560

Utica, Visit the City, www. cityofutica. com/visiting/index

Central New York

Central New York Tourism, http:// www. visitcentralnewyork. com

Cayuga County Tourism, http:// tourcayuga. com, 800-499-9615, 315-255-1658

Madison County Tourism, http:// www. madisontourism. com, 800-684-7320, 315-684-7320

Oneida County Tourism, www. oneidacountytourism. com, 888-999-6560

Onondaga County/Syracuse Tourism, http:// www. visit syracuse. com, 800-234-4797, info@ visitsyracuse. com

North Country

Lewis County Tourism, http:// newyorkvisitorsnetwork. com/lewis/

Jefferson County Tourism, http:// www. co.jefferson. ny. us/index.aspx?page=7

Oneida County Tourism, www. oneidacountytourism. com, 888-999-6560

Oswego County Tourism, http: //visitoswegocounty. com, 315-349-8322, 800-248-4FUN(4386)

Tug Hill (Adirondacks), http:// visitadirondacks. com/regions/adirondacks-tughill

Thousand Islands

1,000 Islands (CAN & USA), http://www.visit1000islands.com 800-847-5264

Ontario Travel, www. ontariotravel. net/, 800-668-2746

Gananoque & The Thousand Islands Visitor Centre, www. travel1000islands.ca, 844-382-8044, 613-382-8044

Jefferson County Tourism, http:// www. co.jefferson. ny. us/index.aspx?page=7

Kingston Tourism, http: //start-up.kingstoncanada. com/en/index.asp, 866-665-3326, 613-544-2725, tourism @kingstoncanada. com

Lyn, See Brokville Tourism, http:// brockvilletourism. com, 888-251-7676, 613-342-4357, tourism @brockvillechamber .com

Southern Tier

Binghamton Tourism, http:// www. visitbinghamton. org, 800-836-6740

Finger Lakes

Finger Lakes Tourism Alliance, http:// www. fingerlakes. org, 800-530-7488, 315–536-7488

Finger Lakes Tourism, http:// fingerlakestravelny. com, 888-408-1693

Cayuga County Tourism, http:// tourcayuga. com, 800-499-9615, 315-255-1658

Ithaca & Tompkins County Tourism, http: //www. visitithaca. com, 800-28-ITHACA, 607-272-1313

Ontario County Tourism, http:// www. visitfingerlakes. com, 877-386-4669, 585-394-3915

Seneca County Tourism, http:// fingerlakesgateway. com, 00-732-1848

Watkins Glen & Schuyler County Tourism, https:// www. watkinsglenchamber. com, 800-607-4552, 607-535-4300

Bare Hill and High Tor

Ontario County Tourism, http:// www. visitfingerlakes. com, 877-386-4669, 585-394-3915

Yates County Tourism, http: //yatesny. com/

Metro Rochester

Ontario County Tourism, http:// www. visitfingerlakes. com, 877-386-4669, 585-394-3915

Monroe County/ Rochester Tourism, www. visitrochester. com/, 800-677-7282, info@visitrochester.com

Western NY

Chautauqua County Tourism, http: //www. tourchautauqua. com/Default.aspx, 866-908-4569

Genesee County Tourism, http: //visitgeneseeny .com, 800-622-2686, 585-343-7440.

Livingston County Tourism, www. fingerlakeswest. com, 800-538-7365, 585-243-2222

Buffalo Niagara Falls (Visit), www. visitbuffaloniagara. com, 800-283-3256

Wyoming County Tourism, www. gowyomingcountyny. com/, 800.839.3919, 585-786-0307

Chautauqua Institute, http: //www. ciweb. org, .800-836-ARTS

Lily Dale, http: //www. lilydaleassembly. com, 716-595-8721

Ontario's Golden Horseshoe

Niagara Canada Tourism, https:// www. visitniagaracanada. com/, 289-477-5344

Ontario Travel, www. ontariotravel. net/, 800-668-2746

Hamilton Tourism, http:// tourismhamilton. com, 800-263-8590, 905-546-2666

St. Catharine's Tourism, http:// www. tourismstcatharines. ca, 905-688-5601 ext 1731, 905-688-4TTY (4889)

Toronto Tourism, http: // www. seetorontonow. com, 800-499-2514, 416-203-2500, toronto@torcvb.com

Pennsylvania

Pennsylvania Tourism, http://www.visitpa.com, 800-847-4872

Allegheny County Tourism, http: //www. visitpittsburgh. com ,412 281-7711, info@visitpittsburgh.com

Erie County Tourism, http:// www.visiteriepa. com 814-454-1000

Lackawanna County Tourism, www. visitwaynecounty. com/, 800-22-WELCOME

Susquehanna County Tourism, http:// susqco. com/tourism/ Wayne County Tourism, www. visitwaynecounty. com/

New England

New England (Visit), http: //www. visitnewengland. com/all/http://, www. discovernewengland. org (International)

Connecticut Tourism, www. ctvisit. com, 888-288-4748

Fairfield County Tourism, http:// visitfairfieldcountyct. com

Litchfield County Tourism, http:// www. litchfieldcty. com

Massachusetts' Tourism, http: //www. massvacation. com, 800-227-MASS, 617-973-8500

Berkshires Tourism, http:// berkshires. org,

Vermont Tourism, https: //www. vermontvacation. com, 800-837-6668

Bennington Tourism, http: //www. bennington. com, 802-447-3311

Brattleboro Activities, http:// www. brattleboro. com

Ohio

Ohio Tourism, www .ohio. org/, 800-BUCKEYE

Lake Erie Tourism, http:// www. shoresandislands. com, 800-255-3743, 419-625-2984, info @shoresandislands. com

Ashtabula County Tourism, http:// www. visitashtabulacounty. com, 800-337-6746

Conneaut Tourism, http:// www. visitconneautohio. com/about_us.htm

Geneva Tourism, http: //genevaohio. com/tourism/

New Jersey

New Jersey Tourism, http:// www. visitnj. org, 800-VISITNJ

Passaic County Tourism, http: //www. discoverpassaiccounty. org, 973-881-4550

Sussex County Tourism, http: //www. sussex. nj. us/Cit-e-Access/webpage.cfm?TID=7&TPID=891

Underground Railroad

Partial Listing of Sites Nationally, https: //www. nps. gov/nr/travel/underground/states.htm

CAN, Niagara Falls Freedom Trail, https: //www. niagarafallstourism. com/blog/niagara-freedom-trail/

CAN, UGRR Sites in SW Ontario, http: //caen-keepexploring. canada.travel/things-to-do/exp/canadas-underground-railroad#/?galleryItemId=200010578

CT, Connecticut Freedom Trail, http: //www.ctfreedomtrail .org/trail/underground-railroad/

MA, Traveling the UGGR in MA, http:// historyofmassachusetts. org/traveling-the-underground-railroad-in-massachusetts/

MA, Western MA Sites, http: //www. bywayswestmass. com/map-markers/national-underground-railroad-sites/

MA, Boston Walking Tour, http: //maah. org/trail.htm

NY, State Map with Listings, http:// www. jimapco. com/eriecanalway/ugrr/

NY, Abolition Hall of Fame, http:// www. nationalabolitionhalloffameandmuseum. org/

NY, Cayuga Cty. & Auburn Freedom Trail, http:// www. auburncayugafreedomtrail. com

NY, Finger Lakes UGRR Sites, http:// www. ilovethefingerlakes. com/history/undergroundrailroad.htm

NY, Madison County's Freedom Trail, http:// www. madisontourism. com/trail_freedom.pdf

NY, Niagara Area Driving Tour, http: //www. greaterniagara. com/driving_tours/underground_railroad_tour.html

NY, Niagara Falls Heritage Area, http: //discoverniagara. org/heritage/underground-railroad/#.WBJ00FdsDww

NY, North Star UGRR Museum, http:// northcountryundergroundrailroad. com/museum.php

NY, NYC Walks of UGRR Sites, https: //www. walksofnewyork. com/blog/underground-railroad-new-york-city

NY, Oneida County's Freedom Trail, http: //www. oneidacountyfreedomtrail. com

NY, Oswego County, http:// visitoswegocounty. com/historical-info/underground-railroad/

NY, Oswego Town of Driving Tour, http: //www.townofoswego. com/pdfs/ugrr.pdf

NY, Seneca County Sites, http:// www. co.seneca. ny. us/wp-content/uploads/2015/02/Uncovering-UGRR-in-Finger-Lakes.pdf

NY, Syracuse's Freedom Trail. http ://pacny. net/freedom_trail/

NY, Utica Walking Tour UGRR, https: //www. utica. edu/academic/institutes/ucsc/doc/Utica%20Walking%20Tour% 202%20Oct%202013.pdf

NJ, NJ's UGRR Heritage, https: //dspace. njstatelib.org/xmlui/bitstream/handle/10929/24563/h6732002.p df?sequence=1

OH, Clermont County Tour, http: //newrichmondugrrtour. weebly. com

OH, Cleveland Listing of UGRR sites, http: //clevelandhistorical. org/tours/show/44#.WBJM2FdsDww

OH, Hubbard UGRR Museum, http:// www. hubbardhouseugrrmuseum. org

OH, National UGGR Freedom Center, http: //www. freedomcenter. org

PA, Blairsville UGRR History Center, http: //www. undergroundrailroadblairsvillepa. com/UGRRCenter.php

PA, Pittsburgh's UGRR, http: //www.v isitpittsburgh. com/about-pittsburgh/underground-railroad/

PA, Traveling PA's UGRR, http ://www. visitpa. com/articles/destination-freedom-traveling-pas-underground- railroad

PA, Traveling the UGGR in PA, http: //www. whereandwhen. com/Articles/Journey+To+Freedom,+The+Underground+Railr oad+In+Pennsylvania/

PA, Lancaster County UGRR, http:// www. susquehannaheritage. org/portals/0/documents/ugrr.pdf

Women's Rights

Where Women Made History, a listing of sites, https: //www. nps. gov/nr/travel/pwwmh/womlist1 .htm

National Women's Hall of Fame, https: //www. womenofthehall. org

464

Women's Rights national Historical Park, https: //www. nps. gov/wori/index.htm

NY Women's Heritage Trail, https: //www. google. com/maps/d/viewer?hl=en&msa=0&z=7&ie=UTF8&mid=1PeJ mtV3tZkZyiM4pN-V6FEcNsE8

Outdoors, Hiking, Parks

CAN Fronteac Biosphere Thousand Islands Trails, http: //www. frontenacarchbiosphere. ca

CAN, Parks Canada, http://www.pc.gc.ca/eng/index.aspx

MA, Hiking MA, http: //www. massvacation. com/explore/outdoors/hiking/

MA, Berkshire Hiking, http:// berkshirehiking .com

NY, ADK (Adirondack Mountain Club), https: //www. adk. org

NY, Finger Lakes Trail System, http:// www. fltconference. org/ trail/

NY, CNY Hiking—Listing of hikes in Upstate NY, http:// www. cnyhiking. com

NY, Catskills Hiking, http: //www .dec. ny. gov/outdoor/77168.html

NY, Western NY Waterfalls, http: //falzguy. com

PA, PA Hikes, http:// www. pahikes. com

PA, Dept of Conservation, http: //www. dcnr.state. pa. us/stateparks/recreation/hiking/

VT, VT State Parks, http: //www. vtstateparks. com/htm/hiking.htm

Hunting Seasons

Be aware these pages may change annually.

NY, http:// www. dec. ny. gov/outdoor/10002.html

PA, http: //www . pic .pa. gov/HuntTrap/Law/Pages/SeasonsandBagLimits.aspx

VT, http:// www. vtfishandwildlife. com/hunt/seasons

Prayers

The following are some prayers, meditations and ceremonies you may to use when visiting sacred sites.

A prayer for the love of Mother Earth

Dear Mother,

You are so ravaged and damaged from the actions of my sisters and brothers, yet you still love them, still nourish them.

They pollute your air with smoke and toxins, and fill it with technological devices that emit damaging rays that harm you and prevent you from healing yourself; still you give.

My sisters and brothers cannot get along; they fight and hurt each other. They stalk and experiment with the little ones and in the process cover your body with sores; still you give.

Teach me that love dear Mother Earth so that I may love you and those that foul you.

Well up compassion in me like a holy spring so that my sisters and brothers may drink from me and be healed, and in the process rejuvenate you, my dear Mother.

Nourish me dear Mother so that I may have your love and forgiveness for all of creation.
Help me dear Mother grow closer to you, to feel and sense you.

Help me grow closer to you dear Mother, so that I may grow from your bounty.

Nourish me dear Mother.
Nourish me.
Fill me.

Nourish me so that I may have your love for all of creation.

Mantra

The illusion of Reality—"The world is not real", or the "It's not real" mantra. This would be a great mantra to do at a mystical place such as Muller Hill, High Tor, or even the Peacemaker's Sanctuary at Onondaga Lake.

The eastern traditions teach that the world is Maya, an illusion, that it is not real. I see this not so much that all of reality is a sham, but that there is a greater truth behind it. Our true being is our soul, not the physical body we parade on the Earth Plane. This illusion tethers us to the Earth Plane and it materiality, creating a host of challenges to our spiritual evolution.

Shortly after I accepted God's call, while I was meditating I was given a mantra—"The world is not real"—to repeat over and over again. I verbally said it, or mentally repeated it endlessly, while I was hiking, walking around or driving my car. Like the Russian Pilgrim who would ceaselessly repeat the Jesus Prayer; "Lord Jesus Christ have Mercy on me."

I eventually shortened it to—"It's not real"—because I had so inculcated in my mind what "it," was.

I now pass this mantra on to you.

We are One Mantra

Another mantra I was given was the "we are one" mantra, which I would also repeat endlessly. The purpose is to educate and fill up the world with we are linked to each other, all of creation and Mother Earth.

Repeat verbally or mentally, "we are one" while at a sacred site, or driving, or walking, sitting.....

Dream of a New Earth, a New World

Contemplate on what a new world would look like. Ask yourself what would Heaven on Earth look like? Visualize a lion lying down with a lamb. See enemies hugging. What would it physically look like? How would it be different? These are only a few suggestions for your contemplative query. Remain open to all possibilities and DREAM!

Ask for Divine Inspiration

Ask for inspiration, or guidance. Ask God to show you the way. Offer your services and ask what you can do? As you focus on this request, remember to pause and be silent at times so that your "ears" may hear. What comes to you might not necessarily be then and there, but you may hear a voice or get a notion later. Be sincere, be genuine.

Be open to all. Do not limit yourself. Back in the nineties, my then wife Susan would talk about energy and other mystical subjects. I would wince. But now here I am writing a book about Mother Earth and Her Fields of Consciousness. Be open and don't limit yourself.

Silence

Be silent and empty your mind and listen. If inconsequential thoughts come up, label them, and get back to silence and an empty mind. Space needs to be available for the new, or for revelation to come in.

The Promised Land

The promised land is an echo of the Israelites dream of finding a homeland, the land of milk and honey. Subsequently, the idea of a promised land has captured and motivated others, whether in this life, or the life thereafter. Many in North Star Country sought not to find a Promised Land, but to make a Promised Land, a proverbial Heaven on Earth. So it is with you Pilgrim; to dream of a Promised Land, to visualize and pray for a world of peace.

Sarah Bradford, in *Harriet, The Moses of Her People* (1991, 1886c) tells how when Harriet Tubman learned she might be sold she decided to escape North. Fearing if she told her family she would put everyone at risk, she instead sang them a song that lingered;

"When dat ar old chariot comes,
　　I'm gwine to lebe you,
I'm boun' for de promised land,
　　Frien's, I qwine to lebe you.

I'm sorry, frien's, to lebe you,
　　Farewell! Oh, farewell!
But I'll meet you in de mornin',
　　Farewell! Oh, farewell!

I'll meet you in de mornin',
　　When you reach the promised land;
On de oder side of Jordan,
　　For I'm boun for de promised land."(page 28)

Water Ceremony

Conduct a water ceremony to heal the water and honor what a precious a gift it is from Mother Earth. It should preferably be performed close to a body of water at one of the sites. Onondaga Lake would be ideal. You will need a receptacle to hold water.

- Say a prayer and ask for guidance in blessing the water.
- Use your receptacle to scoop up some water.
- Bless the water and give thanks by saying why you honor the water; tell a story of how water has helped you, or why you appreciate it.
- Pass the water along to others in your group so that they too can bless the water and give thanks.

- Once everyone has blessed the water, pause and say a prayer asking that this healing water clean and heal all that it comes in contact with.
- Pour the water back to where it came from.

Give Thanks to Mother Earth

Glossary

Antebellum Period—The period before the Civil War and after the War of 1812.

Abolitionism—The movement to end slavery. Ecclesiastical abolitionism is based on religion/spirituality.

Aura—an invisible emanation surrounding our physical body that consists of our several subtle bodies.

Artificial Ley—see Connector.

Chakra—is a spinning wheel, or vortex that facilitates the movement of prana in the human subtle body and Mother Earth. It consists of a vortex which pulls in prana released by a duct at a distance and two nadis, energy lines, below the vortex that are at 90 degrees to each other in the shape of a right angle which then transport the prana. Chakras are often clumped together in a series creating a larger structure, or chakra. A chakra is a permanent structure and is not created through human intention as an energy vortex is.

Chidakasha—the seat of consciousness residing in the forehead area; also called the mind screen. This is where you would feel consciousness.

Christ Consciousness—God's highest aspirations as embodied in Jesus Christ; love, compassion, altruism, self sacrifice…

Connector—a structure that forms in the unseen world connecting two places, or even people, that is a joint venture with Mother Earth.

Consciousness—(for our purposes here) emanations from Fields of Consciousness, consisting of Christ Consciousness. If absorbed, nourishes our soul.

Cosmic Prana—is prana with a high consciousness component. It is the prana that we attract during meditation and from selfless and loving acts. It nourishes our soul.

Cry for a Vision—the Native American tradition of going into the wilderness, usually without food and water, to seek inspiration, guidance or receive a vision from Great Spirit.

Desert Hermits—In the period after Christ's death many of his followers would look to replicate his simple life of love and nonviolence by living in the desert, abandoning all to follow him, as Jesus told the wealthy man (MK 10: 17-31.)

Earth Chakra—is a chakra that facilitates the movement of Earth Prana.

Earth Prana—is a coarse prana(energy) with a low consciousness component. It is the only prana that circulates in both the atmosphere and in the earth.

Energy Healing—Working to heal the physical body by nourishing the Energy Body with energy.

Energy line—is a line that transports prana, or energy. Also called a nadi.

Energy Plane—is the Plane of Existence just above the physical world that gives life and sustenance to it. It is full of moving energy, which has varying degrees of consciousness.

Fields of Consciousness (FOC)—part of Mother Earth's Soul in greater central New York that nourishes us with consciousness. This consciousness has a higher consciousness reading than Cosmic Prana and it nourishes our soul and raises our consciousness. It does this through Spirit lines which absorb the consciousness emanating from the Fields and travel to distant parts of the world. In the process they transport the consciousness emanating from Mother Earth's Soul.

Fourierism—a system of social reform built on communal living.

Handsome Lake—Haudenosaunee (Seneca) prophet, 1735-1815.

Herd Path—A path created by hikers, or animals such as deer by continually walking it, which creates a trail.

Imprints, impressions, land imprints, land memories—our thoughts that attach to the land and objects. They look to grow by having us think or behave in a manner that reinforces their original intent. Over time they can build up and exert a tremendous influence upon us and Mother Earth and the flow of energy.

Ley Line—see Spirit Line.

Line, a Line—A Connector of sorts that links FOC to each other through the energy grid that powers them.

Manitou stone—a stone placed in the ground at an angle, or perpendicular to the earth, that looks like a flying stone that crashed into the ground. Part of it is above ground, the other below. Manitou stones are associated with sacred and ceremonial sites. See *Manitou: The Sacred Landscape of New England's Native Civilization*, by Byron Dix and James Mavor.

Mesmerism—believe that people were affected by animal magnetism that eventually became hypnosis.

Milarepa—11th to 12th century Tibetan Buddhist mystic, considered the most famous. A cave in Nepal where he lived has an imprint of his hand embedded in the rock wall as a testament to the great powers this sage achieved.

Millennialism—the second coming of Christ and a thousand year golden age.

Mother Earth's Soul—made up of Fields of Consciousness and other related divine aspects of our Mother. The heart or center of which is located in central New York between Rochester and Utica, along the route of the old Erie Canal. It extends into southern Ontario, Canada to the north, Vermont/Massachusetts/Connecticut to the east, northern New Jersey/Pennsylvania to the south and northeast Ohio to the west.

Nest—a cluster of several Spirit Lines intersecting each other; or several clusters of intersecting Spirit Lines close to each other.

Orenda— Haudenosaunee term for spiritual power in people and in nature.

Perfectionism—the belief that we are capable of living without sin through self control and religious practices.

Planes of Existence—are alternative realities, or dimensions that exist in the unseen world around us.

Prana—is the life force that exists in the Energy Plane and gives life to everything in the physical plane. It is energy. It is called chi by Daoists.

Pranayama—various yogic breathing exercises to increase, or manipulate, your intake of prana (energy.)

Reiki—a particular healing technique where energy is channeled into body.

Samadhi—is the complete union with an object, or focus during meditation so that all other thoughts are blocked out. In other words the imprint of meditation becomes so dominant that it blocks out all the other imprints/thoughts when we meditate. Samadhi is the goal of Patanjali's yoga and it brings union with God and illumination. In Samadhi our consciousness transcends the physical world and rises to the Collective Plane of consciousness.

Scree—Loose stones on the side of a slope, or mountain, that can act like ball bearings and make climbing difficult.

Soup Theory of Space, or Space is like Soup—The imprints of a space combine to form its vibe. Like a soup, the space has its general overall character, but within it are individual bits—the onions, potatoes, mushrooms…So when you eat soup, a bite of the onions will give you a particular space; similarly a space has distinctive elements.

Spiritualism—a religious movement started with the Fox Sisters in Hydesville, NY (1848) based upon communication with ghosts and spirits.

Swedenborgianism—followers of Emmanuel Swedenborg Swedish philosopher who in his fifties in the 18th century had out of body experiences where he contacted the dead and others in alternative realities. Christian based mysticism.

Spirit Keepers—are those who once maintained and acted as the Keepers of the Fields of Consciousness in greater central New

York. They preceded the Hopewell and Adena, but by how much is not known.

Spirit Line— is a transporter of consciousness emanating from Fields of Consciousness. In traversing Mother Earth it interacts with the consciousness it comes in contact with in different parts of the world. Because this consciousness is often negative it sullies the Spirit Line's cargo of consciousness. They have been traditionally associated with sacred sites. Also called Ley Line, or Line of Consciousness (LOC.)

Steiner, Rudolph—noted Theosophist, associated with spiritual science.

Subtle body—an unseen body, which we have, and that corresponds with, and exist in the various Planes of Existence.

Talisman—is an object that has been charged through focused concentration, often for a specific purpose. The talisman picks up and retains the creator's intention, which gives it its charge and power; basically a samskara attaches to the object.. The term talisman has been traditionally associated with objects created for protection.

Theosophy—a religious philosophy believing in the universality of all religions, the equality of all sexes/creeds/races and alternative realities; although believing in the mystical experience greater emphasis is on knowledge.

Therapeutic Touch—an energy healing technique created by Dora Kunz a well known Theosophist and psychic and Dolores Kreiger (nurse) primarily taught to and practiced by nurses.

Transcendentalism—believe that divinity is inherent in man and Nature, and saw Nature as a source of inspiration and guidance.

Vibe—the cumulative imprints of a place that give it its feel.

Vortex—is a positive indicator for a space, it pulls in extra consciousness, or energy, when you meditate, or pray within it. A vortex forms in response to human intention. It either forms at a specific location, or attaches to an object. Generally a vortex refers to a positive vortex and is a co-creation with Mother Earth; if so it may also be referred to as a natural vortex.

Vortex ring—is the final step before the formation of an energy vortex. It is a circling pattern of energy/consciousness within an imprint.

Welcome circle—is an intention circle created to welcome visiting pilgrims to a sacred site.

Working with stone—is to place and/or charge stones, so that Mother Earth will be healed and or, enhanced. To create a bond with our Mother, and hopefully a new birth.

Western Reserve—Northeastern Ohio; before Ohio became a state (1803) its northeastern tip belonged to the State of Connecticut, and was referred to as the Western Reserve.

Index

V

W

Influence of the
Haudenosaunee Women,
13

Y

Yates County, NY, 292, 323

Z

Zenda Farms, 241
Zoar Valley, 365, 382, 383, 384,
389, 391, 455, 456
Spirit Keeper's Site in the
Creek Bed, 386
Valentine Flats, 384, 385, 388,
389, 390, 391

www.ingramcontent.com/pod-product-compliance
Lightning Source LLC
Chambersburg PA
CBHW060948280326
41935CB00009B/659